Global Environment Outlook

New York   Oxford
Oxford University Press
1997

Published by the United Nations Environment Programme
First edition, 1997

Copyright © 1997, United Nations Environment Programme
ISBN: (PBK) 0-19-521349-1
ISBN: 0-19-521351-3
ISSN: 0-1366-8080

DISCLAIMER

The contents of this volume do not necessarily reflect the views or policies of UNEP or contributory organizations. The designations employed and the presentations do not imply the expressions of any opinion whatsoever on the part of UNEP or contributory organizations concerning the legal status of any country, territory, city or area or its authority, or concerning the delimination of its frontiers or boundaries.

Prepared for printing by the World Resources Institute in the USA.
Cover designed by Pam Reznick, Reznick Design, Washington, D.C.
Printed in the USA by Quebecor Printing Corp.

Distributed by Oxford University Press

Oxford New York Toronto Delhi Bombay Calcutta
Madras Karachi Kuala Lumpur Singapore Hong Kong
Tokyo Nairobi Dar es Salaam Cape Town Melbourne Auckland
and associated companies in Berlin and Ibadan

and
United Nations Environment Programme

P.O. Box 30552
Nairobi, Kenya
This book is printed on recycled paper.

Global Environment Outlook

UNEP

in collaboration with

Thailand Environment Institute

ACKNOWLEDGEMENTS

UNEP would like to thank the many individuals and institutions who have contributed to this report. Full lists of Collaborating Centres, contributors, and reviewers are included in the Appendixes. Specific GEO Collaborating Centres are:

Arabian Gulf University (AGU), Manama, Bahrain

Bangladesh Centre for Advanced Studies (BCAS), Dhaka, Bangladesh

Central European University (CEU), Budapest, Hungary

Centre for Environment and Development for the Arab Region and Europe (CEDARE), Giza, Egypt

Centro Internacional de Agricultura Tropical (CIAT), Cali, Colombia

El Colegio de México (ECM), México DF, México

International Institute for Sustainable Development (IISD), Winnipeg, Canada

Moscow State University (MSU), Moscow, Russian Federation

National Environment Protection Agency (NEPA), Beijing, China

National Institute for Environmental Studies (NIES), Tsukuba, Japan

National Institute of Public Health and the Environment (RIVM), Bilthoven, the Netherlands

Network for Environment and Sustainable Development (NESDA), Abidjan, Côte d'Ivoire

Royal Scientific Society (RSS), Amman, Jordan

Southern African Research and Documentation Centre (SARDC), Harare, Zimbabwe

Stockholm Environment Institute (SEI), Boston, USA

Tata Energy Research Institute (TERI), New Delhi, India

Thailand Environment Institute (TEI), Bangkok, Thailand

University of Chile, Santiago, Chile

World Resources Institute (WRI), Washington, D.C., USA

Wuppertal Institute for Climate, Environment and Energy, Wuppertal, Germany

Our special thanks go to the World Resources Institute, USA, to Deborah Farmer and Maggie Powell in particular, for preparation of the material for printing; to the National Institute of Public Health and the Environment, the Netherlands, for the preparation of the modelling chapter; and to Linda Starke for editorial assistance.

We are also grateful to the following institutes for their specialized contributions: the Asian Institute of Technology, Thailand; the International Centre for Antarctic Information and Research, New Zealand; the International Institute for Environment and Development, UK; the Island Resources Foundation, Virgin Islands; the Norwegian Institute for Nature Research, Norway; and the Regional Environment Centre, Hungary.

In addition we would like to thank Exequiel Ezcurra, Gilberto Gallopin, Allen Hammond, Fred Langeweg, Robert Tiebilé N'Daw, Mike Norton-Griffiths, John O'Connor, Surendra Shrestha, Leena Srivastava, and Mohammad Wahab for their continued support and advice throughout the GEO-1 production process and during the Regional Consultations.

UNEP GEO Team

Veerle Vandeweerd (team leader)

Marion Cheatle

Barry Henricksen

Miriam Schomaker

Megumi Seki

Kaveh Zahedi

Table Of Contents

Foreword

The United Nations Environment Programme (UNEP) is proud and pleased to present the first report in the Global Environment Outlook (GEO) series.

This groundbreaking report presents information on the state of the global environment. It indicates that world-wide, profound changes continue to occur in social, institutional and economic systems. It reports on the continued impoverishment of large parts of the global population. It points to the increased disparities both within and between nations. It describes the environmental implications of rapid globalization, particularly through developments in information technology, transport and trade regimes. It shows us that significant progress has been made in confronting environmental challenges at the local, national, and regional level. In the end, though, *GEO-1* concludes that, during the past decade, the environment has continued to degrade and significant problems still persist.

If there is one conclusion to be drawn from *GEO-1*, it is that despite progress, the pace at which the world is moving toward a sustainable future is simply too slow. Internationally and nationally, the funds and political will dedicated to halting further global environmental degradation are insufficient. We know that the knowledge and technological base to solve the most pressing environmental issues are available. However, the sense of urgency of the early 1990s is lacking.

By reporting on the state of the environment through its GEO series, UNEP is providing the world with an essential tool to speed up the pace of our environmental action, to set priorities, to provide an early warning system, and to support informed decision-making at all levels of society.

Since the Rio Conference in 1992, UNEP has broadened its scientific focus to better address the information requirements of international environmental policy setting and to help bridge the gap between scientific understanding and societal action. The GEO series places high priority on reflecting regional perceptions and realities, while at the same time reporting on the status of the global environment.

GEO-1 is designed to build consensus on critical environmental issues, setting priorities among the plethora of environmental concerns, and identifying issues that the international community needs to address. *GEO-1* addresses regional policy responses and explores the possible future state of the global environment using a scenario of the future in which no major policy or structural changes would be implemented—an unlikely scenario indeed, and one which, we hope, the GEO report will help to divert.

In a single volume, and with a production time of slightly more than one year, not every environmental issue in every region can be covered in great detail. *GEO-1,* thus, should not be read as a comprehensive work on the state of the environment in a specific region. Rather, it should give the reader—whether a policy maker, a corporate leader, a student, an activist, or an interested citizen—a 'feel' for the priority environmental concerns in each region and the overall health of the planet, as well as giving a direction for possible environmental response strategies.

To promote participation and enhance distribution, UNEP is making this report simultaneously available on the Internet in electronic format. This is part of our commitment to improve the accessibility of our information products, by bringing them closer to the people that need them. At the same time, six companion technical reports are being published. These reports enlarge on the model exercises detailed in *GEO-1,* on alternative scenarios, and core data sets. They also highlight the use of remote sensing imagery to evaluate environmental changes over time over large areas, and detail the outcomes of the regional consultations on *GEO-1.*

UNEP hopes that *GEO-1* will give a new impetus to international action on the protection and conservation of the environment, while at the same time promoting and caring for the development aspirations of nations and regions. We hope that the assessment process initiated with the Global Environment Outlook series will find the necessary policy and scientific support to be continued in the future, provide an effective means to link sectoral and regional assessments, and provide an overarching framework for ongoing international assessment activities, thus realising its full potential.

In looking to future reports, UNEP welcomes your comments and suggestions whether they relate to substance or style. Our goal is that by the turn of the century a truly global participatory assessment process may be operational to effectively keep under review the state of the world's environment, as well as to guide international environmental policy setting.

Elizabeth Dowdeswell
Executive Director
United Nations Environment Programme

EXECUTIVE SUMMARY

This first issue of the biennial *Global Environment Outlook (GEO)* is a snapshot of an ongoing world-wide environmental assessment process. It was initiated in response to the environmental reporting requirements of Agenda 21 and to a UNEP Governing Council Decision of May 1995, which requested production of the first in a new, comprehensive State of the Environment Report series in time for the next UNEP Governing Council in January 1997. The decision recognized the need to advance consensus on several essential environmental issues and on the implementation of the recommendations of Agenda 21.

A regional and participatory process was used to produce *GEO-1*. Input was solicited from an extensive array of sources throughout the world: 20 regional Collaborating Centres, United Nations organizations, and independent experts. Draft chapters benefited from discussions and recommendations of participants in regional consultations organized by the UNEP Regional Offices and were extensively amended and reviewed thereafter. (See Figure 1.) Chapter 1 elaborates on this region-based participatory process, and a GEO technical report provides further details on the outcome of the regional consultations.

The regional consultations provided valuable suggestions for the improvement and future direction of the *Global Environment Outlook* series. In later reports, the regional inputs will be strengthened through the further development of the global network of Collaborating Centres. These centres will be called upon to draw more widely on the work of sectoral and national institutes so that the most accurate and up-to-date information is included from the regional level. Analysis of environmental impacts of alternative development scenarios and policy action will be included in future GEO reports as well as more extensive analyses of current policy responses, their impacts, and the reasons for their successes and failures. The introduction of these elements in the continuous GEO assessment process has already started.

SIGNIFICANT PROGRESS HAS BEEN MADE IN CONFRONTING ENVIRONMENTAL CHALLENGES. NEVERTHELESS, THE ENVIRONMENT HAS CONTINUED TO DEGRADE IN NATIONS OF ALL REGIONS. PROGRESS TOWARDS A SUSTAINABLE FUTURE HAS SIMPLY BEEN TOO SLOW.

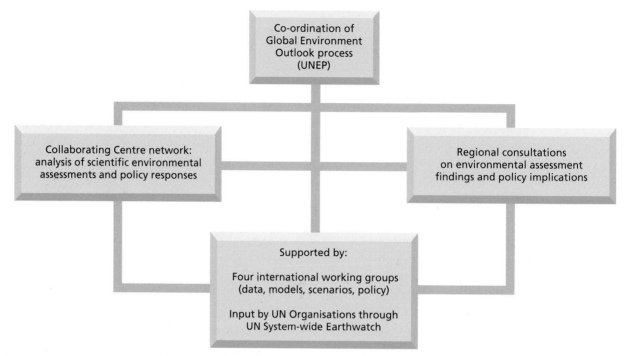

Figure 1. Framework of the global environment outlook process.

Global Overview

The *GEO-1 Report* shows that significant progress has been made in the last decade in confronting environmental challenges in both developing and industrial regions. World-wide, the greatest progress has been in the realm of institutional developments, international co-operation, public participation, and the emergence of private-sector action. Legal frameworks, economic instruments, environmentally sound technologies, and cleaner production processes have been developed and applied. Environmental impact assessments have become standard tools for the initiation, implementation, and evaluation of major development and investment projects in many countries around the world.

As a result, several countries report marked progress in curbing environmental pollution and slowing the rate of resource degradation as well as reducing the intensity of resource use. The rate of environmental degradation in several developing countries has been slower than that experienced by industrial countries when they were at a similar stage of economic development. (See Figure 2.)

Internationally, Agenda 21—the plan of action adopted by Governments in 1992 in Rio de Janeiro—provides the global consensus on the road map towards sustainable development. The Commission on Sustainable Development offers an intergovernmental forum to co-ordinate and monitor progress on the plan's implementation. A financial mechanism, the Global Environment Facility, addresses the incremental costs that developing countries face in responding to selected global environmental problems. UNEP continues to be the environmental voice of the United Nations, responsible for environmental policy development, scientific analysis, monitoring, and assessment. Increasingly, United Nations organizations, the World Bank, and Regional Banks are "greening" their programmes. Recently signed international agreements are entering into force, older treaties are being improved, and new approaches to international policy are being developed, tested, and implemented.

Since Rio, a growing body of actors—Governments, non-governmental organizations (NGOs), the private sector, civil society, and the scientific and research community—have responded to environmental challenges in a variety of ways and have taken great strides towards incorporating environmental considerations in their day-to-day activities. Groups such as the World Business Council for

Sustainable Development, the Earth Council, and the International Council for Local Environment Initiatives provide effective non-governmental forums for world-wide co-operation and information sharing. Increasingly, Government departments are called on to take environmental considerations into account, and consequently environment assumes a more important role in international relations and transactions. The participation of a broad range of ministries (other than those on the environment) in the negotiation and implementation of the Biodiversity, Climate, and Desertification Conventions and the increasing array of voluntary agreements, codes of conduct, and guidelines generated by the industry, banking, and insurance sectors all exemplify the encouraging trend.

Nevertheless, despite this progress on several fronts, from a global perspective the environment has continued to degrade during the past decade, and significant environmental problems remain deeply embedded in the socio-economic fabric of nations in all regions. Progress towards a global sustainable future is just too slow. A sense of urgency is lacking. Internationally and nationally, the funds and political will are insufficient to halt further global environmental degradation and to address the most pressing environmental issues—even though technology and knowledge are available to do so. The recognition of environmental issues as necessarily long-term and cumulative, with serious global and security implications, remains limited. The reconciliation of environment and trade regimes in a fair and equitable manner still remains a major challenge. The continued preoccupation with immediate local and national issues and a general lack of sustained interest in global and long-term environmental issues remain major impediments to environmental progress internationally. Global governance structures and global environmental solidarity remain too weak to make progress a world-wide reality. As a result, the gap between what has been done thus far and what is realistically needed is widening.

Comprehensive response mechanisms have not yet been fully internalized at the national level. The development at local, national, and regional levels of

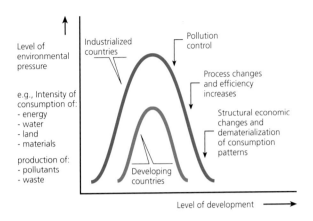

Figure 2. Environmental transitions.

effective environmental legislation and of fiscal and economic instruments has not kept pace with the increase in environmental institutions. In the private sector, environmental advances by several major transnational corporations are not reflected widely in the practices of small- and medium-sized companies that form the backbone of economies in many countries.

In the future, the continued degradation of natural resources, shortcomings in environmental responses, and renewable resource constraints may increasingly lead to food insecurity and conflict situations. Changes in global biogeochemical cycles and the complex interactions between environmental problems such as climate change, ozone depletion, and acidification may have impacts that will confront local, regional, and global communities with situations they are unprepared for. Previously unknown risks to human health are becoming evident from the cumulative and persistent effects of a whole range of chemicals, particularly the persistent organic pollutants. The effects of climate variability and change are already increasing the incidence of familiar public health problems and leading to new ones, including a more extensive reach of vectorborne diseases and a higher incidence of heat-related illness and mortality. If significant major policy reforms are not implemented quickly, the future might hold more such surprises.

GEO-1 substantiates the need for the world to embark on major structural changes and to pursue environmental and associated socio-economic policies vigorously. Key areas for action must embrace the use of alternative and renewable energy resources, cleaner and leaner production systems world-wide, and concerted global action for the protection and conservation of the world's finite and irreplaceable fresh-water resources.

Overview of Regional Status and Trends

Not surprisingly, *GEO-1* confirms both striking similarities and marked differences among regions in terms of which environmental issues are of primary concern today. Chapter 2 elaborates the priorities in the different regions with regard to land, forests, biodiversity, water, marine and coastal environments, atmosphere, and urban and industrial environments.

In regions where food security and poverty alleviation are priorities, such as Africa, West Asia, and parts of Asia-Pacific and Latin America, the primary emphasis regarding land is its availability, the abatement of land degradation, and efficient land and water management. The limited availability of arable land and loss of land to urban expansion are particularly important to small island states and the West Asian region. Degradation of drylands is an urgent global problem, placing some 1 billion people in 110 countries at risk, mainly in developing regions. In highly industrialized regions, ameliorating soil contamination and combating acidification are priorities.

With regard to forests and biodiversity, the impacts of development activities and the advance of the agricultural frontier are of concern in developing regions, while forest and biodiversity conservation receive major attention in the North. The decade 1980 to 1990 witnessed a decline in the world's forests and wooded land of some 2 per cent; while the area of forest in industrial regions remained fairly unchanged, in developing regions natural forest cover declined 8 per cent. In Europe, air pollution (including acid rain), pests and diseases, and forest fires were the main causes for forest degradation. Biodiversity is of particular concern both to Latin America and the Caribbean and to Asia and the Pacific, which together house 80 per

cent of the ecological megadiversity countries of the world. As yet, no region-based assessment of the state of the world's biodiversity is available, and of a working figure of 13 million species, only 13 per cent have been scientifically described. World-wide habitat loss and fragmentation, the lack of biological corridors, and the decline in biological diversity outside protected areas constitute primary threats to overall biodiversity.

All regions experience problems related to either ground water or surface water or both. Every day, 25,000 people die as a result of poor water quality, and waterborne diseases still represent the single largest cause of human sickness and death world-wide. Some 1.7 billion people, more than one third of the world's population, are without safe water supply. In addition, an estimated one quarter of the world will suffer from chronic water shortages in the beginning of the next century. The development and efficient management of water resources is a priority concern in West Asia, Africa, and Asia and the Pacific. In Europe and North America, the protection of water resources from contamination, acidification, and eutrophication are highest on the agenda. Water supply to regions hosting megacities is a concern world-wide, particularly with regard to protection of ground-water resources, intrusion of salt into fresh-water supplies, and land subsidence. More than 1.5 billion people depend on ground water for their drinking water. Other global priorities are the equitable distribution of water among riparian countries sharing international river basins, non-point sources of pollution, and the impacts of major dams and diversion projects. Water will be the major impediment to development in the future in several regions.

About 60 per cent of the world population lives within 100 kilometres of the coastline, and more than 3 billion people rely in some manner on coastal and marine habitats for food, building sites, transportation, recreation, and waste disposal. Around one third of the world's coastal regions are at high risk of degradation, particularly from land-based sources of pollution and infrastructure development. European coasts are most affected, with some 80 per cent at risk, followed by Asia and the Pacific, with

70 per cent of the coast at risk. In Latin America, some 50 per cent of the mangroves are affected by forestry and aquaculture activities. Oil spills are particular threats in West Asia and the Caribbean, while infrastructure development for the tourism industry puts stress on natural coastal areas around the world, particularly in small island developing states. There is widespread alarm in Asia and the Pacific, North America, Europe, and West Asia regarding the overexploitation of marine fisheries and consequent declining stocks of commercial fish species. Globally, more than 60 per cent of marine fisheries are heavily exploited.

Air pollution problems are multifaceted and pervasive. All major cities in the world suffer urban air quality problems; in Eastern Europe, air quality is considered the most serious environmental problem. Acid rain and transboundary air pollution, once problems only in Europe and parts of North America, are now becoming apparent in parts of the Asia-Pacific region as well as parts of Latin America. Large regions are at risk from the effects of both climate change and acidification. Despite co-ordinated action world-wide, damage to the ozone layer continues faster than expected, with the next 10 years predicted to be the most vulnerable. Cases of non-compliance and growth in illegal trade in ozone-depleting substances are emerging problems. All regions express concern over global warming, but special emphasis is placed by developing countries on the need for adaptive mechanisms to cope with accompanying climate variability and sea-level change. The rapidly rising demand for energy to fuel economic development will aggravate these problems, particularly in Asia and the Pacific, where a 100-per-cent increase in energy use is predicted for 1990–2010, and in Latin America, with a predicted energy growth of 50–77 per cent. It is expected that for the near future, fossil fuels—coal, oil, and natural gas—will continue to be the primary energy source.

The impacts of current consumption and production patterns and associated waste generation, particularly on personal health and well-being, are high on the priority list in both North America and Western Europe and are of concern to other regions, particularly with regard to the use of natural re-

sources for production and consumption processes outside the regions. Subregions with emerging economies, such as those of Eastern Europe, South East Asia, and parts of Latin America and West Asia, face problems associated with rapid industrialization. Rising levels of pollutants and greenhouse gases create serious problems of acidification, urban air quality deterioration, and transboundary pollution—all posing increasing health risks. Accumulation of radioactive waste, and the effects of past radioactive spills remain of particular concern in Eastern Europe.

These problems are compounded by rapid urbanization, particularly in coastal zones, and the widening gap between the rich and the poor. More than half of humankind will live in urban areas by the end of the century, a figure that will increase to 60 per cent by 2020, when Europe, Latin America, and North America will have more than 80 per cent of their populations living in urban areas.

The polar regions, representing the largest remaining natural ecosystems on Earth, are also increasingly coming under stress, particularly from long-range pollutant transport and deposition. Their crucial role in climate regulation and the vulnerability of their fauna and flora warrant special attention.

Although poverty and the growing global population are often targetted as responsible for much of the degradation of the world's resources, other factors—such as the inefficient use of resources (including those of others), waste generation, pollution from industry, and wasteful consumption patterns—are equally driving us towards an environmental precipice. Table 1 indicates the relative importance of environmental issues within and across regions. Table 2 reflects trends for the same issues, without depicting the rate of changes in these trends. In many instances, although trends are increasing, the rate of increase over the years has slowed down or was less than the rate of increase in economic growth previously experienced by countries with comparable economic growth. This suggests that several countries are making the transition to a more sustainable environment at a lower level of economic development than industrial countries typically did over the last 50 years.

Table 1

Regional Concerns: Relative Importance Given to Environmental Issues By Regions

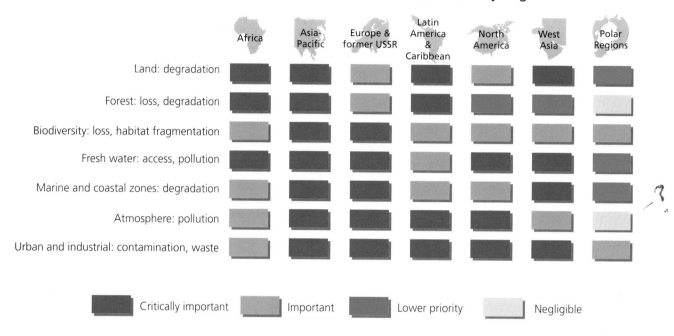

Critically important   Important   Lower priority   Negligible

As nations develop, different sets of environmental concerns assume priority. Initially, prominence is given to issues associated with poverty alleviation and food security and development—namely, natural resource management to control land degradation, provide an adequate water supply, and protect forests from overexploitation and coastal zones from irreversible degradation. Attention to issues associated with increasing industrialization then follows. Such problems include uncontrolled urbanization and infrastructure development, energy and transport expansion, the increased use of chemicals, and waste production. More affluent societies focus on individual and global health and well-being, the intensity of resource use, heavy reliance on chemicals, and the impact of climate change and ozone destruction, as well as remaining vigilant on the long-term protection needs of natural resources. Figure 3 illustrates the observed progression on environmental priority issues.

Overview of Regional Policy Responses

Chapter 3 summarizes policy responses to environmental issues in different regions; it indicates that typically these responses focus first on institutional and constitutional issues, and then on the implementation and enforcement of often disjointed sectoral environmental legislation and regulations. Subsequent actions concentrate on developing comprehensive strategic and integrated plans for the protection of the environment, such as National Environmental Action Plans, and an array of concerted command-and-control measures. Later, attention is given to introducing market-based incentives research, creating conducive environments for voluntary, flexible, and innovative actions, and stimulating increased participation and commitment by all sectors of society. Figure 4 illustrates this pattern in policy responses.

Progression through the cascade of policy responses is often constrained in developing regions by weak institutions, insufficient human and financial resources, ineffective legislation, and a lack of compliance monitoring and enforcement capabilities. In other instances, environmental institutions and regulations have been introduced at the request of external forces, such as international conventions and strategies, donor requirements, and structural adjustment programmes, and are only later internalized by countries.

Table 2
Regional Environmental Trends

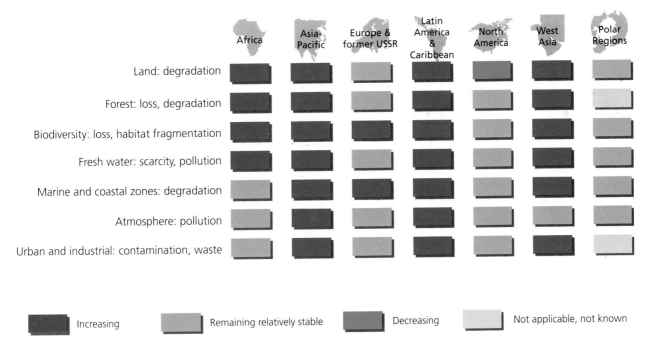

	Africa	Asia-Pacific	Europe & former USSR	Latin America & Caribbean	North America	West Asia	Polar Regions
Land: degradation							
Forest: loss, degradation							
Biodiversity: loss, habitat fragmentation							
Fresh water: scarcity, pollution							
Marine and coastal zones: degradation							
Atmosphere: pollution							
Urban and industrial: contamination, waste							

Increasing   Remaining relatively stable   Decreasing   Not applicable, not known

In the more developed regions of the world, experience with environmental management and conservation is extensive and of longer duration. Adequate safeguards in the initial stages were largely achieved through Government-regulated command-and-control policies. Effective implementation of such policies relied on legislation and measures such as emission standards and limits as well as on maximum permitted rates of resource use. Today, countries are increasingly using a mix of command-and-control policies and market-based incentives to achieve cleaner and more resource-efficient production systems and to modify consumers' attitudes. More integrated approaches that rely on cleaner production processes rather than on end-of-pipe solutions and accounting on a cradle-to-grave basis are being tested in a number of countries, addressing the industrial, agricultural, forestry, transportation, and fishery sectors. These measures have not yet been used to their full potential anywhere.

Although there is repeated acknowledgement of both the "vicious cycle of poverty" and its intrinsic linkages with the environment and the urgency to address poverty alleviation, little evidence emerged from the regional reports that effective and concerted actions have been taken since Rio to ensure that environmental policies benefit the poorest members of society. Only anecdotal evidence suggests striking individual and community solutions, as in income-generating initiatives recounted at the UNEP Global Assembly of Women and the Environment in 1992. A vacuum still remains at the national level for linking environmental protection to social investment, such as

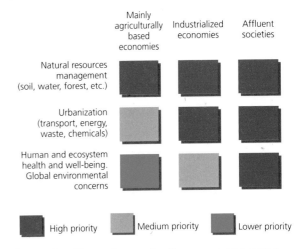

	Mainly agriculturally based economies	Industrialized economies	Affluent societies
Natural resources management (soil, water, forest, etc.)			
Urbanization (transport, energy, waste, chemicals)			
Human and ecosystem health and well-being. Global environmental concerns			

High priority   Medium priority   Lower priority

Figure 3. Changing priority concerns over time.

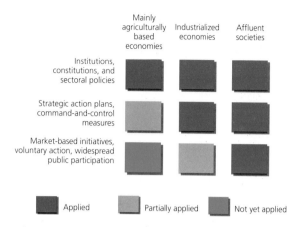

Figure 4. Changing use of policy instruments over time.

education, better health care, and employment generation for the poor, especially women.

Empowerment of communities and the growth of environment-oriented NGOs in civil society are increasingly recognized in all regions as powerful mechanisms to advance sustainable development. However, real participation and commitment to the environmental cause by civil society often follows clear Government action in the implementation of environmental policies. In regions where such governmental policies are weak and ineffective, public participation and empowerment are generally low.

Despite the contradicting tendencies described above, a heartening sign is the tendency to strengthen regional and subregional co-operation world-wide. This might well prove to be one of the most powerful mechanisms to move national and global institutions forward towards sustainable development. Table 3 depicts environmental regional policy responses and their relative importance within and across regions.

Looking to the Future

The first *GEO Report* concludes with a brief exploration, based on model analyses, of what we might expect in the future for a selected number of environmental issues. The results in this final chapter highlight the integrated nature of the environment and underscore the need for more systematic analysis of linkages between environment, social, economic, institutional, and cultural sectors and among different environmental issues, such as biodiversity, climate, land, and water.

Preliminary results from the model analyses confirm trends revealed by the regional chapters. They indicate that, despite both declining global birth rates since 1965 and recent policy initiatives towards more efficient and cleaner resource use in some regions, the large increases in world population, expanding economies in industrializing countries, and wasteful consumption patterns particularly in developed countries of the world will continue to increase global resource and energy consumption, generate burgeoning wastes, and spawn environmental contamination and degradation. Pressures on remaining biodiversity and natural ecosystems will increase accordingly.

If no fundamental changes occur in the amount and type of energy used, global carbon dioxide emissions will increase, and the declining trends in acidifying sulphur and nitrogen concentrations may be reversed. In light of the apparent effects of human activity on climate, contingency plans to adapt to projected climate change will be required in the near future. These include the development of drought-resistant crops, increases in water use efficiency, the avoidance of ecosystem fragmentation, and an improvement of the adaptive capabilities in all regions.

With only moderate application of improved agricultural management and technology in developing regions, the demands of growing populations and the increasing burden of poverty may well lead to substantial expansion of agricultural activities into marginal lands at the expense of remaining wilderness and associated biodiversity. Although the models project adequate availability of water and food on a global basis, regional deficiencies could be aggravated in the near future. The combination of increased pressure on land by expanding urbanization and losses of productive land through degradation and unsustainable management practices may lead to shortages in arable land and water, impeding development in several regions. Global food trade can supplement these regional shortfalls, but will create dependencies and require importing countries to engage in other production activities to finance essential food imports.

Table 3
Environmental Regional Policy Responses

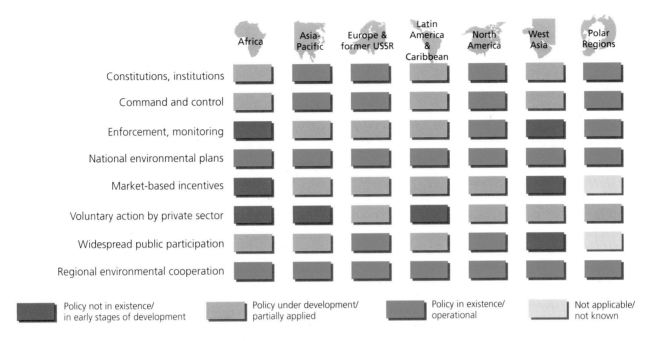

	Africa	Asia-Pacific	Europe & former USSR	Latin America & Caribbean	North America	West Asia	Polar Regions
Constitutions, institutions							
Command and control							
Enforcement, monitoring							
National environmental plans							
Market-based incentives							
Voluntary action by private sector							
Widespread public participation							
Regional environmental cooperation							

Policy not in existence/ in early stages of development
Policy under development/ partially applied
Policy in existence/ operational
Not applicable/ not known

In such a scenario, sharp regional differences will remain and poverty will be aggravated in several regions. If global economic gains are not accompanied more explicitly by investment in education, social development, and environmental protection, a move towards a more equitable, healthy, and sustainable future for all sectors of society will not be realized, and a new spate of urban and pollution-related health impacts may surface.

The chapter's brief exploration into alternative development scenarios illustrates that technology transfer can lead to significant changes in energy consumption, land use, and carbon dioxide emissions. Although the analysis presented is only a first attempt to explore the potential impact of alternative policies, it demonstrates that reductions of human pressures on the global environment are indeed technically feasible if the willingness to implement them globally is found.

The Way Ahead

World-wide, rapid and profound changes are occurring in many social, institutional, and economic systems. Continued impoverishment of large parts of the global population, increased disparities both within and among nations, and rapid globalization—particularly through developments in information technology, transport, and trade regimes—are observed. In many countries, there are trends towards decentralization of environment responsibilities from national to subnational authorities, an increasing role for the transnational corporations in environmental stewardship and policy development, and a move towards integrated environmental policies and management practices. Increased willingness by Governments to co-operate on a global basis is witnessed by the multitude of world summits in the last decade. The question arises, however, as to how this willingness is translated into concrete and effective actions. There is greater recognition and popular insistence that the wealth of nations and the well-being of individuals lie not just in economic capital, but in social and natural capital as well.

Against this background of change, many fundamental global environmental trends are emerging from the diverse regional accounts of priority environmental concerns—global and regional, current and future—summarized in this report:

(trillion dollars 1987)

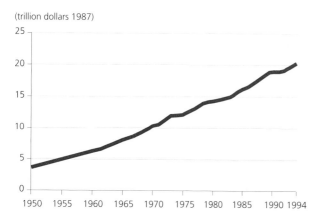

Figure 5. Gross world product, 1950–94.

- The use of renewable resources—land, forest, fresh water, coastal areas, fisheries, and urban air—is beyond their natural regeneration capacity and therefore is unsustainable.

- Greenhouse gases are still being emitted at levels higher than the stabilization target internationally agreed upon under the United Nations Framework Convention on Climate Change.

- Natural areas and the biodiversity they contain are diminishing due to the expansion of agricultural land and human settlements.

- The increasing, pervasive use and spread of chemicals to fuel economic development is causing major health risks, environmental contamination, and disposal problems.

- Global developments in the energy sector are unsustainable.

- Rapid, unplanned urbanization, particularly in coastal areas, is putting major stress on adjacent ecosystems.

- The complex and often little understood interactions among global biogeochemical cycles are leading to widespread acidification, climate variability, changes in the hydrological cycles, and the loss of biodiversity, biomass, and bioproductivity.

There are also widespread social trends, intrinsically linked to the environment, that have negative feedback effects on environmental trends, notably:

- an increase in inequality, both among and within nations, in a world that is generally healthier and wealthier (See Figure 5.);

- a continuation, at least in the near future, of hunger and poverty despite the fact that globally enough food is available; and

- greater human health risks resulting from continued resource degradation and chemical pollution.

If one were to distill four key priority areas that emerge from the *GEO-1 Report* for immediate, enhanced, and concerted action by the international community, energy, environmentally sound technologies, fresh water, and benchmark data are obvious choices. Many other urgent action areas are apparent in the report as well. But these four, although touching on different levels at which action should be taken, address key areas needing attention if the world is to reverse the negative environmental trends highlighted in the *GEO Report*. Economic cost-benefit analyses will need to be conducted in conjunction with concerted international action in these areas.

Energy efficiency and renewable energy resources. Current patterns of energy use require drastic changes because of destructive impacts on land and natural resources, climate, air quality, rural and urban settlements, and human health and well-being. The need for ever higher levels of energy to fuel economic development in all regions of the world and the absence of significant world-wide advances in the development and application of alternative energy sources and increased energy efficiency will inevitably exacerbate environmental degradation. Alternative energy sources are being developed but need to be vigorously pursued and their application enhanced. Energy efficiency—that is, energy density per unit of production, whether industrial, domestic, or agricultural—still needs to be greatly improved, and emissions need to be reduced. Consideration should be given to declaring an Energy Decade, or decades, for that matter, until energy sustainability is reached.

Appropriate and environmentally sound technologies world-wide. Appropriate technological improvements, which result in more effective use of natural resources, less waste, and fewer pollutant by-products, are required in all economic sectors—but particularly in industry, agriculture,

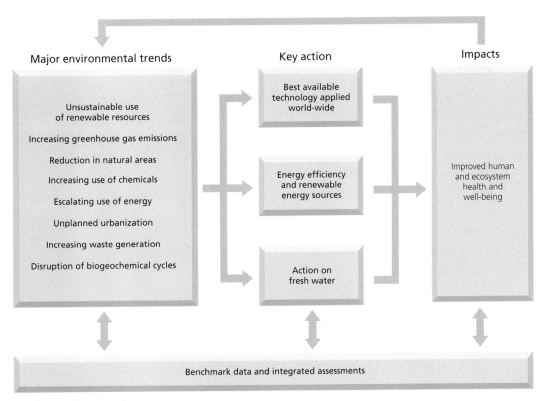

Major environmental trends	Key action	Impacts

Figure 6. The action cycle.

transportation, and infrastructure development. Truly global availability and world-wide application of the best available and appropriate technology and production processes, including best traditional practices, has yet to be ensured through the exchange and dissemination of know-how, skills, and technology and through appropriate finance mechanisms. Despite years of deliberation, countries have yet to agree on how to reach consensus on international mechanisms to serve the vital interests of both developers of technologies and those countries that need access to them, as well as on international finance mechanisms.

Global action on fresh water. Water will be the major impediment for further development in several regions. Not only is unsafe water having a negative impact on human and ecosystem health but also the scarcity of water, together with insufficient arable land, will increasingly pose a threat to food self-sufficiency in several regions, forcing a dependance on food trade. Greater efforts are needed to resolve issues related to land-based sources of pollution, non-point source runoff from agricultural and urban areas, protection of ground-

water reserves, water pricing, the impact of development projects on ecosystems, and competing demands for water among different societal sectors, among rural and urban communities, and among riparian countries. Globally, a much stronger, more integrated, and extensive programme on water is required to address the green (food) and brown (health) fresh-water issues as well as traditional blue water issues.

Benchmark data and integrated assessments. Assessments are required continually to guide rational and effective decision-making for environmental policy formulation, implementation, and evaluation at local, national, regional, and global levels. To improve the global capability for keeping the environment under continuous review, urgent action is required in the following fields:

- investment in new and better data collection, in the harmonization of national datasets, and in the acquisition of global datasets;

- increased understanding of the linkages among different environmental issues as well as of the interactions between environment and development;

- enhanced capabilities for integrated assessment and forecasting and the analysis of the environmental impact of alternative policy options;

- better translation of scientific results into a format readily usable by policy-makers and the general public; and

- the development of cost-effective, meaningful, and useful methods for monitoring environmental trends and policy impacts at local, national, regional, and global levels.

Figure 6 illustrates the relationships among key actions, major environmental trends, and the ensuing overall improvements in environment and human health and well-being. To achieve advances in one or all of these key areas for action, a change in the "hearts and minds" of everyone will be required, along with a world-wide transition towards equity and resource efficiency. The necessary financial resources will have to be made available at national and international levels. Estimates have indicated that if 2–3 per cent of gross domestic product (GDP) could be devoted to environmental education, protection, and restoration, great strides could be made in halting the progress of major negative environmental trends. Implementing the pledges made at Rio to increase development aid to the equivalent of 0.7 per cent of industrial countries' GDP and to provide new additional funding is the prerequisite for initiating action to reverse global environmental degradation.

THE GLOBAL ENVIRONMENT OUTLOOK PROCESS

M ore than two centuries ago, the industrial revolution introduced an age of unprecedented growth in production, consumption, and resource use. The global community has experienced major changes as a result of the unfolding and globalization of that revolution.

The next major global revolution is now under way, mainly driven by innovations in information technology and increased mobility. Accelerated industrialization, economic and cultural globalization, technological innovation, new world political orders, and the communication revolution are apparent everywhere. Liberalized trade, global markets, and capital flows are opening new avenues for the circulation of materials and products. The revolution in telecommunication is leading to unprecedented access to knowledge. The expansion and increase in the economic dominance of transnational corporations affects everyone's life. For many people, these changes mean a broadening of personal horizons, new hope of a more prosperous future, and the opportunity to become part of a global village—with all the perceived benefits that offers. Such changes in society occur subtly and over time. Often they go unnoticed in the day-to-day life of many. These developments will, however, lead to a vastly different future in the decades ahead.

Many of the changes are positive, and progress is being made. Nevertheless, the benefits of economic globalization and technological innovations have bypassed the vast majority of the poor in many countries. The gap between rich and poor is increasing, both between countries and within them. The impact of new technologies on employment is still uncertain. In some parts of the world, strong manifestations of cultural or religious identity are resulting in friction and even fragmentation of society. Environmental degradation still continues unabated in many parts of the world, and adequate control over excessive urban expansion is absent or inadequate in many areas. Marginalization of groups within society and an increase in conflicts, poverty, and massive migration—these are all signs that global development is uneven (Raskin et al., 1996).

COMPREHENSIVE ASSESSMENTS OF THE STATE OF THE GLOBAL ENVIRONMENT, INCLUDING THE LINKAGES BETWEEN ENVIRONMENT ISSUES AND THE SOCIO-ECONOMIC FABRIC OF LIFE, ARE SORELY NEEDED.

The final decade of the twentieth century has witnessed an impressive number of conferences on various aspects of sustainable development—first environment and development, and then human rights, population, social development, women, urbanization, and food security. These gatherings have brought home the message that development is no longer perceived in economic terms alone; the dimension of human well-being is not only important but essential to the equation.

These are today's realities—realities that need to be taken into account in policy formulation and action planning in order to move towards sustainable development, which addresses the social, cultural, institutional, economic, and environmental changes needed for the continuing improvement of human well-being. To ensure success in this process, comprehensive assessments of the state of the global environment, including the linkages between environmental issues and the socio-economic fabric of life, are sorely needed.

A New Era in Environmental Assessment

Against this background of major changes in the world and the global efforts to address them, environmental assessment is changing too. Monitoring progress towards sustainable development and assessing the state of the environment are no longer just static reporting activities. They involve co-operative and frequent interactions of policy-makers and scientists working together to achieve orderly progress towards the implementation of Agenda 21, the blueprint for action adopted in 1992 at the United Nations Conference on Environment and Development in Rio de Janeiro.

Assessments that aim to support sustainable development can no longer report on the environment in isolation. Rather, environmental issues have to be seen as parts of larger systems, closely coupled to socio-economic developments and strongly influenced by political and institutional structures. The current trend is thus towards integrated analyses, including the evaluation of alternative policy options

to provide an improved knowledge base for action, political accountability, and public participation.

Evidence of this new approach is found in the international assessments done on ozone layer depletion, climate change, acidification, biodiversity, land degradation, toxic wastes, and land-based sources of pollution. These studies have supported and still support international negotiations and decision-making. The adoption and the implementation of major global environmental conventions in recent years have relied on such scientific assessments, which involved hundreds of experts, analyses of the latest information and research results, scientific consensus, and translation of the consensus view into policy-relevant action documents.

In addition to these well-publicized assessments, some 200 multilateral agreements target regional and global action to protect the environment (UNEP, 1993; Bergesen and Parmann, 1994; CIESIN, 1996). This multitude of agreements illustrates the inherent complexity of environmental issues and of the mechanisms to deal with them. The complexities also arise from the persistence of changes and their impacts and from the fact that fundamental socioeconomic and institutional aspects of life underlie every environmental problem.

The regional or global nature of environmental problems further complicates the assessment and formulation of effective responses. Even though the contribution of a single country to an environmental problem may seem insignificant taken on its own, the global total of individual contributions can result in degradation that is larger than the sum of the parts. By the same token, unilateral actions to deal with such problems will be less than optimally effective. Finally, different regions and nations have varying perspectives and priorities on the urgency of many environmental issues. These complexities make the production of comprehensive, policy-relevant assessments a challenging task.

The Global Environment Outlook Project

In 1995, the Governing Council of the United Nations Environment Programme (UNEP), at its eighteenth Session, called for the preparation of a new, comprehensive report on the state of the global environment now and in the year 2015 (UNEP, 1995). The document should be prepared, it suggested, in close co-operation with relevant international, regional, and national organizations and institutions. The Governing Council recommended that the report include essential problems of and threats to the environment, basic trends in environmental change, and the global effects of expected economic development, population increase, and consumption and production patterns. It further requested the inclusion of recommended action and measures, such as institutional and legal changes, that could effectively reverse unwelcome trends.

The Global Environment Outlook (GEO) Project is UNEP's response to the Governing Council's request. It addresses five questions:

- What are the major regional and global environmental problems, both current and emerging?

- What are the major demographic, social, and economic driving forces behind the observed problems and trends?

- Where are we heading if we continue doing "business as usual"?

- Where do we want to be heading?

- What is being done to address environmental concerns and what can be done in the future to move forward on the path of sustainable development?

The GEO Project has two main tracks:

- a global environmental assessment process that is cross-sectoral and participatory, incorporating regional views and perceptions and building consensus on priority issues and actions through dialogue among policy-makers and scientists at regional and global levels; and

- a biennial environmental assessment report series that reviews the state of the world's environment through identifying major environmental concerns, trends, and emerging issues—together with their causes, impacts, and societal responses—to provide guidance for international environmental policy formu-

lation, action planning, and resource allocation.

The GEO Assessment Process

To implement its goals, the GEO Project will rely increasingly on a global network of Collaborating Centres, a series of regional consultations, four scientific working groups, and United Nations agency participation through the System-wide Earthwatch co-ordination function of UNEP. (See Box 1.1.)

The process is designed to provide in the long run an effective mechanism for international environmental policy setting, engaging experts and decision-makers from industrial and developing worlds and from international agencies as equal partners. Its primary product will be the *GEO Report Series*. Each report in the series will build on previous ones, expanding on the issues and linkages identified as requiring closer political, public, and scientific scrutiny. The series will include a decadal *State of the Environment Report—2002*.

The process endeavours to gradually become an umbrella for global and regional environmental assessments, providing a framework and a mechanism for wide participation and co-operation that will also help build the capacity in developing countries for conducting integrated, policy-relevant assessments. As such, it should become a way to integrate and link sectoral and regional assessments, as well as a mechanism for aggregating and disseminating their results.

GEO-1

This volume—*GEO-1*—is the first product of the GEO Project. It provides a snapshot of a process in the making and aims to move the process along by documenting its progress. The principal focus of *GEO-1* is a review of major environmental issues from regional perspectives, and an initial evaluation of some existing and a few promising policy responses that address regional priority concerns. It also takes a first glimpse at the future using quantitative analysis techniques.

Box 1.1
The GEO Assessment Process

The process of assessing global environmental trends and policy options in the GEO Project has four major components.

Collaborating Centres

A global co-ordinated network of Collaborating Centres consists of regional multidisciplinary institutes that are at the interface between science and policy. These centres undertake studies with the dual aim of keeping the state of the regional and world environment under review and providing scientific guidance to regional and international policy setting and action planning for sustainable development. Around 20 centres contributed to the production of *GEO-1*. (See Appendix 2.)

Ultimately, these centres of excellence are intended to become regional engines for policy-relevant assessments, providing the information and knowledge base for sustainable development planning and for analysing the long-term consequences of current policy decisions. The centres will communicate with other institutes in their region and bring together the required expertise to cover all environmental sectors pertaining to sustainable development. Through such networking, the best regional knowledge will be brought to bear on issues of regional or global importance.

Working Groups

The four GEO Working Groups are composed of top experts from around the world. Their major goal is to ensure that methodological developments in integrated assessments are globally co-ordinated and that the studies conducted by the individual Collaborating Centres can be compared and compiled. The Working Groups will develop new methodologies as required and provide technical advice and support to the Collaborating Centres. They are implemented jointly by a number of international and national organizations.

The four Working Groups are:

● the Modelling Working Group, developing new models, harmonizing existing modelling activities, and linking integrated assessment models;

● the Scenario Working Group, articulating a range of possible futures and examining their plausibility, desirability, and sustainability;

● the Policy Working Group, reviewing alternative policy and response options for consideration in GEO Project analyses; and

● the Data Working Group, harmonizing and co-ordinating the data compilation, documentation, maintenance, and distribution activities of the GEO Collaborating Centres and of relevant United Nations and international organizations.

Scientific and Policy Consultations

Assessments geared towards policy setting and action planning need to be based on a dialogue between scientists and policy-makers. Regional policy consultations and other consultative mechanisms will promote and contribute to a continuous dialogue between science and policy at the regional and global levels. For *GEO-1,* such consultations were held in the six different UNEP Regions. (See Appendix 3 and Figure 4.2.)

The World-Wide Web is an ideal platform for group review and global document distribution, both of which are important aspects of the GEO process. Therefore, as a complement to the printed versions, the *GEO Report Series* will be available on the Web at <http://www.unep.org/unep/eia/geo1/>.

United Nations Participation

Through the United Nations System-wide Earthwatch, co-operation is sought with major United Nations organizations and bodies. For this first *GEO Report*, close links were maintained in particular with the United Nations Department for Policy Coordination and Sustainable Development, concerning the production of its *Trends Report*. United Nations bodies will increasingly contribute to data, science, and policy issues relevant in the GEO process.

As the logical follow-up to this volume, *GEO-2* will further analyse the priority issues identified in *GEO-1*. This analysis will be done during 1997 and 1998 using, in particular, regionally available data, knowledge, and capacity.

OVERVIEW OF REMAINING CHAPTERS

Chapter 2. Regional Perspectives

Chapter 2 looks at existing key regional State of the Environment reports, action plans, and sectoral reports. It provides a global synthesis of the primary regional environmental problems, the driving forces behind them, and emerging concerns. The issues are analysed against a background of existing development patterns and objectives, operating policies, practices, and institutions.

Inevitably, there are gaps and incompatibilities of data sets and reporting techniques between regions, as each report has a different concept, content, and depth. It is, however, through such a systematic analysis of regional reports that further harmonization of reporting can be achieved, leading to a comprehensive global overview based on regional realities.

Chapter 3. Policy Responses and Directions

This chapter takes the first step in forging the link between assessment and policy. It presents the outcome of regional policy and assessment consultations conducted as part of the GEO Project. The discussions involved policy and sectoral experts using scientific inputs from the Collaborating Centres and the draft *GEO-1* chapters as background material. (See Appendix.)

Chapter 4. Looking to the Future

This chapter explores the future to the year 2015 and beyond using a model-based approach, assuming that no major policy or institutional changes will take place. For a selected number of topics, it attempts quantitative analyses of changes in environmental and socio-economic factors and their interlinkages. It bases the analyses on contemporary situations and trends as well as on data from the past. The possible future impacts on the environment of current development processes are highlighted. A brief example is given of changes in the future if different policies or life-styles were to be applied.

References

Bergesen, H.O., and G. Parmann (eds.). 1994. *Green Globe Yearbook of International Co-operation on Environment and Development.* The Fridtjof Nansen Institute. Oxford University Press. Oxford.

CIESIN. 1996. Environmental Treaties and Resource Indicators (ENTRI) [on line]. Consortium for International Earth Science Information Network. University Center, Michigan. <http://sedac.ciesin.org/entri/>.

Raskin, P., M. Chadwick, T. Jackson, and G. Leach. 1996. *The Sustainability Transition—Beyond Conventional Development.* Polestar Series Report No. 1. Stockholm Environment Institute. Stockholm.

UNEP. 1993. Register of International Treaties and Other Agreements in the Field of the Environment. United Nations Environment Programme (UNEP). Nairobi.

UNEP. 1995. Proceedings of the Governing Council at Its Eighteenth Session. UNEP/GC.18/40. 13 June. UNEP. Nairobi.

chapter 2

REGIONAL PERSPECTIVES

The GEO process has found both striking similarities and marked differences among regional environmental priorities today. Environmental risks to human health are high on the priority list in North America and transboundary regional environmental problems and issues associated with unsustainable consumption and production patterns are major concerns in Europe. Of more immediate concern to Africa, and the less developed areas of West Asia and Asia and the Pacific, are food security and the diminution of poverty.

Regions with emerging market economies, such as those of Eastern Europe, South-East Asia, and parts of Latin America, increasingly face problems associated with rising energy demands and other negative effects of industrialization, such as increasing levels of pollutants and greenhouse gases. This trend will pose serious problems of acidification, transboundary pollution, reduced air quality, and declining health unless lessons of prior industrialization are heeded. Problems of burgeoning populations, rapidly increasing urbanization, and the widening gap between the rich and the poor are concerns shared by most regions.

Poverty and the growing global population are often targetted as responsible for much of the degradation of the world's resources. However, the inefficient use of resources (including those of others), waste generation, pollution and contamination from industry, and high levels of consumption are equally driving the earth toward an environmental precipice. Unfortunately, environmental problems are often disregarded when they interfere with short-term economic impetus; they only attract thoughtful attention when economies are in jeopardy from the very environmental problems economic advancement may bring. The intergovernmental process is also too often slow in catching up with current conditions, and there is an increasing need to encourage greater environmental citizenship and informed voluntary action at all levels in societies.

WHILE MANY MAY ATTRIBUTE THE CURRENT DEGRADATION OF THE WORLD'S RESOURCES TO POVERTY AND BURGEONING POPULATION GROWTH, THE INEFFICIENT USE OF RESOURCES, HIGH LEVELS OF CONSUMPTION, WASTE GENERATION, AND INDUSTRIAL POLLUTION ARE EQUALLY TO BLAME.

In all regions it appears that politics and environment are increasingly inseparable. Widespread access to the media and modern communications in democratic societies, with the associated availability of environmental information empower individuals and interest groups to stimulate public policy response. Political changes sweeping through much of the developing and rapidly industrializing worlds suggest further dissemination of these technologies with accompanying transparency, access to information, and accountability.

Widespread poverty, the burden of increasing population without accompanying development, urbanization, and equity questions still menace sustainable development while acceptance is growing world-wide of the need to seek solutions together on a global scale. And, even though less developed regions have become involved increasingly in international environmental negotiations, survival strategies addressing the immediate needs of the poor often dictate short-term actions. As a result, immediate needs are often met through, for example, uncontrolled expansion of cultivation in wilderness areas and inadequate land management to support food production.

Even when technologies are available, economic pressures tend to slow change in industrial and industrializing countries, retarding the introduction of cleaner and more efficient production methods and reduced consumption. Unfortunately, in most regions there is only embryonic acceptance and application of preventive and remedial actions that—if taken sooner rather than later—would assist sustainable development in all regions.

Interaction of Environmental Problems

Environmental problems are mostly complex in nature with a myriad of interactions occurring both within and between the atmosphere and biosphere. Greenhouse gases and acidifying pollutants produced by industry, for example, have been shown to worsen the problem of ozone layer thinning when they interact. Sulphate aerosols, the by-products of industry and transport systems, have been found to mask the effects of global warming in the short term, particu-

larly in industrialized areas of the northern hemisphere. Integrated solutions are therefore essential to halt complex environmental degradation of these types and to ameliorate their effects.

Although there is overall recognition that many specific environmental problems are inextricably linked to or influenced by one another, North America and western Europe are taking the lead in addressing such complex environmental concerns in an integrated manner through inter-agency approaches and multi-disciplinary teams within agencies. Action is also beginning to be taken in this regard in the industrialized quarters of Asia and the Pacific, Latin America, and West Asia.

Major Issues

Land

Issues pertaining to land are of greatest concern in regions where food security is a priority, notably in Africa and West Asia. Land availability, abatement of land degradation, and efficient land management are driven by the food security demands of growing populations, which result in expanded cultivation and agricultural intensification—unless met by food trade.

In countries with limited economic resources, the food trade option is not generally sufficient to cover the magnitude of growing needs. Rapid introduction and adoption of intensification technologies are also limited by economic and cultural complexities, leaving the expansion of cultivation into marginal lands and wilderness areas as the prime short- to medium-term option for increasing production. As a consequence, forests, woodlands, or grasslands are destroyed or degraded and natural ecosystems are fragmented, with negative impacts on biodiversity. Poor land management further increases susceptibility of soils to erosion, reduces moisture retention, and accelerates leaching of nutrients. Degradation feeds back into a cycle of declining productivity and, in the worst cases, desertification or the irreversible degeneration of marginal lands.

Considerable anxiety still remains in several regions (Africa, Asia-Pacific, and West Asia) where there is a relative scarcity of land per capita and land quality is poor. Waterlogging, salinization, and erosion (by both wind and water) of soil resources are of special concern, while desertification remains a serious worry in the drier zones of the regions. Loss of limited agricultural land to alternative uses is another particular concern in West Asia.

Human-made fire influences land degradation in the woodlands and grasslands of Africa, and the problem is complicated by long-established cultural practices. The residual impacts of civil conflict in Africa also pose problems regarding the availability and degradation of land. Significant tracts of land remain effectively inaccessible due to the widespread laying of mines during past military conflicts and the environmental impact of refugees is substantial in a number of countries.

Limited land availability is also of particular concern to small island states world-wide. Land degradation through erosion and significant desertification of drylands in the past is an ongoing problem in Latin America. Despite the remaining high number of natural ecosystems in Latin America, unrestrained expansion of the agricultural frontier there could have serious impacts on wilderness areas.

In Europe, problems of land degradation relate mainly to irreversible erosion, acidification, and pollution of soils and the subsequent economic impacts. Generally speaking, soil degradation is no longer a priority concern in North America, given the widespread adoption of conservation-based farming practices. More attention is placed on problems relating to land pollution, and water contamination. Improving poor agricultural practices, where evident, is vigorously targetted in order to reduce erosion and productivity losses.

Forests

The decline of natural forest in developing regions has been considerable between 1980 and 1990. Total losses in the tropics have been greatest in Latin America and the Caribbean, followed by those in Africa and in Asia and the Pacific. Industrialization, population growth and related agricultural expansion, and forest product trade are the main driving forces in reducing forest cover in these regions. Rates of deforestation are of particular concern in Asia and the Pacific, and in the highland states of West Asia. In West Asia, the opening up of woodlands has caused increased susceptibility to erosion and land degradation in general.

In Africa, remaining forests are under great pressure from agricultural expansion and the use of wood as fuel, with pressure likely to increase with rising population, continued dependence on subsistence agriculture, and an absence of alternatives to wood as fuel. Declining productivity, increased climatic variability, and greater susceptibility to flooding have also been attributed in part to accelerated deforestation on the African continent.

Forest area is currently rather stable in Europe and North America, as it has been for the past century. However, forests in Europe suffer from acidification, and the boreal (northern) forests in Siberia are being heavily exploited. The removal of old-growth forests raises protests in North America and Europe.

Biodiversity

Conservation of biodiversity is of concern in all regions, with most countries having adopted the principles of the Convention on Biological Diversity. As a result, many have taken steps domestically to protect and conserve natural habitats and related biodiversity. The degree of success and national priority accorded to biodiversity varies widely across regions, however.

Latin America accords biodiversity a high priority, while Asia and the Pacific more recently accepted its legitimacy as an issue of both national and international concern. Both Europe and North America accord a high priority to the conservation of biodiversity, although the United States has not signed the Convention on Biological Diversity. Many African countries, with a view toward the economic potential of revenues from wildlife tourism, also recognize the need for biodiversity conservation.

Yet competition for scarce land resources and the rising demand for food production represent important constraints. Habitat loss caused by development pressure and the overexploitation of fisheries, ground-water depletion, and hunting are threatening biodiversity. Fish stocks in parts of North America and Europe have also been seriously depleted. One of the more pernicious effects worldwide of deforestation and the conversion of other natural lands such as woodlands and grasslands is the fragmentation of habitats and the negative effect this has on biodiversity.

Water

On a global scale, the problem of water is more a case of distribution and quality than one of quantity. Water is rarely a region-wide concern, with some notable exceptions, but all regions have some problems related to either ground-water or surface water resources.

The development and efficient management of water resources is of particular concern in West Asia and parts of Africa, particularly the Sudano-Sahelian belt and the Horn of Africa. Not only is there relative scarcity of water resources, but these locations also face high evaporation rates, high levels of anticipated future demands, and the transboundary problems associated with water resources. Measured against the future requirements of urban centres, agriculture, and industry, access to adequate quantity and quality of water will soon become problematic in those areas of West Asia, Africa, and the parts of Latin America that have mega-cities. In some cases, competition for water may lead to conflicts over transboundary resources.

In other regions, overexploitation of surface waters disrupts flow regimes, affecting aquatic ecosystems and the quantity and quality of water supplies downstream, a situation that can lead to hostility between water users. Overexploitation of ground water lowers water tables, which may damage wetlands, cause ground subsidence, and induce saltwater intrusion in coastal aquifers.

Many cities world-wide that depend on ground water as the primary water supply are experiencing problems caused by the deterioration of these reserves. In large cities in many regions, the discharge of inadequately treated sewage subjects aquatic communities to severe deoxygenation and possibly ammonia toxicity. Humans risk microbial infection if recycled water is not adequately treated, as happens in areas marginal to cities, including those mega-cities in the less developed parts of Asia and Latin America.

Europe also suffers from contamination of much-needed ground-water resources as well as shared surface water resources as a result of excessive agricultural fertilizer and pesticide use. Concerns over water in North America relate mainly to municipal supplies and rural water quality and their consequent impact on health.

Marine and Coastal Environments

A high proportion of the world's population resides in coastal areas, and many more derive benefit from marine resources such as food, employment, or tradable commodities. Marine coastal ecosystems and the accompanying biodiversity are particularly vulnerable to land-based sources of contamination.

An estimated one third of the world's coastal regions are at high risk of degradation, with the greatest threat apparent in Europe. Asia and the Pacific, the wider Caribbean, and West Asia also face problems related to land-based sources of urban waste discharge and industrial pollution. Shipping traffic and oil spills represent a particular threat in West Asia and the Caribbean. Threats to the coastal and marine resources in Latin America and the Caribbean rise considerably with tourism, infrastructure development, and the discharge of sediment, waste, and industrial contaminants. Coastal erosion is a growing problem in a number of African countries where local communities are adversely affected by changing sedimentation patterns due to upstream dam construction or increased erosion in degraded catchments. Eutrophication in the Baltic, Black, and North seas is also a problem—and a severe one in localities bordering the Mediterranean and Caspian seas.

The overexploitation of marine fisheries and the economic impact of such practices cause widespread concern in parts of Asia and the Pacific, North America, Europe, and West Asia. In addition, small island states and coastal communities of South-East Asia, the Pacific, the Caribbean, and low-lying areas of Europe have special concerns over the future impacts of climate change on sea level, especially as the precise local effects cannot yet be determined. Climate change may also affect ocean mixing and circulation patterns, with significant repercussions on the productivity of marine ecosystems and the location of fisheries.

Atmosphere

Polluted air has many adverse impacts: on human health, through inhalation of harmful gases and particulates; by damaging biotic and ecosystem functions; through accelerated deterioration of building materials; and by inducing climatic disturbances. In the short term, it is the human health risks, especially chronic respiratory illnesses, that are of greatest concern.

Damage to ecosystems through acidification and acid rain is also causing growing anxiety in some regions. Once regarded only as a problem in Europe and parts of North America, airborne pollution has become apparent in parts of Asia and the Pacific and in Latin America—fuelled literally by the by-products of industrialization. The cause lies largely in the burning of fossil fuels for industry and transport in countries with developed and rapidly growing market economies. The long-range transportation and transboundary effects of such atmospheric processes are increasingly of global concern.

The concentration of people and activities close to urban and industrial areas is of particular concern in Europe—especially in eastern Europe, where poor air quality is considered the most common environmental problem. Large cities in Asia and the Pacific, Latin America, and North America also experience problems of local air pollution. The rapid growth of a number of African cities points to emerging problems of poor urban air quality there in the near future.

The Montreal Protocol clearly illustrated the ability of the international community to quickly mobilize and respond to a scientifically identified environmental problem stemming from ozone de-

pleting substances. Despite coordinated action world-wide, damage to the ozone layer continues faster than expected. The resulting increase of ultra-violet-B radiation in the lower atmosphere has adverse impacts on human health (skin cancer, cataracts, and reduced immune efficiency), on terrestrial and aquatic ecosystems (reduced species survival and productivity), and on building materials (faster deterioration). While ozone depletion continues in the upper atmosphere, rising ozone concentrations in the troposphere have focused world attention on the extent of the human contribution to this problem.

Global warming is yet another universal problem emanating from a changing atmosphere. All regions express concern over global warming and place emphasis on the need for adaptive mechanisms to cope with accompanying climate variability and sea level change.

Urban and Industrial Environments

Developing and rapidly industrializing regions, faced with rapidly increasing populations as a result of high birth rates and in-migration, are battling with the accompanying environmental problems of unplanned urban growth and emerging mega-cities (those with more than 10 million inhabitants). Estimates indicate that by the year 2000, 21 cities will fall in this category. The rise of such cities in Asia and the Pacific, Latin America, and Africa has been accompanied by the proliferation of slums and squatter settlements without access to basic infrastructure, water, or sanitation. Eastern Europe is also affected to some degree by this phenomenon, as are a number of cities in West Asia, especially those experiencing massive rural-to-urban migration.

The resultant concentration of people and of industrial and domestic effluents and waste impose unwieldy demands on urban environments. Poor urban and solid waste management in African cities is particularly problematic in view of the potentially damaging effects on human health. At the same time, there is a move in western Europe and North America toward greening cities and encouraging reduced urban population densities. The increasing number of single-person households in these latter regions, however, is placing increased demands on energy resources and the management of wastes.

Wherever management and disposal of industrial and domestic waste is inadequate, these sources of soil and water contamination pose potential hazards to human and ecosystem health. Consequently, improved waste management is a priority in urban and industrial areas of Europe. Changing consumption patterns and recycling are encouraged by governments, but thousands of contaminated sites remain due to improper waste disposal, particularly in Eastern Europe and the former Soviet Union.

Investment in new technologies is helping improve waste management in much of western Europe. In the Asia-Pacific region, rapidly growing economic activity and populations have stimulated solid and industrial waste generation to the extent that it now poses a serious environmental health problem.

In the industrializing countries of Latin America, industrial effluent and solid wastes pose increasing hazards to human health because of the close proximity of large populations to the contaminants. Waste management receives serious attention throughout North America due to the ever increasing quantities of municipal and industrial waste generated. The region is the leading producer of waste on the planet.

Chemical pollutants are emerging world-wide as a pervasive environmental concern of highest priority. Environmental emergencies involving chemicals appear to be steadily increasing, and mounting evidence is being put forth about serious health risks posed by persistent organic pollutants. Radioactive pollution remains a top environmental concern of countries in northern and eastern Europe, particularly those of the former Soviet Union.

Polar Environments

The Arctic and Antarctic regions represent the world's largest remaining natural areas and pristine environments. Polar regions have long been recognized as important indicators of the planet's overall health, especially with regard to global warming, long-range transport of pollutants, and, in the case of Antarctica, atmospheric ozone concentrations. For these reasons, universal concern generated international action regarding the state of the environment in both regions.

In the Arctic, overexploitation of fisheries, mining, the presence of forest industries, and infrastructure development all threaten natural habitats and open the possibility for direct degradation and pollution of resources. A fragile ecosystem, the region is particularly sensitive to land degradation and erosion. Biodiversity is also fragile, with few but highly specialized and adapted species.

Military and industrial interest in the Arctic has had a negative impact through dumping of radioactive wastes and accidents involving similar materials. While radioactivity of Arctic seas is low compared with other north European seas, it is still considered one of the main threats to the Arctic environment. Traditional societies have also increased their exploitation of resources through a shift towards non-traditional activities.

The vast extent of Antarctica's sea ice and continental ice sheet are especially important with regard to the modelling and assessment of climate change and sea level rise. Its unique geographical location and pristine environment also enable the monitoring of air pollution against a background of minimum interference and high sensitivity to change. Antarctica has unique marine and terrestrial life forms that require protection from growing international interest in the continent. Related tourism is a growing industry that can have a serious impact if not controlled.

AFRICA

Major Environmental Concerns

Africa is a large continent with many different dynamics. Since the 1960s, it has experienced persistent and severe economic and environmental problems, as well as political and social turmoil in some countries. Its population growth rate—the world's highest—has placed additional strains on all systems. Poverty has perpetuated underdevelopment and mismanagement of resources in the region. Furthermore, deterioration in the terms of trade and lack of financial resources for investment have made it difficult for several countries to develop patterns of livelihood that would reduce pressure on the natural resource base.

However, this is only a part of African reality. Other significant changes have also occurred, including the dramatic demise of apartheid in South Africa, the end of civil wars and the subsequent accession of elected Governments to power in Angola and Mozambique, implementation of structural adjustment programmes in 35 countries that have successfully put in place economic reform measures, a surge towards political liberalization, and emergence of an increasingly strengthened civil society (UNDP, 1996). These are examples of social and political transitions towards peace and economic progress, although their impacts on the environment are yet to be assessed. Africa is at a critical turning point.

Amid these changes, environmental degradation continues. One of the major problems common to the countries of Africa relates to the great imbalance in the use of its natural resources: those such as soil and vegetation are overexploited, while water, energy, minerals, and organic resources are underused or exported raw. Striking a balance between economic development and sustainability for the growing number of people remains the major environment and development challenge. The two are interlinked, requiring a coherent and integrated regional approach for their solution. The difficulty of finding the right path is compounded by the region's great variance in cultural heritage and natural resource endowments.

Various regional fora of African Government leaders have consistently mentioned the following priority environmental concerns (UNECA, 1992, 1993a, 1993c; OAU, 1995; UNEP, 1996a):

- land degradation and desertification problems, particularly in relation to the need for food security and self-sufficiency;

- the protection and sustainable use of forests;

- effective management and protection of biodiversity;

- water resources issues, including the problem of water scarcity and efficient water management;

- pollution problems, particularly those affecting freshwater resources as well as urban, coastal, and marine areas;

- climatic problems, including drought and climate change; and

- demographic change and population pressures on natural resources and in urban areas.

Land

This continent contains the world's largest expanse of drylands, covering roughly 2 billion hectares of the continent or 65 per cent of Africa's total land area (UNEP, 1991a). One third of this area is hyperarid deserts, while the remaining two thirds consists of arid, semi-arid, and dry sub-humid areas—home to about 400 million Africans, two thirds of the continent's total. Recurrent droughts are a permanent fact of life throughout the drylands of Africa.

Severe droughts have seriously affected both agriculture and wildlife and caused deaths and severe malnutrition. With each drought cycle, desertification increases. Currently, 36 countries in Africa are affected by drought and some degree of desertification (UNEP, 1994). The risk of drought is high in the Sudano-Sahelian belt and in southern Africa.

Land degradation, which includes degradation of vegetation cover and soil degradation, has been identified as a major problem in Africa. The extent of the problem continent-wide is difficult to determine precisely due to lack of data, particularly on vegetation cover degradation. The Global Assessment of Soil Degradation (UNEP/ISRIC, 1990; UNEP, 1991c) estimated that about a half-billion hectares in Africa are moderately to severely degraded, corresponding to one third of all cropland and permanent pasture on the continent. Some national reports, especially in northern Africa, indicate much higher percentages of degradation.

The main causes of the soil degradation are overgrazing, particularly in drylands; extensive clearing of vegetation for agriculture; deforestation; extensive cultivation of marginal lands; the use of inappropriate agricultural technology; poor management of arable lands; and droughts (UNECA, 1992; Thomas and Middleton, 1993; Ohlsson, 1995). (See also Figure 2.1.) Other contributors, particularly in the southern African countries, are thought to include land shortages, usually due to the unequal distribution of land, and the modernization of agriculture that has led to marginalization of subsistence farming (Dahlberg, 1994). All these activities lead to depletion of soil fertility, water and wind erosion, and salinization (UNEP/ISRIC, 1990; Thomas and Middleton, 1993).

Land degradation is exacerbating the existing natural constraints on agricultural production, including poor soil quality, variable climatic conditions, and reliance on rainfed agriculture. About 90 per cent of African soils are deficient in phosphorus, a key nutrient in the production of biomass. These soils also have low content of organic matter, and low water infiltration and retention capacity due to surface crusting. Moreover, about half the cultivable land (or three quarters of land already cultivated) is under arid and semi-arid conditions, so potential for irrigation is limited (World Bank, 1995).

Agriculture is the fundamental economic activity in most African countries, averaging 20–30 per cent of gross domestic product (GDP) in sub-Saharan Africa, and 55 per cent of the total value of exports (excluding the oil-producing countries). Yet land degradation, coupled with rapid population growth, is increasing deficits in food production and food insecurity. Although a serious information gap exists regarding the productivity impacts of degradation, rough estimates indicate that, on average, land areas affected by degradation have lost about 20 per cent of their productivity during the last decade (World Bank, 1995).

Forests

The 1990 Forest Resources Assessment by the United Nations Food and Agriculture Organization estimated the extent of forests and other wooded land in Africa as about 1.14 billion hectares (approximately 38 per cent of total land area) some of which is in drylands.

The total area of tropical forests in Africa in 1990 was estimated to be approximately 530 million hectares, compared with 569 million hectares in 1980 (the average annual rate of deforestation was 0.7 per cent). (See Figure 2.2.) Africa's rainforests covered about 7 per cent of the land surface in 1992, representing slightly less than 20 per cent of the total remaining global rainforests. The forests of Africa are the most depleted of all the tropical regions, with only 30 per cent or so of the historical stands still remaining (UNEP, 1994).

Africa's closed canopy tropical moist forests range from the mangroves of Senegal on the west coast to the montane forests of Jevel Hantara near the eastern tip of Somalia. Most of the countries of western Africa were once clothed in forest from the coast to deep inland. Central Africa still contains vast and more or less continuous stretches of rainforest. Around 80 per cent of the rainforest on the continent is concentrated in this area, particularly in Zaire (see also Box 2.1, on the Congo Basin). Moving to the south of the continent, the main forest block

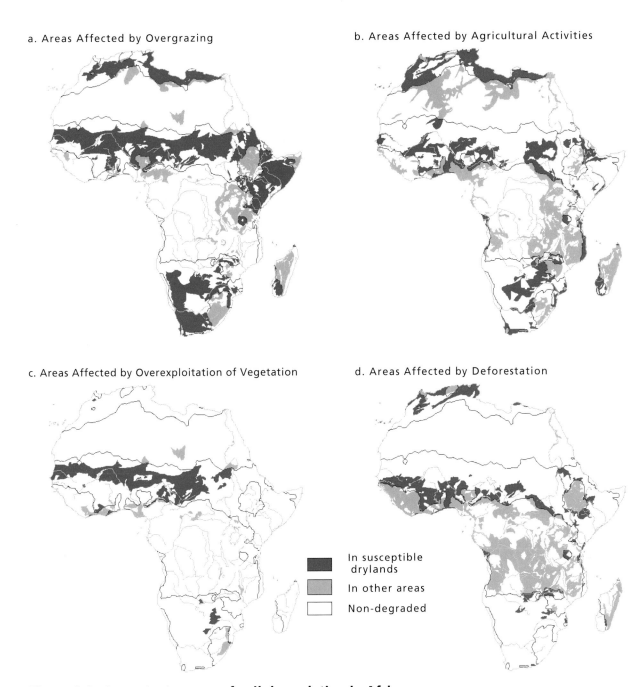

a. Areas Affected by Overgrazing

b. Areas Affected by Agricultural Activities

c. Areas Affected by Overexploitation of Vegetation

d. Areas Affected by Deforestation

In susceptible drylands

In other areas

Non-degraded

Figure 2.1. Important causes of soil degradation in Africa.

Source: UNEP (1992).

gives way to dense miombo woodlands with scattered patches of dry deciduous type forest. In eastern Africa, the moist forest gradually disappears as the climate becomes more arid. In these areas, forests occur only in strips bordering rivers, along the tops or slopes of mountains, or on the wet coastal hills.

The total area of temperate forests in 1990 was approximately 13 million hectares, compared with 14.3 million hectares in 1980, indicating an average annual rate of decrease of 0.9 per cent (FAO, 1995). This was the highest rate of temperate-forest decline of all developing regions.

Deforestation is a major problem throughout Africa, although its causes and magnitude vary by region. The major cause is related to forest clearance for agriculture (particularly commercial farming

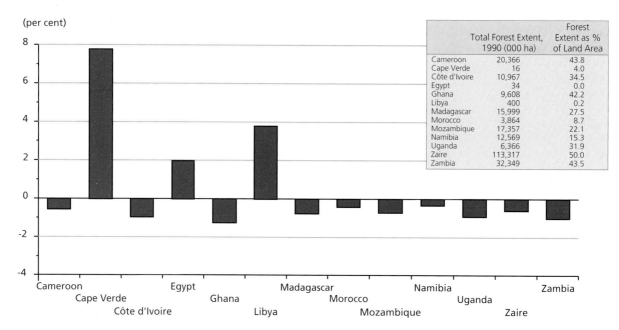

(per cent)

	Total Forest Extent, 1990 (000 ha)	Forest Extent as % of Land Area
Cameroon	20,366	43.8
Cape Verde	16	4.0
Côte d'Ivoire	10,967	34.5
Egypt	34	0.0
Ghana	9,608	42.2
Libya	400	0.2
Madagascar	15,999	27.5
Morocco	3,864	8.7
Mozambique	17,357	22.1
Namibia	12,569	15.3
Uganda	6,366	31.9
Zaire	113,317	50.0
Zambia	32,349	43.5

Figure 2.2. Average annual change in the extent of forest in selected African countries, 1981–90.

Sources: FAO (1993, 1995).
Note: Forest consists of the sum of natural forest and plantation area categories for tropical and temperate developing countries.

and to some extent shifting cultivation) and the harvesting of fuelwood (SARDC, 1994a; UNECA, 1992). In 1980, one study estimated that cultivation accounted for 70 per cent of the deforestation (WCMC, 1992). In sub-Saharan Africa, 70 per cent of total energy consumed and 90 per cent of household energy are derived from wood fuel, and it has been estimated that in Africa each family uses at least 7 metric tons of wood a year (SADC ELMS, 1993).

An extensive shortage of fuelwood is already particularly apparent in the Sudano-Sahelian belt, including in Burkina Faso, Chad, The Gambia, and Niger (World Bank, 1995). Commercial logging is limited, but settlement and agriculture around roads built to transport timber has resulted in additional clearing of forest areas (World Bank, 1995). In northern Africa, deforestation is particularly severe in Algeria, Morocco, and Tunisia (World Bank, 1994). What remains of the forests in humid West Africa are disappearing at the alarming rate of about 2 per cent a year, and exceeding 5 per cent in the extreme case of Côte d'Ivoire (World Bank, 1995). In eastern Africa, severe encroachment and exploitation are destroying the forests that occur in fragmented patches (UNEP, 1994). Additional causes of

deforestation in southern Africa include clearing of land for refugee camps, construction materials, tobacco curing, and tsetse fly controls (SARDC, 1994b; Babu and Hassan, 1995).

Biodiversity

Africa offers a wide spectrum of habitats and ecosystems. Biological diversity varies in complex ways, depending on local moisture regimes, topography, vegetation, and soil type. Countries such as Zaire, which has large areas of land in the humid tropics, and South Africa, Kenya, and Tanzania—with impressively variable landscapes—are famous for their high species diversity and impressive wildlife populations. Some island States in the Indian Ocean are rich in endemic species (UNEP, 1994).

Savannahs (consisting of savannah woodland, tree savannah, shrub savannah, and grass savannah) are the most extensive ecosystem in Africa and provide a home for the majority of humans, livestock, and wildlife. They are the richest grassland regions in the world, with a high incidence of indigenous plants and animals and the world's greatest concentration of large mammals, particularly in northern Tanzania (WCMC, 1992).

Box 2.1
Some Areas of Rich Biodiversity and Forests in Africa

Western Africa

The relic blocks of forests left at Gola in Sierra Leone, at Sapo in Liberia, and at Tai in Côte d'Ivoire are now of global importance as the last significant remains of the structurally complex and species-rich forests of the upper Guinea zone (UNEP, 1994). Some areas—such as Fouta Djallon, Mount Nimba, and Loma at the head of major watersheds in western Africa (the Niger, Senegal, and Gambia rivers)—encompass areas of exceptional biodiversity. These remaining centres of biodiversity are at risk (World Bank, 1995).

The Congo Basin

This area constitutes the second largest contiguous primary tropical rainforest area in the world. It has the lowest population density in Africa but the highest level of urbanization (52 per cent). One of the main economic activities is forest exploitation; others include mining, gas and oil exploration, and related industrial activities. Although the environment problems of the subregion are less severe compared with others on the continent, a future development challenge is to maintain the primary forest intact while drawing benefits from its local use (World Bank, 1995).

Islands of the Indian Ocean

The biodiversity of some of the island countries of the Indian Ocean are of global significance. The diversity of the landscapes in Madagascar and the extremely high level of endemism of its flora and fauna have put this country on the list of environmental priorities in the world (World Bank, 1995). Most of these species are found in the remaining forest areas.

It has been estimated that there were originally about 11.2 million hectares of eastern rainforest, which was reduced to 7.6 million hectares by 1950 and to 3.8 million hectares by 1985. The main causes of the deforestation are slash-and-burn (or tavy) agriculture and cutting of fuelwood to sustain the growing population. The population is still rural, surviving by subsistence agriculture (WCMC, 1992). Madagascar and parts of southern Africa were the home of the giant ostrich, or elephant bird, a huge, 3-metre-tall flightless creature whose 11 known species have long been extinct. The mummified bodies and gigantic eggs of this bird have been found in the Madagascar swamps. Their demise was probably caused by human activities (UNEP, 1994).

Other endemic species of the Indian Ocean islands include the red colobus monkey, found only on Zanzibar Island, and the different species of fruit bats or "flying foxes" found in the forests of Seychelles and Mafia and on the Pemba Islands of Tanzania.

References

UNEP. 1994. The Convention on Biological Diversity: Issues of Relevance to Africa. Regional Ministerial Conference on the Convention on Biological Diversity. October. UNEP/AMCEN/RCU 7/1 (A), 27 July.

WCMC. 1992. *Global Biodiversity: Status of the World Living Resources*. World Conservation Monitoring Centre. Chapman and Hall. London.

World Bank. 1995. *Toward Environmentally Sustainable Development in Sub-Saharan Africa*.

Several African mountains and highlands have unique and rich biodiversity, with a number of endemic animal and plant species. These areas include mountain ranges or chains such as the Atlas, Rwenzori, and Aberdare mountains; more uniform volcanic cones such as Mount Kenya, Mount Kilimanjaro, and Mount Cameroon; valleys and escarpments such as the Rift Valley and the Nile gorge; and highlands and plateaus such as those found in Ethiopia, Kenya, and southern Africa. Particularly in the tropical and subtropical regions of Africa, the sloping areas surrounding high altitudes are of great importance for development (UNEP, 1994).

Wetlands cover about 1 per cent of Africa's total surface area and are found in every country (WCMC, 1992). The largest include the Zaire swamps, the Sudd in the Upper Nile, the Lake Victoria and Chad basins, the Okavango Delta, and the floodplains and deltas of the Niger and Zambezi rivers. The diversity of flora and fauna of wetlands in Africa is immense and in many places unknown, with endemic and rare plant species and wildlife, including migratory bird species (UNEP, 1994). Many wetlands are under threat from conversion (drainage and filling), overuse, pollution from farm runoff and untreated urban and industrial effluents, and unplanned development. Also, the fact that freshwater fish are a primary source of protein and income in many local communities can threaten biodiversity. Furthermore, a substantial number of species in water masses are threatened with extinction from new species that were introduced in the absence of environmental impact assessments (WCMC, 1992), as happened in Lake Victoria (Roest, 1992).

The African coastal region is vast, and includes a variety of habitats. Diversity of fish species is high, with more than 4,000 species reported. Some of the most numerous and economically most important fish species are tuna, marlin, and billfish; tuna is a significant source of foreign exchange for a number of countries.

Various kinds of human activities are harming biodiversity in terms of habitat loss and degradation, resulting in, for example, loss of medicinal and aromatic plants of high value. Cultivation is perhaps the most significant cause of damage to ecosystems, involving large land areas and alteration of the landscape. The savannah was also greatly enlarged (usually at the cost of forests) through burning to improve grazing for livestock and to facilitate wild game hunting, forest clearance, and massive increases in the number of cattle (WCMC, 1992).

The margins of the seas are affected by humans almost everywhere. Habitats are being lost forever to the construction of harbours and industrial installations, the development of tourist facilities and mariculture, and the growth of settlements and cities. Increasing coastal erosion as well as pollution is also evident.

The adverse effects of poverty on biological resources are compounded by exploitation by a small but influential and affluent segment of the African population and by commercial firms hastening to satisfy market demands that often originate in other regions (UNEP, 1994).

African countries have taken steps over the years to conserve their biodiversity in its various forms. Protected areas have been established, for example, although they do not cover the full spectrum of biodiversity in the major ecosystems. The continent has 727 protected terrestrial areas (approximately 5 per cent of the total land area) and 112 protected marine areas (WRI/UNEP/UNDP/WB, 1996).

A few countries (in particular, Kenya, Zimbabwe, and South Africa) have used one aspect of biodiversity—wildlife—for tourism development. Africa's share of international tourism was only 2 per cent in 1990 (World Bank, 1995), but it is a growing economic activity: for example, in southern Africa the number of tourists doubled between 1990 and 1994, and tourism contributed to about 3.4 per cent of the region's economy in 1994 (Hulme, 1996).

Although Africa's biodiversity generates considerable revenue, both for Governments and businesses as well as for industrial countries' commercial interests, more equitable distribution of these revenues to landowners adjacent to protected areas is needed to ensure the full and effective participation of local populations in the tasks of conservation and sustainable use of biological resources (UNDP/FAO, 1980; Makombe, 1993).

Water

The availability of water in Africa is highly variable both in space and in time. Precipitation over the continent varies from practically zero over the Horn of Africa and the Namibian Desert to more than 4,000 millimetres a year in the western equatorial region. A large proportion of the continent is semi-arid, receiving between 200 and 800 millimetres a

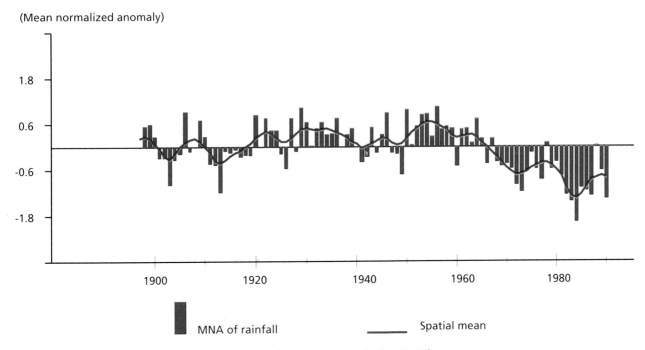

(Mean normalized anomaly)

■ MNA of rainfall   —— Spatial mean

Figure 2.3. Trends in mean annual rainfall in the Sahel (1897–90).

Source: UNEP (1992).

Note: The number of stations from which data are taken and averaged varies for each year up to about 100. The annual rainfall series for each station is normalized by taking away the long-term (1951–80) mean from each value and dividing the difference by the long-term (1951–80) standard deviation. The smooth curve is a 10-year Gaussian filter that suppresses variations of less than 10 years, giving an indication of trends in the rainfall anomalies.

year of variable rainfall. Droughts that last between one and five years occur frequently.

The rainfall records from the early 1900s to mid-1980s show that the continent's average annual rainfall has decreased since 1968, and has been fluctuating around a notably lower mean level (UNEP, 1985). (See Figure 2.3.) The impact of variable rainfall and drought has been accentuated by land degradation and deforestation, which have led to more soil erosion and hence increased sediment transport—which adversely affects water quality, aquatic ecology, reservoir volumes, estuaries, ports, and hydroelectric dams (World Bank, 1996).

In Africa some 4 trillion (4,000 billion) cubic metres of renewable water is available annually, but only about 4 per cent is used (WRI/UNEP/-UNDP/WB, 1996). (See Table 2.1.) The infrastructure and technical and financial means do not exist to use effectively the water available (UNEP, 1996b). Runoff is concentrated in limited upland areas (such as Fouta Djallon in Guinea, the Jos Plateau in

Nigeria, the Cameroon Mountains, the Ethiopian Highlands, the Aberdares and the slopes of Mount Kenya, and Mount Kilimanjaro and Lesotho and Swaziland Highlands), and relatively few lengthy rivers run through downstream dry terrain (for example, into Sudan and Egypt for the Nile River). The fresh water available to downstream countries, often with a dry climate, depends on actions taken by upstream countries to develop their own water resources (World Bank, 1996).

The continent's ground-water resources, although widespread, are limited. In sub-Saharan Africa, about 15 per cent of the renewable water resources is ground water and more than three quarters of the population uses this as their main source of supply (World Bank, 1996). There are a few large sedimentary basins in the region with substantial renewable ground-water reserves and numerous smaller sedimentary aquifers along the major rivers, coastal deltas, and plains.

Ground-water quality is deteriorating in some areas due to lack of proper assessment and manage-

Table 2.1

Annual Internal Renewable Water Resources and Water Withdrawals in Selected African Countries

	Annual Internal Renewable Water Resources[a]		Annual Withdrawals			Sectoral Withdrawals (percent)[b]		
	Total (cubic kilometres)	1995 Per Capita (cubic metres)	Year of Data	Percentage of Water Resources[a]	Per Capita (cubic metres)	Domestic	Industry	Agriculture
Algeria	14.8	528	1990	30	180	25	15	60
Burundi	3.6	563	1987	3	20	36	0	64
Congo	832.0	321,236	1987	0	20	62	27	11
Egypt	58.1	923	1992	97	956	6	9	85
Ethiopia	110.0	1,998	1987	2	51	11	3	86
Kenya	30.2	1,069	1990	7	87	20	4	76
Libya	0.6	111	1994	767	880	11	2	87
Morocco	30.0	1,110	1992	36	427	5	3	92
Nigeria	280.0	2,506	1987	1	41	31	15	54
Tunisia	3.9	443	1990	78	381	9	3	89
Zaire	1,019.0	23,211	1990	0	10	61	16	23

Source: WRI/UNEP/UNDP/WB (1996).
Notes: a. Annual internal renewable water resources usually include river flows from other countries. b. Sectoral percentages date from the year of other annual withdrawal data.

ment, which leads, for example, to overexploitation (World Bank, 1996). This is particularly true in northern Africa.

The proportion of people without access to adequate water is greater here than anywhere else: Africa has 19 of the 25 countries in the world with the highest percentage of populations without access to safe drinking water (WRI/UNEP/UNDP/WB, 1996). West and central Africa have more than enough water on a per capita basis, but in most other areas, population growth and economic development create excess demand over supply.

For example, Algeria, Egypt, Morocco, and Tunisia suffer water scarcity and stress (Population Action International, 1994). In Libya, more than 100 per cent of the renewable water supply is already being consumed, and fossil water is also being tapped. The freshwater supply is particularly limited in the Sudano-Sahelian belt and parts of southern Africa. (See also Figure 2.4.)

All the countries in continental sub-Saharan Africa share one or more river basins. There are at least 54 rivers or water bodies cross or form international boundaries in the region. However, few are effectively managed jointly. The Nile, Zambezi, Volta, and Niger rivers and Lake Victoria all have the potential to create serious conflicts as well as cooperation and economic integration.

The various activities competing to use fresh water include individual consumption, agriculture, fisheries, industry, power supply, livestock, wildlife resources and recreation, and watershed protection. The competition is becoming more intense, increasing the potential for conflicts at local, national, and regional levels (World Bank, 1996). The most important issue for Africa is to increase investment and cooperation among riparian States to manage the freshwater resources in an efficient and sustainable manner (UNEP, 1996b).

Rapid population growth, urbanization, industrialization, and the drive for food security are putting pressures on water resources, both in terms of quantity and quality. Domestic wastewater, industrial effluents, and agrochemicals are polluting both freshwater and coastal resources, causing health hazards, eutrophication, and stress on aquatic and marine ecosystems. For example, diarrhoeal deaths from consumption of contaminated water in Africa are the highest in the world, and other water-related diseases such as schistosomiasis, malaria, onchocerciasis, and filariasis are also common (World Bank, 1996).

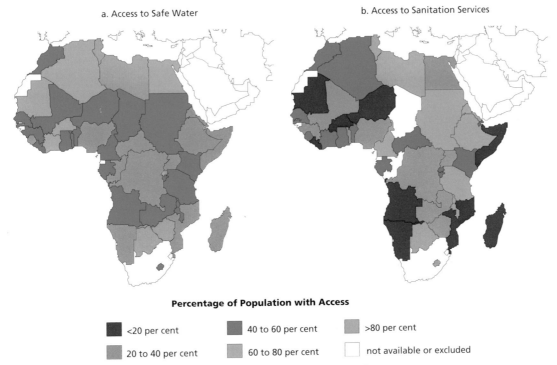

a. Access to Safe Water

b. Access to Sanitation Services

Percentage of Population with Access

- <20 per cent
- 40 to 60 per cent
- >80 per cent
- 20 to 40 per cent
- 60 to 80 per cent
- not available or excluded

Figure 2.4. Access to safe water and sanitation services in Africa.

Source: UNCHS (Habitat) (1996).
Notes: *Access to safe water:* Proportion of the population with access to an adequate amount of safe drinking water located within a convenient distance from the user's dwelling. *Access to sanitation services:* Proportion of the population with access to a sanitary facility for human extreta disposal in the dwelling or located within a convenient distance from the user's dwelling. *Access, sanitary facility,* and *convenient distance* are defined at the country level.

Marine and Coastal Environments

The African coastline is vast and traces a variety of habitats—from open ocean, near-shore waters, and sandy and rocky islands to beaches, lagoons, sand dunes, mud and sand flats, rocky cliffs, sea grass beds, coral reefs, and mangroves. Some of the waters surrounding Africa, particularly those from the Straits of Gibraltar to Guinea, are among the richest fishing grounds in the world, and the marine areas from Angola south to the Cape also contain great wealth (UNEP, 1985). Fish species diversity is high, including some of the most numerous and economically important fish. For many countries, especially in western Africa, fish is the main source of protein; Nigeria consumes the continent's largest quantities of fish (UNEP, 1994). The east coast of Africa, with the possible exception of Somalia, is not as fortunate; there the resources range from moderate to poor (UNEP, 1985).

Fishing and tourism are the main forms of marine resource use in Africa. Tourism is having an increasing impact, for example, in North Africa [Centre for Environment and Development for the Arab Region and Europe (CEDARE), personal communication, 1996]. Exploitation of mangrove forests is also an important economic and subsistence activity in many countries (SARDC, 1994c), and the cutting of these forests causes serious threats to the habitat. Dynamite fishing, the most environmentally destructive fishing method, is used along the coast. Although it is illegal in many countries, the laws are not actively enforced (UNEP, 1996b).

Several eastern African countries are constructing dams for hydroelectric power (UNEP, 1990) and in western Africa nearly all the main rivers have been dammed in at least one location (UNEP, 1989), blocking sediments and nutrients as well as fresh water. Excessive erosion of river mouths and delta areas (often the site of mangrove forests) and recession of shorelines and even disappearance of islands and towns (such as the town of Keta on the western coast) have occurred because of a reduced supply of sediment. The reduction in sediment and nutrient

Figure 2.5. African coastal ecosystems threatened by development.

Source: Bryant, D., *et al.* (1995).
Notes: a. Threat ranking depicts potential risk to coastal ecosystems from development-related activities. b. Coastal areas falling within a city or major port footprint or having a population density exceeding 150 persons per square kilometre, a road network density exceeding 150 metres of road per square kilometre, or a pipeline density exceeding 10 metres of pipeline per square kilometre. c. Coastal areas with a population density of between 75 and 150 persons per square kilometre, a road network density of between 100 and 150 metres of road per square kilometre, or a pipeline density of between 0 and 10 metres of pipeline per square kilometre. d. Coastal areas with a population of less than 75 persons per square kilometre, a road network density of less than 100 metres of road per square kilometre, and no pipelines known to be present.

supply also affects the spawning and growth cycles of marine fish and prawn species as well as fisheries further offshore (UNEP, 1990).

The decrease in freshwater discharge in the estuarine areas alters the extent of salt-water intrusion, with significant effects on the coastal ecosystems. For example, the mangrove swamps and rainforests of the Niger Delta have been damaged by salt-water intrusion (UNEP, 1990). The possible impact of sea level rise is also a high concern in the coastal and island countries of Africa (UNEP, 1996b).

Marine and coastal pollution problems do exist in Africa, although the scale of industrial activities is relatively limited and the size of population in relation to the length of coastline is also relatively small compared with other regions (UNEP, 1989 and 1990). (See Figure 2.5.) The Mediterranean Sea, however, is one of the most polluted water bodies (CEDARE, personal communications, 1996). In Africa, little sewage is treated, and effluents from growing industries are discharged into city sewage systems, rivers, and the coastal environment (including the sea, estuaries, and lagoons) mainly untreated and unchecked.

Pollution has many impacts on major coastal systems, such as the Niger Delta, where aquatic life and habitats are damaged (World Bank, 1996). In eastern Africa—for example, in Madagascar—soil erosion and consequent siltation as well as agrochemical pollution are increasing as a result of the development of irrigation, rice cultivation, and expanded and intensified agriculture into marginal, often sloping, areas (UNEP, 1990). In countries such as Mozambique and Tanzania, expanded, relocated, and new settlements in coastal areas and river plains, as well as overexploitation of mangroves for timber and fuelwood, are also increasing soil erosion problems and habitat loss for aquatic species, including shrimp and prawns (the largest contributor to the Mozambique's foreign exchange) (UNEP, 1990; Dalal-Clayton, 1995; Dejene and Olivares, 1991).

A number of other development activities are leading to major changes in coastal areas. The growth of towns and seaports and the dredging of harbours are some examples. Most coastal countries of western Africa have exploitable oil reserves. The main exploitation takes place in the area between Nigeria and Gabon. The cases of oil spillage in Nigeria have caused some significant local problems (UNEP, 1990). Environmental impacts from oil production, transportation, and related industrialization is also a concern in some North African countries, particularly Egypt, Libya, and Algeria (CEDARE, personal communication, 1996). In addition, the Iraq-Kuwait conflict had negative environmental impacts (UNEP, 1991b).

Urban and Industrial Environments

Urbanization is increasing rapidly in Africa. With only 35 per cent of its population living in cities, Africa is the least urbanized continent in the world.

Yet the urban population soared from 83 million in 1970 to 206 million in 1990 (Morna, 1996), and the number of cities with more than a million inhabitants increased from only one 30 years ago to 18 by 1990 (World Bank, 1995). Lagos in Nigeria and Cairo in Egypt are the world's fifteenth and eighteenth largest cities, with average annual population growth rates in 1990–95 of 5.68 and 2.24, respectively (WRI/UNEP/UNDP/WB, 1996). In the least developed countries, urban growth rates are among the highest in the world, at nearly 5 per cent a year. Between 1990 and 1995, some of these countries, including Burkina Faso and Mozambique, registered urban growth rates of more than 7 per cent a year (WRI/UNEP/UNDP/WB, 1996).

The main causes of urbanization are rapid population growth, natural disasters, ethnic tensions, and armed conflict. With 7 million refugees and 17 million internally displaced people, Africa has the highest number of people in the world forced to leave their homes (Morna, 1996). Additional reasons for rural-urban migration, which are generally true for developing countries, include the prospect of jobs and higher incomes in urban areas, poverty and lack of land in rural areas, and declining returns from agricultural commodities. (See also the discussion of social causes of environmental deterioration later in this section.)

Most African cities have not been able to develop the basic environmental services (such as solid waste disposal systems, sewage treatment, and adequate industrial and vehicle pollution control) to keep pace with the rapid growth of new urban dwellers. This has led to a steady deterioration of the urban environment, with a particularly strong impact on poorer people. For instance, urban health hazards resulting from a lack of clean water and proper sanitation particularly affect the poor. Reliable data are lacking on the scale and intensity of urban poverty in Africa. Although the incidence of rural poverty is still significantly higher, it seems that the difference is narrowing (WRI/UNEP/UNDP/WB, 1996).

Much of the urban population growth is in coastal cities. In North Africa, for example, the coastal zones along the Mediterranean are the most inhabited areas (Serhal et al., 1994). The rapid growth of coastal cities is one of the most pressing environmental concerns in the subregion (CEDARE, personal communication, 1996). Coastal zones bring all the pressing environmental issues together in one place—those related to agriculture, fisheries, water management at the interface between marine and river systems, infrastructure, and urban and industrial development. Most Governments, even in industrialized countries, do not have robust institutional mechanisms to deal with such complex systems in an integrated manner (World Bank, 1995).

Air pollution levels in the region are still low, but are emerging as a problem at local levels, particularly in major cities. In most countries and cities, pollution is neither monitored nor controlled. There is virtually no long-term study of pollutant impacts at the local or regional level. The primary sources of air pollution are coal and biomass burning, mining and manufacturing industries, and vehicles. Household burning of fuelwood, charcoal, and coal creates indoor pollution and local health hazards, and the burning of grasslands and forests also contributes to particulates and elevated levels of carbon dioxide in the atmosphere. The harmful effects of pollution are exacerbated by poor nutrition. Air pollution is emerging as a major problem in South Africa and to some extent in Zimbabwe, in areas where energy use and industrial development are essentially based on mineral coal (SARDC, 1994a; Ohlsson, 1995; Dalal-Clayton, 1995).

Underlying Causes

Environmental deterioration in Africa is intricately linked to poor economic performance and poverty. The chain of dependencies is all too familiar: rapid population growth and poverty accelerate deforestation and the expansion of agriculture into marginal areas, leading in turn to land degradation, which exacerbates food insecurity, loss of biodiversity, decline in water quality, and decrease in health status (UNEP, 1995).

Taken in isolation, any one link in the chain is neither entirely irrational nor perverse. Large families, for example, ensure an adequate labour force to cope with increasing time costs for gathering fuel and water, clearing of new land, or moving herds farther afield in the dry season (World Bank, 1995). Clearing a patch of forest and selling the timber to buy improved agricultural technology may be the most sustainable form of conversion in that situation.

The largest unknowns in the equations of environmental degradation are not the states and magnitudes but the relative importance of the driving forces and what actually drives what. Such knowledge would allow progress beyond the usual truisms and tautologies—for example, that economic development is a key to protecting and improving the environment and that growth must be environmentally sustainable to achieve the necessary economic development.

Social

The population of Africa is approaching 700 million (UNFPA, 1994). The current annual average growth rate is about 2.9 per cent and nearly half the population is below 16 years of age, yielding a population doubling time of 20–30 years. At this rate, the regional population will exceed 1 billion by 2005 (World Bank, 1995).

The African Common Position on Environment and Development (UNECA, 1992) states that the regional problem is not so much the high population growth rate but its distribution: a number of countries in Africa are underpopulated, and their resources are underexploited. Nevertheless, rapid population growth may frustrate Government efforts at meeting future demands for services and jobs, and slowing it will not necessarily minimize or eliminate existing levels of poverty, unemployment, and unevenness in income distribution (UNECA, 1993a).

While there is admittedly no evidence to show that reducing the population growth rate would solve poverty problems and regenerate abused environments, failure to do so will certainly worsen the situation. A precautionary principle seems to be emerging, and the consensus is that socio-economic development and population programmes should be planned and implemented simultaneously to

ensure that the benefits of each are fully realized (UNECA, 1993a).

Sub-Saharan Africa is home to an estimated 35 million international migrants, including some 4 million refugees. Out-migration from the inland countries of the Sudano-Sahelian belt to the coastal countries in West and Central Africa has been considerable. In West Africa, for example, the coastal countries are thought to have absorbed about 8 million people in the last three decades. These trends are likely to continue and even to expand (World Bank, 1995).

In several countries, migrants are not only pulled towards cities by the prospect of jobs and higher incomes, they are also pushed out of rural areas by such factors as poverty, lack of land, declining returns from agricultural commodities, war, and famine. Migration is also often part of a complex household survival strategy, in which families minimize risk by placing family members in different labour markets. An estimated 40–60 per cent of the annual urban population growth in developing countries is due to rural-urban migration, particularly where rural poverty is rampant (WRI/UNEP/UNDP/WB, 1996; SARDC, personal communication, 1996).

Africa still needs to improve in the areas of education and health. Since the promise of the 1990 Jomtien Conference on Education for All, slow but steady progress is being made in most regions of the world. In Africa, however, the downward trend in educational enrollment of the 1980s has not been reversed (UNDP, 1996). Repetition rates are excessive, retention is poor, and the gender gap is high. The health situation in Africa is cause for some satisfaction, in that life spans have increased significantly, in part from the impacts of concerted health initiatives. Yet it remains a cause of outrage in that preventable deaths, suffering, and loss of human potential are still high (UNDP, 1996).

Conflict arising from political instability has been a primary impediment to development in a number of African countries. The social, economic, and environmental impacts can be immense, as demonstrated in the recent armed conflicts that resulted in massive displacements and loss of human life. The causes for these outbreaks have been largely internal to the countries in question. Although such conflicts may be more amenable to intervention and management before they lead to violence, they also have wider implications: violence spillover, refugee flows, and regional destabilization. For example, the influx of Mozambican refugees into Malawi had a catastrophic effect on land and forest resources (Babu and Hassan, 1995). Some conflicts and social unrest were the result not only of political instability but also of ethnic tensions, food insecurity, poverty, limited access to resources, and land pressures.

Economic

Of the 30 poorest countries of the world, 21 are in Africa (World Bank, 1995). The United Nations Economic Commission for Africa points to the scarcity of a financial capital base for the initiation, stimulation, promotion, and sustenance of development activities as being the root of underdevelopment and environmental degradation in Africa (UNECA, 1992). Availability and suitability of imported technology to local situations is also a problem (SARDC, personal communication, 1996).

Lack of or slow growth, particularly in central and northern Africa, has contributed significantly to the overall low aggregate regional output. The annual average growth rate from 1990 to 1993 was a mere 1.5 per cent, barely half of the regional population growth rate (UNECA, 1993b). Western Africa did better (2.7 per cent), while central Africa stagnated (UNECA, 1993b). In the last few years, however, nearly half the countries have diverged from the general trend, reaching rates between 3 and 8 per cent, with three of them exceeding even the 8 per cent level (UNDP, 1996).

Poor people are most at risk from environmental damage, whatever the cause. In economies based on natural resources, which most African countries are, resource degradation reduces the productivity of the poor, increases their susceptibility to extreme weather, economic and civil events, and environmental health threats. Poverty also makes recovery from such events even more difficult. Extreme events, especially those related to weather,

appear to be increasing in frequency in Africa (World Bank, 1995).

Most African countries depend on primary commodities for a significant part of their export income. Yet the values of the continent's agricultural and mineral raw material exports have been falling dramatically from the combined effects of stagnation in industrial countries, substitution by synthetics, and competition from, for example, the Commonwealth of Independent States (UNECA, 1993b).

Africa's external debt continues to be a major impediment to the achievement of accelerated economic growth and development. The total debt stock stood at US$313 billion in 1994, equivalent to 234 per cent of export income and 83 per cent of GDP. The debt burden was higher than that of any other region. Four fifths of severely indebted low-income countries (as designated by the World Bank) are in sub-Saharan Africa, and the number is increasing. In sub-Saharan Africa, the average per capita debt servicing load was US$43, compared with US$35 spent on health and education. Nineteen African countries have manageable debt burdens, but even under the most optimistic assumptions, 24 countries will continue to face an unsustainable debt burden (by World Bank criteria) well into the twenty-first century.

There are also problems of high dependence on foreign aid and marginalization in the flow of foreign direct investment (FDI). African development has had very heavy involvement by donors, who in some cases have provided the full funding for long-term development investment activities (UNDP, 1996). But donor-driven development has not always been co-ordinated or fully appreciative of Africa's development efforts and priorities. While FDI increased to Latin America and Asia, Africa's share of FDI remains at less than 2 per cent of total flows (UNDP, 1996). A study by the United Nations Conference on Trade and Development concluded that, contrary to common perceptions, FDI in Africa can be profitable and at a level above the average in other developing regions (UNDP, 1996).

In the face of declining export earnings and debt burdens, many Governments have tried to boost their cash crop production and timber sales. This has led to further environmental damage as well as forced poor farmers to move further onto marginal lands (UNECA, 1993a). Many of the institutions and infrastructure supporting agriculture often operate inadequately, with little impact on food supply and a lack of support for agricultural technologies (UNECA, 1993a).

Thirty-five African countries have been implementing structural adjustment programmes for more than a decade, and have put in place economic reform measures in an attempt to correct some fundamental economic imbalances and to support private-sector development. Although African Governments are committed to removing obstacles to growth, current projections indicate that socio-economic recovery is still not in sight for most countries (UNDP, 1996). It has also been argued that structural adjustment programmes have been leading to wider gaps between rich and poor (Ohlsson, 1995).

Institutional

Political liberalization is spreading across Africa (UNDP, 1996); pluralism and accountability are more evident. In the last five years, 30 sub-Saharan countries held national pluralistic elections. In the wake of such changes, civil society is growing in strength, with significant movements towards more open communication, a freer press, decentralization, attention to human rights, social justice, and popular participation in the development process; evidence of this includes the fuller inclusion of women in positions of economic and political prominence (UNDP, 1996). Grassroots participation and initiatives are playing an increasingly important role in the process of policy-making and implementation (UNEP, 1996b).

Yet institutional infrastructures to support democratic changes often lag behind. Physical as well as institutional infrastructures were designed to support the colonial economy, not to promote production diversity and industrial development in general. Given a long history of dependence on imported technological inputs, African countries have only relatively recently begun to be involved in acquiring appropriate technological capability (UNECA, 1993a), thereby increasing both local capacity and competitiveness.

Financial institutions, too, need attention. In many African countries, the banking system is weak and in some cases bankrupt (UNDP, 1996). There is dominance of State-owned banks, with Government control of credit markets and interest rates. In many countries, Government expenditures outstrip revenues: 30 countries have fiscal deficits of nearly 10 per cent of GDP, draining savings from the rest of the economy (UNDP, 1996).

A number of Governments, centres of commerce and learning, non-governmental groups, and private and public donors, including United Nations agencies, are actively working to expand the information and telecommunication infrastructures in Africa, so that Africans can become full actors in the global information revolution. As the rest of the world also adapts to this, the resistance of African central Government and parastatal institutions to communications entrepreneurship is fading, thereby creating opportunities for information exchange rather than information hoarding and exploitation. The ensuing participation by a wide range of community sectors offers great opportunities for Africa to compete effectively in an international marketplace and thereby bolster and accelerate development.

Environmental

Some underlying natural environmental factors in Africa reinforce the effects of the human-driven causes of environmental degradation. One major factor that affects the continent is the climate, which is generally dry with frequent severe droughts and highly variable rainfall. Droughts and the great unevenness in the distribution of natural resources (such as water and vegetation) are the predominant impediments to development and are intrinsic to environmental degradation. It is clear that Africa is endowed with diverse and rich natural resources; the greatest problem lies in the imbalance in the use of these resources as a result of a combination of factors discussed already. These include a lack of investment capital, inappropriate technologies, and poor management.

Little can be done about the natural climate variability save discovering, teaching, instilling, and encouraging behavioural changes to adapt to prevailing conditions. Global climate change could disrupt the weather patterns and contribute to the worsening of the natural climatic conditions. The potential impact of climate change is a concern in Africa.

The poor quality of soils is another constraining environmental factor. In addition to the climatic conditions, phosphorus deficiency, low content of organic matter, and low water infiltration and retention capacity on much of the African soils have been a limiting factor in agriculture. Unlike climate variability, however, this problem can be addressed: soil quality can be augmented through considerable investment in careful management and importation of nutrients.

Natural disasters other than droughts that have negative impacts on the environment and the sustainability of economic growth include invasion by desert locusts, storms, and floods. Although the need is global, in Africa there is a particular sense of urgency about understanding the causal links and the relationships between the various driving forces behind environmental problems in order to help formulate policies that will work.

References

Babu, S.C., and R. Hassan. 1995. International migration and environmental degradation—the case of Mozambican refugees and forest resources in Malawi. *Journal of Environmental Management.* No. 43. International Food Policy Research Institute. Washington.

Bryant, D., *et al.* 1995. Coastlines at risk: An index of potential development-related threats to coastal ecosystems. World Resources Institute (WRI) Indicator Brief. WRI. Washington.

Dahlberg, A. 1994. *Contesting Views and Changing Paradigms: The Land Degradation Debate in Southern Africa.* Nordiska Afrikainstitutet. Uppsala, Sweden.

Dalal-Clayton, B. 1995. *Environment and Ecology in Southern Africa: Current Trends and Scenarios to 2015.* International Institute for Environment and Development. London.

Dejene, A., and J. Olivares. 1991. *Integrating Environmental Issues into a Strategy for Sustainable Agricultural Development: In the Case of Mozambique.* World Bank. Washington.

FAO. 1993. *Forest Resources Assessment 1990: Tropical Countries.* FAO Forestry Paper 112. Food and Agriculture Organization of the United Nations (FAO). Rome.

FAO. 1995. *Forest Resources Assessment 1990. Global Synthesis.* FAO Forestry Paper 124. Rome.

Hulme, M. (ed). 1996. *Climate Change and Southern Africa: An Exploration of Some Potential Impacts and Implications in the SADC Region.* University of East Anglia/WWF. Norwich/Gland, Switzerland.

Makombe, K. (ed). 1993. *Sharing the Land: Wildlife, People and Development in Africa.* IUCN/ROSA. Harare, Zimbabwe.

Morna, C.L. 1996. Serving cities—or all settlements? Africans on Africa Series—Cities and Citizenry: Urbanized Communities in Africa. Supplement to *IDOC Internazionale.* April-June.

OAU. 1995. Relaunching Africa's economic and social development: the Cairo agenda of action. Adopted at the Extraordinary Session of the OAU Council of Ministers on 28 March 1995. Endorsed by the June 1995 Summit of African Heads of State and Government in Addis Ababa.

Ohlsson, L. 1995. *Water and Security in Southern Africa.* Publications on Water Resources No. 1, Department for Natural Resources and the Environment. Stockholm, Sweden.

Population Action International. 1994. *Sustaining Water: An Update.* Washington.

Roest, F.C. 1992. *Conservation and Biodiversity of Lake Tanganyika.* CTA Bulletin, Courier No. 132. CTA. Wageningen. The Netherlands.

SADC ELMS. 1993. The Biowaste gas stove. *Splash—Newsletter for the SADC ELMS.* September–December. Lesotho, Maseru.

SARDC. 1994a. *The State of the Environment in Southern Africa.* Penrose Press, for Southern African Research and Documentation Centre (SARDC), the World Conservation Union (IUCN), and Southern African Development Community (SADC). Johannesburg.

SARDC. 1994b. Deforestation. CEP Factsheet—Southern African Environmental Issues, No. 5. Harare, Zimbabwe.

SARDC. 1994c. Facts About Fish in Southern Africa. CEP Factsheet—Southern African Environmental Issues, No. 4. Harare, Zimbabwe.

Serhal, A., M. El-Khawlie, M. Fawaz, and H. Malat. 1994. *Towards an Environmental Action Plan for Lebanon.* Friedrich Ebert (in Arabic). pp 208.

Thomas, D.S.G., and N.J. Middleton. 1993. Salinization: new perspectives on a major desertification issue. *Journal of Arid Environments*. Vol. 24, pp. 95–105. University of Sheffield, U.K.

Tognetti, S.S., R. Constanza, L. Arizpe, C. Cleveland, H. Daly, A. Gupta, J. Martiney-Alier, P.H. May, M. Ritchie, J. Ruitenbeek, and O. Segura. 1995. *Poverty and the Environment*. UNEP. Nairobi.

UNCHS (Habitat). 1996. Habitat Atlas: Graphic Presentation of Basic Human Settlement Statistics. United Nations Centre for Human Settlements (UNCHS). Nairobi.

UNDP. 1996. The United Nations system-wide special initiative on Africa. United Nations Development Programme (UNDP). New York.

UNDP/FAO. 1980. Wildlife management in Kenya: project findings and recommendations. Kenya Wildlife Management Project Terminal Report. FO: DP/KEN/71/526. FAO. Rome.

UNECA. 1992. African common position on environment and development. June.

UNECA. 1993a. African strategies for the implementation of the United Nations Conference on Environment and Development; Conference of Ministers of Economic Planning and Development at its 19th session, 3–6 May 1993. June. Addis Ababa.

UNECA. 1993b. Preliminary assessment of the performance of the African economy in 1993 and prospects for 1994, end of year statement. December.

UNECA. 1993c. Proposals for the implementation of the Abuja Treaty Establishing the African Economic Community of the 14th Meeting of the Technical Preparatory Committee of the Whole, 12–16 April 1993, and the 28th session of the commission/19th meeting of the Conference of Ministers, 19–22 April.

UNEP. 1985. Report of the Executive Director of the United Nations Environment Programme. African Environmental Conference, 16-18 December 1985. United Nations Environment Programme (UNEP), in consultation with UNECA and OAU. Cairo.

UNEP. 1989. State of the marine environment: West and Central African region. Prepared by Portmann, E., C. Biney, A.C. Ibe, and S. Zabi. UNEP Regional Seas Reports and Studies No. 108. UNEP. Nairobi.

UNEP. 1990. *State of the Marine Environment in the Eastern African Region*. Prepared by Bryceson, I., T.F. De Souza, I. Jehangeer, M.A.K. Ngoile, and P. Wynter. UNEP Regional Seas Reports and Studies No. 113. UNEP. Nairobi.

UNEP. 1991a. Status of desertification and implementation of the United Nations Plan of Action to Combat Desertification. Report of the Executive Director. UNEP/GCSS.III/3. Nairobi.

UNEP. 1991b. A rapid assessment of the impact of the Iraq-Kuwait conflict on terrestrial ecosystems.

UNEP. 1991c. Global digital datasets for land degradation studies: a GIS approach. GRID Case Study Series No. 4. UNEP. Nairobi.

UNEP. 1992. *World Atlas of Desertification*. Edward Arnold. London.

UNEP. 1994. The Convention on Biological Diversity: Issues of Relevance to Africa. Regional Ministerial Conference on the Convention on Biological Diversity. October. UNEP/AMCEN/RCU 7/1 (A), 27 July.

UNEP. 1996a. African Ministerial Conference on the Environment (AMCEN), 6th Session, Ministerial Session. Report of the Session of the Conference. 14–15 December 1995. Nairobi.

UNEP. 1996b. Report of the Regional Consultations held for UNEP's first Global Environment Outlook. Nairobi.

UNEP/ISRIC. 1990. World map of the status of human-induced soil degradation. Wageningen, the Netherlands.

UNFPA. 1994. The State of World Population 1994: Choices and Responsibilities. United Nations Fund for Population Activities (UNFPA). New York.

WCMC. 1992. *Global Biodiversity: Status of the World Living Resources*. World Conservation Monitoring Centre. Chapman and Hall. London.

WHO. 1984a. *The International Drinking Water Supply and Sanitation Decade: Review of National Baseline Data: December 1980*. World Health Organization (WHO). Geneva.

WHO. 1984b. *The International Drinking Water Supply and Sanitation Decade: Review of National Progress (as at December 1983)*. World Health Organization (WHO). Geneva.

WHO. 1987. *The International Drinking Water Supply and Sanitation Decade: Review of Mid-Decade Progress (as at December 1985)*. World Health Organization (WHO). September. Geneva.

WHO. 1989. *Global Strategy for Health for All: Monitoring 1988–1989: Detailed Analysis of Global Indicators*. May. World Health Organization (WHO). Geneva.

WHO. 1991. unpublished data. World Health Organization (WHO). Geneva.

WHO. 1992. *The International Drinking Water Supply and Sanitation Decade: End of Decade Review (as at December 1990)*. World Health Organization (WHO). Geneva.

WHO/UNICEF. 1995. Unpublished data. WHO/UNICEF Joint Water Supply and Sanitation Monitoring Programme. World Health Organization (WHO) and the United Nations Children's Fund (UNICEF). Geneva.

World Bank. 1994. *Forging a Partnership for Environmental Action. An Environmental Strategy Toward Sustainable Development in the Middle East and North Africa.*

World Bank. 1995. *Toward Environmentally Sustainable Development in Sub-Saharan Africa.*

World Bank. 1996. African water resources: challenges and opportunities for sustainable development (draft). January.

WRI/UNEP/UNDP/WB. 1996. *World Resources 1996–97.* World Resources Institute (WRI), UNEP, UNDP, and the World Bank. Oxford University Press. New York and London.

ASIA AND THE PACIFIC

Major Environmental Concerns

The Asia and Pacific region extends from Mongolia in the north to New Zealand in the south and from the Cook Islands in the east to Iran in the west. It embraces the world's largest ocean, the Pacific (165 million square kilometres), as well as the third largest ocean, the Indian (73 million square kilometres), and a range of important seas (ESCAP, 1992; ESCAP, 1995a). It contains three of the largest and most populous countries in the world (China, India, and Indonesia), several mountainous and land-locked states (such as Bhutan and Nepal), and 22 small archipelagic states, territories, and protectorates. With only 23 per cent of the world's total land area, the region is home to about 58 per cent of the world's population (ESCAP, 1992; ESCAP, 1995a).

The economies of this region have witnessed high growth rates in the recent past: in 1994, the total GDP growth was 8.2 per cent (ADB, 1995a). Despite this, poverty persists. Estimates indicate that, of the world's 1.2 billion people who live in absolute poverty (with a per capita income of less than US$1 a day), more than two thirds reside in this region (ADB, 1994a). High population growth is exerting pressure on the environment and on natural resources in the region. Urbanization and industrialization have also had deleterious impacts, leading not only to high pollution loads but also social stress.

The major environmental concerns vary widely across the region. (See Table 2.2.) The major issues include:

- land degradation,

- deforestation,

- declining availability of fresh water and deteriorating water quality, and

- the degradation of marine and coastal resources.

The general recognition in the region is that deforestation, inadequate water supply, and water quality need to be addressed on a priority basis (ADB, 1994a).

In the large megacities of the region, such as Bombay, Bangkok, Jakarta, and Manila, air pollution is an increasingly serious problem. The small island states such as Fiji, Maldives, and Western Samoa are grappling with solid waste disposal problems with irregular and inadequate disposal facilities. Furthermore, the burden on women resulting from environmental degradation needs to be recognized. Women are the primary natural resource managers in developing countries of Asia and the Pacific, yet this important role is often ignored by governments and agencies. They do most of the work to reap food and fuel from the environment to sustain their families. When the environment is degraded, it is the women who first feel the crunch.

Land

The region's land resources have been divided into low and high agricultural production potential. The region is characterized by relative land scarcity and poorer land quality than other regions. Due to increasing population, the available land decreased from 0.27 hectares per person in 1976 to 0.25 hectares in 1986 (ESCAP, 1992). Land availability in the small island developing countries is severely limited.

In most developing countries in the region, soils suffer from varying degrees of erosion and degradation mainly due to rapid rates of deforestation, poor irrigation and drainage practices, inadequate soil conservation, steep slopes, and overgrazing. According to the Global Assessment of Human-Induced Soil Degradation, of the world's 1.9 billion hectares affected by soil degradation, the largest area (850

Table 2.2

Relative Significance of Resource and Environmental Issues in Selected Countries in Asia and the Pacific

	Land & soil resources	Pesticide & fertilizer	Deforestation	Water resources	Industrial pollution	Acid rain	Marine & coastal degradation	Sea level rise	Urban congestion & pollution	Waste disposal
Bangladesh	▪	▪	▪	■	▪		▪	▪	▪	
China	▪	▪	■		■	■	▪	▪	■	▪
India	■	▪	■	■	■	▪	▪	▪	■	▪
Myanmar	▪		▪					▪		
Nepal	■	▪	■	▪			n.a.	n.a.	▪	
Pakistan	■	▪	▪	▪	▪				■	▪
Sri Lanka	▪	▪	■		▪		■		▪	
Cambodia	▪		■	▪	▪		▪			▪
Indonesia		▪	■				▪	▪		
Lao PDR					▪		n.a.	n.a.	▪	
Malaysia	▪	▪	▪	▪	▪		▪		▪	
Philippines	■	▪	■	▪	▪		▪	▪	■	▪
Thailand	▪	▪	■	▪	▪	▪	▪	▪	■	
Vietnam	▪	▪	■	▪	▪		▪	▪	▪	
Pacific Islands	▪	▪	▪	■	▪		■	■	▪	■

■ High priority
▪ Medium priority
▫ Low priority
n.a. not applicable

Source: ADB, 1994a.

Notes: Waste disposal includes industrial and toxic wastes. Marine and coastal degradation includes driftnet fishing, coral mining, and coastal development. Land and soil resource problems include desertification, salinization, soil erosion, and water logging. Water resource problems include shortage, ground-water depletion, flooding, and water pollution. Deforestation includes industrial wood production, fuelwood collection, watershed degradation, and loss of biological diversity.

million hectares) is in Asia and the Pacific, accounting for about 24 per cent of the land in the region. Thirteen per cent of arable land in the region is considered to be severely degraded, 41 per cent moderately degraded, and 46 per cent lightly degraded (WRI/UNEP/UNDP/WB, 1996).

Land degradation in the region results from displacement of soil material, mainly through water erosion (61 per cent) and wind erosion (28 per cent), and from biophysical (2 per cent) and chemical (9 per cent) deterioration (UNEP/ISRIC, 1990).

Water erosion is extensive and severe throughout the Himalayas, South Asia, South-East Asia, large areas of China, Australia, and the South Pacific. In India alone, 12.62 million hectares out of a total of 32.77 million hectares of agricultural land is affected by strong water erosion; in Sri Lanka, 845,000 hectares are affected; and in Iran, 45 per cent of agricultural land is affected by light to moderate water erosion (FAO/UNDP/UNEP, 1994).

Wind erosion is extensive and severe in the dry belt stretching from central Iran to the Thar Desert

of Pakistan and India. The wind-eroded land in eight countries of South Asia alone is about 59 million hectares (FAO/UNEP/UNEP, 1994). More than half of the world's irrigated land affected by water-logging and salinization is located in Asia and the Pacific, while some 75 million hectares of soil in the region have deteriorated chemically over the past 45 years.

Overall, 86 million hectares of land in the arid, semi-arid, and dry subhumid zones—70 million hectares of rainfed cropland and 16 million hectares of irrigated croplands—have been affected by desertification (ESCAP, 1995a). This implies that altogether 35 per cent of productive land in Asia is now desertified. The region has the largest population in the world affected by the process. The countries suffering most from desertification are China, Afghanistan, Mongolia, Pakistan, and India.

The contribution of human activities to land degradation in the region has been estimated as follows: removal of vegetation cover, 37 per cent; overgrazing by livestock, 33 per cent; unsustainable

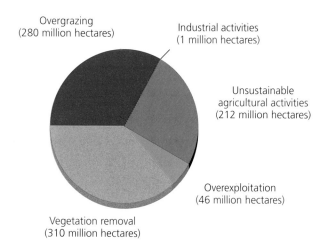

Overgrazing
(280 million hectares)

Industrial activities
(1 million hectares)

Unsustainable
agricultural activities
(212 million hectares)

Overexploitation
(46 million hectares)

Vegetation removal
(310 million hectares)

Figure 2.6. Causes of land degradation in Asia-Pacific.

Source: UNEP/ISRIC (1990).

agricultural practices, 25 per cent; and overexploitation through construction of infrastructure, 5 per cent (UNEP/ISRIC, 1990). (See Figure 2.6.)

Population pressure on arable land in various subregions of Asia and the Pacific is considerable. The average population density for the region is 90 persons per square kilometre, and 15 per cent of the total land area is considered arable. The equivalent figures for the four subregions are as follows:

- 186 persons per square kilometre and 39 per cent arable land for South Asia;

- 104 persons per square kilometre and about 18 per cent arable land for South-East Asia, which also has more than half the land area under forest cover;

- 120 persons per square kilometre and 9 per cent arable land for East Asia, where approximately 45 per cent of the land area is pasture and 15 per cent is under forest or woodland; and

- 3 persons per square kilometre and less than 10 per cent arable land in the Pacific subregion, with more than half being permanent pasture (FAO/RADA, 1994; ESCAP, 1993a and 1993b).

Population growth will continue to pressure land resources. Increased dependence on intensive agriculture and irrigation may result in salinization,

alkalization, and waterlogging, particularly in irrigated lands that are not managed properly. This is a serious concern in the region, especially since irrigated lands are expected to increase significantly in the near future.

Forests

The forest and woodlands in the Asia and Pacific region cover approximately 655 million hectares—some 17 per cent of the world's total (FAO/RAPA, 1993). About 33 per cent of this is found in South-East Asia, and just three countries—Australia, Indonesia, and China—account for 52 per cent of forest cover in the region (FAO/RAPA, 1993).

Most of the other countries have at least 20 per cent forest cover, with the least forest cover being found in South Asia and the small island developing states. Due to industrialization, agricultural expansion, and forestry product trade, deforestation remains one of the major environmental issues in the region.

Deforestation in the region increased from 2 million hectares per year during 1976–81 to 3.9 million hectares per year in 1981–90 (FAO, 1993). The countries experiencing the fastest deforestation are Bangladesh, Pakistan, the Philippines, and Thailand (FAO, 1993). (See Figure 2.7.) The average per capita forest area for the whole region is 0.21 hectares. Yet 13 countries have higher rates than the world average of 0.71 hectares per person (FAO/RAPA, 1994).

South-East Asia has a per capita forest cover of 0.48 hectares per person and also the highest absolute deforestation rates, with continental and insular South-East Asia losing some 1.3 million and 1.9 million hectares per year. Indonesia alone in the early 1990s had an average annual deforestation rate of 0.6 million hectares (equivalent to around 0.5 per cent of forest cover), while Malaysia, Myanmar, the Philippines, and Thailand were each losing more than 300,000 hectares per year, representing 2, 1.3, 4, and 4 per cent of their forest cover, respectively, for the period 1981–90 (FAO, 1995). About 980,000 hectares of forest area had been depleted from 1989 to 1993 in Thailand alone (Government of Thailand, 1994). Cambodia, Lao PDR, and Vietnam each lost in excess of 100,000 hectares per year, representing 1, 0.9 and 1.6 per cent of their total forest cover, respectively, for the period 1981–90 (FAO, 1995). (See Figure 2.7.)

The lowest per capita forest cover is found in South Asia, at 0.08 hectares, while the Pacific subregion has the highest per capita forest cover (5.88 hectares) and the lowest rate of deforestation (around 130,000 hectares per year), of which about 113,000 hectares are removed in Papua New Guinea. This country also has the highest forest cover, at 9.4 hectares per person, in the entire region (FAO/RAPA, 1994).

From 1981–90, it is estimated that, within total forest area, tropical forests decreased by 6.7 per cent while temperate forest area increased by 5.2 per cent. The percentage decrease in the natural tropical forest area was 11.1 (the highest rate observed for this type of forest as compared with other regions). The figure for natural temperate forest area was 3.4 (the lowest rate) (FAO, 1995).

Rapid population growth has contributed to depletion of forests not only through land-clearing for cultivation but also through overharvesting of forests for fuelwood, roundwood, and fodder. At the current rate of harvesting, the remaining timber reserves in Asia may not last for more than 40 years.

Water

The region has arid and semi-arid areas as well as humid tropical areas with high precipitation. It has some of the world's largest rivers—the Ganges (Ganga), Brahmaputra, Chang Jiang (Yangtze Kiang), and Yenisei—and numerous small rivers in the insular countries of South-East Asia and the Pacific. There are also a substantial number of natural lakes. Among the largest are Dongting-hu in China, Tonle Sap in Cambodia, and Kasumigaura in Japan. The region is also characterized by extensive ground-water resources; in some of the small island states, such as Maldives, Kiribati, Tuvalu, and the Federated States of Micronesia, ground water is the main source of fresh water.

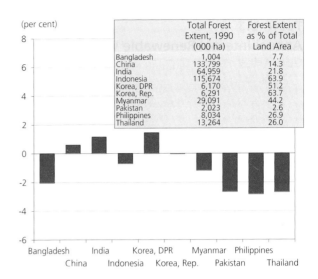

	Total Forest Extent, 1990 (000 ha)	Forest Extent as % of Total Land Area
Bangladesh	1,004	7.7
China	133,799	14.3
India	64,959	21.8
Indonesia	115,674	63.9
Korea, DPR	6,170	51.2
Korea, Rep.	6,291	63.7
Myanmar	29,091	44.2
Pakistan	2,023	2.6
Philippines	8,034	26.9
Thailand	13,264	26.0

Figure 2.7. Average annual change in the extent of forest in selected Asia-Pacific countries, 1981–90.

Source: FAO (1993, 1995).
Note: Forest consists of the sum of natural forest and plantation area categories for tropical and temperate developing countries.

Though comparatively well endowed with water resources, only a part of the renewable water resources can be extracted and used, owing to the high variability of streamflow between low water and flood seasons, the inaccessibility of some watercourses, and the lack of storage sites on many catchments (ESCAP, 1995a). The total average annual renewable water resource in the region is estimated to be approximately 13,000 cubic kilometres (WRI/UNEP/UNDP, 1994).

The per capita availability of water varies from about 186,000 cubic metres per year in Papua New Guinea to just over 200 cubic metres in Singapore (WRI/UNEP/UNDP/WB, 1996). (See Table 2.3.) Countries such as Afghanistan and Iran suffer from chronic water shortages due to aridity, while parts of China and India experience the same problem primarily due to high population density.

Water pollution in countries in Asia and the Pacific is caused mainly by domestic sewage, industrial effluents, and runoff from activities such as agriculture and mining. The severity of water quality problems in the region is summarized in Table 2.4.

The problem of pathogenic pollution is quite severe in South Asia, South-East Asia, the Pacific Islands, and China; only in industrial countries such

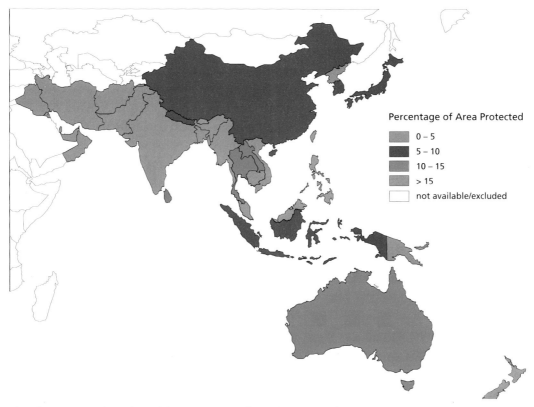

Figure 2.9. National and international protection of natural areas in Asia and the Pacific.
Source: WCMC (1995).
Note: Protected areas include areas falling within World Conservation Union (IUCN) protected area categories I-V.

runoff and drainage from port areas, domestic and industrial effluents, and various contaminants from ships. River waters are generally heavily contaminated by municipal sewage, industrial effluent, and sediments. Asian rivers account for nearly 50 per cent of the total sediment load (13.5 billion tons) transported by the world's rivers each year (UNEP, 1992).

As much as 70 per cent of the waste effluent discharged into the Pacific Ocean has no prior treatment (Fuavo, 1990). More than 40 per cent of marine pollution in the region is derived from land-based activities through riverine discharge, with maritime transport contributing a further 12 per cent (Weber, 1993). The Government of Korea estimates that at least 80 per cent of pollutants in the Yellow and South seas of the Korean Peninsula come from inland activities (domestic and industrial) through the four largest Korean rivers (Government of Korea, 1994).

The major sources of heavy metal contamination are industrial effluent and dumping of land-based solid waste into the sea. In India, for example, exceptionally high concentrations of lead, cadmium, and mercury have been observed in Thane creeks on the Bombay Coast, and sediment along the creeks and offshore stations was reported to contain significant concentrations of lead (India, 1993). In Pakistan, heavy metal contaminations have been detected in water and sediment from the coastal area within the mouth of the Indus River (Tariq *et al.*, 1993). Moreover, there is increasing evidence of these toxic substances getting into the food chain.

The sources of marine pollution from sea-based activities include marine transportation and off-shore mineral exploration and production activities. Accidental oil spills have been frequently reported along these routes.

In the Straits of Malacca alone, 490 shipping accidents were reported in 1988–92, resulting in a considerable amount of oil spillage (*Straits Times*, 1993). It has been reported that beach tar along the west coast of India is a severe problem, with total

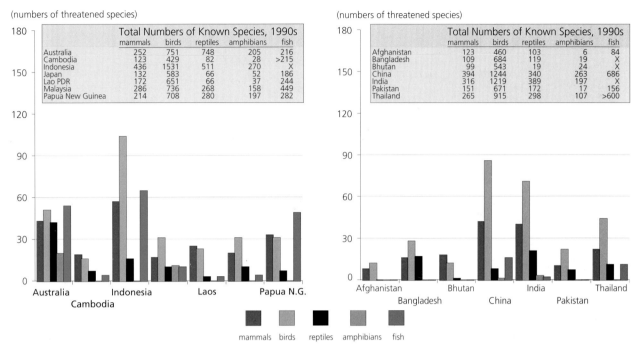

(numbers of threatened species)

Total Numbers of Known Species, 1990s					
	mammals	birds	reptiles	amphibians	fish
Australia	252	751	748	205	216
Cambodia	123	429	82	28	>215
Indonesia	436	1531	511	270	X
Japan	132	583	66	52	186
Lao PDR	172	651	66	37	244
Malaysia	286	736	268	158	449
Papua New Guinea	214	708	280	197	282

(numbers of threatened species)

Total Numbers of Known Species, 1990s					
	mammals	birds	reptiles	amphibians	fish
Afghanistan	123	460	103	6	84
Bangladesh	109	684	119	19	X
Bhutan	99	543	19	24	X
China	394	1244	340	263	686
India	316	1219	389	197	X
Pakistan	151	671	172	17	156
Thailand	265	915	298	107	>600

mammals   birds   reptiles   amphibians   fish

Figure 2.8. Numbers of threatened species in selected Asia-Pacific countries, 1990s.

Source: IUCN (1993).

Note: The number of threatened species listed for all countries includes full species that are classified by the World Conservation Union (IUCN) as endangered, vulnerable, rare, and indeterminate, but excludes introduced species, species whose status is insufficiently known, or those known to be extinct. X = not available.

Biological diversity is recognized as a legitimate issue at national and international levels in Asia and the Pacific, and there has been a considerable response (such as the implementation of the Convention on Biological Diversity and designation of protected areas). (See Figure 2.9.) However, patterns of unsustainable use and conflicting policies contribute to continued losses of biodiversity throughout the region. With only 10–30 per cent of natural habitats left in many countries, any further decrease could have much more serious consequences for biodiversity than the initial stage, when 50 per cent of the original habitat was lost (ESCAP, 1995a).

Marine and Coastal Environments

Most people in the region live along the coasts, with one quarter of the world's 75 largest cities being near or on the region's coastlines (ESCAP, 1995a). Growth rates of coastal populations are generally higher than the national average due to migration to coastal urban areas and industrial centres. Most of these large cities and industrial areas are located in highly productive low-lying estuarine areas.

The marine resources of the region are economically important to most countries, with 47 per cent of world fisheries production being found in this region. Of this, marine and fresh-water fisheries account for 76 per cent and 24 per cent of production, respectively (FAO/RAPA, 1994). The region is also the centre of global mariculture (87 per cent of total world production) (FAO/RAPA, 1994), with major consequences for coastal habitats and water quality.

For insular and archipelagic states, marine resources are the key source of external earnings for development and marine-based tourism is playing an increasingly important role. Several countries rely almost exclusively on fisheries products for dietary protein. Trends show that the marine fish catch is rising steadily in almost all subregions. The average annual fish catch is comparatively higher in South-East Asia.

Coastal and marine pollution in this region is mainly due to direct discharge from rivers, surface

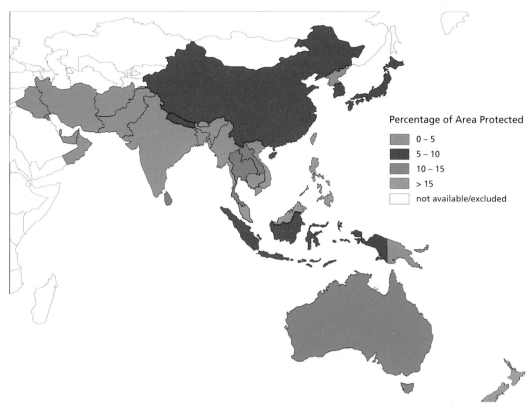

Figure 2.9. National and international protection of natural areas in Asia and the Pacific.
Source: WCMC (1995).
Note: Protected areas include areas falling within World Conservation Union (IUCN) protected area categories I-V.

runoff and drainage from port areas, domestic and industrial effluents, and various contaminants from ships. River waters are generally heavily contaminated by municipal sewage, industrial effluent, and sediments. Asian rivers account for nearly 50 per cent of the total sediment load (13.5 billion tons) transported by the world's rivers each year (UNEP, 1992).

As much as 70 per cent of the waste effluent discharged into the Pacific Ocean has no prior treatment (Fuavo, 1990). More than 40 per cent of marine pollution in the region is derived from land-based activities through riverine discharge, with maritime transport contributing a further 12 per cent (Weber, 1993). The Government of Korea estimates that at least 80 per cent of pollutants in the Yellow and South seas of the Korean Peninsula come from inland activities (domestic and industrial) through the four largest Korean rivers (Government of Korea, 1994).

The major sources of heavy metal contamination are industrial effluent and dumping of land-based solid waste into the sea. In India, for example, exceptionally high concentrations of lead, cadmium, and mercury have been observed in Thane creeks on the Bombay Coast, and sediment along the creeks and offshore stations was reported to contain significant concentrations of lead (India, 1993). In Pakistan, heavy metal contaminations have been detected in water and sediment from the coastal area within the mouth of the Indus River (Tariq *et al.*, 1993). Moreover, there is increasing evidence of these toxic substances getting into the food chain.

The sources of marine pollution from sea-based activities include marine transportation and offshore mineral exploration and production activities. Accidental oil spills have been frequently reported along these routes.

In the Straits of Malacca alone, 490 shipping accidents were reported in 1988–92, resulting in a considerable amount of oil spillage (*Straits Times*, 1993). It has been reported that beach tar along the west coast of India is a severe problem, with total

number of quantitative analyses of transboundary air pollution have been done in the past.

Although acidification of the environment has until recently been regarded as a problem only in Europe and North America, the problem has also started to emerge in parts of Asia and the Pacific region. It has been estimated that 38 million tons of sulphur dioxide were emitted in 22 countries of Asia in 1990, almost 56 per cent more than in North America, and this is expected to be much higher in the coming decades if effective mitigation measures are not adopted (Shrestha *et al.*, 1996). About 78 per cent of these emissions originated from North-East Asia (China, Republic of Korea, Japan, Hong Kong, Mongolia, and Chinese Taipei).

A study done in a project sponsored by the World Bank and the Asian Development Bank (Hettelingh *et al.*, 1995) on acid rain and emissions reduction in Asia shows that the areas with critical loads of up to 320 milligrams per square metre per year (that is, areas that are most susceptible to acid deposition) are located in South China, the areas south-east of Thailand, Cambodia, and southern Vietnam. In 1990, the areas with an acid loading in large excess of critical loads were located in south-east China, north-east India, Bangladesh, Thailand, parts of Indonesia, South Korea, southern Japan, and small parts of the Philippines.

Biodiversity

The region encompasses parts of three of the world's eight biogeographic realms and includes the world's highest mountain system, the second largest rainforest complex, and more than half of the world's coral reefs. Five of the 12 "mega-diversity" countries identified by McNeeley *et al.* are in this region (McNeeley *et al.*, 1990). The rainforests of South-East Asia contain some 10 per cent of the flora of the world. The region as a whole encompasses two thirds of the world's flora. Almost all the nations in the region (with the exception of Singapore and Brunei Darussalam) depend heavily on direct harvesting from nature.

The flora and fauna of the region are more threatened now than ever before. (See Figure 2.8.)

The drive for increased agricultural production has resulted in the loss of genetic diversity. Land under rice cultivation rose between 1960 and 1970 by only 25 per cent, but production rose by 77 per cent due to the replacement of traditional varieties with higher-yielding, semi-dwarf varieties. By 2005, India is expected to produce 75 per cent of its rice from just 10 varieties compared with the 30,000 varieties traditionally cultivated. In Indonesia, 1,500 varieties of rice disappeared during the period 1975–90 (WRI/UNEP/IUCN, 1992). Terrestrial biodiversity loss in various ecosystems has been identified as a major concern, but losses have still to be quantified. Overall habitat losses have been most acute in the Indian sub-continent, China, Vietnam, and Thailand (ESCAP, 1995b).

The Indo-west Pacific is the centre of shallow-water marine biodiversity. Coastal habitat loss and degradation, combined with increased sediment, nutrient, and pollutant discharge into coastal areas, are a major cause of concern, particularly in the insular countries of the region. Thailand alone lost about 200,000 hectares of mangrove from 1961–93 (Government of Thailand, 1994). Conversion of mangroves to shrimp mariculture and unsustainable fishing practices such as blast fishing are widespread. Although the impacts of such practices on regional biodiversity are difficult to quantify, it has been estimated that the rates of loss of coral reef and mangrove habitats are among the highest in the world.

The underlying causes of losses of biological diversity in the region include international trade, particularly in timber (which results in forest habitat losses); population growth (leading to accelerated rates of land use change); poverty (in conjunction with demand leading to unsustainable consumptive use of "common access resources"); the introduction of non-native species (leading to destruction of predator/prey equilibrium); and improper use of agrochemicals (leading to loss of aquatic species). Other major reasons for biodiversity loss include loss of keystone species, extensive deforestation and habitat loss, increased trafficking in animals and animal body parts, large-scale conversion of land for agriculture, and the construction of large-scale dams.

Table 2.4

Water Quality Issues in the Asia-Pacific Region

Quality Issues	South Asia	South-East Asia	Pacific Islands	People's Republic of China	Japan
Pathogenic agents	1-3	1-2	2-3	1-3	0-1
Organic matter	1-3	0-2	0-1	1-3	0-1
Salinization	0-1	0-1	0-3	0-2	0-1
Nitrate	0-1	0-1	1-2	0-2	0-1
Fluoride	0-1	0	0	0-2	0
Eutrophication	0-1	0-3	0	0-2	0-1
Heavy metals	0-1	0-2	0-1	0-2	0-2
Pesticides	0-1	0-1	0-1	0-1	0-1
Sediment load	0-2	0-2	0-1	0-1	0-1
Acidification	0	0-1	0	0-1	0-1

Source: ESCAP (1991).

Notes:
0 = No pollution or irrelevant.
1 = Some pollution (water can be used if appropriate measures are taken).
2 = Major pollution.
3 = Severe pollution affecting basic water uses.

available per year, while Iran and India are heading in that direction. India is among the countries projected to fall into the water-stress category before 2025. Its situation is well illustrated by the case of Rajasthan, which is home to 8 per cent of India's population but claims only 1 per cent of the country's total water resources. China is expected to only narrowly miss the water-stress benchmark by 2025 (WRI/UNEP/UNDP, 1992).

Atmosphere

One of the important implications of economic growth in Asia and the Pacific over the last three decades has been the increased demand for energy. The region, excluding Japan, Australia, and New Zealand, accounted for 21 per cent of the world's primary commercial energy demand in 1992 as compared with 51 per cent for members of the Organisation for Economic Co-operation and Development (OECD) and 28 per cent for the rest of the world. The growth in energy demand for the whole region was 3.6 per cent per year between 1990 and 1992, compared with an average 0.1 per cent growth of the whole world (ADB, 1994b). In particular, the region accounted for about 41 per cent of world coal consumption in 1993 (EIA, 1995).

The rapid growth in energy demand and especially the region's reliance on coal translate into a significant increase in air pollutants if appropriate technological interventions are not made (such as the use of scrubbers). Urban air pollution is a serious problem in many major cities of the region. Significant health threats also arise from indoor air pollution resulting from the use of low-quality solid fuels, such as coal, wood, crop residues, and dung for cooking and heating in lower-income urban households and in rural areas throughout the region.

Fly ash generated from the mining of coal is also a significant problem in the region, particularly in India, where the problem is as serious as acid rain is elsewhere. An estimated 35–40 million tons of fly ash are generated by thermal power plants every year, and only 2–3 per cent is being reused (India, 1993). Fly ash can be reduced through better washing techniques. In addition, it can be reused as fertilizer, to make bricks and roads, or to replace sand used to refill mines.

Transboundary air pollution is a problem that has accompanied economic growth and high energy consumption. The effects of coal burning tend to spread over a large area, resulting in acid deposition in areas near the coal burning plants as well as further away. The accumulation of fly ash adds suspended particulate matter into the air and leads to air quality deterioration. In addition, slash–and–burn agriculture leads to haze problems that extend beyond national boundaries. Unfortunately, only a limited

to 1993 in Thailand alone (Government of Thailand, 1994). Cambodia, Lao PDR, and Vietnam each lost in excess of 100,000 hectares per year, representing 1, 0.9 and 1.6 per cent of their total forest cover, respectively, for the period 1981–90 (FAO, 1995). (See Figure 2.7.)

The lowest per capita forest cover is found in South Asia, at 0.08 hectares, while the Pacific subregion has the highest per capita forest cover (5.88 hectares) and the lowest rate of deforestation (around 130,000 hectares per year), of which about 113,000 hectares are removed in Papua New Guinea. This country also has the highest forest cover, at 9.4 hectares per person, in the entire region (FAO/RAPA, 1994).

From 1981–90, it is estimated that, within total forest area, tropical forests decreased by 6.7 per cent while temperate forest area increased by 5.2 per cent. The percentage decrease in the natural tropical forest area was 11.1 (the highest rate observed for this type of forest as compared with other regions). The figure for natural temperate forest area was 3.4 (the lowest rate) (FAO, 1995).

Rapid population growth has contributed to depletion of forests not only through land-clearing for cultivation but also through overharvesting of forests for fuelwood, roundwood, and fodder. At the current rate of harvesting, the remaining timber reserves in Asia may not last for more than 40 years.

Water

The region has arid and semi-arid areas as well as humid tropical areas with high precipitation. It has some of the world's largest rivers—the Ganges (Ganga), Brahmaputra, Chang Jiang (Yangtze Kiang), and Yenisei—and numerous small rivers in the insular countries of South-East Asia and the Pacific. There are also a substantial number of natural lakes. Among the largest are Dongting-hu in China, Tonle Sap in Cambodia, and Kasumigaura in Japan. The region is also characterized by extensive ground-water resources; in some of the small island states, such as Maldives, Kiribati, Tuvalu, and the Federated States of Micronesia, ground water is the main source of fresh water.

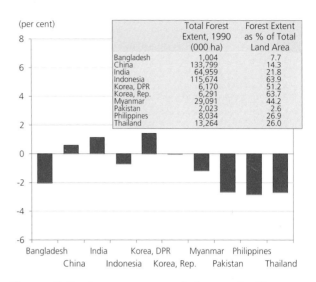

	Total Forest Extent, 1990 (000 ha)	Forest Extent as % of Total Land Area
Bangladesh	1,004	7.7
China	133,799	14.3
India	64,959	21.8
Indonesia	115,674	63.9
Korea, DPR	6,170	51.2
Korea, Rep.	6,291	63.7
Myanmar	29,091	44.2
Pakistan	2,023	2.6
Philippines	8,034	26.9
Thailand	13,264	26.0

Figure 2.7. Average annual change in the extent of forest in selected Asia-Pacific countries, 1981–90.

Source: FAO (1993, 1995).
Note: Forest consists of the sum of natural forest and plantation area categories for tropical and temperate developing countries.

Though comparatively well endowed with water resources, only a part of the renewable water resources can be extracted and used, owing to the high variability of streamflow between low water and flood seasons, the inaccessibility of some watercourses, and the lack of storage sites on many catchments (ESCAP, 1995a). The total average annual renewable water resource in the region is estimated to be approximately 13,000 cubic kilometres (WRI/UNEP/UNDP, 1994).

The per capita availability of water varies from about 186,000 cubic metres per year in Papua New Guinea to just over 200 cubic metres in Singapore (WRI/UNEP/UNDP/WB, 1996). (See Table 2.3.) Countries such as Afghanistan and Iran suffer from chronic water shortages due to aridity, while parts of China and India experience the same problem primarily due to high population density.

Water pollution in countries in Asia and the Pacific is caused mainly by domestic sewage, industrial effluents, and runoff from activities such as agriculture and mining. The severity of water quality problems in the region is summarized in Table 2.4.

The problem of pathogenic pollution is quite severe in South Asia, South-East Asia, the Pacific Islands, and China; only in industrial countries such

Table 2.3
Annual Internal Renewable Water Resources and Water Withdrawals in Selected Asia-Pacific Countries

	Annual Internal Renewable Water Resources [a]			Annual Withdrawals				
	Total (cubic kilometres)	1995 Per Capita (cubic metres)	Year of Data	Percentage of Water Resources [a]	Per Capita (cubic metres)	Sectoral Withdrawals (per cent) [b]		
						Domestic	Industry	Agriculture
Afghanistan	50.0	2,482	1987	52	1,830	1	0	99
Bhutan	95.0	57,998	1987	0	14	36	10	54
China	2,800.0	2,292	1980	16	461	6	7	87
India	2,085.0	2,228	1975	18	612	3	4	93
Indonesia	2,530.0	12,804	1987	1	96	13	11	76
Iran	117.5	1,746	1975	39	1,362	4	9	87
Japan	547.0	4,373	1990	17	735	17	33	50
Korea, Rep.	66.1	1,469	1992	42	632	19	35	46
Malaysia	456.0	22,642	1975	2	768	23	30	47
Papua New Guinea	801.0	186,192	1987	0	28	29	22	49
Singapore	0.6	211	1975	32	84	45	51	4

Source: WRI/UNEP/UNDP/WB (1996).

Notes: a. Annual Internal Renewable Water Resources usually include river flows from other countries. b. Sectoral withdrawal percentages are estimated for 1987.

as Japan, Australia, and New Zealand is the problem relatively minor. Pathogens generally come from domestic sewage that is discharged untreated into watercourses. South Asia and China are most severely affected by organic matter pollution, the main source of which is effluent from the pulp and paper and food industries.

Lake eutrophication is a significant but localized concern in a number of countries. A survey by UNEP and the International Lake Environment Committee (ILEC) shows that 54 per cent of the lakes in South-East Asia suffer from eutrophication problems (UNEP, 1994). This subregion's inland water bodies are also affected by the presence of pathogenic agents, while many rivers carry enhanced nutrient and pollutant loads resulting from changes in land use, industrialization, and urbanization.

Discharge of mine tailings and development of industrial areas with direct discharge of pollutants into neighbouring river systems has resulted in hot spots of heavy metal pollution throughout the region.

In the small island countries, salinization affects the ground-water resources severely due to the intrusion of sea water. In Thailand, the rapid lower-

ing of the water table due to excessive extraction of ground water has caused the shallow aquifers in Bangkok to become contaminated with sea water. The overwithdrawal of ground-water reserves has also caused land subsidence in cities such as Bangkok and Jakarta. In Bangkok, for instance, land has subsided in some places by 0.5–0.6 metres over the last 20–25 years, which has aggravated the city's flood problems (ESCAP, 1995a). In countries like Bangladesh, salinity and sedimentation are occurring largely as a result of upstream water withdrawal.

The fresh-water withdrawals in Asia and the Pacific range from 15 to 1,400 cubic metres per person per year (WRI/UNEP/UNDP, 1994). Agriculture accounts for 60–90 per cent of the annual water withdrawal in most countries of the region, with the highest proportion in Afghanistan (99 per cent). (See Table 2.3.) The demands for domestic and industrial uses are increasing in the region due to the high rates of urbanization and industrialization. The demand for water will continue to rise in the region in parallel with population growth.

Fresh-water availability of below 1,000 cubic metres per capita per year indicates water scarcity. Singapore is already water-scarce, with considerably less than 1,000 cubic metres per capita of water

deposits of up to 1,000 tons per year (GESAMP, 1991). In the port of Chittagong in Bangladesh, an estimated 6,000 tons of crude oil is spilled annually, while crude oil residue and wastewater effluent from land-based refineries amount to about 50,000 tons per year (Khan, 1993). Approximately 5 million tons of oil enter the Arabian Sea each year, while the Bay of Bengal receives some 400,000 tons from similar sources (ESCAP, 1995a). Similarly, oil pollution from shipping and offshore oil rigs is a concern in East Asian seas.

Increased use of agro-chemicals in this region is also a matter to be considered. Fertilizer consumption rose 74 per cent in 1982–92, from 33.3 million to 57.8 million tons (ESCAP, 1995a). Use of pesticides, which contribute to enhanced agricultural productivity, appears to be increasing, especially in developing countries. An estimated 1,800 tons of pesticides enter the Bay of Bengal annually (Holmgren, 1994), and increased use of pesticides in some areas has resulted in contamination of shell- and finfish.

Loss of coastal habitats includes substantial loss of mangrove forests in South-East Asia, particularly for the construction of shrimp ponds and for paddy rice cultivation, with negative impacts on commercial fisheries that rely on species using the mangroves as nursery areas. Thailand and the Philippines are clear examples: some 208,218 hectares and 200,000 hectares of mangroves, respectively, were cleared between 1961 and 1993 (GESAMP, 1993). Identical problems because of shrimp culture have occurred in Bangladesh, India, and Sri Lanka. One example of this destructive sequence of events is the Chakaria Sundarbans in eastern Bangladesh, which have been almost completely cleared for aquaculture (ESCAP, 1995a).

Similarly, coastal construction (particularly for tourist facilities), inland mining, and poor land use practices have increased sediment loads in coastal waters in countries such as Fiji, Indonesia, Malaysia, and Thailand, with adverse impacts on sensitive coral reef systems. At present, the status of coral reefs has been significantly improved in Thailand, thanks to the efforts of non-governmental organizations and local people (OEPP, 1996).

Occurrences of "red tides," a special plankton bloom, has been an environmental problem of major concern in the coastal areas of the region. In addition to severely depleting oxygen levels, leading to the mass death of aquatic organisms, the red tides also cause a paralytic shellfish poisoning, with serious risks to human health. For example, an outbreak of red tides in the Philippines in 1990 proved costly for the fisheries and shellfish industries (ESCAP, 1995a). The frequency of the appearance of red tides in Tolo Harbour, Hong Kong, ranged from 2 in 1977 to 9 in 1994. China is also experiencing an increasing threat of red tides in its coastal waters; there were a total of 19 incidents of red tide in 1993 (ESCAP, 1995a).

A major cause for concern throughout the region is overfishing and the use of destructive fishing techniques, particularly in the highly diverse coral reef systems. Most stocks throughout the region are currently being fully harvested, while a number are being exploited at unsustainable levels. Increasingly frequent and severe toxic algal blooms and the eutrophication of bays and semi-enclosed water bodies are growing problems throughout the region. Coastal erosion resulting from increased land subsidence from ground-water extraction, sediment starvation as a consequence of inland dam and irrigation barrage construction, and offshore mining of sand are notable problems in some localities. The high volume of maritime traffic and rising numbers of international tourist arrivals pose additional threats to marine and coastal environments.

Though the consequences of marine environmental pollution are becoming increasingly evident, the level of pollution in most coastal waters is still reasonably manageable. Countries of the Asia and Pacific region have joined various international and regional agreements to resolve the problem. Over the past five years, the situation in the coastal zone has improved in a few localities. This has been helped along by extensive use of remote sensing on a pilot project basis to obtain data on suspended sediments in a water column, topography, bathymetry, sea state, water colour, chlorophyll-a, sea-surface temperature, fisheries, oil slicks, and submerged and emergent vegetation, including mangroves and seagrass.

Table 2.5

Urban Water and Sanitation Coverage in the Asia-Pacific Region, 1994

Access to Safe Drinking Water		Access to Sanitation Services	
Per cent of population covered	80.9	Per cent of population covered	69.8
Per cent served by:		Per cent served by:	
House connection	48.4	House connection to sewer/septic system	42.7
Public standpipe	24.0	Pour-flush latrine	43.1
Other	27.6	Ventilated improved pit latrine	2.7
		Simple pit latrine	8.5
		Other	3.0

Source: G. Watters, 1995. Personal communication. Health and Environment, World Health Organization. Geneva.

Note: WHO defines reasonable access to safe drinking water in an urban area as access to piped water or a public standpipe within 200 meters of a dwelling or housing unit. "Safe" drinking water includes treated surface water and untreated water from protected springs, boreholes, and sanitary wells. Urban areas with access to sanitation services are defined as urban populations served by connections to public sewers or household systems such as latrines, pour-flush latrines, septic tanks, communal toilets, and other such facilities. Definitions of safe water and appropriate access to sanitation and health services vary depending upon location and condition of local resources. Application of these definitions may vary, and comparisons can therefore be misleading.

Urban and Industrial Environments

In 1995, the Asia and Pacific region was home to 3.3 billion people, with an average annual population growth rate of 1.7 per cent and an average density (in 1990) of 95 people per square kilometre, equivalent to that of Europe (UN, 1993). Countries range in population size from a few thousand in some of the smaller Pacific island nations to China (1.2 billion), India (900 million), and Indonesia (200 million).

The urban populations in the developing countries grew between 3 and 6.5 per cent a year in the mid-1990s. About 35 per cent of the region's population is urban, compared with 43 per cent for the world as a whole. The region contains 13 of the 25 largest cities of the world. By 2015, some 903 million people in Asia are expected to live in cities with a population of more than 1 million (WRI/UNEP/UNDP/WB, 1996).

The environmental stress generated by urbanization in the region has been categorized as relating to poverty and arising from economic growth and affluence. The rise of cities has been accompanied by a proliferation of slums and squatter settlements without access to basic infrastructure, clean water, and sanitation, with associated health risks. (See Table 2.5.) Further, the lack of basic infrastructure results in local environmental degradation. It is expected that a large share of the world's urban poor will continue to live in South Asia (WRI/UNEP/UNDP/WB, 1996).

Environmental concerns resulting from the economic growth and affluence of urban areas include congestion; increasing air and water pollution; loss of productive agricultural land; loss of coastal habitats to conversion and land reclamation; overextraction of ground-water resources, resulting in land subsidence; and deforestation as a consequence of increased demand for construction timber.

The problems of urbanization are not confined to continental or large archipelagic states but also occur in small island states such as Maldives, Tuvalu, and Tonga, where in-migration to the capital islands has resulted in severe land and, in some instances, freshwater shortages, and in hot spots of coastal pollution.

About 700 million tons of solid waste and 1,900 million tons of industrial waste are generated each year in Asia and the Pacific (ESCAP, 1995a). Among the various subregions, East Asia generates the largest share of municipal solid waste. Broad calculations indicate that its share may increase to 60 per cent by the year 2000 because of the large population base and high economic growth rate (ESCAP, 1995a).

The key issues regarding solid waste management are the environmental health implications due to inadequate coverage of waste collection; improper storage prior to collection; and poor standards of disposal (ESCAP, 1995a). It is estimated that 30–50 per cent of municipal solid waste is uncollected (ESCAP, 1995a).

The disposal of domestic and industrial waste is given relatively low priority in many countries, with only around 70 per cent of the waste in urban municipal areas being collected and only some 5 per cent of this being treated (ESCAP, 1995b). Solid waste disposal is a particular problem in the small island states due to their limited land area; disposal areas have been used for land reclamation in some of these countries, resulting in contamination and pollution of surrounding coastal areas.

Extensive and reliable data on the generation of hazardous wastes in the region are not available. Rough estimates indicate that about 100 million tons are produced annually, with as much as 90 per cent generated in China and India (ESCAP, 1995a). About 60–65 per cent of these wastes end up in landfills; 5–10 per cent are dumped in the oceans; and only about 25 per cent are either incinerated or undergo physico-chemical treatment (ESCAP, 1995a). However, there is growing awareness in the region, especially in Japan, China, and India, about the detoxification of wastes and about immobilization by fabrication into bricks and other usable products (ESCAP, 1995a). Another issue of concern is wastes being brought into the region for disposal.

Wastewater disposal poses another problem. In many places, untreated domestic and industrial wastes are discharged directly into canals and rivers. Some Governments are in the process of taking measures to increase the treatment of wastewater. In 1992, about 68.6 per cent of industrial wastewater and 18.5 per cent of municipal wastewater generated in China was treated (WRI/UNEP/UNDP, 1994). The Government of Thailand has agreed in principle to establish a Central Waste Water Management Authority to consolidate policies and institutions to deal with this matter. The Government is also envisaging a role for private investments in setting up treatment plants (Government of Thailand, 1994). In Singapore, 36 industries were prosecuted in 1993 for discharging acidic effluents into the sewers (ASEAN, 1995). Singapore has significantly improved its facilities for handling wastes and is ensuring a stringent enforcement of standards.

With growing economic activities and consumerism, the quantity of solid wastes generated is growing rapidly. Furthermore, large quantities of industrial and hazardous wastes accompanying the expansion of industries that use chemicals in the region has exacerbated the waste management problem.

Underlying Causes

The root causes of different environmental problems vary considerably in Asia and the Pacific. Much of the increasing severity of problems is driven by the demographic situation, although other aspects of the human condition—such as cultural, social, and economic status; traditional and acquired technologies; institutional and legal systems; and changing consumption patterns—have all played a significant role. Although high economic growth is being achieved in many countries in the region, poverty is still a problem at the root of several environmental problems. Impacts on the environment caused by the developed and the newly industrialized countries in the region, as well as the unsustainable use of natural resources by those countries (and other developed countries outside the region), have also been considerable (NEPA, personal communication, 1996).

Social

Population size, growth rate, and distribution have contributed significantly to shaping the environment in this region. Looking at demographic trends (population growth rates and densities), the countries most likely to face environmental problems include Maldives, Pakistan, and Bangladesh, closely followed by Nepal, Vietnam, India, and the Philippines (ESCAP, 1995a).

The levels of consumption in Asia and the Pacific vary significantly among countries, but in general as a region, the consumption levels are modest—for instance, with regard to energy consumption (and hence, lower per capita carbon dioxide emissions) (ESCAP, 1995a). Nevertheless, the high population growth rate has been found to strongly correlate with rates of deforestation, expansion of agricultural land, and increasing water scarcity in some countries (ESCAP, 1995a). In recent decades, pressure on arable land resulting from expansion of human settlements, the clearing of land for cultivation, intensive agriculture for intensified food production, and overgrazing has been noted, and has led to the expansion of agricultural areas into forest areas and marginal lands.

Migration from rural to urban areas has accounted for some 40 per cent of urban population growth during 1970–90 in most developing countries of the region (ESCAP, 1995a). The major environmental problems associated with urban development, as described earlier, are increasing pollution levels due to the concentrated discharge of gaseous, liquid, and solid wastes into the environment and the consequent destruction of fragile ecosystems.

Deforestation is also a major problem associated with urban expansion. For example, fuelwood meets 50 per cent of the cooking energy needs of the urban population in many countries (ESCAP, 1995a). Coastal areas with sensitive ecosystems have fallen victim to the continued pressure of urbanization in the region. In the Pacific subregion, urban residents are running short of fuelwood as coastal mangroves and inland forests are depleted. In Tuvalu, pressure on the coastal environment has also followed the migration of people from the outer islands to the dense shanty areas in the capital city on the Fogafale Islet (Thistlewaite and Votaw, 1991).

Economic

The developing countries of Asia and the Pacific are economically the fastest growing group of countries in the world, with an average growth rate in GDP of 7 per cent during 1991–94 compared with the world economic growth rate of 1.1 per cent (ES-CAP, 1995a). Although growth of this order and magnitude has been instrumental in reducing the incidence of poverty, particularly in East Asia and among the Association of South-East Asian Nations, it has been accompanied by serious environmental problems (ESCAP, 1995a).

The impact of industry on the environment has become increasingly evident: resource depletion; contamination of water, air, and land; health hazards; and degradation of natural ecosystems. Industrial

sources contribute a relatively high share to air pollution in this region because the main source of industrial energy is fossil fuels, with a high share of coal, and the major air polluting industries, such as iron, steel, fertilizer, and cement, are growing in the region. Similarly, water-polluting industries are expanding very rapidly. For instance, in 1992, approximately 64 per cent of the total wastewater generated in China was from the industrial sector (ESCAP, 1995a).

Both the quality and the quantity of industrial solid waste is problematic from the environmental point of view. For example, China has had the most waste-intensive production process in this region; in 1990, more than 2 kilograms of industrial waste were generated for every US dollar (in constant 1980 prices) of industrial production (ESCAP, 1995a). However, since 1990, the rate of waste generation has slowed down and even decreased in the case of industrial solid waste (NEPA, personal communication, 1996).

The transportation sector has become a key accelerating factor for economic growth as well as environmental degradation. A relatively heavy concentration of road networks and vehicles in a few cities has resulted in high levels of pollution. For example, road transport accounts for a major share of the air pollution load in Delhi (57 per cent), Beijing (75 per cent), Manila (70 per cent), and Kuala Lumpur (86 per cent) (WRI/UNEP/UNDP, 1994).

With regard to coastal and marine environments, port and harbour projects primarily have impacts on sensitive coastal ecosystems. Construction affects, in varying degrees, the hydrology and surface-water quality in the coastal zones, fisheries, coral reefs, and mangroves, as noted earlier. China, Hong Kong, India, Japan, Malaysia, the Philippines, Singapore, Thailand, and Papua New Guinea are making substantial investments in expanding their maritime transport. Also, these countries are undertaking dredging operations for the maintenance of port transportation facilities (UN, 1994).

Agriculture in the Asia and Pacific region has witnessed accelerated structural changes in the past 40 years. In terms of direct impact on the environment, farming activities are major contributors to soil erosion, land salinization, and loss of nutrients. For example, it has been estimated that about 25 per cent of the soil degradation in the region has occurred directly from agricultural activities. Shifting cultivation has been an important cause for land degradation in many countries of this region: Bangladesh, Brunei Darussalam, Fiji, India, Indonesia, the Lao PDR, Malaysia, Myanmar, Nepal, Papua New Guinea, the Philippines, Solomon Islands, Sri Lanka, Thailand, and Vietnam (Dent *et al.*, 1992). As noted earlier, natural habitats are being destroyed, degraded, and depleted, accompanied by significant loss of wild species.

The largest water user on a regional scale is the agricultural sector, with more than two thirds of the water abstracted from the region's rivers, lakes, and aquifers being used for irrigation. With regard to the impacts of agro-chemicals, there is now considerable evidence that the leaching of fertilizer into water bodies is a significant source of water pollution. In particular, excessive levels of nitrates and other nutrients resulting from fertilizer application are a major cause of eutrophication in surface water throughout the region. The region's use of fertilizers increased from 11 million tons in 1968–70 to 52 million tons in 1988–90 (FADINAP, 1992). In 1990, an average of 125 kilograms of fertilizer were used per hectare, although this figure was exceeded in the Republic of Korea, Korea DPR, China, and Malaysia (ESCAP, 1995a). The intensification of agriculture in recent years has also been accompanied by the extensive use of pesticides (herbicides, insecticides, and fungicides). Data on unintended pesticide poisonings are not currently available.

Over the past two decades, there has been an impressive growth in tourism in this region. This has generally led to the creation of additional employment, increased flows of foreign exchange and infrastructural development, and the restoration of cultural, religious, and heritage sites. Of 500 million international tourist arrivals world-wide in 1993, 14.5 per cent (72.4 million) were registered in this region, compared with 1.3 per cent in 1960 (WTO, 1994a, 1994b, 1994c).

Tourism growth has also had significant environmental impacts, however, particularly in relation to important ecosystems such as mangroves, forests, and coral reefs. Impacts on the physical environment are largely related to tourism infrastructure development (including resorts, hotels, and coastal zone management activities), inducing soil erosion, landslides, sedimentation, and water pollution. For example, unplanned development of infrastructure too close to the shoreline has affected coastal natural processes and led to beach erosion, particularly in Fiji, Indonesia, Maldives, Malaysia, and Sri Lanka. With the introduction of environmental impact assessments (EIAs), such unplanned developmental activities are being checked.

Coral reefs are one of the primary tourist attractions in the region. Damage to coral reefs from sedimentation is widespread, particularly in Thailand, where 51 per cent of coral reefs are under threat (ESCAP, 1995a). Also, mangrove forests in Thailand, Fiji, and the Philippines are currently under threat from tourism-related development and activities, including direct encroachment from hotel and resort construction, exploitation for fuelwood, and clearance for shrimp farming (OEPP, 1996).

Promoting liberal trade while maintaining and strengthening protection of the environment and natural resources is one of the great policy challenges of the decade. There has been a widespread inflow of polluting industries and hazardous waste from industrial nations, and an outflow of raw materials and resource-intensive industrial products to them.

The direct effects of agricultural trade liberalization on Asian environmental resources are less clear. However, increasing product prices are likely to lead to greater demand of agro-chemicals. Demand for water could also rise, an important consideration in countries with seasonal water scarcity, such as Thailand. Studies of the impact of trade on land resources have shown a positive correlation between rate of forest conversion and crop prices (Barbier and Burgess, 1992).

Similarly, the principal direct environmental impact of manufactured goods and their export is industrial pollution. While almost 75 per cent of total world exports of "dirty" industries originates from industrial countries, South-East Asia's share increased from 3.4 per cent in 1965 to 8.4 per cent in 1988, reflecting the region's rapid expansion of manufactured exports (Low and Yeats, 1992). South Asia's share of the world total, based on India, Pakistan, and Sri Lanka, rose from 2.1 per cent to 2.8 per cent over the same period (Low and Yeats, 1992).

Institutional

In this region, Government responsibility for the environment rests with environment ministries, with a division or unit in another ministry, with independent environment agencies, or with departments created to assist the environment ministries. Most of the environment institutions in developing countries are relatively small and far from satisfactory in terms of staffing and financial resources. Command and control is the main environmental policy instrument in the region. Strategic environmental planning, legislative means, and regulatory standards and planning procedures are the most commonly used tools of environmental control. The least used instruments are those related to economic incentives.

A common problem is that environmental institutions have no power to audit the environmental performance of sectoral institutions. Thus, they are attempting to strengthen performance through improvement of existing tools or by developing additional tools for use by other institutions. Two major shortcomings with regard to the greening of industry and business in the region are weak monitoring and enforcement capabilities of environment institutions and the lack of green consumerism.

Moderate progress was made during the last five years on the effective implementation of the environmental impact assessment process. The overall quality of EIAs in the region suggests a need for more legislation, regulations, and guidelines. There is also an urgent need to create Government environment management units that can enforce the EIA's procedure. In addition, the federal system of some Governments makes it difficult to enforce EIAs for activities related to resource exploitation because these are usually under the jurisdiction of a provincial Government.

Institution-strengthening measures (which include training of key professionals, especially engineers and economists, on EIA techniques) are needed to make the EIA procedure a more effective instrument for sustainable development in the region. For example, in India there was an initiative to develop responsibility for EIA in the State Governments, but most projects are now once again under the responsibility of a unit in the Ministry of Environment and Forests because many States lacked the institutional capacity to handle EIAs of large and complex projects (ESCAP, 1995a).

Similarly, using risk assessment in developing countries entails many problems, including the lack of trained personal and comprehensive databases—whether industrial, medical, or environmental.

Developing countries of the region are only moderately involved in international agreements on the environment, and the least developed countries are barely participating. In most cases, non-implementation is due to inadequate availability of the professional and administrative expertise and resources needed to formulate and implement relevant domestic legislation.

Environmental

Many of the developing countries in this region are situated in the world's hazard belts of floods, droughts, cyclones, earthquakes, windstorms, tidal waves, and landslides. The major natural disasters faced periodically are largely due to climatic and seismic factors. The region has been one of the worst hit in terms of natural disasters, suffering 50 per cent of the world's major emergencies (ESCAP, 1995a). Since the International Decade for Natural Disaster Reduction began in 1990, the total number of deaths in the region due to these causes has exceeded 200,000, with the damage to property over this period estimated at US$100 billion (ESCAP, 1995a). Vulnerability has increased due to growing urban populations, environmental degradation, and a lack of planning and preparedness.

Disasters are the result of meteorological phenomena such as typhoons, hurricanes, sheet flooding, and marine- and river-based floods; of geological processes such as volcanic eruptions, earthquakes, and tsunamis; and of climatic phenomenon such as the El Niño–Southern Oscillation that results in a lower mean sea level in the east, failure of the monsoon rains in India, and drought in Indonesia and Australia. Vulnerability to natural hazards has been increased in many coastal areas due to the loss of habitats such as mangroves and coral reefs that provided natural protection against marine-based flooding.

Tropical cyclones, or typhoons, which are common in Asia and the Pacific, occur most frequently over the north-west Pacific during June and November just east of the Philippines, with an average of 30 typhoons per year (38 per cent of the world's total) (ESCAP, 1995a). In the Bay of Bengal, tropical cyclones usually form over the southern end during April–December and then move to the east coast of India and Bangladesh, causing severe flooding and, often, devastating tidal surges. The cyclones generated in the South Pacific Ocean frequently cause devastation in small island countries such as Fiji, Tonga, Vanuatu, Solomon Islands, and Samoa. Overall, the Philippines, Bangladesh, and Vietnam appear to suffer most frequently from these large events.

Floods, which are the most common climate-related disasters in the region, include seasonal flooding, flash flooding, urban flooding due to inadequate drainage facilities, floods associated with tidal events induced by typhoons in coastal areas, and so on. In Bangladesh, one of the most flood-prone countries in the region, as many as 80 million people are vulnerable to flooding each year (ESCAP, 1995a). Another example is India, where 40 million hectares are at risk from flooding each year, and the average annual direct damage has been estimated at US$240 million, although this can exceed US$1.5 billion when flooding is severe (ESCAP, 1995a).

It has been observed that the impact of droughts differs widely between industrial and developing countries because of such factors as water supply efficiency and behavioural patterns such as water use efficiency. Most of the estimated 500 million rural poor in this region are subsistence farmers occupying mainly rainfed land (ESCAP, 1995a). The

drought-prone countries in this region are Afghanistan, Iran, Myanmar, Pakistan, Nepal, India, Sri Lanka, and parts of Bangladesh. In India about 33 per cent of the arable land—14 per cent of the total land area of the country—is considered to be drought-prone, and a further 35 per cent can also be affected by drought when rainfall is exceptionally low for extended periods (ESCAP, 1995a). Nepal has experienced severe droughts in the past. Also, the Philippines, Thailand, Australia, and the Pacific islands of Fiji, Vanuatu, and Samoa contain drought-prone areas.

Landslides, which are very common in the hills and mountainous parts of the region, occur frequently in India, China, Nepal, Thailand, and the Philippines. In addition to the primary cause—the topography—landslides are aggravated by human activities, such as deforestation, cultivation, and construction, which destabilize the already fragile slopes. For instance, as a result of combined actions of natural (mostly heavy rainfall) and human factors, as many as 12,000 landslides occur in Nepal each year (ESCAP, 1995a).

The region has recorded 70 per cent of the world's earthquakes measuring 7 or more on the Richter scale, at an average rate of 15 per year (ESCAP, 1995a). The countries badly affected by earthquakes include Afghanistan, India, Iran, Japan, Nepal, the Philippines, and the Pacific Islands.

Many of the countries in the region are located along or adjacent to the Pacific Ocean Seismic Zone and/or the Indian Ocean Seismic Zone. For instance, 50–60 per cent of India is vulnerable to seismic activities of varying intensity (ESCAP, 1995a). These areas are essentially located in the Himalayan region and in the Union Territory of the Andaman and Nicobar Islands. The September 1993 earthquake in Maharashtra State in Western India claimed more than 12,000 lives (ESCAP, 1995a).

Similarly, about 80 per cent of China's territorial area (with 60 per cent of its large cities and 70 per cent of its urban areas with populations over 1 million) is located in seismic zones (ESCAP, 1995a). The most devastating earthquake in the world in recent history, the Tangshan earthquake in China on 28 July 1976, claimed more than 240,000 lives

(ESCAP, 1995a). Japan is located in the Pacific Rim seismic zone.

Japan suffers a massive earthquake (Richter scale 8 or over) on average once every 10 years, and a large-scale earthquake (magnitude 7 class) on average once a year (ESCAP, 1995a). In January 1995, Japan suffered one of the worst earthquakes in recent years at Kobe, which claimed 5,000 lives (ESCAP, 1995a). The Philippines, which lies between two of the world's most active tectonic plates, experiences an average of five earthquakes a day, most of which are imperceptible (ESCAP, 1995a). And in New Zealand, an average of 200 perceptible earthquakes occur each year, with one at least exceeding 6 on the Richter scale (ESCAP, 1995a).

Tsunamis, the tidal waves generated by earthquakes, affect many of the coastal areas of the region, including those of Japan, Indonesia, and the Philippines. For example, the infamous Krakatau volcanic eruption during 1883 in Sunda Straits, Indonesia, generated a 35-metre-high tsunami, which claimed 36,000 lives (ESCAP, 1995a). Furthermore, the tsunami of 17 August 1976 in the Moro Gulf area of the Philippines caused some 8,000 deaths (ESCAP, 1995a).

Volcanoes, like earthquakes, are located mainly along the Pacific Rim. Countries of the region at risk from volcanic eruptions include Indonesia, Japan, New Zealand, Papua New Guinea, the Philippines, Solomon Islands, Tonga, and Vanuatu. Those most frequently affected are Indonesia (129 active volcanoes), Japan (77 active volcanoes), and the Philippines (21 active volcanoes) (ESCAP, 1995a; Government of Japan, 1987).

Notable examples include the eruptions of Mount Pinatubo in Central Luzon, during the period 12–15 June 1991, which affected about 1–2 million people (Lewinson, 1993), demolished the surrounding forests, caused massive siltation of rivers and coastal areas, and deposited volcanic ash in surrounding areas and even across continents. In New Zealand, Mount Tarawera had a severe eruption in 1886, and the Ngauruhoe, which erupted in 1974, emits steam and vapour constantly (ESCAP, 1995a). In Papua New Guinea, the volcanic eruption in 1994 near the city of Rabaul damaged about

40 per cent of the houses in the area (ESCAP, 1995a).

Environmental degradation and disasters are very closely linked in this region. The countries that suffer most from disasters are the same ones in which environmental degradation is proceeding most rapidly. Similarly, poverty and vulnerability to disasters are closely linked. There are some 3,000 deaths per event in low-income countries, and less than 400 per event in middle- and high-income countries (ESCAP, 1992). This reflects the absence of a sufficient infrastructure in low-income economies to mitigate the impact of natural disasters. Both Japan and Pakistan are prone to earthquakes, for example. The people of Japan, however, are far less vulnerable because that Government has strictly enforced building codes, zoning regulations, and earthquake emergency training and communication systems; in Pakistan, most people still live in top-heavy mud and stone houses built on hillsides, increasing their vulnerability.

Encroachment of disaster-prone lands due to rapid population growth is accelerating the vulnerability to disasters. It has been estimated that annual flood losses in some countries are 40 times more today than what they were in the 1950s (ESCAP, 1992). According to the Indian Government, one out of every 20 people in the nation is vulnerable to flooding (ESCAP, 1992). Similarly, in China more than 85 per cent of the population is concentrated on alluvial plains or basins along river courses that constitute one third of its total land area (ESCAP, 1992).

References

ADB. 1994a. *The Environment Program: Past, Present and Future.* Asian Development Bank (ADB). Manila.

ADB. 1994b. *Energy Indicators of Developing Member Countries of ADB.* Energy and Industry Department. Manila.

ADB. 1995a. *Asian Development Outlook, 1995 and 1996.* Manila.

ASEAN. 1995. Draft. *ASEAN State of the Environment 1995.* Unpublished. Association of South-East Asian Nations.

Barbier, E., and J. Burgess. 1992. Agricultural Pricing and Environmental Degradation. Background paper for World Bank, *World Development Report, 1992*. Oxford University Press. Oxford and New York.

Dent, F.J., Y.S. Rao, and K. Takeuchi. 1992. *Womb of the Earth: Regional Strategies for Arresting Land Degradation*. Occasional Paper 2. FAO. Bangkok.

EIA. 1995. *International Energy Annual: 1993*. Energy Information Agency, U.S. Department of Energy. Washington.

ESCAP. 1991. *Groundwater Quality and Monitoring in Asia and the Pacific*. Water Resources Series No. 70. Economic and Social Commission of the Asia-Pacific (ESCAP). Bangkok.

ESCAP. 1992. *State of the Environment in Asia and the Pacific 1990*. Bangkok.

ESCAP. 1993a. *Asia-Pacific in Figures 1993*. Bangkok.

ESCAP. 1993b. *Population Data Sheet 1993*. Bangkok.

ESCAP. 1995a. *State of the Environment in the Asia-Pacific, 1995*. Bangkok.

ESCAP. 1995b. Preparatory Meeting for the Ministerial Conference on Environment and Development in Asia-Pacific. Bangkok.

FADINAP. 1992. Trends in the Nutrient Consumption Ratios in the Region. Fertilizer Advisory, Development and Information Network for Asia and the Pacific (FADINAP). Bangkok.

FAO. 1993. *Forest Resources Assessment 1990: Tropical Countries*. FAO Forestry Paper 112. Food and Agriculture Organization of the United Nations (FAO). Rome.

FAO. 1995. *Forest Resource Assessment: 1990: Global Synthesis*. FAO Forestry Paper No. 124. (FAO). Rome.

FAO/RAPA. 1993. *Selected Indicators of Food and Agricultural Development in Asia and the Pacific Region, 1982–1992*. Publication 1993/26, Bangkok.

FAO/RAPA. 1994. *Selected Indicators of Food and Agricultural Development in Asia and the Pacific Region, 1983–1993*. Publication 1994/24, Bangkok.

FAO/UNDP/UNEP. 1994. Land degradation in South Asia: Its severity, causes and effects upon the people. World Soil Resources Report No. 78. FAO. Rome.

Fuavo, V. 1990. *Areas of Environmental Concerns in the South Pacific Region*. SPREP.

GESAMP (IMO, FAO, UNESCO, WMO, WHO, IAEA, UN, UNEP). 1991. Joint group of experts on the scientific aspects of marine protection, reducing environmental impacts of coastal aquaculture. Reports and Studies No 47. FAO. Rome.

GESAMP. 1993. Joint group of experts on the scientific aspects of marine protection, impact of oil and related chemicals and wastes on the marine environment. Reports and Studies No. 50. IMO. London.

Government of India. 1991–92. *Annual Report, 1991–92*. Ministry of Environment and Forests, New Delhi.

Government of India. 1993. *Environment Action Programme*. Ministry of Environment and Forests, New Delhi.

Government of Japan. 1987. Volcanic Disaster Counter Measures in Japan. National Land Agency. Tokyo.

Government of Korea. 1994. Country Paper presented at the Regional Meeting on State of the Environment in Asia-Pacific, 26–30 July 1995.

Government of Thailand. 1994. *Thailand State of the Environment Report*. Bangkok.

Hettelingh, J.P., M. Chadwick, H. Sverdrup, and D. Zhao. 1995. RAINS-ASIA: an assessment model for acid rain in Asia (Chapter 6). Report from the World-Bank sponsored project Acid Rain and Emissions Reduction in Asia.

Holmgren S. 1994. An environmental assessment of the Bay of Bengal region. Bay of Bengal Programme. BOPG/REP/67. BOBP. Madras.

IUCN. 1993. *1994 IUCN Red List of Threatened Animals*. World Conservation Union (IUCN). Gland, Switzerland.

Khan, M.A. 1993. *Problem and Prospect of Sustainable Management of Urban Water Bodies in the Asian and Pacific Region*. Bangkok.

Lewinson, J. 1993. Mount Pinatubo rehabilitation programme. *Asian Disaster Management News*. January.

Low, P., and A. Yeats. 1992. Do dirty industries migrate? In: Patrick Low (ed.). *International Trade and the Environment*. World Bank. Washington.

McNeeley, J.A., K.R. Miller, W.V. Reid, R.A. Mittermeier, and T.B. Werner. 1990. *Conserving the World's Biological Diversity*. WRI, World Conservation Union, World Bank, WWF-U.S., and Conservation International, Washington and Gland, Switzerland.

NEPA. 1993. *China Environment News*. National Environment Protection Agency of China (NEPA). June. Beijing.

OEPP. 1996. Communication submitted after GEO/ASEAN consultation. Office of Environmental Policy and Planning (OEPP). Bangkok.

Shrestha, R.M., S.C. Bhattacharya, and S. Malla. 1996. Energy use and sulfur dioxide in Asia. *Journal of Environmental Management*. No. 46.

Straits Times. 1993. 3 June 1993. Indonesia.

Tariq, J., M. Jaffar, M. Ashraf, and M. Moazzam. 1993. Heavy metal concentration in fish, shrimp, seaweed, sediments and water from the Arabian Sea, Pakistan. *Marine Pollution Bulletin*, Vol. 26, No. 11.

Thistlewaite, R., and G. Votaw. 1991. *Environment & Development: A Pacific Island Perspective*. Asian Development Bank, Manila.

UN. 1993. *World Population Prospects, 1992 Revision*. New York.

UN. 1994. Infrastructure development as key to economic growth and regional economic cooperation. ST/ESCAP/1364, New York.

UNEP. 1992. Marine pollution from land-based sources: facts and figures. *UNEP Industry & Environment*. Paris.

UNEP. 1994. *Environmental Data Report 1993–94*. United Nations Environment Programme. Oxford.

UNEP/ISRIC. 1990. *World Map of the Status of Human-Induced Soil Degradation*. UNEP and the International Soil Reference and Information Centre (ISRIC). Wageningen, the Netherlands.

WCMC. 1995. Protected Areas Data Unit of the World Conservation Monitoring Centre. Unpublished data. World Conservation Monitoring Centre (WCMC). Cambridge.

Weber, P.C. 1993. *Abandoned Seas*. Worldwatch Paper 116. Washington.

WRI/UNEP/IUCN. 1992. *Global Biodiversity Strategy: Guidelines for Action to Save, Study and Use Earth's Biotic Wealth Sustainably and Equitably*. World Resources Institute (WRI). Washington.

WRI/UNEP/UNDP. 1990. *World Resources 1990–91*. Oxford University Press. New York and London.

WRI/UNEP/UNDP. 1992. *World Resources 1991–92*. Oxford University Press. New York and London.

WRI/UNEP/UNDP. 1994. *World Resources 1994–95*. Oxford University Press. New York and London.

WRI/UNEP/UNDP/World Bank. 1996. *World Resources 1996–97*. Oxford University Press. New York and London.

WTO. 1994a. Tourism Market Trends: East Asia and the Pacific 1980–93. Madrid.

WTO. 1994b. *Yearbook of Tourism Statistics*. Vol 1. Madrid.

WTO. 1994c. *Yearbook of Tourism Statistics*. Vol 2. Madrid.

EUROPE AND CIS COUNTRIES

Major Environmental Concerns

The first pan-European conference of environmental ministers, held at Dobříš Castle, Czechoslovakia, in 1991, requested that a comprehensive state of the environment report be done for the whole of Europe. Prepared by the European Environment Agency Task Force in cooperation with Governments and intergovernmental bodies, the Dobříš Assessment was published in 1995 (EEA, 1995a). Without indicating priorities, the report identified the following as the 12 most significant environmental problems of concern to Europe:

- climate change,
- stratospheric ozone depletion,
- the loss of biodiversity,
- major accidents,
- acidification,
- tropospheric ozone and other photochemical oxidants,
- the management of fresh water,
- forest degradation,
- coastal zone threats and management,
- waste reduction and management,
- urban stress, and
- chemical risks.

The Dobříš Assessment has been an important source of information for this section. Additional documents that were of use related to specific sectoral issues and supplemented the information contained in the Dobříš report on Central and Eastern Europe (CEE) and the Commonwealth of Independent States (CIS). It is noteworthy that the relatively prolific and detailed documentation available for much of the region contains frequent references to the inadequacy of existing data for reliable environmental monitoring and assessment.

The region is vast, covering more than a fifth of the earth's land area and extending further than 11,000 kilometres between the Atlantic and Pacific oceans. The Russian Federation makes up more than 60 per cent of this total area. Some 15 per cent of the world's population live in Europe and the CIS countries.

Land

Land degradation has been identified as a crucial and increasing environmental problem in the region, the most severe forms being the irreversible processes of erosion, acidification, and pollution. Soil compaction, loss of organic matter, overgrazing, improper irrigation, salinization, and waterlogging are other, less common forms of land degradation in the region (EEA, 1995a). Parts of Europe also suffer from desertification. Both physical and chemical degradation are expected to continue unless low-input agriculture and erosion control measures are widely adopted (CEC, 1992).

Soil erosion is increasing in Europe. Mediterranean areas are particularly susceptible, and parts of CEE and the CIS have also been widely affected. For example, 56 per cent of agricultural lands in Russia are subject to erosion of different types (Min. of Env. Prot. and Nat. Res. of the Russ. Fed., 1995a); equivalent figures for the Ukraine and Kazakstan are 34 per cent and 42 per cent respectively (Min. of Env. Prot. of Ukraine, 1994; Min. of Ecol. and Biol. Res., Kazakstan, 1993). West of the Urals, an estimated 12 per cent (115 million hectares) of the total land area is affected by water erosion and 4 per cent by wind erosion (EEA, 1995a). Major problems include the loss of humus, production losses, the cost of replacing lost nutrients, and damage to areas that receive the eroded materials (EEA, 1995a).

Pollution of land from a variety of contaminants (heavy metals, persistent organic pollutants, nitrates, phosphates, artificial radionuclides, and so on) is widespread, though the area affected is not accurately determined. Among other effects, pollutants may lower plant yields; enter food chains and water supplies, rendering them unfit for human consumption; and inhibit soil micro-organisms, thereby disturbing natural decomposition processes.

Pesticides and fertilizers are major sources of these pollutants. Industrial processes, fossil fuel combustion, waste and wastewater sludge disposal, and accidental release contribute significantly (EEA, 1995a). The Chernobyl disaster is a case in point. After the event in 1986, over 23 per cent of the territory of Belarus alone was affected by radioactive fallout (Republic of Belarus, 1995). Large areas remain contaminated more than 10 years after the event, including 430,000 hectares of the worst affected areas of Belarus, Russia, and the Ukraine, which remain an "alienation zone," and a further 9.4 million hectares of agricultural land that remain contaminated with long-lived radionuclides (IAEA, 1996). Additional, less well-known cases of serious radionuclide soil contamination in eastern Europe and the CIS countries are associated with other nuclear installations and test sites.

Other serious cases of contamination include oil and heavy-metal pollution of soils around abandoned military sites in the CIS countries, and oil leakages into land and aquatic ecosystems during oil extraction and transportation activities in western Siberia. It is estimated that some 7–20 per cent of all oil extracted ends up in these ecosystems (Mnatsakanian, 1994).

Acidification is frequently a transboundary problem. Whereas the main emission sources are in north-western and central Europe, the greatest impacts are in the industrialized, densely populated zone that extends from Poland and the Czech Republic through Germany and the Benelux countries to the United Kingdom and Scandinavia. Present loads of acidic deposition are higher than critical loads in roughly 60 per cent of Europe, with central parts of Europe receiving 20 times more acidity than the ecosystem's critical loads (EEA, 1995a).

Sulphur deposition predominates in the more northerly countries whereas nitrogen leaching and associated problems are typical for central Europe and the Netherlands. Although long-term trends in acid deposition are not yet available, there is an indication that the Long Range Transboundary Air Pollution (LRTAP) Convention prepared under the auspices of the United Nations Economic Commission for Europe (UN-ECE) is effectively reducing sulphur-related acidification in the region, as discussed later in this section (EEA, 1995a).

In agricultural areas, the application of chemicals has tended to offset acid deposition, but outside these areas the effects are not mitigated. Acid deposition is a problem in most countries in western Europe where soils have low buffering capacity. At present, 30 per cent of the forested area of Europe is thought to be degraded from this, with a further 15 per cent at risk if acid deposition continues (EEA, 1995a). Acidification of soil and water has been particularly serious in the Scandinavian countries because of prevailing winds and the high natural acidity of soils (EEA, 1995a; Bernes, 1993).

A third of Europe's 300 million hectares of drylands suffers some degree of desertification and the reduction in biological and economic productivity that goes with it (UNEP, 1992a). Desertified areas are mainly uncultivated and abandoned lands (15 million hectares), drylands (13 million hectares), and irrigated lands (1.6 million hectares) (UNEP, 1992a). Changes in agricultural practices, particularly the intensification of land use, are thought to have been the prime causes (EEA, 1995a). The affected areas are mainly in southern and central Europe and the southern parts of the Former Soviet Union (FSU) (UNEP, 1996).

Forests

Forests cover 27 per cent of the region west of the Urals and 35 per cent of the FSU—a total of 900 million hectares (FAO, 1995b). Combined, they contain almost 15 per cent of the world's forest biomass (FAO, 1995b). A large proportion of the region's forests are in the Russian Federation (FAO, 1995b). The region, however, has little left of its mature, biodiversity-rich natural forest ecosystems due to centuries of exploitation (EEA, 1995a).

Since the early 1960s, Europe's total forest area has increased by more than 10 per cent, mainly in the south and west (EEA, 1995a). Though small in percentage terms, there have been some huge areal increases in the east as well: from 1988 to 1993, registered forestlands in Russia increased by 3.9 million hectares (0.33 per cent) (Min. of Env. Prot. and Nat. Res. of the Russ. Fed., 1995a). Increases have been due to reforestation policies and spontaneous tree growth in marginal areas (EEA, 1995a).

While there is an overall increase in growing stock and forest productivity in the region (FAO, 1995b), large-scale deforestation is currently under way in the boreal forests of the Russian Federation. Much of the logging there is fostered by large timber companies from outside the area; the extensive timber removal is causing serious erosion problems and habitat changes that have negative impacts on biodiversity (EEA, 1995a). In addition, in some CEE countries such as Georgia, thousands of hectares of mountain forests have been felled to provide fuel (REC, 1994). However, the region's forests are reportedly increasingly valued for their environmental and other non-wood functions (FAO, 1995b).

Forest degradation is of more widespread concern in Europe than deforestation. Crown defoliation and discolouration indicate a general worsening in forest conditions in many parts of the region, although no reliable correlation has been established yet between tree growth and defoliation. The forests most severely affected by defoliation are in central, north, and south-east Europe. In a 1993 transnational survey, 22.6 per cent of trees were found to be defoliated by more than 25 per cent (EC/UN-ECE, 1994). Recent research has demonstrated a number of causative factors, including adverse weather conditions, air pollution, pests and pathogens, and forest fires rather than just acid rain, as previously suspected (EC/UN-ECE, 1994; EEA, 1995a).

Nevertheless, a number of the most affected countries consider air pollution the major reason for catastrophic dieback in local areas including the Black Triangle on the borders of Poland, Germany,

and the Czech Republic; Upper Silesia in Poland; and the Kola Peninsula and Norilsk areas of Russia (Nowicki, 1993; Min. of Env. Prot. and Nat. Res. of the Russ. Fed., 1993; Min. of Env. of the Czech Republic, 1996). It is believed that emissions of sulphur dioxide (SO_2) and nitrogen oxides (NO_x) from coal-fuelled power plants are largely responsible for the 35–50 per cent of CEE forests that are damaged or dying, while non-ferrous smelting is a major contributor to the degradation of the Russian sites (Environmental Resources Ltd., 1990). Fires damage some 700,000 hectares of forest each year, mainly in parts of the FSU and southern Europe, although in the latter area a certain frequency of burning is necessary to maintain vegetation types like chaparral and maquis (EEA, 1995a).

Biodiversity

Europe is estimated to have more than 2,500 habitat types, which are home to some 215,000 species, more than 90 per cent of which are invertebrates (EEA, 1995a). Many of these species are currently threatened by extinction: 52 per cent of fish are under threat, 45 per cent of reptiles, 42 per cent of mammals, 30 per cent of amphibians, and 15 per cent of birds (EEA, 1995a). Of Europe's 12,500 species of higher plants, 21 per cent are threatened, although only 27 species are known to have become extinct (EEA, 1995a). The countries with the highest percentage of threatened plant species are Slovakia (36 per cent), the Netherlands (35 per cent), and Romania (at least 30 per cent) (EEA, 1995a). In comparison with the rest of the world, the total number of species in Europe is relatively small but the percentage of threatened species is large (EEA, 1995a).

Natural ecosystems, which sustain a high proportion of plant and animal species, are best preserved in the extremities of the region—the far North, parts of eastern Europe, and the Mediterranean Basin. This latter area boasts the highest species diversity in the region, whereas eastern Europe has particularly high species endemism. Natural ecosystems are sparse and fragmented in western and central Europe, which are also the areas with the highest percentages of threatened species (EEA, 1995a).

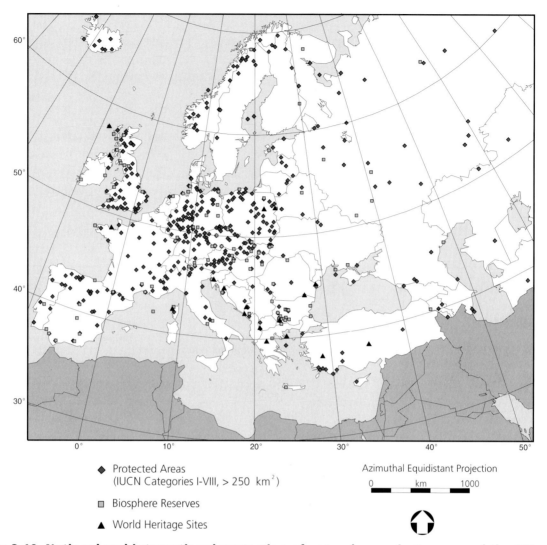

♦ Protected Areas
(IUCN Categories I-VIII, > 250 km²)

▢ Biosphere Reserves

▲ World Heritage Sites

Azimuthal Equidistant Projection

0   km   1000

Figure 2.10. National and international protection of natural areas in Europe and the CIS countries.

Source: WCMC (no date).
Note: About 2 per cent of the part of Russia not portrayed in this map is covered by protected areas.

Every country in Europe has passed legislation to protect sites for nature conservation, though some Mediterranean and CEE countries have lagged behind in this respect. The Russian Federation alone has more than 65 million hectares of national parks and protected areas (IUCN, 1994). Figure 2.10 shows the distribution of protected areas in Europe. The total extent of these protected areas has increased rapidly: two thirds of the more than 40,000 sites have been designated since the Stockholm Conference in 1972, and 10 million hectares have been added since 1982 (EEA, 1995a).

As elsewhere, forests are an important reservoir of biodiversity and play a central role in wildlife conservation. Many countries now protect part of their natural forest primarily for this purpose (EEA, 1995a). Slovenia, for example, has established a network of natural forest reserves, some of which have remained undisturbed for more than 100 years and introduced a system of unique-habitat "eco-cells" to protect particular species (A. Velkavrh, Ministry of Environmental Protection, Slovenia, personal communication, July 1996).

Unfortunately, the designation of protected areas does not automatically guarantee their success;

Table 2.6

Annual Internal Renewable Water Resources and Water Withdrawals in Selected European and CIS Countries

	Annual Internal Renewable Water Resources[a]			Annual Withdrawals		Sectoral Withdrawals (per cent) [b]		
	Total (cubic kilometres)	1995 Per Capita (cubic metres)	Year of Data	Percentage of Water Resources[a]	Per Capita (cubic metres)	Domestic	Industry	Agriculture
Albania	21.3	6,190	1970	1	94	6	18	76
Austria	90.3	11,333	1991[c]	3	304	33	58	9
Belgium	12.5	1,236	1980	72	917	11	85	4
Estonia	17.6	11,490	1989	21	2,097	5	92	3
Iceland	168.0	624,535	1991[c]	trace	636	31	63	6
Italy	167.0	2,920	1990	34	986	14	27	59
Lithuania	24.2	6,541	1989	19	1,190	7	90	3
Romania	208.0	9,109	1994	13	1,134	8	33	59
Russian Federation	4,498.0	30,599	1991	3	790	17	60	23
Spain	111.3	2,809	1991[c]	28	781	12	26	62
Turkmenistan	72.0	17,573	1989	33	6,390	1	8	91
United Kingdom	71.0	1,219	1991[c]	17	205	20	77	3

Source: WRI/UNEP/UNDP/WB (1996).

Notes: a. Annual Internal Renewable Water Resources usually include river flows from other countries. b. Sectoral percentages date from the year of other annual withdrawal data. c. Data are from the early 1990s.

overall in Europe, management of protected areas is considered to be currently inadequate to retain the integrity of the ecosystems that they represent (EEA, 1995a). It is interesting to note the unexpected side effect of the cold war in this respect, where nature flourished in the closed areas on the former East-West border (UNEP, 1996).

Coastal and marine ecosystems are habitats for an enormous number and range of species, including millions of birds. Many of Europe's remaining marine and coastal sites of ecological importance have no protected status; of 135 sites evaluated for the Dobříš Assessment, nearly half were considered under threat from coastline development (EEA, 1995a). In France, for instance, natural coastal areas are being lost at a rate of 1 per cent a year; 15 per cent have disappeared since 1976, and 90 per cent of the French Riviera is now developed (EEA, 1995a).

Managed ecosystems also contain an important cross-section of species and landscape types. Intensive, monocultural forestry and agricultural practices have been detrimental to both types of biodiversity, although for the most part forestry now contributes to preserving biodiversity and habitats (EEA, 1995a).

Depending on the geographical location, Europe's biodiversity is under pressure from mass tourism (affecting coasts and mountains), intensification of agriculture (grasslands and wetlands), deteriorating water quality (freshwater and coastal ecosystems), forest management geared towards economic gains (forests), and industrial, transport, and energy policies (coasts, major rivers, and mountains) (EEA, 1995a).

Water

Both the quantity and the quality of fresh water present major problems over much of the region, and the issue is of growing importance (UNEP, 1996).

Although there is no overall water shortage in Europe, water availability varies considerably. (See Table 2.6.) Malta has the least water available (100 cubic metres per person a year), while Iceland has more than 600,000 cubic metres available a year for each resident (EEA, 1995a). Low availability is a characteristic of the relatively dry, southern countries of the region and those with high population densities and moderate precipitation in the west. Some 70 per cent of all water withdrawals west of the Urals are from surface supplies, many of which are transboundary sources (EEA, 1995a). Rivers are also the principal source of water in Russia although occurrence does not closely match demand. While more than 80 per cent of the population lives in the basins of the Caspian and Azov seas, with high agricultural and industrial potential, these basins contain only 8 per cent of the nation's water resources (Min. of Env. Prot. and Nat. Res. of the Russ. Fed., 1994). Some 90 per cent of Russia's surface runoff drains to the Arctic and Pacific oceans (EEA, 1995a).

Withdrawal as a percentage of available water resources, or water use intensity, ranges from 0.1 per cent in Iceland to more than 70 per cent in Belgium (EEA, 1995a). Annual per capita withdrawal rates range from 156 cubic metres (Luxembourg) to more than 4,000 cubic metres (Uzbekistan and Turkmenistan) (WRI/UNEP/UNDP/WB, 1996). The breakdown into supplies for industry, agriculture, and domestic use varies widely; in European Union (EU) countries, the average ratio is 53:26:19 (EEA, 1995a). Total water withdrawal has stabilized or even decreased in some countries in recent years, including Austria, Bulgaria, the Netherlands, Spain, and Switzerland, and there are some encouraging signs of increased water use efficiency due to improved technology in industrial and agricultural sectors. On the other hand, large amounts of water are being lost through leakages, particularly in urban water systems where losses of up to 80 per cent have been reported (UN-ECE, 1996). On balance, water use is still increasing in the region (EEA, 1995a and 1995b).

The regional imbalance between water supply and demand is a major concern, as it leads to unsustainable exploitation of water resources in many areas. The noticeable increase in frequency and severity of droughts in the region, possibly an early sign of climate change, could exacerbate this situation (UNEP, 1996). Ground water is of enormous importance for public water supplies in the region, providing around 65 per cent of the total (EEA, 1995a). About 60 per cent of European industrial and urban centres are close to areas where ground water is overexploited, and some are experiencing water shortages as a result: 25 per cent of wetlands west of the Urals are threatened by lowered ground-water tables, and extensive tracts of the Mediterranean,

Baltic, and Black sea coasts are suffering from salt intrusion in ground-water supplies (EEA, 1995a). The availability of clean water for all sorts of uses has become a topic of intergovernmental and international disputes in the CEE countries (EEA, 1995a).

Water quality is the second freshwater concern. The range of possible contaminants and the mobility of water in the environment makes this a complex issue. Acidification of fresh water has already been mentioned in the context of land degradation above.

European waters tended to show a marked increase in both phosphorus and nitrogen loadings during the 1960s and 1970s, making them more prone to eutrophication and toxicity (EEA, 1995a). While point sources, particularly municipal sewage outflows, make a major contribution to phosphorus levels, in some areas, agriculture is estimated to be responsible for up to 80 per cent of the nitrogen loading and 20–40 per cent of the phosphorus loading in surface waters (EEA, 1995a). Despite a levelling off in average inputs of nitrogen fertilizer to agricultural land and a drastic fall in countries such as Poland, nitrogen levels have continued to rise in more than two thirds of the European rivers measured (EEA, 1995a). In ground water, nitrate concentrations are frequently above levels considered safe for human consumption. Rural communities are particularly at risk from this source. However, for phosphorus the trends have now reversed where countries, mainly in the west and south, have taken positive measures to reduce discharges (EEA, 1995a; WHO, 1995). The phosphorus concentration in the Rhine is a good example of the decrease that followed efforts initiated in the 1960s to collect and treat sewage before discharge into the river (UNEP, 1995). (See Figure 2.11.)

Loadings of organic matter have decreased in many European rivers as sewage treatment practices have improved. However, this form of freshwater contamination is still widespread in some parts of the region. The worst affected countries in western Europe and CEE are Belgium, Bulgaria, the Czech Republic, Denmark, Italy, the Netherlands, and Poland (EEA, 1995a). A recent 10-year study in the

Russian Federation showed that only 21 per cent of 245 rivers were acceptable in terms of bacteriological pollution (WHO, 1995).

Incidents of diseases linked to contamination of water supplies have been recorded in many countries, but especially in CEE and the CIS. Drinking-water samples tested in 1990 illustrate the widespread nature of this problem. In Belarus, 30 per cent of samples did not meet chemical standards and 8 per cent did not meet biological standards; equivalent figures for Uzbekistan were 37 per cent and 15 per cent; for Turkmenistan, they were 31 per cent and 26 per cent (Info. Centre of Goskomstat, USSR, 1991). There are indications that the situation is worsening. In Russia, 30.5 per cent of drinking-water samples from all over the country in 1993 failed to meet acceptable chemical quality standards and 28.25 per cent failed to reach biological ones (Min. of Env. Prot. and Nat. Res. of the Russ. Fed., 1994). The corresponding figures for 1980 were 15.4 per cent and 22.9 per cent (Min. of Env. Prot. and Nat. Res. of the Russ. Fed., 1994).

Recent information shows that the regulations introduced in response to the alarming concentrations of heavy metals in many European lakes and rivers in the 1970s have been effective. In general, concentrations today are well below standards for drinking water; only mercury and cadmium exceed drinking-water standards in some rivers. There are, however, still some heavy-metal "hot spots" associated with mining areas and industries using large quantities of metals that pose a risk to human health. Aquatic communities may still be affected by the lower concentrations prevailing more widely (EEA, 1995a).

Ground and surface water contamination from industrial, communal, and agricultural sources has been identified as one of the three environmental priorities for CEE (REC, 1994). The whole of Lake Baikal, containing 20 per cent of the earth's fresh water, is now affected by pollutants, including oil, even in its most remote and open parts, with only a minor amount (15 per cent) of effluents being treated satisfactorily (Min. of Env. Prot. and Nat. Res. of the Russ. Fed., 1994 and 1995b). In Hungary, large quantities of nitrogen annually seep into ground-water supplies (Environmental Resources

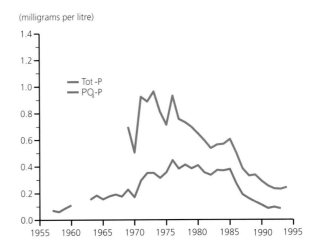

(milligrams per litre)

Figure 2.11. Observed mean annual concentration of phosphorus species for the Rhine River at Lobith Station (German–Dutch border).

Source: Van Dijk *et al.* (1996).

Ltd., 1990). In the former Czechoslovakia, mining wastes, SO_2, nitrates from fertilizers, and oil are the main causes of water contamination (Environmental Resources Ltd., 1990). In addition, much of the sewage discharge is untreated. Similar situations exist in other CEE countries and significant portions of some major waterways are not fit even for industrial use.

The need for water treatment facilities is critical. Those that do exist function poorly and have inadequate capacity to cope with the level of treatment necessary. Instances of radionuclide contamination in waters associated with nuclear installations and nuclear waste disposal sites have also been reported for this part of the region. The multiple functions of surface waterways, such as the Danube, Elba, and Vistula rivers, also create conflict among users (Environmental Resources Ltd., 1990; EEA, 1995a; REC, 1994).

Ground-water pollution is expected to become increasingly widespread and acute in coming years, particularly because of uncontrolled waste deposits, leakage from petrochemical tanks, and continuing percolation of untreated sewage, pesticides, and other pollutants into aquifers. As the already high proportion of Europe's drinking water from this source is expected to increase, ground-water quality is a priority issue (EEA, 1995a).

Many wetland habitats have been severely disturbed by freshwater-focused tourism and recreation activities together with the extensive physical and chemical modification of lakes and rivers in the region. Wildlife support functions and water purification capacities are particularly at risk. Only a small proportion of wetlands in the region are protected (EEA, 1995a).

Marine and Coastal Environments

Although the scale of problems has not been fully assessed, the key environmental problems in European seas and coastal areas have been identified as coastal zone pollution, eutrophication, overexploitation of resources, and the longer-term effects of climate change and sea level rise. In addition, important wildlife habitats in some coastal areas continue to be degraded or lost; one frequent consequence is the decline in populations that depend on these habitats for reproduction and other processes.

Europe has a range of different sea types, but its semi-enclosed and closed seas are a distinctive feature of the region. Their basins and shores are heavily affected by human activities. The physical characteristics of each sea, combined with the nature and intensity of the human activities changing it, determine which problem dominates. The seas most at risk from human activity are the Caspian Sea, the Black Sea, and the Sea of Azov. The Mediterranean, with its heavy imbalance in population growth, economic development, and pollution loads between north and south shores, is also a cause for concern (UNEP, 1996). Least affected are the North Atlantic Ocean and the Norwegian and Barents seas (EEA, 1995a). West of the Urals, almost 30 per cent of the population lives within 50 kilometres of coastal waters (EEA, 1995a). It is estimated that 86 per cent of the coastal ecosystems in this part of the region are at high or moderate risk from development. (See Figure 2.12.) In FSU, 62 per cent of coastlines are in the same risk categories (WRI/UNEP/UNDP/WB, 1996).

The most significant contaminants in the coastal zone are synthetic organic compounds, microbial organisms, oil, nutrients, litter, and, to a lesser extent, heavy metals and radionuclides. They originate from a wide range of land-based sources and activities in the marine catchment, sometimes hundreds or thousands of kilometres away from the sea, as well as from shipping and other offshore activities. Depending on type, the contaminant can harm marine organisms through physical damage or toxicity, turn bathing water and seafood into a human health hazard, and decrease the amenity value of beaches, thereby damaging local tourist industries.

The Black Sea and the Sea of Azov have the largest and most populated catchments in the region. Together with the Mediterranean, Baltic, and North seas, they consistently receive the highest loads of land-based contaminants—loads that are 10 to 100 times greater than those in the White, Barents, and Norwegian seas. In these areas, catchments and catchment populations are relatively small (EEA, 1995a).

Despite these differences and recent reductions in some of the riverine pollutant discharges [such as a 50-per-cent drop in phosphorus and heavy metal discharges by North Sea States between 1985 and 1995 (EEA, 1995b)], pollution of coastal waters is still considered to be a significant problem in all European seas (EEA, 1995a). Some consider the drying up of the Aral Sea to be the world's single greatest man-made environmental disaster (UNEP, 1996). (See Box 2.2.)

Bathing waters in the region's tourist resorts tend to be closely monitored for compliance with microbial standards. Although there are many examples of beaches being closed to bathers because of contamination from inadequately treated sewage (EEA, 1995a), there are also indications of improvements. Nevertheless, bathing water contamination is still expected to result in more than 2 million cases of gastrointestinal diseases annually in Europe in a wide range of locations (WHO, 1995).

Eutrophication is considered a major problem in the Baltic, Black, and North seas and locally in the Mediterranean and Caspian. Recent evidence suggests that eutrophication of near-shore waters is occurring more frequently and seriously than in the past in many areas, including the Adriatic, Black, and Baltic seas; the west coast of Sweden; and the coast of Denmark (EEA, 1995a).

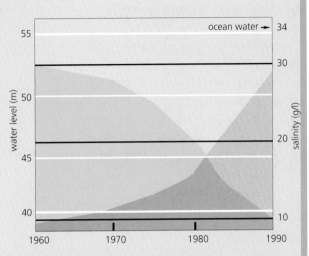

Box 2.2
The Aral Sea Catastrophe

The Amu Dar'ya and Syr Dar'ya rivers, flowing from the mountains of Tian Shan and Pamirs, are the principal water sources for Uzbekistan, Kyrgyzstan, Tajikistan, Turkmenistan, and the southern part of Kazakstan. Traditionally, about half of the water was used for irrigation and the other half flowed into the Aral Sea. However, intensive development of irrigation, mainly for cotton, over the last few decades reduced the inflow of these rivers to around 3 per cent, causing severe shrinking of the Aral Sea.

Since 1960 the Aral Sea has lost two thirds of its volume, the surface area has halved, the water level has dropped by 16 metres, and the salinity level is now approaching that of sea water. (See Figures 1 and 2.) Almost all the native organisms have died out, devastating the sea-based portion of the economy.

The 3.3 million hectares of exposed seabed have become a source of aerosols containing salt and agricultural residues that are then deposited by wind over surrounding areas. The resulting poor drinking-water quality and exposure to toxic airborne substances is believed to account for a dramatic deterioration in the health of inhabitants in peripheral areas; significant increases in malnutrition, diarrhoeal and kidney diseases, anaemia, cancers, and several other health problems have all been recorded.

In 1992, the five republics came to a water distribution agreement. In 1994, for the first time since the sea started shrinking, there was no decrease in sea level in comparison

Figure 1. Water level and salinity change in the Aral Sea.
Source: UNEP (1994).

to the previous year. In early 1995, implementation of the Aral Sea Programme began. It aims to:

- stabilize the environment of the Aral Sea,
- rehabilitate the disaster zone around the Sea,
- improve the management of international waters in the basin, and
- build the capacity of regional institutions to plan and implement these programmes.

Sources: UNDP (1995), UNEP (1992b and 1994), and State Comm. for Nat. Prot. of the Rep. of Uzbekistan (1995).

Figure 2. Chronology of the Aral Sea changes.
Source: UNEP (1994).

Threat potential[a]

High[b]

Moderate[c]

Low[d]

Figure 2.12. European coastal ecosystems threatened by development.

Source: Bryant, D., *et al.* (1995).
Notes: a. Threat ranking depicts potential risk to coastal ecosystems from development-related activities. b. Coastal areas falling within a city or major port footprint or having a population density exceeding 150 persons per square kilometre, a road network density exceeding 150 metres of road per square kilometre, or a pipeline density exceeding 10 metres of pipeline per square kilometre. c. Coastal areas with a population density of between 75 and 150 persons per square kilometre, a road network density of between 100 and 150 metres of road per square kilometre, or a pipeline density of between 0 and 10 metres of pipeline per square kilometre. d. Coastal areas with a population of less than 75 persons per square kilometre, a road network density of less than 100 metres of road per square kilometre, and no pipelines known to be present.

While some national marine fisheries have increased annual catches since the early 1980s, unsustainable harvesting of fish stocks and shellfish has led to the decline of many and the collapse of several fisheries in European seas. (See Figure 2.13.) North Sea catches, for example, were around 2 million tons in 1960; by the early 1970s, they had doubled to 4 million, but in recent years they have dropped back to around 2.5 million (EEA, 1995a). In addition to the direct economic repercussions of lower catches, overfishing and damaging fishing techniques have adverse impacts on non-target fish species such as benthic organisms and some cetaceans (EEA, 1995a).

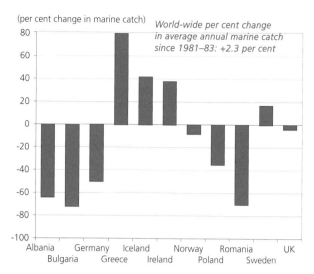

(per cent change in marine catch)

World-wide per cent change in average annual marine catch since 1981–83: +2.3 per cent

Figure 2.13. Percent change in average annual marine catch from 1981–83 to 1991–93.

Source: FAO (1995a).
Note: Marine catch data refer to marine and freshwater fish killed, caught, trapped, collected, bred, or cultivated for commercial, industrial, and subsistence use. Crustaceans and molluscs are included. Base figures used to calculate percentages are national fish catch totals averaged over a three-year period.

In the Caspian Sea, construction of numerous dams on the Volga and Kura rivers has prevented sturgeon fish from reaching their main spawning grounds. This has combined with waterway pollution and more damaging fishing methods to decimate the fish population. Landings decreased from 30,000 metric tons in 1985 to 2,100 metric tons in 1994 (UNDP/UNEP/WB, 1995). As the catch was formerly worth around US$6 billion annually, this has had a major impact on the economies of the riparian countries (UNDP/UNEP/WB, 1995).

The deterioration of the Caspian Sea area, the largest landlocked body of saltwater on earth, is a matter of great ecological and economic significance because of its extensive reserves of oil, gas, and populations of migrant birds and fish. The main factor affecting the state of the ecosystem is the sea level rise, a recurrent phenomenon throughout history, which is not yet understood. Since the late 1970s, the Caspian has risen by about 2.5 metres due to natural oscillations; surrounding countries are having problems coping with this rapid and continuous change (UNDP/UNEP/WB, 1995). All five countries of the Caspian Sea suffer from inundation of human settlements, roads, and other infrastructure (UNDP/UNEP/WB, 1995). The oil fields of Azerbaijan and Kazakstan are particularly at risk, and flooding of these areas, of agricultural land, and of waste dumps is posing a water pollution problem (UNDP/UNEP/WB, 1995).

Of more general concern is the potential sea level rise throughout the region from global warming, as the costs of protecting coastlines against inundation are likely to far outweigh any benefits from increased agricultural yields and tourism. Additionally, changes in sea surface temperatures and a reduction in sea ice as a result of global warming would have profound effects on fish migration and production patterns, particularly in the Nordic Seas (EEA, 1995a; IPCC, 1996).

Atmosphere

Air pollution is a long-standing problem in Europe. The large-scale concentration of people and activities in urban/industrial areas has been accompanied by high emissions of a wide range of air pollutants. These are supplemented by additional pollution from dispersed sources throughout the region, including agricultural activities. Urban air quality and long-range transboundary air pollution are both major concerns in Europe. Air quality is cited as the top environmental priority by the majority of experts in CEE countries (REC, 1994). On the global level, Europe is thought to be responsible for a high proportion of many harmful substances being added to the atmosphere, including 36 per cent of chlorofluorocarbons (CFCs), 30 per cent of carbon dioxide (CO_2), 25 per cent of SO_2 and volatile organic compounds (VOC), and 21 per cent of NO_x (EEA, 1995a).

For many European cities and rural areas, the information required to obtain a reliable timely overview of air pollution and its effects is still not available (EEA, 1995a). Harmonized data reporting could significantly improve understanding of current air pollution, and reliable data are needed to monitor and verify the effectiveness of control measures (WHO, 1995).

The main sources of emissions to the atmosphere are fossil fuel combustion and industry, in CEE countries, along with road transport in western cities and increasingly in cities in the rest of the region. Fossil fuel emissions include CO_2, SO_2, NO_x, and particulate matter (PM) as well as metals and radionuclides. In the industrial sector, the producers of power, petroleum, chemicals, pulp and paper, cement, steel, and non-ferrous metal are all major emitters, with SO_2, PM, and heavy metals being the most significant pollutants (EEA, 1995a). Road traffic currently accounts for 80 per cent of total traffic emissions in western Europe: it contributes over half of total NO_x, 35 per cent of VOC emissions, and about 25 per cent of total energy-related CO_2 emissions (EEA, 1995a). Air transport is also a cause for concern because of the relatively high energy consumption per kilometre travelled and the introduction of NO_x and CO_2 high up in the atmosphere, which may enhance their impact on global warming (EEA, 1995a). Other major anthropogenic sources of CO_2 are combustion for power generation and land use change. Europe is responsible for around a third of global CO_2 emissions, with Russia, Germany, Ukraine, and the United Kingdom being major emitters. Per capita emissions also tend to be high compared with other regions (EEA, 1995a; WRI/UNEP/UNDP/WB, 1996). (See Figure 2.14.)

Industrial emission "hot spots" have shifted during this century from western Europe towards the east and south (EEA, 1995a). In CEE countries, the prevalence of heavy industry, the intensive use of low-quality fuels, and the substantial lack of modern production technologies have resulted in continued high emission levels (REC, 1994). Sulphur dioxide emissions are particularly high in the northern countries, where brown coal is burned for energy. In contrast, southern CEE countries typically experience lower levels of SO_2 emissions due to a greater dependence on oil and gas for energy (Environmental Resources Ltd., 1990).

The transboundary movement of air pollutants is a problem leading to wet and dry deposition of harmful substances, to smog episodes, and to reduced air quality in locations far from their emission sources. Up to 45 per cent of Hungary's SO_2 emissions are transported to neighbouring countries

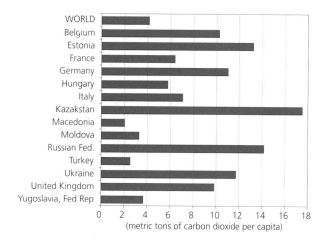

Figure 2.14. Per capita carbon dioxide emissions in selected European countries, 1992.

Source: CDIAC (1995).

(Environmental Resources Ltd., 1990). The atmospheric deposition of heavy metals in Europe is generally well below emission levels, indicating that Europe contributes to deposition outside the region (EEA, 1995a). Airborne radioactivity is another pollutant prone to long-range distribution. Material released into the atmosphere from the Chernobyl accident in 1986 was measurable over practically the entire northern hemisphere (IAEA, 1996).

During the past 20 years, successful measures for reducing urban SO_2, particulates, and lead emissions have included regulations on fuel for domestic heating (such as low sulphur content), the promotion of low and unleaded fuel, and restrictions on the use of cars in city centres. A series of European Community directives (see Chapter 3) to tackle emissions of acidifying substances from transport and industry led to a significant reduction in SO_2 emissions in many countries (EEA, 1995b).

Parties to the Helsinki (Sulphur) Protocol of the UN-ECE LRTAP Convention were required to bring their SO_2 emissions at least 30 per cent below 1980 levels by 1993 (EEA, 1995a). (See Chapter 3.) These reductions have been achieved through such measures as increased use of nuclear power, switching from coal and oil to natural gas, emission controls on large combustion installations, and technological improvements such as desulphurization of petroleum products. As Table 2.7 shows, the eco-

nomic recession in CEE and the CIS has also served to lower total emissions. Over the next 20 years, dust emissions from power generation and industry are expected to decrease in CEE by at least 30 per cent as a result of technological changes and a shift in fuel use (EEA, 1995a).

In contrast, European NO_x emissions have shown a slight increase in recent years (UN-ECE, 1995). Although many countries have made progress in reducing outputs from stationary sources and individual vehicles, this has been offset by increased total emissions from vehicles as overall vehicle numbers and distance travelled per vehicle have risen. A further legal instrument under the UN-ECE LRTAP Convention, the Sofia Protocol, addresses NO_x emissions and is expected to lead to overall NO_x reductions of 20–30 per cent during the next 10 years (EEA, 1995a).

A VOC Protocol under the UN-ECE LRTAP Convention is bringing in a stepped-up approach to controlling VOC (an ozone precursor) emissions. It has not yet been possible to detect clear trends in recent emissions, but the protocol should lead to a 15-per-cent reduction in European VOC emissions by 1999, compared with levels in the 1980s (EEA, 1995a).

Poor air quality is characteristically, though not exclusively, an urban problem. It is likely that all cities with more than 50,000 residents have air pollution problems, though exceeding the World Health Organization (WHO) guidelines for both short- and long-term exposures is more common in central, eastern, and southern Europe.

Large-scale winter smog episodes, caused by SO_2 and PM, are most common and severe in central Europe and in all the major Siberian cities in Russia, with serious repercussions for the health of the population. The incidence of lung cancer among males living for an average of 30 years in polluted parts of Cracow, Poland, was 46 per cent higher than in residents of less polluted areas (WHO, 1995). Czech Republic records reveal 20–30 per cent higher rates of post-neonatal mortality in areas with high concentrations of total PM and SO_2 (WHO, 1995). Average concentrations of the associated pollutants are up to 10 times higher in densely

Table 2.7

Changes in Total Emissions to the Atmosphere from Stationary Sources in Selected Countries of the Former Soviet Union

1993 Emissions as a Percentage of 1990 Emissions	
Armenia	11.6
Azerbaijan	73.0
Belarus	64.0
Kazakstan	81.0
Moldavia	48.0
Russia	73.0
Tajikistan	56.0
Turkmenistan	115.0
Ukraine	77.0

Source: Statistical Commission of CIS (1994) and Ministry of Nature and Environment Protection, Government of Armenia, personal communication (1996).

populated parts of the Czech Republic, eastern Germany, and southern Poland than in western Europe as a result of the high use of sulphur-rich coal and lignite for power generation and steel production (EEA, 1995a).

High tropospheric ozone concentrations (photochemical smog) tend to develop in the summer over large areas of Europe when high-pressure conditions prevail. The main precursors for this buildup are NO_x and VOC emissions. In recent years, concentrations of ground-level ozone have exceeded the WHO air quality guideline for one-hour average human exposure at nearly all existing European stations (EEA, 1995a). Health problems associated with high ozone concentrations include breathing difficulties and decreased lung function (WHO, 1995). The ozone precursors themselves can induce cancers and respiratory diseases.

Long-term overshooting of critical values of harmful air constituents (SO_2, PM, benzene, heavy metals, and so on) is another health hazard in the region (EEA, 1995a). While this problem has been less studied, it is known that long-term exposure can affect human health in many ways, including longevity and the incidence of cancers (WHO, 1995). Indoor air pollution may also be a significant health hazard, especially for old people and very young children, but it has not yet been clearly assessed (EEA, 1995a).

On the positive side, major improvements have occurred in the level and composition of some air pollutants in the region's cities over the past 20 years. Concentrations of SO_2 in most cities are lower than in the late 1970s, in some cases by as much as 80 per cent (EEA, 1995a). As a result, the total population experiencing pollution episodes (exceeding 250 micrograms of SO_2 per cubic metre) has decreased dramatically during the 1980s, from 71 per cent to 33 per cent in western countries and from 74 per cent to 51 per cent in Russia (WHO, 1995). Many cities also show downward trends in particulate concentrations.

In countries that have reduced the lead content in petrol, lead concentrations have substantially declined (EEA, 1995a). The remaining hot spots are in eastern Europe and are associated with lead-emitting industries as well as with leaded fuel (WHO, 1995). Regarding tropospheric ozone, it is anticipated that implementation of the VOC Protocol should result in a 40–60 per cent reduction in high ozone peak values and a smaller reduction (1–4 per cent) in annual average ozone concentration (EEA, 1995a).

West of the Urals, stratospheric ozone depletion is a cause for concern as densely populated areas are under direct risk from the substantial ozone decline recently detected in northern high-latitude regions. The resulting increased ultraviolet-B radiation in the lower atmosphere can have adverse impacts on human health (skin cancer, cataracts, reduced immune efficiency), on terrestrial and aquatic ecosystems (reduced species survival and productivity), and on building materials (faster deterioration). As a region, Europe is in a prime position to contribute to remedial action, as it produces 35–40 per cent of the global emissions of CFCs, which destroy stratospheric ozone (EEA, 1995a).

The increase in airborne caesium-137 levels following Chernobyl has had severe consequences. In human terms, it is estimated that the accident had a devastating impact on the well-being of the 600,000 "liquidators" who worked to contain the spread of radioactivity immediately after the event; in addition, up to 9 million additional ordinary people have also been affected socially and psychologically (UNESCO, 1996). In Belarus alone, the incidence of thyroid cancer increased five times over the 10 years following the accident (Republic of Belarus, 1995). Genetic and other long-term effects may continue to reveal themselves for generations in the populations of the nations affected. Although wildlife in the vicinity of the reactor received lethal radiation doses at the time of the disaster, no sustained severe impacts on populations or ecosystems have been observed. Possible long-term effects remain to be studied (EEA, 1995a; IAEA, 1996; UNESCO, 1996).

Urban and Industrial Environments

Some of the environmental problems that arise in urban and industrial areas, such as air quality, aquifer contamination, ground-water overexploitation, and land degradation, have been addressed earlier in this section. But there are additional concerns that tend to be closely associated with urban and industrial areas. Waste management is one such issue. It has been identified as a particular priority in CEE (REC, 1994), with hazardous wastes seen as a main concern throughout the region (UNEP, 1996).

Waste generation has been on the increase in Europe and the CIS. Many urban areas, particularly in western Europe, have introduced measures for reducing waste and for recycling it when appropriate and economically viable. The average European produces between 150 and 600 kilograms of municipal waste per year, with East Europeans tending to produce less than West Europeans (EEA, 1995a). The rate of increase in municipal waste among members of the Organisation for Economic Co-operation and Development (OECD) in Europe was 3 per cent a year between 1985 and 1990 (EEA, 1995a). In CEE, the adoption of western-style consumption patterns has resulted in an increasing amount of throwaway packaging. This, in turn, has resulted in larger waste streams, consisting of plastics and non-biodegradable materials, that overburden existing waste management systems. Illegal dumping of waste exacerbates the problem in some areas.

The growing quantities of municipal waste require new landfills or alternative methods of waste disposal, such as incineration, composting, reuse, and recycling (REC, 1994). In turn, these measures may generate new problems. Incineration, for example, is instrumental in the release into the environment of some heavy metals, like mercury, and products of incomplete combustion, which include highly toxic dioxins and other persistent organic compounds (EEA, 1995a).

Agricultural and industrial wastes are produced in even greater quantities (EEA, 1995a), a significant proportion of which are considered to be hazardous. For example, 80 billion tons of solid waste have accumulated in the Russian Federation, 1.1 billion of which are toxic and environmentally dangerous (Min. of Env. Prot. and Nat. Res. of the Russ. Fed., 1994). Most countries in Europe have many thousands of contaminated sites due to improper waste disposal. Several FSU countries have a legacy of waste from industrial and abandoned military sites that received little processing (EEA, 1995a). Large quantities of waste, including toxic and even radioactive substances, were just stored in the environment, often with very weak protection. As a result, leakage and further migration of pollutants from storage places has occurred. The worst situations are found in northeast Estonia, the Donbas region of Ukraine, the Moscow region, the Urals, and Kuzbas in West Siberia (REC, 1995b).

Many contaminated sites are now being cleaned up—but at high cost. In addition, the increasing adoption of cleaner production technologies and industrial waste minimization and recycling is a positive trend. The disposal of hazardous wastes continues to be a particular cause for concern. One strategy used particularly by western European countries, which has received much attention recently, is the export of waste to other countries. There are two clear directions in the movement of hazardous European wastes: from west to east within the region and from Europe to developing countries. In 1985, OECD countries adopted some waste movement principles that were later included in the Basel Convention on the Transboundary Movement of Hazardous Wastes and Their Disposal (EEA, 1995a; WHO, 1995).

Accidents are an additional threat to humans and the environment. They are frequently linked to urban and industrial activities. A major industrial accident reporting system has shown that most recent accidents have occurred in the petroleum industry and that highly inflammable gases and chlorine were the substance most often involved. The impact of such accidents can be very widespread if the substances permeate through food chains. Specific risks to the environment or to human health vary according to the location and nature of the accident, and accidental risk management must focus on these variables (EEA, 1995a).

Life in built-up areas brings with it a number of stresses not present elsewhere—particularly those associated with air and noise pollution and traffic congestion. Being a highly urbanized region, a very large number of people are potentially at risk. For example, it is estimated that more than 20 per cent of the European population is habitually exposed to stressful noise levels (above 65 decibels) from road traffic (WHO, 1995). The urban infrastructure also has a bearing on human well-being. In many parts of Europe, the pattern of urban decline prevalent in the 1980s has been replaced by programmes of urban renewal and restructuring, to revitalize economies and improve the quality of life. Most large cities in CEE have yet to reach this stage, however (EEA, 1995a).

Underlying Causes

Social

Europe and the CIS have relatively stable populations. Annual population growth rates are low, ranging from slightly negative up to 1 per cent (World Bank, 1996). National populations tend to be rather static, though a wave of migration, mainly east to west, has occurred since the breakup of the centrally planned economies (EEA, 1995a).

The region, apart from the FSU, is relatively densely populated and highly urbanized. With two thirds of Europeans in western and central countries already living in urban areas, current urbanization rates are low except in Turkey with around 4.5 per cent urban growth per annum (WRI/UNEP/UNDP/WB, 1996). Europe's urban

population lives on around 1 per cent of the total land area (EEA, 1995a). A European city of 1 million inhabitants typically consumes about 11,500 metric tons of fossil fuels, 320,000 metric tons of water, and 2,000 metric tons of food daily. It also produces 300,000 metric tons of wastewater and 1,600 metric tons of solid waste plus 25,000 metric tons of carbon dioxide (EEA, 1995a).

Many of Europe's major concerns are linked to the highly concentrated consumption of resources and production of wastes of these densely populated areas, and to the fact that per capita production and consumption rates are among the highest in the world. For example, with less than a quarter of the world's population, the region accounts for some 40 per cent of the world's energy consumption (EEA, 1995a). Excluding the FSU, consumption of energy in Europe is greater than production; Europe is therefore contributing to energy resource depletion elsewhere in the world. The new democratic and open societies in CEE are now establishing western-style consumption patterns. In addition, the increasing number of households and the small average household size (2.7 people) in Europe tend to exacerbate this situation. Smaller households use water and energy less efficiently and require more land per household member, which leads to greater per-capita resource use (EEA, 1995a).

The enormous consumption of natural resources has now been recognized as one of the root causes for the destabilization of the ecosphere. Not only do the nature and magnitudes of inputs into human economies determine all outputs (emissions, effluents, wastes, material goods), but the very displacement of resources from natural settings by technical means leads inevitably to ecological changes. Displacements can be huge. In the former West Germany, for example, it has been calculated that more than 530 million tons of construction materials alone were moved from one location in the country to another during 1990 (Schütz and Bringezu, 1993). Therefore, precautionary environmental policies must be very much concerned with resource productivities on all levels.

The distribution of goods to meet demands is having a significant and increasing impact on the environment, especially where motor vehicles are the main form of transport (UN-ECE, 1995). Concerning private transport, western Europe now has more cars than households since the number of cars almost doubled between 1970 and 1990 (EEA, 1995a). In CEE, increasing private car ownership has overwhelmed the existing transportation infrastructure. While new road networks are now being built, the preservation and further development of public transport systems that are already in place in many cities could be better for the environment (REC, 1994).

Economic

There is an enormous dichotomy between the economies of western Europe and the rest of the region. This is key to interpreting economic root causes. Almost all of western Europe falls in the high-income group of the most recent World Bank classification—their gross national product (GNP) per capita was $8,956 or above in 1994 (World Bank, 1996). The countries of CEE and the FSU are mainly in the lower-middle-income bracket (GNP per capita between $725 and $2,895) (World Bank, 1996). Agriculture and heavy industry predominate in these economies, in contrast to the manufacturing and service industries in the west.

In 1994, GNP per capita—adjusted by the United Nations purchasing power parity—ranged from less than $1,000 for Tajikistan to more than $25,000 for Switzerland, with obvious implications for the spending power and living standards of people (World Bank, 1996). At present rates of economic growth, it has been estimated that it will take countries like Hungary and Poland 20 more years to reach the average 1994 income level of the EU countries (World Bank, 1996).

Where wage-earners are well off, it is conceivable that they will become increasingly willing to work fewer hours. In OECD Europe, the average amount of time actually devoted to work has fallen from some 3,000 hours per year a century ago to around 1,700 today (OECD, 1994). Researchers foresee this trend continuing even in countries with already relatively low average working hours. In

Norway, for instance, worktime per employee is projected to fall from about 1,400 in 1991 to around 1,300 in 2010 (OECD, 1994).

Estimates of economic growth to 2002 suggest annual increases in the range of 2.5–2.7 per cent for EU, 2.6 per cent for EFTA, 3.4 per cent for CEE, and 1.3–2.0 per cent for the FSU (EEA, 1995a). More significant at the moment is the enormous difference between the long-established, buoyant, prosperous economies of western Europe and the economies in various stages of transition to the east. The political reforms in CEE and the FSU in the late 1980s and early 1990s have led to the replacement of centrally planned economies by market-oriented systems. Rates and degrees of adjustment have varied between countries, from the almost instantaneous changeover in the former East Germany to more hesitant modification in many FSU countries. The changes are all in a similar direction, however: towards price and trade liberalization, privatization, demonopolization, and the reform of tax, legal, and financial systems (World Bank, 1996).

These changes have had enormous short-term repercussions. National output fell dramatically in many transition countries. In CEE as a whole, for example, industrial output fell by over 40 per cent from 1989 to 1992 (WHO, 1995). At the same time, there was generally a sudden burst of inflation. At the personal level, poverty has increased, living standards have dropped, and inequality has reached levels similar to or greater than those of many west European countries (World Bank, 1996). Some of the transition countries, like Poland and Hungary, now appear to have passed through these stages. The Czech Republic, Hungary, and Poland are, for example, now OECD members and the Baltic countries, Slovenia and the Slovak Republic are considered to be market economies. Output and productivity have begun to increase again, and poverty rates have stabilized. Other countries, especially in the FSU, are still experiencing declines in output and high inflation.

Combined with individual sectors of the economy, these east-west differences manifest themselves in varying ways as economic drivers. The region is a major focus of industrial activity; it contains around half the world's countries with the largest outputs of industrial products, chemicals, machinery, and transport equipment and processed food (WHO, 1995). In western Europe, efficiency in energy and material use has improved substantially over the past 20 years with the introduction of improved production processes. The oil price rises of the 1970s provided a major incentive for some of these changes.

In contrast, in CEE, which was buffered from world energy prices until the late 1980s and then went into several years of economic depression, similar efficiencies have not yet been realized, although there have been marked improvements. While the per capita consumption of energy in CEE is often lower than the western European average, the relative consumption of energy per unit of product is several times higher (World Bank, 1996) due to the preponderance of heavy industry and obsolete technologies. Recent market reforms in transition economies have been accompanied by the appearance of a great many small, aggressive businesses in industrial, agricultural, and service sectors. These new enterprises often lack experience in responsible environmental management; landscapes have been marred and natural resources abused in the process (REC, 1994 and 1995b).

Data for 1994 show the share of agriculture in national economies to range from 1–3 per cent for most West European countries to more than 50 per cent for Albania and Georgia (World Bank, 1996). Although there are subregional variations, Europe is characterized by high-input farming systems. Large increases in the use of nitrogenous fertilizers and pesticides over recent decades have been major factors in increasing food production in western Europe as well as a major source of environmental contamination. In the eastern part of the region, however, applications of agricultural chemicals have dropped sharply during the economic depression of the last five years and following the breakup of collective farms.

The passenger transport sector in the region grew by 3.1 per cent a year between 1970 and 1990 (EEA, 1995a). Road transport for both passengers and freight is expected to nearly double between 1990 and 2010 (EEA, 1995a). Air passenger transport is also undergoing a rapid increase, although with the trend towards larger aircraft, the number of aircraft movements has not increased as fast as the number of passengers (EEA, 1995a).

Tourism and recreation have become important social and economic activities in Europe. Sixty per cent of the global tourist traffic is destined for Europe, with Japan and the United States being the main source areas (EEA, 1995a). The current growth in European tourism is expected to reach around 6 per cent per year by 2000, by which time there are expected to be at least 380 million arrivals per year in the region (EEA, 1995a). A large number of additional tourists originate from within the region. Although tourism may have adverse impacts on the environment in local areas, such as the degradation of mountainous tracts in the Alps or the destruction of habitats in the coastal areas of the Mediterranean, there are also positive, albeit minor, spin-offs that may indirectly benefit the environment, such as increased environmental awareness by the general public (EEA, 1995a).

References

Bernes, C. 1993. *The Nordic Environment—Present State, Trends and Threats*. Prepared by the Nordic Council of Ministers: Nordic Environment Report Group. Nord 1993:12. Copenhagen.

Bryant, D., *et al.* 1995. Coastlines at Risk: An Index of Potential Development-Related Threats to Coastal Ecosystems. *World Resources Institute Indicator Brief*. Washington.

CDIAC. 1995. *1992 Estimates of CO_2 Emissions from Fossil Fuel Burning and Cement Manufacturing Based on United Nations Energy Statistics and U.S. Bureau of Mines Cement Manufacturing Data*. Carbon Dioxide Information Analysis Center (CDIAC), Oak Ridge National Laboratory. Oak Ridge, Tennessee.

CEC. 1992. *The state of the environment in the European Community*. Accompanying document to the proposal from the Commission of the European Communities for a community programme of policy and action in relation to the environment and sustainable development. Commission of the European Communities (CEC). Brussels.

EC/UN-ECE. 1994. *Forest Condition in Europe: Results of the 1993 Survey*. International Co-operative Programme on Assessment and Monitoring of Air

Pollution Effects on Forests. Convention on Long-Range Transboundary Air Pollution. European Commission (EC) and United Nations Economic Commission for Europe (UN-ECE). Brussels and Geneva.

EEA. 1995a. *Europe's Environment: The Dobříš Assessment*. D. Stanners and P. Bourdeau (eds.). European Environment Agency (EEA). Office for Official Publications of the European Communities. Luxembourg.

EEA. 1995b. *Environment in the European Union 1995*. Report for the Review of the Fifth Environmental Action Programme. K. Wieringa (ed.).

Environmental Resources Ltd. 1990. *Eastern Europe: Environmental Briefing*. Briefing Document. January. ERL. London.

FAO. 1995a. *Fishstat-PC*. Food and Agriculture Organization of the United Nations (FAO). Rome.

FAO. 1995b. *Forest Resources Assessment 1990. Global Synthesis*. FAO Forestry Paper 124. Rome.

Government of the Russian Federation. 1993. Governmental report on the state of the environment in the Russian Federation in 1992. Moscow.

IAEA. 1996. The International Conference "One Decade After Chernobyl: Summing up the Consequences of the Accident." Information circular plus five attachments. INFCIRC/510. International Atomic Energy Authority (IAEA). 7 June.

Information Centre of Goskomstat of the USSR. 1991. *Nature Protection and Use of Natural Resources: Statistical Yearbook*. Moscow.

IPCC. 1996. *Climate Change 1995. The Science of Climate Change*. Contribution of WG1 to the Second Assessment Report of the IPCC. Intergovernmental Panel on Climate Change (IPCC). Cambridge University Press. Cambridge.

IUCN. 1994. *1993 United Nations List of National Parks and Protected Areas*. Prepared by WCMC and CNPPA. The World Conservation Union (IUCN). Gland, Switzerland.

Ministry of Ecology and Biological Resources, Kazakstan. 1993. National report of Kazakstan on the state of the environment in the Republic. *Eurasia* 6(15). Moscow.

Ministry of Environment of the Czech Republic. 1996. *Environmental Yearbook of the Czech Republic—1995*.

Ministry of Environment Protection and Natural Resources of the Russian Federation. 1993. *Report on the State of the Environment of the Russian Federation in 1992*. Moscow.

Ministry of Environment Protection and Natural Resources of the Russian Federation. 1994. *Report on the State of the Environment of the Russian Federation in 1993*. Moscow.

Ministry of Environment Protection and Natural Resources of the Russian Federation. 1995a. Environment of Russia (brief review). *Ekos* 1995, p. 16 (based on national reports on the state of the environment in Russia in 1991, 1992, and 1993).

Ministry of Environment Protection and Natural Resources of the Russian Federation. 1995b. *National Report on the State of the Environment in the Russian Federation in 1994*. Moscow.

Ministry of Environmental Protection of Ukraine. 1994. *The State of the Environment and Activities in Ukraine: Report of the Environment 1992/93*. Rayevsky Scientific Publishers. Kiev.

Mnatsakanian, R. 1994. L'Héritage Écologique du Communisme dans les Républiques de L'ex-URSS. Éditions Frison-Roche. Paris.

Newman, O., and A. Foster (compilers). 1993. *European Environmental Statistics Handbook*. Manchester Business School, Library and Information Service. Gale Research Int. Ltd.

Nowicki, M. 1993. *Environment in Poland. Issues and Solutions*. Ministry of Environmental Protection, Natural Resources and Forestry. Kluwer Academic Pubs. The Netherlands.

OECD. 1994. OECD societies in transition: the future of work and leisure. Main issues and summary of discussions of a conference held on 20th January 1994 in Paris. OECD Forum for the Future. Organisation for Economic Co-operation and Development (OECD), General Distribution Document OECD/GD(94)39, by B. Stevens and W. Michalski, OECD Secretariat, Advisory Unit to the Secretary-General.

REC. 1994. *Strategic Environmental Issues in Central and Eastern Europe*. Vol. 1. Regional Report. Regional Environmental Center for Central and Eastern Europe (REC). Budapest.

REC. 1995a. *Competing in the New Environmental Marketplace*. Proceedings of Workshops for Environmental Professionals: the Czech Republic, Hungary, Poland, the Slovak Republic. Budapest.

REC. 1995b. *Status of National Environmental Action Programmes in Central and Eastern Europe. Case Studies of Albania, Bulgaria, the Czech Republic, Croatia, Hungary, Latvia, Lithuania, FYR Macedonia, Poland, Romania, the Slovak Republic, and Slovenia*. Budapest.

Republic of Belarus. 1995. *National Report on Environmental Conditions in the Republic of Belarus.* Minsk.

Schütz, H., and S. Bringezu. 1993. Major material flows in Germany. *Fresenius Environmental Bulletin* 2(8):443–448. Birkhauser Verlag. Basel, Switzerland.

State Committee for Nature Protection of the Republic of Uzbekistan. 1995. *National Report: On the State of the Environment and Use of Natural Resources in the Republic of Uzbekistan in 1994.* Ukituvchi Publishing House. Tashkent.

State Committee of the Russian Federation on Land Resources and Land Management. 1995. *National Report on the State and Use of Lands in the Russian Federation in 1994.* Moscow.

Statistical Commission of the Common Independent States. 1994. Statistical Bulletin No. 40. November.

UNDP. 1995. *The Aral in Crisis.* United Nations Development Programme (UNDP). Tashkent.

UNDP/UNEP/WB. 1995. Mission to the Caspian Littoral States. Joint mission report. Prepared by J.B. Collier, H. Dumont, M. Taghi Farvar, P. de Swart, P. Tortell, and I. Zrajevskij, with assistance of B. Schultz and A. Timoshenko. UNDP/United Nations Environment Programme (UNEP)/World Bank (WB).

UN-ECE. 1995. *Effects and Control of Long-range Transboundary Air Pollution.* Air Pollution Studies No. #11. ECE/EB-AIR/43. United Nations.

UN-ECE. 1996. *Press Release.* ECE/GEN/12, ECE/ENV/2. 15 March 1996. United Nations.

UNEP. 1992a. *World Atlas of Desertification.* UNEP. Edward Arnold. London.

UNEP. 1992b. The Aral Sea. Diagnostic study for the development of an action plan for the conservation of the Aral Sea.

UNEP. 1994. The pollution of lakes and reservoirs. UNEP Environment Library No. 12. Nairobi.

UNEP. 1995. Water quality of world river basins. UNEP Environment Library No. 14. Nairobi.

UNEP. 1996. Report of the Regional Consultations held for UNEP's first Global Environment Outlook. Nairobi.

UNEP/WHO. 1992. *Urban Air Pollution in Megacities of the World.* UNEP and World Health Organization (WHO). Blackwell. London.

UNESCO. 1996. Community development centres for social and psychological rehabilitation in Belarus, Russia and Ukraine. UNESCO Chernobyl Programme.

Van Dijk, G.M., P. Stalnacke, A. Grimvall, A. Tonderski, K. Sundblad, and A. Schafer. 1996. Long-term trends in nitrogen and phosphorus concentrations in the Lower River Rhine. *Arch. Hydrobiol. Suppl. 113. Large Rivers 10.* pp. 99–109.

WCMC. No date. Biodiversity Map Library. Computerized geographic information system for mapping global data on habitat and species. World Conservation Monitoring Centre (WCMC). Cambridge.

WHO. 1995. *Concern for Europe's Tomorrow: Health and Environment in the WHO European Region.* WHO European Centre for Environment and Health. Wiss. Verl.-Ges. Stuttgart.

World Bank. 1996. *World Development Report 1996.* Oxford University Press. New York and London.

WRI/UNEP/UNDP/WB. 1996. *World Resources 1996–97.* World Resources Institute (WRI), UNEP, UNDP, and the World Bank. Oxford University Press. New York and London.

LATIN AMERICA AND THE CARIBBEAN

Major Environmental Concerns

The Latin America and Caribbean (LAC) region encompasses countries with great economic, social, and environmental diversity. It is not easy to summarize concerns that are common to large and multi-ecosystem nations such as Brazil, the Andean States, and the Caribbean Island States. Yet the region also has a number of common environmental characteristics that distinguish it from other regions of the world. These include immense hydrological systems, such as the Amazon, Orinoco, and Rio de la Plata; a global importance as a carbon sink, particularly in the Amazon Basin; and unique and vast biological diversity and ecosystem heterogeneity.

In addition, the region has other features common to many of its countries. These include high proportions of urban populations, high ethnic diversity coupled with the existence of native indigenous populations, rapidly expanding agricultural frontiers, national economies that are being or have been subjected to structural adjustment programmes, a changing role for the State and its functions, an emerging active civil society, and increasing inequality and poverty.

The common and overlapping environmental concerns in the LAC region have been grouped and summarized by the Commission on Development and Environment for LAC (LAC CDE, 1992) under the following themes:

- land use,
- forest resources,
- ecosystems and biological patrimony,
- water resources,
- sea and shoreline resources,
- the environment in human settlements,
- energy,
- non-energy mineral resources, and
- industry.

Land

The LAC region includes 23 per cent of the world's potential arable land, 12 per cent of current cropland, and 17 per cent of all pastures (Gallopin et al., 1991). In contrast with other regions, LAC still maintains a high percentage of natural ecosystems that have been little disturbed by human activities, particularly in the Amazon region and the southern tip of South America. These ecosystems are currently being degraded at a high rate, however, particularly at their margins.

Some 306 million hectares (72.7 per cent) of the agriculturally used drylands in South America (that is, irrigated lands, rainfed cropland, and rangelands) suffer from moderate to extreme degradation (UNEP, 1991). (See Figure 2.15.) And some 47 per cent of the soils in grazing lands have lost their fertility (LAC CDE, 1992). This land degradation includes erosion and soil degradation in hillsides and mountain areas and in tropical pasturelands, desertification brought on by overgrazing, and salinization and alkalization of irrigated soils.

The acceleration of the erosion process in LAC is mainly due to the expansion of the agricultural frontier and the overuse or unsustainable use of land for cultivation or grazing and deforestation. Some of the best land is also being lost through urban expansion. Much of the unsustainable use of the land, particularly the overgrazing, is due to mismanagement. The expansion of the agricultural frontier, especially in the Andean highlands, has led to the use of fields whose altitude and gradient render them particularly fragile. In other areas, the overuse of land, especially in the form of single-crop farming, has damaged the soil structure and left land vulnerable during periods when it lacks plant cover (Gligo, 1995).

In the Argentine Patagonia, for example, the introduction of unsustainable numbers of sheep along with inappropriate management policies has resulted in changes in pastureland composition and desertification. This is causing the loss of approximately 1,000 square kilometres a year (LAC CDE, 1992), with 35 per cent of pastureland having been transformed into desert (Winograd, 1995). Other arid and semi-arid zones in the region also suffer from desertification, including Mexico, where water erosion alone affects 85 per cent of the territory (Gligo, 1995).

For the region to maintain its current food self-sufficiency and expand export crops to earn badly needed foreign exchange, countries will need to farm more intensively and increase the land under agriculture. Intensification will lead to increasing inputs in agriculture, which will in turn have important environmental implications (pollution, use of pesticides and fertilizer, and so on). The potential consequence of the expansion of agricultural land is that forests in the region will diminish and more of the marginal lands will become degraded.

Forests

The LAC region has both the world's largest unfragmented tropical forests (in Amazonia) and some of the most fragmented and most endangered tropical forests (such as the Mata Atlantica). At the end of 1990, some 28 per cent of the world's total forested area and 52 per cent of its tropical forest were in Latin America and the Caribbean. In 1990, these forests covered 968 million hectares, or 48 per cent of the land in the region (FAO, 1993).

The accelerated transformation of tropical and other forests into permanent pasture and other forms of land use constitutes a critical environmental problem for the region. Not only is the

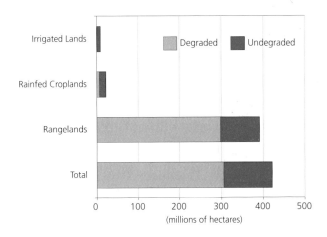

Figure 2.15. Desertification and land degradation in agriculturally used drylands of South America.

Source: Dregne (1991).

extent of the land involved immense, but also effects on ecosystems are practically irreversible (Winograd, 1995).

As with land degradation, deforestation is mainly due to the expansion of the agricultural frontier, which is in turn the outcome of a number of factors. Among these are the displacement of peasant farmers from traditional farming areas, large-scale settlement programmes such as in Rondônia in Brazil, and the use of tax exemptions to promote the expansion of livestock raising activities in the Amazon. In addition, commercial logging, collection of firewood for household use, and road construction have all led to the unsustainable exploitation of the region's forests (Gligo, 1995).

Forest cover in the region declined from 992 million hectares in 1980 to 918 million hectares in 1990, yielding an annual deforestation rate of 0.8 per cent over this period. Average annual deforestation rose from 5.4 million hectares in 1970 to 7.4 million hectares in 1990 (FAO, 1993). (See Figure 2.16.)

Tropical deforestation was also quite rapid. Its rate increased from 5.6 per cent over the period 1960–70 to 7.4 per cent for the period 1980–90 (FAO, 1993). The tropical forests of the Pacific coast of Central America once covered 550,000 square kilometres, but now less than 2 per cent is intact. However, some countries, such as Costa Rica, have preserved and protected some of their forests under

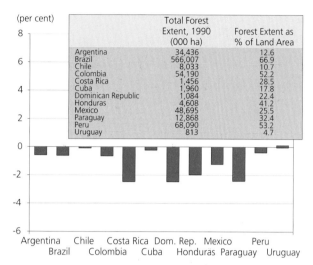

(per cent)	Total Forest Extent, 1990 (000 ha)	Forest Extent as % of Land Area
Argentina	34,436	12.6
Brazil	566,007	66.9
Chile	8,033	10.7
Colombia	54,190	52.2
Costa Rica	1,456	28.5
Cuba	1,960	17.8
Dominican Republic	1,084	22.4
Honduras	4,608	41.2
Mexico	48,695	25.5
Paraguay	12,868	32.4
Peru	68,090	53.2
Uruguay	813	4.7

Figure 2.16. Average annual change in the extent of forest in selected Latin American and Caribbean countries, 1981–90.

Source: FAO (1993, 1995).
Note: Forest consists of the sum of natural forest and plantation area categories for tropical and temperate developing countries.

national park or reserve status. Similarly, the Atlantic forest of Brazil (also marginally present in Paraguay and Argentina) only maintains 4 per cent of its original 1 million square kilometres as pristine forests, and an additional 6 per cent as secondary forests (UNEP, 1995b). The rapid loss of highly diverse native forests is of particular concern, because they are often replaced by induced pastures or by monocultures of exotic timber species. Most of the endangered tropical plants in Brazil (65 per cent) are found in this highly endangered tropical forest ecosystem (CDEA, 1992).

Most of the primeval forests of the Caribbean were stripped in the early colonial period. Since then, an increasing problem has been the introduction of exotic species into successional forests and scrubs. This is a problem of both forestry management and biodiversity conservation.

While deforestation figures are disputed by many national Governments, studies indicate that the annual increase in deforestation in the Amazon Basin countries increased until the late 1980s; the most serious loss was in Rondônia, where the rate increased 128 per cent between 1980 and 1984 and 51 per cent in 1985 alone (LAC CDE, 1992). The situation in Rondônia has improved considerably in the recent years since Brazil abolished the subsidies,

tax incentives, and special credits that encouraged deforestation. The private project of Precious Woods in the Brazilian Amazon as well as other initiatives in the region are also helping address the situation. Nevertheless, deforestation in the region continues as the agricultural frontier expands, albeit at a lower rate.

Biodiversity

Latin America and the Caribbean are characterized by their high species and ecosystem diversity. Five of the 10 richest countries in the world in terms of terrestrial plant and animal species, the so-called ecological megadiversity countries, are in Latin America: Brazil, Colombia, Ecuador, Mexico, and Peru (LAC CDE, 1992). The region contains 40 per cent of the plant and animal species of the world's tropical forests and 36 per cent of the main food and industrial cultivated species (LAC CDE, 1992). Colombia alone, with 0.77 per cent of the world's area, contains 10 per cent of the world's animal and plant species (McNeely et al., 1990).

The region's biota, in addition to being enormously diversified, provide important opportunities for economic development. This heritage, which has medicinal, industrial, and food potential, can generate sustainable benefits for the local population now and into the future (LAC CDE, 1992). In the Amazon, about 1,000 known plant species have economic potential, and at least 300 species have forestry potential (LAC CDE, 1992). This does not even scratch the surface of the potential of unknown and uncatalogued flora and fauna. In 1960, the discovery of two varieties of tomato in Peru provided economic benefits to the industry estimated at US$5 million a year due to improvement in pigment and final product (LAC CDE, 1992). The potential of the region in terms of biodiversity and genetic resources is enormous not only for agriculture, but also for the ever-expanding pharmaceutical industry.

This vital biological reserve, which is of major importance both to the region and the world, is highly threatened. (See Figure 2.17.) In LAC, as elsewhere in the world, habitat loss is the biggest

(numbers of threatened animal species)

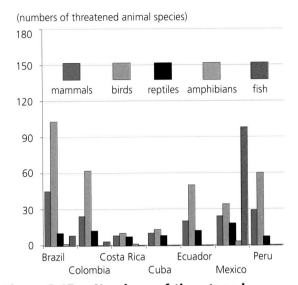

(numbers of threatened plant species)

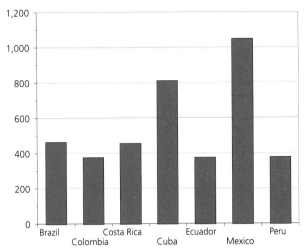

Figure 2.17a. Numbers of threatened animal species in selected Latin American and Caribbean countries, 1990s.

Source: IUCN (1993).
Note: The number of threatened species listed for all countries includes full species that are classified by the World Conservation Union (IUCN) as endangered, vulnerable, rare, and indeterminate, but excludes introduced species, species whose status is insufficiently known, or those known to be extinct.

Figure 2.17b. Number of threatened plant species in selected Latin American and Caribbean countries, 1990s.

Source: WCMC (1992, 1994, 1995).
Note: The number of threatened species listed for all countries includes full species that are classified by the World Conservation Union (IUCN) as endangered, vulnerable, rare, and indeterminate, but excludes introduced species, species whose status is insufficiently known, or those known to be extinct.

threat to biodiversity. Many of the threatened species and habitats are located in areas such as high-mountain habitats, tropical drylands, desert ecosystems, and cloud forests as well as tropical moist forests. Not only has Latin America lost more than 7 per cent of its tropical forests during the 1980s, but its savannah-grasslands are also under continuous threat (FAO, 1993).

Despite the importance of habitat loss other than in forests, most research on biodiversity loss still concentrates on forest ecosystems. General estimates indicate that at current rates, the conversion and deforestation of tropical forests and dry forests may wipe out 100,000–450,000 species within the next 40 years (Winograd, 1995). Of these, some 5,000–20,000 species are estimated to be plants and some 1,000–5,000 vertebrate species according to calculations based on recent studies (May, 1989; Western and Pearl, 1989). Most of the species that are becoming extinct have not been inventoried or described adequately.

In addition to habitat loss, habitat fragmentation is also a major concern. The annual rate of habitat fragmentation in the Brazilian Amazonia, for exam-

ple, is thought to be 2.5 times higher than the rate of deforestation. The effects of this loss on plant and animal species diversity is of critical concern to the region because habitat fragmentation has not been accompanied by adequate concern for the planning and conservation of biological corridors.

Biodiversity conservation in the densely populated islands of the Caribbean is a special problem because of the extremely small area of some local habitats, the high incidence of endemism throughout the islands, and the high regional vulnerability to natural disasters such as hurricanes, tsunamis, volcanoes, and earthquakes. The highly diverse marine ecosystems of the wider Caribbean and the rich biodiversity housed within these ecosystems are also under considerable stress. (See Box 2.3 and Marine and Coastal Environments below.)

Water

Some 13 per cent of the world's continental waters are found in Latin America and the Caribbean, but the distribution within the region is highly variable. (See Table 2.8.) Many areas have great difficulties meeting their water needs, including northern Mexico, north-eastern Brazil, and southern Chile. Two thirds of the territory of the LAC region is arid or semi-arid including large portions of Argentina, Chile, Bolivia, Peru, north-eastern Brazil, Ecuador, Colombia, and central and northern Mexico. Approximately 334 million hectares in South America are classified as semi-arid, arid, or hyper-arid (UNEP, 1992; SEDESOL, 1993).

Furthermore, many areas that are classified as subhumid present a marked water deficit during the seasonally dry periods. In other areas, the hydrological cycle is so variable that it generates a ruinous sequence of prolonged droughts and destructive floods that make agriculture impractical (LAC CDE, 1992).

Water quality problems that are common to the whole region include toxic contamination from industry, waste disposal, and eutrophication from human sewage. Bacterial pollution of water supplies in the region is a continuing problem with adverse effects on human health. The major concerns caused by high bacterial and organic loads range from poor-quality drinking water, eutrophication, and disappearance of aquatic life to food contamination and the prevalence of waterborne diseases (UNEP, 1991).

Forest cutting also has a negative effect on the production and regulation of water flows, while the ensuing soil erosion increases the amount of suspended sediments, which affects the quality of the water resources and the functioning of dams and reservoirs.

The rivers of this region are being polluted by a number of different sources, but the most important ones are industrial and urban wastewaters from large industrial cities, wastewater from mining industries, and agricultural runoff. As a result, many of the region's water resources are today chemically and biologically contaminated. Several rivers in Colombia—among them, the Medellín and the Bogotá—are as good as biologically dead (totally lacking dissolved oxygen). Waters in the Sogamosa Valley and in the Magdalena, Dagua, and Nechi rivers have been contaminated by industry and mining.

Large quantities of agricultural contaminants are disposed of in streams flowing into the Caribbean Sea, where there is clear evidence of elevated levels of phosphorous, nitrates, potassium, pesticides such as DDT, and highly organic effluents (LAC CDE, 1992). These elevated levels of pollutant concentrations are caused by the indiscriminate discharge of highly pollutant-loaded effluents into the region's

Table 2.8
Annual Internal Renewable Water Resources and Water Withdrawals in Selected Latin American and Caribbean Countries

	Annual Internal Renewable Water Resources[a]			Annual Withdrawals		Sectoral Withdrawals (per cent)[b]		
	Total (cubic kilometres)	1995 Per Capita (cubic metres)	Year of Data	Percentage of Water Resources[a]	Per Capita (cubic metres)	Domestic	Industry	Agriculture
Argentina	994.0	28,739	1976	4	1,043	9	18	73
Brazil	6,950.0	42,957	1990	1	246	22	19	59
Chile	468.0	32,814	1975	4	1,626	6	5	89
Colombia	1,070.0	30,483	1987	0	174	41	16	43
Cuba	34.5	3,125	1975	23	870	9	2	89
Ecuador	314.0	27,400	1987	2	581	7	3	90
Haiti	11.0	1,532	1987	0	7	24	8	68
Mexico	357.4	3,815	1991[c]	22	899	6	8	86
Peru	40.0	1,682	1987	15	300	19	9	72
Venezuela	1,317.0	60,291	1970	0	382	43	11	46

Source: Compiled by the World Resources Institute.
Notes: a. Annual internal renewable water resources usually include river flows from other countries. b. Sectoral withdrawal percentages are estimated for 1987. c. Data are from the early 1990s.

water bodies. Finally, the transformation of coca leaves into basic cocaine paste is heavily polluting some small tributaries of the Marañon and Amazon rivers in Bolivia, Colombia, and Peru.

In the wider Caribbean, many coastal aquifers are contaminated by pollutants or salt-water intrusions due to overextraction of ground-water reserves. In Venezuela, for example, the overuse of aquifers has already resulted in widespread salt-water intrusion (UNEP/SCOPE, 1993). This limits future uses of ground water for development and also affects extensive areas of near-shore habitats where fresh water springs emerging from these ground-water reserves have previously nourished reef areas.

In the LAC region, continental waters are crucially important for agricultural production. The arid conditions and seasonal water deficiencies that characterize large parts of the region have led to the development of large irrigated agricultural areas that generate a high proportion of the region's agricultural product in artificially transformed ecosystems. The irrigated areas have grave environmental problems, including soil salinization, alkalization, and water pollution from organic and chemical sources. Organic pollution in the region originates mostly from urban and agro-industrial wastewater that is used for irrigation. The chemical pollution is the result of using pesticides with a long residual life, as well as industrial and mining wastewater.

The great hydroelectric dams in the region, while important for electricity generation, have transformed large fluvial systems into chained lakes, such as the upper and middle Paraná system in Brazil, Paraguay, and Argentina. These large waterworks have generated a number of substantial environmental disruptions, including the erection of often unsurpassable obstacles for fish, the explosive growth of floating aquatic plants, and the eutrophication of dam reservoirs. The large development projects that connect watersheds and improve continental navigation networks, such as the Hidrovia Project in the Paraná-Paraguay fluvial system, also affect some of the most important wetlands of the region, like the Pantanal.

Marine and Coastal Environments

Twenty-five per cent of the people in the region live in coastal areas (and nearly 100 per cent in the smaller islands of the Caribbean), and marine and coastal resources are seen as an important part of the development pattern of numerous countries (Winograd, 1995). The total population of coastal dwellers in the wider Caribbean is estimated at 50 million, which is expected to increase to some 60 million by the year 2000 (UNEP, 1994).

According to some estimates, 26 per cent of the LAC coastlines are under high potential threat of degradation, and a further 24 per cent are under moderate potential threat due to coastal development (including tourism and infrastructure works); discharge of sediments, wastes, and contaminants from urban and industrial areas; sewage; industrial pollution; and oil spills (WRI/UNEP/UNDP/WB, 1996). (See Figure 2.18.) Coastal habitats within the Caribbean region, an area with a high level of biodiversity, are also under stress from development, pollution, sedimentation, and dredging. (See Box 2.3.)

The discharge is concentrated in zones with high economic activity, such as Cartagena, Coatza Coalcos, Havana, and Kingston, where the volume of the discharge exceeds the ecosystem's absorptive capacity. This damage has had an adverse impact on beaches, coral reefs, and seagrass beds. Few Latin American cities have effective waste and sewage treatment facilities or water treatment plants (Gligo, 1995). Industrial and hazardous wastes from the region as a whole flow straight into the ocean, while the river basins act as catchment areas for agricultural wastes, which then drain into the sea.

In the wider Caribbean, oil is a significant marine contaminant, damaging the important tourist industry. The specific threats include loading, unloading, and transporting petroleum products; the cleaning of tanks; and the accidents, spills, and fires that often accompany these activities (LAC CDE, 1992). Many beaches in the Caribbean now have average tar levels 10 times higher than that estimated to adversely affect the use of beaches by tourists—levels at which beaches become virtually unusable for recreation (GESAMP, 1990).

Box 2.3
Coastal Pollution and Biodiversity in the Wider Caribbean Region

The unique, diverse, and threatened environment of the Caribbean region warrants special attention. This is particularly so given the vulnerability of the region's ecosystem to climate change and sea level changes, as well as natural disasters. The prominent tourist industry depends heavily on maintaining this unique environment and its rich biodiversity. There is an urgent need to address the threatened marine and coastal areas of the region in a comprehensive and multisectoral manner, dealing with complete watershed and coastal areas.

Marine and Coastal Environments

Marine and coastal erosion and pollution in the wider Caribbean region are reaching a critical state. Industrial waste, mining runoff, domestic sewage, heavy river sediment loads, and tourism are all increasing stress on marine and coastal environments. The impacts include deterioration of the region's biodiversity, declining fish stocks, and polluted beaches.

The major source of coastal and marine pollution is the discharge of untreated waste and sewage from human settlements, agricultural runoff, and industrial activities, especially the oil and tourist industries. According to the Pan American Health Organisation (PAHO), only 10 per cent of the sewage generated in Central America and the Caribbean Island countries was properly treated in the early 1980s (Archer, 1984). A more recent study by PAHO showed that in the 11 Caribbean Common Market (CARICOM) countries, the percentage of the population served by sewage systems varied between 2 and 16 per cent (Vulgman, 1992). With the population of coastal dwellers in the wider Caribbean region estimated to reach 60–65 million by 2000 (UNEP, 1994), pollution impacts are likely to increase.

Mining operations are an important source of particulate materials entering the coastal areas of the wider Caribbean region. The mining of bauxite is particularly significant for the economies of Jamaica, Suriname, and Guyana, and to a lesser extent for the Dominican Republic and Haiti. Ore mining for the production of nickel oxide in Cuba and the Dominican Republic is another source of contaminants. Few of these operations have treatment and recycling facilities. Much of the waste from mining ends up in the marine and coastal environments of the region, either directly or through rivers.

The oil industry is the largest industrial polluter in the wider Caribbean region. Oil refineries contribute approximately 70 per cent of the total biological oxygen demand load and more than 80 per cent of the total oil and grease discharged from industrial point sources in the region. Other industries that produce large pollutant loads in the region are sugar factories and distilleries, food processing plants, beverage manufacturers, pulp and paper plants, and chemical plants.

The considerable number of tourists visiting resort areas of the wider Caribbean region year-round also has implications for the region's environment. Between 1983 and 1993, the insular Caribbean alone attracted an average of 11 million visitors a year. In addition, daily visitors from cruise vessels in the region numbered some 8 million in 1991–92. (Simmons et al., 1994).

To respond to the increasing influx of tourists, hotels and recreational facilities are still being built throughout the region, often in locations lacking municipal sewage systems. Because much of the current and projected income of the Caribbean comes from tourism, the maintenance of a unique environment is of paramount importance for the sustained economic development and growth of the region.

More than 50 per cent of the mangroves in the region have been degraded by pollution and infra–structure services or have been altered by forestry activities and the conversion to agriculture or aquaculture; this is of particular concern to most of the Caribbean region (WRI/UNEP/UNDP/WB, 1996). Mangroves provide a variety of habitats that serve as nurseries for great numbers of reef and coastal species, and as critical reserves for migratory birds under increasing stress at both ends of their

Box 2.3 continued

The transport of eroded soils to the sea by rivers has led to the increased turbidity of coastal waters, placing an increasing amount of stress on coastal ecosystems such as coral reefs, particularly along the Caribbean coast of Panama, Costa Rica, and Nicaragua (UNEP, 1994). Most of the suspended and dissolved materials carried by these rivers are derived from natural geochemical processes. However, human activities significantly contribute to this load through the erosion of river basin watersheds caused by deforestation, urbanization, agriculture, industry, and the discharge of a variety of pollutants into these waters.

Biodiversity

The Caribbean region contains a rich variety of complex ecosystems with many endemic species. Along the coast of Belize, for example, lies the second largest coral reef in the world and the longest in the northern hemisphere, stretching some 220 kilometres. In many parts of the region, however, coral reefs are severely damaged or are in danger of being lost. For example, the coral cover on the reefs along the north coast of Jamaica has declined from 52 percent to 3 percent over the period from the late 1970s to early 1990s (Hughes, 1994). The Caribbean Sea itself is being subjected to severe environmental stresses, from increased opacity from suspended sediments to marine debris and overharvesting of key commercial species such as lobster, shrimp, grouper, conch, and gamefish.

Habitat destruction due to aggressive coastal zone development, particularly to serve the expanding tourist industry, seems to be the main cause of pressure on the region's biodiversity. Overexploitation and harvesting of species, coral reef and seagrass degradation, and mangrove deforestation (for large-scale land reclamation schemes, in particular) also contribute to the pressure, as do various sources of pollution.

The decades-long efforts to preserve, protect, and restore the five species of endangered and threatened sea turtles in the Caribbean illustrate the difficulty and complexity of the region's environmental problems. The remaining sea turtle populations are being put under enormous stress by the destruction of nesting beaches during coastal development; the destruction of eggs and nests by harvesting; hunting of adults and high mortality as by-catch of fishing nets and trawlers; poisoning by toxic chemicals; ingestion and entanglement in plastic debris in the open ocean; and the destruction of feeding areas by trawling, dredging, and coastal pollution.

Despite ongoing efforts, sea turtle populations are declining throughout most of the region. In some areas, the trends are dramatic and are likely to be irreversible during our lifetimes. According to IUCN—the World Conservation Union—persistent overexploitation, especially of adult females on nesting beaches, and the widespread collection of eggs has resulted in five turtle species in the region being classified as "endangered" and a sixth classified as "vulnerable" (IUCN, 1993).

References

Archer, A.B. 1984. Land Based Sources of Pollution in Coastal, Marine and Land Areas of the CARICOM States. UNEP/CARICOM/PAHO Project for the Protection of the Coastal and Marine Environment of the Caribbean Islands.

Hughes, T.P. 1994. Catastrophes, phase shifts and large scale degradation of a Caribbean coral reef. *Science* 265:1547-1551.

IUCN. 1993. *IUCN Red List of Threatened Animals*. B. Groombridge (ed). World Conservation Union (IUCN), Gland, Switzerland, and World Conservation Monitoring Centre, Cambridge, UK.

Simmons and Associates. 1994. The impact of tourism on the marine environment of the Caribbean; with special reference to cruise and other types of marine based tourism. Prepared for the Caribbean Tourism Organisation, Barbados.

UNEP. 1994. *Regional Overview of Land Based Sources of Pollution in the Wider Caribbean Region*. CEP Technical Report No. 33, UNEP Caribbean Environment Programme. Kingston.

Vulgman, A.A. 1992. CEHI/PAHO Assessment of Operational Status of Wastewater Treatment Plants in the Caribbean.

migration routes. As a combined result of these stresses as well as overfishing, the catch of commercial species such as shrimp, grouper, Caribbean lobster, and bass in semi-tropical areas is diminishing (Winograd, 1995).

Atmosphere

Although Latin America and the Caribbean produce only 14.8 per cent of the world's greenhouse gas emissions and a similarly low proportion of

Threat Potential [a]

High[b]

Moderate[c]

Low[d]

Figure 2.18. Latin American and Caribbean coastal ecosystems threatened by development.

Source: Bryant, D., et al. (1995).
Notes: a. Threat ranking depicts potential risk to coastal ecosystems from development-related activities. b. Coastal areas falling within a city or major port footprint or having a population density exceeding 150 persons per square kilometre, a road network density exceeding 150 metres of road per square kilometre, or a pipeline density exceeding 10 metres of pipeline per square kilometre. c. Coastal areas with a population density of between 75 and 150 persons per square kilometre, a road network density of between 100 and 150 metres of road per square kilometre, or a pipeline density of between 0 and 10 metres of pipeline per square kilometre. d. Coastal areas with a population of less than 75 persons per square kilometre, a road network density of less than 100 metres of road per square kilometre, and no pipelines known to be present.

chlorofluorocarbons (Winograd, 1995), the region will bear a disproportionate portion of the consequences of climatic and atmospheric change.

The southern latitudes of South America are the areas closest to the seasonal ozone hole that opens up over Antarctica each spring and summer. As a result, Argentina, Brazil, Chile, Paraguay, and Uruguay experience the effects of increased ultraviolet-B radiation due to ozone depletion more acutely than any other inhabited region on earth (UNEP, 1995c).

At the same time, sea level rise will affect the Caribbean countries as well as low-lying coastal regions of LAC. Because of regional differences in regimes of storm surges, the increase of flooding risk

due to sea level rise is greater than average for the coasts of the Caribbean and other small island States (IPCC, 1994).

In addition, the effect of natural hazards such as flooding, drought, and hurricanes could be magnified by global climatic change. A potential change in the frequency of occurrence of natural, large-scale anomalies in atmospheric circulation, such as tropical hurricanes and El Niño events, is of particular relevance in a region that is already naturally subject to these contingencies. These changes are likely to affect the small island States of the Caribbean disproportionately.

Urban and Industrial Environments

Cities in Latin America, which are home to 78 per cent of the region's population (UN, 1995a), are particularly vulnerable to environmental problems such as urban air pollution, water pollution, disposal of solid and liquid wastes, and industrial contamination. Domestic and industrial discharges in urban areas contaminate air, land, and water with nutrients and toxins. In turn, degraded air, land, and water harm flora and fauna and pose health risks to city dwellers. Although most of the megacities are affected in similar ways, data on urban environmental conditions are available mainly from a few large cities such as Mexico City, São Paulo, and Santiago. Much of this pollution stems from economic growth and industrialization, which have been highly concentrated in the large cities of the region, rather than from urbanization itself.

In the last decades, rural abandonment and poverty have accelerated the growth of urban areas. (See Figure 2.19.) Many of the cities in LAC were not conceived or planned for the current demographic densities. As a result, the sprawling megacities have generated peripheral belts of fragile human settlements, usually located in environmentally unsuitable areas such as hill slopes or floodable grounds. People living in these areas are particularly vulnerable to disasters and health hazards. Additionally, some of the larger cities, such as Mexico City and Santiago, are located in valleys and surrounded by mountain ranges, which exacerbate their urban pollution problems and make them inappropriate for further industrialization and urban expansion.

Air pollution is a constant fact of life for 81 million urban residents of Latin America, leading to an estimated 2.3 million cases of chronic respiratory illness every year among children, to 105,000 cases of chronic bronchitis among the elderly, and to nearly 65 million lost workdays (LAC CDE, 1992). Mexico City, São Paulo, and Santiago all have very high pollution indexes. Buenos Aires, Bogotá, Rio de Janeiro, and Caracas are not free of this problem either, although due to their geographical locations and climatic conditions they are less seriously affected (ECLAC, 1993a).

Mexico City has probably experienced one of the worst air pollution problems in the world. The weather and topography greatly hamper dispersal of the enormous volumes of pollutants that are emitted into the air, especially during the dry season (Gligo, 1995). World Health Organization guidelines for sulphur dioxide, suspended particulate matter, and carbon monoxide were all regularly exceeded in the city during the 1970s and 1980s (UNEP and WHO, 1992), although there has been a marked improvement over the past five years. According to estimates in 1992, suspended particulate matter in Mexico City from vehicles and other sources increased mortality rates about 0.038 per cent, and thus contributed to 6,400 deaths (Margulis, 1992). In addition, it was estimated that elevated ozone concentration contributed to the loss of around 6.4 million workdays a year, and that 29 per cent of children had unhealthy blood lead levels (Margulis, 1992). Similar patterns have been observed in many other cities of the region.

Two main factors are causing an increase in urban air pollution in the region: the mounting number of motor vehicles in use, and the expansion of industrial activity. Mexico City alone has more than 4.2 million motor vehicles (Cevalos, 1996), while in Santiago, the number of motor vehicles has tripled over the past 15 years (ECLAC, 1991). The use of motor vehicles produces more air pollution than any other single human activity, with an estimated 80–90 per cent of lead in ambient air coming from the combustion of leaded gasoline, despite the fact that unleaded gaso-

line has been introduced in most Latin American countries (WRI/UNEP/UNDP/WB, 1996). The growth of industrial activity has been especially marked in the larger countries and major cities. Following the slowdown in the 1980s due to economic stagnation, industrial activities are once again picking up (ECLAC, 1996), and with them, environmental pollution is increasing.

Although few countries aside from the smaller ones in the Caribbean face water supply problems on a national scale, many must deal with such problems in urban areas. Local water shortages are particularly acute in the region's megacities. The supply of drinking water is also a major environmental, technological, and financial challenge in many of the smaller cities.

Lima, Peru, for example, is located in an area where not enough water is available, which has forced the costly extraction of water from distant watersheds. In other large urban centres, water supply is based on the unsustainable exploitation of underground aquifers. In Buenos Aires, some 55 per cent of the population obtains its drinking water from underground sources, some of which have serious levels of pollution. In Mexico City, around two thirds of the water used in the city is obtained from aquifers at a rate of extraction more than double the recharge rate (Gligo, 1995).

The concentration and increases in urban population in the region have also generated difficulties in the supply of water of adequate quality. In most cities, piped drinking water is not available to everyone. The mounting demand for drinking water has outstripped its supply, causing serious problems (ECLAC, 1992). Access to safe water in the region is highly variable, ranging from 100 per cent for the urban dwellers of Cuba and Chile to 63 per cent for those in the urban areas of Ecuador (UNICEF, 1994). Some 10 per cent of urban households in Bolivia, 25 per cent in Ecuador, 30 per cent in Guatemala, and 13 per cent in Honduras are without access to piped water—inside or outside (UN, 1995a).

The absence of sewage treatment, especially in rapidly expanding urban areas, creates problems. Approximately 80 per cent of the urban population

(per cent urban population)

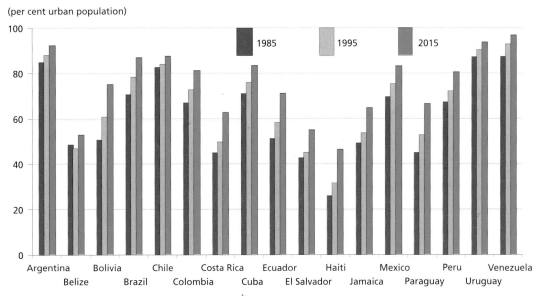

Figure 2.19. Percentage of population residing in urban areas in selected countries in Latin America and the Caribbean, 1985–2015.

Source: UN (1995a).

in the region has access to adequate sanitation and sewerage services (collection, but not treatment), although there is great variation among the countries—from 100 per cent in Chile and 97 per cent in Venezuela to 40 per cent in Bolivia and 56 per cent in Ecuador (UNICEF, 1994). This relatively high percentage of sewage collection coupled with the low share receiving any treatment before discharge into rivers, lakes, and seas has resulted in water quality problems not only in cities, but also on downstream areas, coastal areas, and beaches.

Many of the megacities, such as Mexico City and São Paulo-Santos, contain large concentrations of industry with correspondingly high levels of contamination. Such cities are often highly polluted and lack adequate social and sanitation infrastructure and proper policies for the treatment of hazardous industrial waste. At the same time, land pressures and urban poverty mean that communities are often built near industrial plants that dump their wastes into the rivers, the seas, or onto the nearby land, and that pollute the air. The inhabitants of these low-income neighbourhoods are consequently exposed to hazardous waste and face health risks.

In addition, increasingly stringent environmental standards in the industrial world, particularly in North America, have driven industries to transfer some of their most polluting technologies to developing countries such as Mexico (LAC CDE, 1992). The need to develop a local industry has forced many LAC countries to accept polluting technologies and, in some cases, also the transboundary traffic of hazardous wastes. The largest proportion of hazardous wastes coming into the region does so under the terms of agreements between the United States and Mexico. As of 1988, Mexico had accepted 30,000 tons of such waste for industrial recycling (ECLAC, 1993b).

Underlying Causes

Social

The population in Latin America grew from 179 million to 481 million between 1950 and 1995 (UN, 1993). Cuba and a few small Caribbean islands have birth rates below replacement level. Other nations, including Argentina, Brazil, Chile, Colombia, Jamaica, and Uruguay, are growing at less then 3 per cent a year (UN, 1995b). The concentration of population growth in urban areas and marginal agricultural lands is the main factor responsible for pressures exerted by human population on the environment.

An important characteristic of the regional population dynamics in LAC is urbanization. By 1995, 78 per cent of the population of South America and more than 70 per cent of the population of LAC as a whole lived in urban areas; by 2020, this figure is expected to increase to well over 80 per cent (UN, 1995a). The region has seven urban centres with populations of more than 5 million. Mexico City and São Paulo are among the five largest cities in the world and will remain so at the end of the century. (See Table 2.9.) Such concentrations of population put incredible stresses on the immediate environment.

The concentration of human activity affects the environment in three major ways: land use and land cover change, the extraction and depletion of natural resources, and the production of wastes such as untreated wastewater (WRI/UNEP/UNDP, 1994). The infrastructure in urban areas is already stretched to the limit and will, in the future, be unable to support further growth in population unless considerable investments in services are made.

The tropical moist forest regions have also experienced a population growth rate higher than the 3 per cent regional average (CEUR, 1988). The population growth rate has had implications with regard to the expansion of agricultural frontiers and the associated deforestation discussed earlier.

Economic

The long-term environmental challenges of the region are to a large extent the delayed consequence of the fast economic growth, industrialization, urbanization, agricultural modernization and expansion, and heavy public investments in transportation and energy infrastructure that took place between 1950 and 1982. After the oil crisis of 1973, private foreign financing contributed to the continuation of these trends, adding to a strong consumption boom. This lead to the debt crisis and the consequent adjustment and restructuring process, which included reduction of Government spending, privatization of State companies and services, and liberalization of national and international markets of goods, services, and factors of production. These

later developments brought about a decline of internal demand, a fall in the production of nontradeable goods and services, and an increase in underemployment and unemployment, poverty, and inequality (UNEP, 1996). They also stimulated the expansion of natural-resource-based exports to earn foreign currency leading to deforestation and land degradation (UNEP, 1996).

The economic situation improved during the early 1990s, with most economies reversing the trends of negative growth seen in the 1980s. The Gross Domestic Product (GDP) grew by 3.8 per cent in 1991, 3 per cent in 1992, and 3.2 per cent in 1993, while per capita GDP was up by 1.8 per cent, 1.1 per cent, and 1.3 per cent in those same years (ECLAC, 1996). At present, however, the situation is unclear, as most countries have encountered financial difficulties during 1995 and 1996, which have enhanced the spiral of inequity, unemployment, and poverty.

All these developments have had complex and sometimes contradictory consequences for the environment. On the one hand, the economic changes have brought additional international pressure to implement environmental policies, while increased competition and technological modernization may have stimulated a more efficient use of resources and lower emissions. On the other hand, the liberalization of the economies brought less Government investments in infrastructure and reduced spending to prevent or mitigate environmental damage. The reduction of public spending, and the transference of public services to the private sector, in many cases put the preservation of the environment as a second-order priority.

Because the region is almost exclusively a producer of raw materials, the new market-economy model and the globalization of trade have accelerated the tapping of the region's natural resources. Coupled with a generalized deterioration of the relative price of these commodities, this phenomenon has meant an additional pressure on the environment and natural resources of the region.

The rising foreign debt, which led to a net transfer of capital from the region of $200 billion between 1982 and 1989 (LAC CDE, 1992), encour-

Table 2.9

Population Estimates, Projections, and Growth Rates for the Seven Largest Cities in Latin America and the Caribbean, 1995 and 2000

Agglomeration	Population (millions)		Growth rate	World rank in size
	1995	2000		
São Paulo, Brazil	26.8	27.9	0.8	2
Mexico City, Mexico	15.6	16.4	0.9	4
Buenos Aires, Argentina	11.0	11.4	0.7	12
Rio de Janeiro, Brazil	9.9	10.2	0.7	16
Lima, Peru	7.5	8.4	2.4	25
Bogota, Colombia	5.6	6.3	2.4	32
Santiago, Chile	5.1	5.4	1.4	38

Source: UN (1995).

aged overexploitation of natural resources to increase exports and meet pressing short-term needs.

In the Caribbean, where economic health is often determined by the volatile tourism industry, rapid economic cycles and the prolonged recessions in Europe have led to resort failures (sometimes with abandonment of important infrastructure, such as water, sewer, and transport systems). This has weakened both local planning and management capabilities of Government and its willingness to implement control and disaster mitigation actions for developments in critical habitat areas, such as coasts and barrier islands.

The austerity policies of the 1980s and 1990s helped initiate a recovery of many of the region's economies, but they have also contributed to an increase in poverty. The economic restructuring programmes led to cuts in public spending, thereby increasing unemployment. Between 1980 and 1985, real per capita income dropped 14 per cent, pushing a high proportion of the population below the poverty line (Winograd, 1995). Eighteen per cent of the urban population and 49 per cent of the rural population of the region fell below the absolute poverty level between 1980–89 (UNICEF, 1994). And in 1990, 40 per cent of the households did not get the minimum of calories needed for an adequate diet, unemployment and underemployment affected 44 per cent of the labour force, and 68 per cent of the housing could be considered inadequate (LAC CDE, 1992).

The aggravation of poverty in the region had serious implications for the environmental base; extreme poverty compelled people to exploit vulnerable ecosystems through short-term survival strategies or to migrate to the cities to inhabit marginal shelters. The concentration of poverty belts around the large cities of the region, coupled with the current reduction in Government spending, has increased the vulnerability of the population to environmental problems in general, and to hazards of epidemics and health in particular. Forests in particular and natural resources in general bore the brunt of growing social and ecological impoverishment and of reduced investment funds for development in the region.

A complex loop of interactions therefore exists in the region among poverty, population, and environment. The inequity in the distribution of wealth and resources, more than the problem of population growth, is putting strong pressures on the sustainability of the natural resources. The regressive distribution of resources has also meant a concentration in the ownership of land, resulting in more environmental pressure being put on the remaining small properties.

Institutional

Following the paradigm of sustainable development that the United Nations Conference on Environment and Development (UNCED) initiated in 1992 at a global scale, many Governments in the region have created specific high-ranking offices at the ministerial level to take care of environmental issues. Examples of this trend include the Ministerio de Desarrollo Sustentable y Medio Ambiente in Bolivia, and the Secretaría de Medio Ambiente, Recursos Naturales y Pesca in Mexico. Although the change towards specific administrative offices for environmental matters is in general positive, it has also meant that environmental awareness and the paradigm of sustainable development remain alienated from the traditional sectors of Government in certain countries.

There has also been a trend towards the decentralization of governmental functions to provinces

and municipalities, which meant the transfer of decision-making to lower administrative levels. At times, however, these local Governments have lacked the technical capacity to assume environmental responsibilities.

A number of multilateral agreements with the objective of preserving the environment and promoting sustainable development were signed or reactivated. For example, the Amazon Cooperation Treaty was moved forward, and a permanent secretariat was established; the Central American countries formed the Central American Commission for Sustainable Development; and the Caribbean countries formed the Confederation of Caribbean States.

Also as a result of UNCED, regional Governments have begun to view environmental issues more as a problem of social and economic development, closely related to the problem of poverty and social progress. And some have started to take an active interest in the protection of their natural patrimony through specific organisms created for that purpose, such as the National Commission for the Knowledge and Use of Biodiversity (CONABIO) in Mexico and the National Biodiversity Institute (INBIO) in Costa Rica, two organizations devoted to the survey of the biological richness of their respective national ecosystems.

The changes in the regional economies and the shift towards market systems and liberalization have had mixed results on the environmental institutions and policy as well. The reduced Government spending has meant a decrease in State-promoted, large-scale development projects, and this in turn has lessened their impact on the environment. The widespread reduction in governmental spending has, however, also decreased the capacity of the State to establish environmental regulations and has lowered the capacity to enforce them. In other cases, the diminution of the State functions and responsibilities has also meant the elimination or downscaling of regulatory, research, and administrative organisms such as the National Forestry Institute (IFONA) in Argentina. So research on environmental issues and sustainable development problems has declined significantly.

One favourable development in the institutional context has been the rise of environmentally active non-governmental organizations (NGOs) in the region. As an example, the number of NGOs in Colombia rose from 26 in 1990 to more than 400 in March 1994 (Winograd, 1995). These groups have had a positive impact at local and regional levels in terms of natural resource management, the appraisal of and respect for native knowledge and cultures, and the implementation of alternative production models. They have also acquired a voice at the international level regarding how projects and funds need to be managed, and have emerged as a strong force in guiding popular participation and producing important changes in development policies and actions (Winograd, 1995).

Another promising endeavour is the creation of national councils for sustainable development or similar initiatives in many countries of the region, including Bolivia, Costa Rica, Mexico, and Peru. These councils are often tripartite in nature, being composed of the private sector, government, and NGOs. Such councils allow a more systematic participation of civil society and the private sector.

References

Bryant, D., *et al.* 1995. Coastlines at Risk: An Index of Potential Development-Related Threats to Coastal Ecosystems. *World Resources Institute Indicator Brief.* Washington.

CDEA. 1992. Amazonia without myths. Comisión de Desarrollo y Medio Ambiente para la Amazonía; Commission on Development and Environment for Amazonia (CDEA). Inter-American Development Bank, United Nations Development Programme, Amazon Cooperation Treaty.

CEUR. 1988. Proyecciones de población por ecosistema en América Latina. Proyecto Prospectiva Ecológica para América Latina (PEAL) y Grupo de Análisis de Sistemas Ecológicos (GASE). Centro de Estudios Urbanos y Regionales. Bariloche, Argentina.

Cevalos, D. 1996. "El Reino del auto," Tierramerica: Suplemento de Medio Ambiente para América Latina y El Caribe. A Publication of UNEP Regional Office for LAC. Year 2, No. 3. June.

Dregne, H. 1991. Desertification Costs: Land Damage and Rehabilitation. Consultant's Report prepared for UNEP and International Centre for Arid and Semi-arid Land Studies (ICASALS). Nairobi.

ECLAC. 1991. Principales emisiones de contaminantes atmosféricos y algunos medios para su control. Elementos para la discusión. Economic Commission for Latin America and the Caribbean (ECLAC). LC/R.983. Sem. 61/5. Santiago, Chile.

ECLAC. 1992. Water management in metropolitan areas of Latin America. Santiago, Chile. LC/R.156.

ECLAC. 1993a. Ciudades medianas y gestión urbana en América Latina. LC/L.747. Santiago, Chile.

ECLAC. 1993b. Hazardous products and wastes: Impact of transboundary movement towards the Latin America and the Caribbean Region and possibilities for preventing and controlling it. LC/R.1303. Santiago, Chile.

ECLAC. 1996. *Statistical Yearbook for Latin America and the Caribbean. 1995 edition*. United Nations Publication No. E.96.II.G.1. Santiago, Chile.

FAO. 1993. *Forest Resources Assessment 1990. Tropical Countries*. Forestry Paper 112. Food and Agriculture Organization of the United Nations (FAO). Rome.

FAO. 1995. *Forest Resources Assessment 1990: Global Synthesis*. Forestry Paper 124. FAO. Rome.

Gallopin, G., M. Winograd, and I. Gomez. 1991. Ambiente y Desarrollo en América Latina y el Caribe: Problemas, Oportunidades y Prioridades, GASE. Bariloche, Argentina.

GESAMP. 1990. The State of the Marine Environment. IMO/FAO/UNESCO/WMO/IAEA/UN/UNEP Joint Group of Experts on the Scientific Aspects of Marine Pollution. Blackwell Scientific Publications. Oxford.

Gligo, N. 1995. Situación y perspectivas ambientales en América Latina y el Caribe. *Revista de la CEPAL* 55:107–122.

IPCC. 1994. Preparing to meet the coastal challenges of the 21st century. Conference Report, World Coast Conference 1993.

IUCN. 1993. *1994 IUCN Red List of Threatened Animals*. World Conservation Union (IUCN). Gland, Switzerland.

LAC CDE. 1992. *Our Own Agenda*. Latin American and Caribbean Commission on Development and the Environment (LAC CDE). UNDP and IDB in collaboration with ECLAC and UNEP.

Margulis, S. 1992. Back-of-the-envelope estimates of environmental damage costs in Mexico. World Bank, Policy Research Working Papers, Washington.

May. R.M. 1989. How many species are there on earth? *Science* 241:1441–1448.

McNeely, J., K. Miller, W. Reid *et al*,. 1990. *Conserving the World's Biological Diversity*. World Bank, WRI, IUCN, WWF. Washington.

SEDESOL. 1993. Plan de Acción Para Combatir la Desertificación en Mexico. Comisión Nacional de Zonas Aridas. Mexico.

UN. 1993. *Annual Populations (The 1994 Revision)*. United Nations (UN) Population Division. New York.

UN. 1995a. *Compendium of Human Settlement Statistics 1995*. 5th Issue. DESIPASD and Habitat UN Publications. New York.

UN. 1995b. *World Population Prospects: The 1994 Revision*. United Nations (UN) Population Division. New York.

UNEP. 1991. Status of Desertification and Implementation of the United Nations Plan of Action to Combat Desertification. United Nations Environment Programme (UNEP). Nairobi.

UNEP. 1992. World Atlas of Desertification. Edward Arnold. London.

UNEP. 1994. Regional overview of land based sources of pollution in the wider Caribbean region. CEP technical report no. 33. UNEP. Caribbean Environment Programme. Kingston, Jamaica.

UNEP. 1995a. Final Report of the Ninth Meeting of Ministers of the Environment of LAC. 21-26 September. Havana, Cuba.

UNEP. 1995b. *Global Biodiversity Assessment; summary for policy-makers*. Cambridge University Press.

UNEP. 1995c. Monitoring Ozone Depletion and UV Radiation in South America. In: *Our Planet*. Vol. 7. No. 2. UNEP. Nairobi.

UNEP. 1996. Environmental Impacts of Structural Adjustment Programmes: Synthesis and Recommendations. UNEP Environmental Economics Series Paper No. 21. June.

UNEP/WHO. 1991. *Water Quality: Progress in the Implementation of the Mar del Plata Action Plan and a Strategy for the 1990s*. UNEP and World Health Organization (WHO). Earthwatch GEMS.

UNEP/WHO. 1992. *Urban Air Pollution in Megacities of the World*. Blackwell, United Kingdom.

UNEP/SCOPE. 1993. Groundwater Contamination in Latin America. Proceedings of a SCOPE/UNEP Workshop. July 26–30. San Jose, Costa Rica.

UNICEF. 1994. *The State of the World's Children 1994*. United Nations Children's Fund (UNICEF) and Oxford University Press for UNICEF. New York.

WCMC. 1992. *Global Biodiversity Status of the Earth's Living Resources*. World Conservation Monitoring Centre (WCMC). Chapman and Hall. London.

WCMC. 1994. *Biodiversity Data Sourcebook*. World Conservation Press. Cambridge.

WCMC. 1995. Unpublished data. July.

Western, D., and M. Pearl (eds.). 1989. Conservation for the 21st Century. Wildlife Conservation International, New York Zoological Society, Oxford University Press. New York.

Winograd, M. 1995. Environmental indicators for Latin America and the Caribbean: Toward land use sustainability. GASE in collaboration with the Organisation of American States, IICA/GTZ, and WRI.

WRI/UNEP/UNDP. 1994. *World Resources 1994–95*. World Resources Institute (WRI), UNEP, and United Nations Development Programme (UNDP). Oxford University Press. New York and Oxford.

WRI/UNEP/UNDP/WB. 1996. *World Resources 1996–97*. Oxford University Press. New York and Oxford.

NORTH AMERICA

Major Environmental Concerns

The two countries considered in this section, Canada and the United States, rank among the wealthiest in the world, not only in per capita income but also in richness of natural resources. With its high standard of living, North America is the leading producer and consumer of goods and services—and of waste—on the planet. Both nations are concerned about global, regional, and national implications of today's resource use patterns, with the increasingly obvious negative feedback on the quality of life.

In both countries, major Government policy statements are made to bring environmental issues to public attention (Marchi, 1996; Christopher, 1996). Some of the priority environmental concerns in the region have also been expressed by the Commission for Environmental Cooperation (CEC), set up in 1994 under the environmental side agreement of the North American Free Trade Agreement (NAFTA), which includes Mexico. The CEC concentrates on five areas: environmental conservation; protecting human health and the environment; environment, trade, and economy; enforcement co-operation and environmental law; and information and public outreach (CEC, 1996).

This section draws on official reports and statements of the Canadian and U.S. Governments as well as reports from Government agencies and the private, non-governmental sector, including public opinion surveys.

Together, Canada and the U.S. cover nearly 18.8 million square kilometres, some 14 per cent of the world's land area. The two countries contribute 49 per cent and 51 per cent to this total area respectively. With one of the longest common borders in the world, transboundary, multimedia environmental issues are also important. Environmental deterioration in the Great Lakes Basin and transboundary air pollution are two such areas of concern.

Land

The major land-related problems in the region are erosion; soil contamination resulting from industrial and agricultural activities, including the overuse of fertilizer and pesticide use; and water contamination from agricultural practices.

Canada depends on the land for its economic well-being more than most other industrialized nations. One in three workers is employed directly or indirectly in agriculture, forestry, mining, energy generation, and other land-based activities (Government of Canada, 1996). In the United States, while dependence on primary production is lower, agricultural production and marketing account for 16 per cent of employment, and almost half of the total land area (excluding Alaska) is dedicated to agriculturally related purposes (PCSD, 1996).

U.S. agriculture is in transition. While total cropland has stayed nearly constant since 1945 at 186 million hectares, much of the best farmland is adjacent to major metropolitan areas and is being converted to non-agricultural uses (PCSD, 1996; USDA, 1996). The number of farms declined by almost 31 per cent, from 2.9 million in 1970 to 2 million in 1994, as the average size of farms increased by about 28 per cent in the same period (PCSD, 1996). New strategies are needed to address the changing situation.

Throughout North America, then, the management of farms and rangeland is a key part of sustainable development. Poor agricultural practices result in hazards to human health. Although the pesticide DDT has been banned in Canada and

the United States, residues of DDT, such as DDE, are still found in the serum and fat tissues of the majority of North Americans due to its persistence in the environment and to continued inputs from other regions through long-range transport. High DDE levels in women have been associated with an increased risk of breast cancer. The presence of other chlorinated compounds in human tissues has raised concerns about their possible harmful effects on endocrine and reproductive functions (Pohl and Chivian, 1996; Canadian Dept. of Foreign Affairs and International Trade, 1996b).

Some measures are being taken to address key problems. For example, by 1992, U.S. farmers had reduced soil erosion on croplands by around one billion metric tons per year from 1982 levels (NSTC, 1996). Soil erosion savings have come about through the Conservation Reserve Program (635 million metric tons), conservation technical assistance (272 million metric tons), and conservation compliance (90 million metric tons) (PCSD, 1996).

To mitigate the use of persistent organic pollutants (POPs), Canada and the U.S. have developed and implemented pesticide management programmes nationally and regionally.

Forests

Forests are a dominant feature of the North American landscape, covering almost half of Canada (Natural Resources Canada, 1996) and a third of the United States (Brooks, 1993). They provide a great diversity of economic, ecological, recreational, cultural, and spiritual benefits. These two countries are the world's two leading exporters of forest products (Brooks, 1993). In Canada alone, more than 880,000 people rely on the forest industry for their livelihood (Canadian Dept. of Foreign Affairs and International Trade, 1996b). Important steps—including both public and private action—have been taken to put the region on an effective course for achieving sustainable forestry management (PCSD, 1996; Natural Resources Canada, 1996).

Pressures for commercial logging are expected to intensify in the U.S. in the years to come. In Canada, commercial logging is not expected to

increase, and annual harvests are currently running at almost a quarter below the annual allowable cut (Canadian Dept. of Foreign Affairs and International Trade, 1996b). While deforestation and loss of forested area are not among the priority concerns, the depletion of old-growth forests and of the last remaining rainforests in British Columbia, Canada, and the Pacific Northwest in the United States are serious concerns of the public and often trigger discussions and legal measures for their conservation. Recently there has been a movement to stop logging of old-growth forests on public lands in order to promote biodiversity conservation.

Although most forests in the United States are managed for multiple use, private forests are often managed with a stronger emphasis on fibre production than is found in public forestlands. Private forests also produce higher wood yields at a lower cost per unit than public timberlands. Because of these factors, private forest areas figure significantly in market-based approaches to promoting natural resources stewardship (PCSD, 1996). There are nearly 8 million private landowners engaged in non-industrial forestry in the United States. Together they planted 41 per cent of the trees planted in 1993 and care for 59 per cent of U.S. timberland (Comanor, 1994).

In Canada, although more than 425,000 landowners are engaged in private forestry, only 6 per cent of the nation's forests are growing on private property. Provincial governments are responsible for managing 71 per cent of Canadian forests; the remaining 23 per cent are managed by Federal and Territorial governments (Natural Resources Canada, 1996).

Biodiversity

Canada's wildlife heritage is estimated to encompass 138,000 species, including 4,000 vascular plants, 1,800 vertebrates, and more than 44,000 invertebrates (Environment Canada, 1996b). As of 1996, 254 species, subspecies, or populations in Canada were considered endangered, threatened, or vulnerable; another 21 species were already nationally or globally extinct (Government of Canada, 1996b).

(per cent of species threatened)

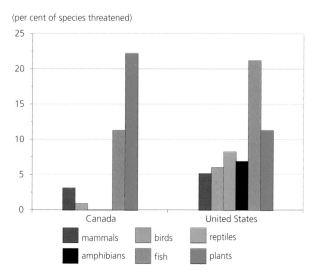

Figure 2.20. Percentage of known species threatened in North America, 1990s.

Sources: IUCN (1993); WCMC (1992, 1994, 1995).
Note: The number of threatened species listed for all countries includes full species that are classified by the World Conservation Union (IUCN) as endangered, vulnerable, rare, and indeterminate, but excludes introduced species, species whose status is insufficiently known, or those known to be extinct.

(See Figure 2.20.) Pressures on native wildlife are also reflected in the presence of toxic contaminants in tissues of living organisms and in the ongoing invasions of non-native species, such as the purple loosestrife and the zebra mussel. Encouraging signs include an increase in populations of ducks and some species of geese; progress in efforts to restore endangered species such as the peregrine falcon, swift fox, and whooping crane; and declining levels of toxins in tissues of living organisms (Government of Canada, 1996).

There are about 2,800 protected areas in Canada, excluding private lands and cultural heritage sites. Nearly two thirds of their total area is strictly protected, but most sites are smaller than 10 square kilometres. Of the 217 terrestrial eco-regions in Canada, 71 have no protected sites (Government of Canada, 1996). Preliminary modelling has suggested that 7 per cent of Canada is at high risk of biodiversity loss, and only 25 per cent is at low risk (Environment Canada, 1996a). In an effort to protect biodiversity, Canada continues to add to its networks of parks and other protected areas, as well as to legislation (Government of Canada, 1996).

The United States has also made strides in the protection of its natural resources. By 1994, for example, 5.7 million hectares across the country were protected through land trusts. Private and voluntary efforts have resulted in a 49-per-cent increase in the area under conservation since 1990. While public lands play an important role in this respect, private lands are also critical because they account for 64 per cent of the continental United States. Moreover, of the 728 species listed as endangered or threatened (under the Endangered Species Act), about half are found on a combination of public and private lands. To date, existing laws and regulations have not been entirely adequate to safeguard the nation's biological diversity (PCSD, 1996).

Water

Water is one of the most common concerns of Americans and Canadians. Despite an overall relative abundance, water shortages occur periodically in some localities, such as the more arid sections of the western United States, the Canadian prairie, and some of the valleys in the interior of British Columbia.

Canadians and Americans are among the world's largest per capita consumers of water (See Table 2.10.) especially where prices are relatively low. For example, Canadian households use twice as much water as European households, but they pay half as much for it. (See Table 2.11.) In 1994, Canadian households that paid volume-based water rates used 258 litres per person per day, nearly 40 per cent less than those charged a flat rate (Environment Canada, 1996d).

Eleven per cent of all surface and ground water withdrawn in Canada is used for municipal purposes. While one in four Canadians relies on ground water for domestic supply and the remainder depend on surface water, both sources are coming increasingly under threat in terms of quantity and quality (Environment Canada, 1996d). Because of increasing demand, municipal water supply is becoming one of the most critical water issues in the region (Environment Canada, 1996d; EOP, 1993). For example, in 1991, one in five Canadian municipalities reported problems with water availability

Table 2.10

Annual Internal Renewable Water Resources and Water Withdrawals in North America

	Annual Internal Renewable Water Resources[a]		Annual Withdrawals			Sectoral Withdrawals (per cent)		
	Total (cubic kilometres)	1995 Per Capita (cubic metres)	Year of Data	Percentage of Water Resources[a]	Per Capita (cubic metres)	Domestic	Industry	Agriculture
Canada	2,901.0	98,462	1991[b]	2	1,602	18[c]	70[c]	12[c]
United States	2,478.0	9,413	1990	19	1,870	13[d]	45[d]	42[d]

Source: WRI/UNEP/UNDP/WB (1996).
Notes: a. Annual Internal Renewable Water Resources usually include river flows from other countries. b. Data are from the early 1990s. c. Sectoral percentages estimated for 1987. d. Sectoral percentages date from the year of other annual withdrawal data.

(Environment Canada, 1996d). Linked to this is a growing concern for how to prevent resource depletion and reduce the environmental burden caused by the use of water for both industrial and community needs.

Compared with most other countries, Canada and the United States enjoy relatively good water quality. Nevertheless, basic delivery problems remain in some rural areas. Improper agricultural production practices have in some areas contributed significantly to impaired water quality of rivers, lakes, and estuaries (PCSD, 1996). In Canada, recent surveys suggest that 20 to 40 per cent of rural wells may be affected by faecal coliform bacteria (Government of Canada, 1996). A U.S. Department of Agriculture study in 1995 concluded that 2.4 million rural Americans, including a million without piped water, had a critical need for safe, dependable drinking water; supplies to a further 5.6 million did not meet Safe Drinking Water requirements (EPA, 1996a). The cost of meeting "highest priority" safe drinking water needs in rural America was estimated at US$3.5 billion.

One in five U.S. citizens receives water from a facility that violates a national safety standard. Surface water treatment standards were not met in 9 per cent of the systems while total coliform bacteria levels exceeded permitted levels in 8 per cent of the systems. Lead and copper treatment violations occurred in 1 per cent, as did chemical or radiological contamination violations. Through aggressive action under the Surface Water Treatment Rule by respon-

sible authorities, the risk of human exposure to microbiological contaminants is being reduced. In 1993, 1,000 water systems serving 12 million residents were not in compliance; by 1995, the number of non-compliant systems had been reduced to 400, serving 9.9 million (EPA, 1996a). Since 1972, the United States has invested a total of US$350 billion to control water pollution (NSTC, 1996).

Most Canadians get their drinking water from municipal water supplies, which generally meet high provincial and territorial safety standards. However, a 1995 report entitled "Community Drinking Water and Sewage Treatment in First Nation Communities" indicates that in those Aboriginal communities, about 20 per cent of the water systems require action to eliminate the risk of potential health problems while 9 per cent of the sewage systems have problems that could put human health at risk (Canadian Dept. of Foreign Affairs and International Trade, 1996).

The largest system of fresh surface water on earth, containing approximately 18 per cent of the world supply, is situated on the Canada–U.S. border. The Great Lakes—Superior, Michigan, Huron, Erie, and Ontario—together with the St. Lawrence River system, are a vital part of the physical and cultural heritage of North America. Spanning more than 1,200 kilometres from east to west, these inland fresh-water seas provide water for consumption, transportation, power, and recreation. The basin ecosystem is home to more than one tenth of the population of the U.S. and one quarter of the

Table 2.11

Water Prices in Selected Countries

	Price of Water (US dollars per 1,000 litres)	Average Residential Use (litres per person per day)
Canada	0.29	370
France	0.60	150
Germany	0.94	150
Sweden	0.56	210
United Kingdom	0.45	220
United States	0.30	430

Source: Environment Canada (1996c).

population of Canada. Some of the world's largest concentrations of industrial capacity are located in the Great Lakes region. Nearly 25 per cent of the total Canadian agricultural production and 7 per cent of the American production are located in the basin (Environment Canada and U.S.-EPA, 1995).

Beginning in the 1950s, concerns arose about the increasing eutrophication of the lakes, loss of wetlands and other habitats, the impact of exotic species on native fish stocks and aquatic ecosystems, and environmental contamination by persistent toxic chemicals. Concerted, system-wide efforts by both governments over the intervening years have done a great deal to restore environmental quality. Nutrient stresses are no longer the widespread problem that they were in the 1970s. There has been a general decline in the concentrations of persistent organic substances in all media throughout the Great Lakes. The aquatic community in Lake Superior is in good health again.

Despite these and other improvements, the latest *State of the Great Lakes* report, issued by the governments of Canada and the U.S. (Environment Canada and U.S.-EPA, 1995), concludes that the health of the Great Lakes Basin ecosystem is still variable. For instance, many toxic contaminant loadings remain above acceptable levels in water, aquatic organisms, and fish-eating birds. Aquatic habitats and wetlands are considered to be in a generally poor state due to huge losses acquired over the years in both quality and quantity. The ecosystem balance and reproductive impairment of native species in Lakes Michigan, Ontario, and eastern Erie are still worrying. Joint efforts are continuing to

address, in an integrated manner, the Great Lakes environment. (See Chapter 3.)

Marine and Coastal Environments

By the year 2000, more than three quarters of the U.S. population is expected to reside in coastal communities, with concomitant effects on land use (PCSD, 1996). The figure is much lower in Canada, about 25 per cent. Canada has the longest coastline in the world, fronting on three oceans (Government of Canada, 1996). Not surprisingly, the sustainable use of marine ecosystems is thus crucial to the future of both nations. (See Figure 2.21.)

The populations of some estuarine, inshore, and offshore fisheries have been reduced to drastically low levels in North America by overfishing, loss of habitat, and land-based pollution. From 1980 to 1989, reports from more than 3,650 events with disastrous impacts on fish populations cited the loss of 407 million fish in coastal and near-coastal locations in the United States (EOP, 1993; EPA, 1996a). In eastern Canada, acid rain is responsible for habitat degradation and the loss of fish in thousands of lakes and rivers, including a number of former salmon streams (EPA, 1996a). Pollution has also caused the disappearance of some formerly fished species and the decline of some others in the Great Lakes–St. Lawrence River system (EPA, 1996a).

Approximately 1,000 species of fish live in Canadian waters; fewer than 200 live in fresh water, the others live in salt water along the Atlantic, Arctic, and Pacific coasts. Four stocks or species are thought to be extinct, two are no longer found in Canadian waters, and 49 are listed as endangered, threatened, or vulnerable. Declining fish stocks have resulted in the collapse of the East Coast fisheries, with a devastating impact in eastern Canada (Environment Canada, 1996c).

Atmosphere

Concentrations of some atmospheric pollutants have been noticeably reduced in North America. Over the period 1970 to 1993, among the six pollutants used to monitor National Ambient Air

Quality in the U.S., lead showed the most dramatic improvement, with virtual outdoor elimination since the 1970s following the changeover to unleaded fuel (Government of the United States of America, 1995). Emissions of four of the other five critical pollutants also declined: carbon monoxide (by 24 per cent), volatile organic compounds (VOCs) (by 24 per cent), fine particulate matter (PM-10) (by 78 per cent), and sulphur dioxide (by 30 per cent). Only nitrogen oxide registered an increase (of 14 per cent) (Government of the United States of America, 1995). Although nitrogen oxide emissions from vehicles have declined during the last 10 years, these gains have been offset to a large extent by increased fuel combustion for electricity generation.

In Canada, industrial emissions of sulphur dioxide were cut by nearly half while emissions of total particulate matter from industrial plants declined by nearly 36 per cent between 1970 and 1985 (Environment Canada, 1996d). As in the United States, ambient concentrations of lead have dropped dramatically and, by the early 1990s, were only a small percentage of the concentrations present 20 years earlier (Environment Canada, n.d.).

Despite these improvements, air pollution is still a concern in both countries. Twenty years after the passage of the Clean Air Act in the United States, one in three Americans still lives in an area where the air is too polluted to meet Federal health standards (Browner, 1996). The major air quality issues in the United States have been identified as health risks from air pollutants in the ambient air, especially ozone and toxic chemicals; ecosystem damage from regional air pollution, including ozone and acid deposition; transboundary air pollution; and radon and other indoor air pollutants (US-UNCED, 1992).

Some central Canadian cities continue to experience unacceptable air quality, especially in summer. The most frequent causes are ground-level ozone and airborne particulates (Environment Canada, 1996d). Canadian and U.S. emissions of ozone-forming volatile organic compounds (VOCs) and nitrogen oxides, the precursors of ground-level ozone, are still close to the levels of the mid-1980s

Threat potential [a]
- High [b]
- Moderate [c]
- Low [d]

Figure 2.21. North American coastal ecosystems threatened by development.

Source: Bryant, D., *et al.* (1995).
Notes: a. Threat ranking depicts potential risk to coastal ecosystems from development-related activities. b. Coastal areas falling within a city or major port footprint or having a population density exceeding 150 persons per square kilometre, a road network density exceeding 150 metres of road per square kilometre, or a pipeline density exceeding 10 metres of pipeline per square kilometre. c. Coastal areas with a population density of between 75 and 150 persons per square kilometre, a road network density of between 100 and 150 metres of road per square kilometre, or a pipeline density of between 0 and 10 metres of pipeline per square kilometre. d. Coastal areas with a population of less than 75 persons per square kilometre, a road network density of less than 100 metres of road per square kilometre, and no pipelines known to be present.

(Government of Canada, 1996). Pulmonary disease from air pollution, especially from small particulates, has been estimated to cause 50,000–60,000 deaths each year in the United States and to cost the economy a total of US$40 billion to US$50 billion in direct health care expenditures and lost productivity (Pohl and Chivian, 1996). Some experts have suggested that 6 per cent of all respiratory admissions to hospitals in Canada are smog-related (Marchi, 1996).

In recent years, comparative risk studies performed by EPA have consistently ranked indoor air pollution among the five top environmental risks to public health in the U.S. Studies of human exposure to air pollution indicate that indoor air levels of many pollutants may be two to five times—and, on some occasions, more than 100 times—higher than outdoor levels (EPA, 1994). Over the past several decades, exposure to indoor air pollutants is believed to have increased due to a variety of factors, including the construction of more tightly sealed buildings, reduced ventilation rates to save energy, the use of synthetic building materials and furnishings, and the use of chemically formulated personal care products, pesticides, and household cleaners. EPA, in close cooperation with other Federal agencies and the private sector, has begun a concerted effort to better understand indoor air pollution and to reduce people's exposure to air pollutants in offices, homes, schools, and so on (EPA, 1996b).

Electricity generation accounts for about 70 per cent of annual sulphur dioxide emissions and 30 per cent of nitrogen oxide emissions in the United States (EPA, 1996d). The largest source of sulphur dioxide emissions in Canada is the smelting of metal ores, which accounts for 50 per cent of eastern Canadian emissions. Power generation contributes 20 per cent (Environment Canada, 1996d).

Airborne acidic pollutants are often transported by large-scale weather systems thousands of kilometres from their point of origin before being deposited. In eastern North America, weather systems generally travel from southwest to northeast. Thus, pollutants emitted from sources in the industrial heartland of the midwestern states and central Canada regularly fall on the more rural and comparatively pristine areas of northeastern U.S. and southeastern Canada (Environment Canada, 1996).

Acidification of surface waters is a further cause for concern. Many lakes and streams in Canada and the United States suffer from chronic acidity because they rest atop soil with a limited capacity to neutralize acidic compounds (called "buffering capacity"). The U.S. National Surface Water Survey found that acid rain causes acidity in 75 per cent of acidic lakes and about half the acidic streams (EPA, 1996d). The Canadian Government has estimated that 14,000 lakes in eastern Canada are acidic (Government of Canada, 1996d). About 43 per cent of Canada's land, mainly in the east, is highly sensitive to acid rain (Environment Canada, 1996d). Acidification in Canada is, to a large extent, a transboundary problem because half the acid rain falling in Canada originates in the U.S. (Environment Canada, 1996). "Episodic" acidification is an added

concern, particularly since it can cause large "fish kills." In the United States, for example, approximately 70 per cent of sensitive lakes in the Adirondacks of New York state and 30 per cent of streams in the mid-Appalachians of the eastern United States are likely to become acidic during such an episode (EPA, 1996d).

Recent extreme weather events, including heat waves and heavy flooding, have helped citizens to understand the possible impacts of climate change and how they could affect North America. The region produces more greenhouse gas emissions than any other region and has among the highest per capita emission levels (WRI/UNEP/UNDP/WB, 1996). Total U.S. emissions increased by 13 per cent between 1970 and 1990 (EOP, 1993) and currently comprise 22 per cent of the world total (WRI/UNEP/UNDP/WB, 1996). Both Canada and the United States are pursuing ways to reduce their contributions as part of concerted efforts under the United Nations Framework Convention on Climate Change.

Urban and Industrial Environments

Health threats to children in urban and industrial environments are of particular concern in the region (NRC, 1993; Needleman and Landrigan, 1994; OTA, 1990; Schewiz and Harris, 1993; Canadian Dept. of Foreign Affairs and International Trade, 1996a). Four million one- to six-year-olds in the United States—including two thirds of poor, minority, inner-city pre-school children—have levels of lead in their blood high enough to cause brain damage (Pohl and Chivian, 1996). The U.S. Public Health Service has concluded that toxic lead exposure costs the country tens of billions of dollars in health expenditure and productivity loss (Pohl and Chivian, 1996). This lead is primarily from indoor pollution (e.g., from paint) and from mother-to-child transfer during pregnancy. (Lead remains in the body, in bones, for example, for a long period of time.)

The remedies adopted to upgrade environmental quality during the past two decades have not always benefited all communities or all populations within a community equally. Many minority, low-income, and Native American communities have raised concerns that they suffer a disproportionate burden of health consequences due to the proximity to industrial plants and waste dumps, and from exposures to pesticides or other toxic chemicals at home and on the job. They argue that environmental programmes do not adequately address these disproportionate exposures or the underlying "environmental justice" issues (Greenwire, 1996).

Reducing overall chemical loads on North America's environment is one of the region's major concerns. The dramatic growth in the number and variety of chemical products since the Second World War has led to an increasing concern for the health of both wildlife and humans. More than 35,000 chemicals are reported to be in use in Canada today (Environment Canada, 1996d). Just how many of these are toxic is unclear. Today, one in four U.S. citizens lives within four miles of a toxic waste dumpsite (EPA, 1996c). Restoration and remediation of hundreds of thousands of contaminated ground sites will cost the United States an estimated US$100 billion to US$1 trillion over the next 30 years (NSTC, 1996). In 1991, Canadians produced an estimated 5.9 million tons of industrial hazardous wastes, most of which came from industrial sources. It is estimated that as many as 1,000 sites in Canada are contaminated by hazardous wastes (Government of Canada, 1991).

The United States is the largest producer of wastes in the world (PCSD, 1996). Per capita generation of solid waste has increased 65 per cent over the last 25 years (NSTC, 1996). Some 195 million tons of municipal waste were generated annually in 1992 and 1993; by the year 2000, total municipal waste generation is projected to reach 222 million tons per year (Government of the United States of America, 1995). Throughout North America, urban centres are having increasing problems finding sites for new sanitary landfills. Campaigns to save resources and encourage recycling or waste separation by local, regional, and national public institutions have already led to the implementation of stricter rules in certain communities. Canada is committed to a 50-per-cent waste-reduction target established

by the Canadian Council of Ministers of the Environment (Canadian Dept. of Foreign Affairs and International Trade, 1996b).

Underlying Causes

The driving forces behind North America's environmental concerns vary considerably and are undergoing important changes.

The single most important driving force in North America has been economic growth and the pattern of production and consumption that has come to be associated with it. In the last 25 years, for instance, the gross national product (GNP) of the U.S. economy increased fivefold (PCSD, 1996). The United States, with a GNP of more than US$6.4 trillion in 1994, is the world's largest economy and the largest consumer of natural resources (PCSD, 1996). The nation consumes more than 4.5 billion metric tons of materials annually to produce goods and services (PCSD, 1996).

North Americans are among the world's heaviest consumers of energy. With just 5 per cent of the world's population, the United States accounts for 25 per cent of global energy use on an annual basis (PCSD, 1996). Canada has a per capita consumption of energy similar to the U.S. (319 gigajoules per capita per year in 1993) (WRI/UNEP/UNDP/WB, 1996). These consumption patterns have an impact on global climate and could, through global warming impose severe problems in the future for drinking water supply as well as for the agricultural and forestry sector of North America's economy.

The trend towards single family households and the growing number of private cars in use (an average of one for every two people) have contributed most significantly to increasing energy consumption. In 1990, more than half the dwellings constructed in Canada were single-family homes (Government of Canada, 1991). The corresponding increase in energy demands in Canada is being tempered through energy conservation programmes, increased energy efficiency, and consumer awareness. In the United States between 1950 and 1990, there was a 400-per-cent increase in the number of vehicles in the country and a 270-per-cent increase in the number of licensed drivers. Here also, emphasis is now being placed on energy efficiency and on renewable resources.

There are signs that patterns of production and consumption may be shifting and that a "de-materialization" of GNP may occur, as the service sector expands rapidly. There is also evidence that production processes are becoming less resource-intensive even for conventional industrial products (Wernick et al., 1996). Moreover, changes seem to be taking place in the way people work and spend their leisure time. If harnessed, these changes could fundamentally alter the trade-off between economic and social welfare and environmental stewardship.

A recent survey suggests that North American attitudes to materialism are changing. For example, 83 per cent of those surveyed believe that the United States consumes too much, and 88 per cent believe that protecting the environment will require "major changes in the way we live." However, only 51 per cent agree that their own buying habits have a negative impact on the environment. (Merck, 1996). The survey also found that millions of Americans are already "downshifting," or choosing to scale back their salaries and life-styles to reflect a different set of priorities. Twenty-eight per cent of the survey respondents said that, in the last five years, they had voluntarily made changes in their lives (not including regularly scheduled retirements) that resulted in making less money (Merck, 1996).

References

Brooks, D.J. 1993. U.S. Forest in a Global Context, U.S. Forest Service.

Browner, C.M. 1996. Remarks by Carol M. Browner, U.S.-EPA Administrator, at Watershed '96. U.S. Environmental Protection Agency. June 12.

Bryant, D., et al. 1995. Coastlines at Risk: An Index of Potential Development-Related Threats to Coastal Ecosystems. World Resources Institute Indicator Brief. Washington.

Canadian Dept. of Foreign Affairs and International Trade. 1996a. Global Agenda—Canada's Foreign Policy and the Environment. Vol. 4, No. 1. Ottawa. June.

Canadian Dept. of Foreign Affairs and International Trade. 1996b. Communication to the Director, UNEP Regional Office for North America. 15 October.

CEC. 1996. CEC Discussion Papers. Unpublished. Commission for Environmental Cooperation (CEC).

CEPA. 1996. Canadian Environmental Protection Act. Part III, Chapter 8: International Air Pollution. Ottawa. (Address on World Wide Web: <http://www.ec.gc.ca/cepa/govtresp/echap08.html>.

Christopher, W. 1996. Speech by Warren Christopher, U.S. Secretary of State, on 6 April 1996 at Stanford University.

Comanor, J.M. 1994. Ecosystem Management and Its Influence on Private Forest Landowners. Joan M. Comanor, Deputy Chief, State and Private Forestry, Alaska. Presented at the SAF National Convention. September 18–22, 1994.

Environment Canada. 1996a. Science and Technology Report. Environment Canada (EC). Address on World Wide Web: <http://www.doe.ca/SciencePol/homepg.html>. March.

Environment Canada. 1996b. Achievements of the Past, Commitments to the Future. EC. Address on World Wide Web: <http://www.doe.ca/ec25/pastfuture_e.html>.

Environment Canada. 1996c. Environmental Initiatives, Invest in Science and Technology Advances. EC. Address on World Wide Web: <http://www.doe.ca/EnvironIni/index.html>.

Environment Canada. 1996d. Canada's National Environmental Indicators Series: Stratospheric Ozone Depletion; Urban Water; Toxic Contaminants in the Environment—Persistent Organochlorines. Ottawa. Address on World Wide Web: <http://199.212.18.12/folio.pgi/txt.nfo/query=/doc/>.

Environment Canada. No date. Pollution Data Branch Database. Environmental Protection Service.

Environment Canada and U.S.-EPA. 1995. The Great Lakes. An Environmental Atlas and Resource Book. 3rd edition. Government of Canada. Toronto. United States Environmental Protection Agency (U.S.-EPA) Great Lakes National Program Office. Chicago.

EOP. 1993. Environmental Quality—24th Annual Report of the Council on Environmental Quality. Executive Office of the President of the United States (EOP). U.S. Government Printing Office. Washington.

EPA. 1994. 1994 Annual Urban Air Quality Trends Report. EPA. Washington. Address on World Wide Web: <http://politicsusa.com/CVC/cafe/air_quality.html>.

EPA. 1996a. Water Indicators Project. Address on World Wide Web: <http://www.epa.gov/epahome/programs.html>

or <http://www.fsu.edu/~cpm/segip/products/perform _agree/goalsort.html>.

EPA. 1996b. The Inside Story: Indoor Air—Basic Facts. EPA. Address on World Wide Web: <http://www.medaccess.com/pollution/con_polltoc. html>.

EPA. 1996c. The New Generation of Environmental Protection: EPA's Five-Year Strategic Plan. EPA. 1996. Address on World Wide Web: <http://www.epa.gov/docs/strategic_plan/>.

EPA. 1996d. Acid Rain Program: Environmental Benefits; Allowance System. U.S.-EPA. 1996. Address at World Wide Web: <http://www.epa.gov/epahome/Programs.html>.

Government of Canada. 1996. *The State of Canada's Environment Report*. Government of Canada. Ottawa. Address on World Wide Web: <http://199.212.18.12/folio.pgi/soereng/query=★ /doc.>

Government of the United States of America. 1995. US Government Draft Interim 1995 Indicators Report, April.

Greenwire. 1996. Greenwire, The Environmental News Daily. July 16, Vol. 6, No. 52. Alexandria, Virginia.

IUCN. 1993. *1994 IUCN Red List of Threatened Animals*. World Conservation Union (IUCN). Gland, Switzerland.

Marchi, S. 1996. Speech by Sergio Marchi, Canadian Minister of the Environment. Municipal Clean Air Summit. June 4. Toronto.

Merck. 1996. Merck Family Fund: Yearning for Balance. Harwood Group. Address on World Wide Web: <http://www.futurenet.org/pfinweb/yol/b1arts/yfb. html>.

Natural Resources Canada. 1996. *The State of Canada's Forests 1995–1996*. Government of Canada. Ottawa.

Needleman, H.L., and P.J. Landrigan. 1994. Raising children toxic free. F. Strauss & Giroux. New York.

NRC. 1993. National Register of Chemicals: Pesticides in the diets of infants and children. National

Research Council (NRC). National Academy Press. Washington.

NSTC. 1996. National Environmental Technology Strategy. Address on World Wide Web: <http://vm1.hqadmin.doe.gov/nepp/ch6bx2.html>.

OTA. 1990. Neurotoxicity: Identifying and controlling poisons in the nervous system. Office of Technology Assessment. U.S. Government Printing Office. Washington.

PCSD. 1996. Sustainable America. A New Consensus for Prosperity, Opportunity, and a Healthy Environment for the Future. The President's Council on Sustainable Development. U.S. Government Printing Office. Washington.

Pohl, R.L. and E. Chivian. 1996. Human Health and the Environment: The Neglected Equation. In: *Voice of Human Services Philanthropy—Grant Scene.* Spring 1996. Grantmakers in Health. Washington.

Schewiz, B.A. and M.W. Harris. 1993. Developmental toxicology: Status of the field and contribution of the National Toxicology Program. *Environ. Health Perspect.* 100:269–282.

USDA. 1996. 1996 Farm Bill Conservation Provisions, Summary. USDA Natural Resources Conservation Service.

US-UNCED. 1992. United Nations Conference on Environment and Development, United States of America National Report.

WCMC. 1992. *Global Biodiversity Status of the Earth's Living Resources*. World Conservation Monitoring Centre (WCMC). Chapman and Hall. London.

WCMC. 1994. *Biodiversity Data Sourcebook*. World Conservation Press. Cambridge.

WCMC. 1995. Unpublished data. July.

Wernick, I.K., *et al.* 1996. Materialization and Dematerialization: Measures and Trends. *Daedalus.* Summer. 1996. Address on World Wide Web: <http://www.amacad.org/su96rel.html>.

WRI/UNEP/UNDP/WB. 1996. *World Resources 1996–97*. Oxford University Press. New York and London.

WEST ASIA

Major Environmental Concerns

The West Asia region [Bahrain, Iraq, Jordan, Kuwait, Lebanon, Oman, Qatar, Saudi Arabia, Syria, United Arab Emirates (UAE), Palestine, and Yemen] represents a diverse group of countries and territories surrounding four regional seas—the Mediterranean, the Persian Gulf, the Arabian Sea, and the Red Sea. The countries are characterized by great differences of surface area, natural resources endowment, population, income, and level of socio-economic development.

All West Asian countries are located in the arid and semi-arid zones, with more than 70 per cent of the region being arid (UNEP/WHO, 1991). The region is characterized by low, unpredictable, and variable rainfall, and by high evaporation rates. Most of the rainfall occurs during winter, with the summer lasting 5–9 months each year. There is considerable rainfall variability, making it difficult to plan for rainfed agricultural activities (UNEP/WHO, 1991).

The countries face serious problems of environmental degradation that must be addressed immediately because failure to act now will greatly compound the cost and complexity of later remedial efforts, and because environmental degradation is beginning to pose a major threat to human well-being, especially among the poor in the region.

The West Asia region has varied environmental priorities and concerns; the major ones identified by the West Asia Region (UNEP, 1996) are:

- land degradation, desertification, and deforestation;

- management of marine and coastal environments and their resources;

- development and management of water resources;

- human settlements;

- conservation of biodiversity;

- industrial pollution; and

- toxic chemicals, and hazardous and radioactive wastes.

Of these, the most pressing environmental concerns have been identified as development and management of water resources, the management of marine and coastal environments and their resources, and land degradation and desertification.

Land

Land degradation is a common problem throughout most of West Asia, resulting both from natural environmental factors and from the misuse of land. Periodic droughts along with extensive pressure from overgrazing, uncontrolled cultivation, fuelwood gathering, wind-blown soil materials, inappropriate use of irrigation water, uncontrolled urbanization, and sand encroachment have all contributed to the process of land degradation in the region (LAS/UNEP, 1992).

More than three quarters of West Asia is desert, and an increasing part of the permanent pasture areas is subject to erosion because of reduced vegetation cover (LAS/AOAD, 1995b). Additionally, much of the cropland is losing its inherent productivity due to poor agricultural practices. (See Figure 2.22.) The direct loss of agricultural land is most acute in Jordan, Iraq, Lebanon, the Syrian Arab Republic, and Yemen, where fertile land is scarce and concentrated in the narrow coastal strip and river valleys (ESCWA, 1995). In the irrigated areas close to the main urban centres in Jordan, Iraq, Yemen, Lebanon, and the Syrian Arab Republic, established agricultural land is being lost to alternative uses, including urbanization, industrialization, and transport infrastructure. To compensate for this, new land is being brought into production through reclamation. The productivity of the reclaimed land, however, is in many cases only a fraction of the old, and new land is being brought into production more slowly than old land is being lost.

In Lebanon, land degradation is most acute on fragile steeplands with extensive deforestation and soil erosion (Government of Lebanon, 1996).

Overgrazing in desert areas is a major cause of plant cover loss, particularly in the northern regions of Saudi Arabia and the southern parts of Oman. Countries such as Bahrain have also lost substantial vegetation cover as a result of urbanization (UNEP/ESCWA, 1991a). The coastal plains of Oman have suffered a particularly severe loss of vegetation as a result of overgrazing, off-road vehicles, construction, and tourist activities (UNEP/ESCWA 1991).

Dry land salinity, mainly due to high evaporation, is another serious problem, particularly in the low-lying parts of West Asia. In Iraq, for example, salinity and waterlogging are problems in more than 50 percent of the lower Rafidain Plains (El-Hinnawi, 1993).

Fragile, marginal lands cover extensive areas in West Asia and constitute an important resource for animal husbandry. Rapid change in life-styles and the introduction of modern production systems in such areas have triggered an increasing imbalance between the exploitation of such areas and their carrying capacity. This has led to increasing land degradation and desertification, with negative impacts on traditional life-styles of nomads and desert inhabitants (UNEP, 1991). Existing statistics for Yemen show that the average annual rate of cultivated land abandoned due to soil degradation has increased from 0.6 per cent in 1970–80 to about 7 per cent in 1980–84 (UNEP, 1991).

Desertification and land degradation, including soil erosion, have implications for the region's food security. West Asia had a food gap estimated at US$10.7 billion in 1993, up nearly 4 per cent from the previous year (FAO/ESCWA, 1994). With increased desertification coupled with the high population growth rates, this food gap will increase dramatically in the future, along with the high levels

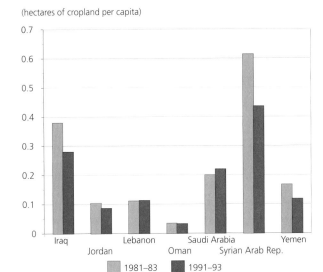

(hectares of cropland per capita)

1981–83   1991–93

Figure 2.22. Loss of cropland in selected West Asian countries, 1981–83 and 1991–93.

Source: UN (1994a).
Note: Cropland includes land under temporary and permanent crops, temporary meadows, market and kitchen gardens, and temporary fallow. Permanent crops are those that do not need to be replanted after each harvest, such as cocoa, coffee, fruit, rubber, and vines. It excludes land used to grow trees for wood or timber.

of dependency on food imports for most countries of the region (FAO/ESCWA, 1994).

Biodiversity

Indigenous plant and animal life in West Asia is under increasing threat due to the impact of development (LAS/UNEP, 1992). Overgrazing and mismanagement of rangelands have led to the loss of natural plant cover. Deforestation is now a major concern in the highlands of Yemen, Oman, and Jordan. Overfishing, pollution, and destruction of habitat (from land reclamation and filling in of wetlands) have all had a negative impact on marine biodiversity. As a result, declining fish and shrimp harvests have become a common feature in the Persian Gulf region (ROPME/IMO, 1996).

The depletion of underground water levels on the western side of the Gulf is leading to the loss of a unique ecosystem of natural fresh-water springs, affecting large numbers of plants and animals. This ecosystem was once widely distributed in the eastern province of Saudi Arabia and in Bahrain (UNEP, 1996). The Azraq Oasis in Jordan was declared a wetland under the RAMSAR Convention because it was endangered due to the overextraction of ground water. The overextraction is not only depleting the ground water, it is leading to increased salinity, which in turn negatively affects wildlife and plant species in the area.

In West Asia, wildlife such as fallow deer, ostrich, wild goat, and antelope have been threatened with extinction due to indiscriminate hunting. The threat to wildlife is worsened through the destruction of their habitats, particularly deforestation. The region lost 11 per cent of its remaining natural forest during the 1980s, and natural forest cover now averages less than 1 per cent of the total land area (FAO, 1995b).

On the whole, there is little information on species, and good data are generally limited to certain mammals and birds. Species inventories are currently being undertaken in a number of countries in the region [such as Jordan and some Gulf Cooperation Council (GCC) countries].

Water

Water availability in the West Asia region depends on the physiographical and hydrogeological setting. Iraq, the Syrian Arab Republic, and Lebanon have relatively dependable surface water sources in the form of rivers and springs. (See Table 2.12.) This supply is supplemented through extraction from ground-water reserves in Jordan, Lebanon, the Syrian Arab Republic, and Palestine. Jordan is faced with water deficits, with demand outstripping supply. Palestine, with limited surface water and renewable ground-water reserves, also faces problems in meeting water needs, particularly in view of the unbalanced use of available water resources. The Euphrates and Tigris rivers in Iraq and the Syrian Arab Republic, the Orients and Latani rivers in Jordan and the Syrian Arab Republic, and the lower Jordan River in Jordan represent major water sources for domestic, industrial, and agricultural requirements within these countries.

In contrast, the GCC countries and Yemen are characterized by a harsh desert environment devoid of rivers and lakes. The water resources consist of limited quantities of runoff resulting from flash floods,

ground water in the alluvial aquifers, and extensive ground-water reserves in deep sedimentary formations. Some of these countries also rely on non-conventional water sources such as desalinization of sea and brackish water and limited use of renovated wastewater. Ground water in the shallow aquifers in Bahrain, Kuwait, Oman, Qatar, Saudi Arabia, the United Arab Emirates, and Yemen is the only renewable water source in these countries.

Water requirements for all sectors in Iraq are met mainly from river flow, while Jordan, Lebanon, the Syrian Arab Republic, and Palestine use ground water to satisfy water demand. The major problem associated with the management of renewable water, particularly rivers, is its transboundary nature. The lack of formal agreements for sharing rivers such as the Euphrates have created shortcomings in the efficient utilization of water. The problem is also apparent for ground-water resources, with the Palestinian territories, for example, unable to use the totality of their renewable resources.

Total water demand for agriculture, industrial, and domestic purposes in West Asia in 1990 was about 82 billion cubic metres. (See Table 2.13.) Agriculture accounts for the bulk of water use, followed by the industrial sector. The agricultural sector uses approximately 68 billion cubic metres of water, while the water demand for industrial activities in the region reached 6 billion cubic metres. Domestic water demand accounts for about 7.7 billion cubic metres (ESCWA, 1995).

Human water consumption per capita in the region, including for domestic, agricultural, and industrial uses, is now very high, ranging from 300 to 1,500 litres per day (UNEP/WHO, 1991). Rapidly rising incomes in some countries, with the resultant increase in living standards, and water losses in the network have led to higher per capita water consumption. Intensive agriculture under arid conditions is also demanding an ever-increasing quantity of water.

Based on current trends, water shortage is expected to increase as a result of increased demand and limited renewable supplies in most West Asian countries. Current water resources such as perennial surface water, renewable ground water, desali-

Table 2.12

Water Resources in the West Asia Region

Country	Population (millions)[a] 1994	Conventional Water Resources (million cubic metres)		Non-Conventional Water Resources (million cubic metres)		Total (million cubic metres)
		Surface Water[b]	Ground Water[c]	Desalinization	Wastewater Reuse	
Bahrain	0.55	0.20	90.00	75.00	9.50	174.70
Iraq	19.09	76,880.00	1,500.00	7.40	n.a.	78,387.40
Jordan	4.06	660.00	275.00	2.50	52.00	989.50
Kuwait	1.62	0.10	182.00	240.00	83.00	505.10
Lebanon	3.48	2,500.00	12,000.00	1.70	n.a.	14,501.70
Oman	2.05	918.00	10,500.00	32.00	25.00	11,475.00
Qatar	0.53	1.35	2,500.00	92.00	25.00	2,618.35
Saudi Arabia	18.18	2,230.00	84,000.00	795.00	217.00	87,242.00
Syrian Arab Republic	13.73	22,688.00	3,000.00	2.00	50.00	25,740.00
United Arab Emirates	2.15	125.00	20,000.00	385.00	110.00	20,620.00
West Bank and Gaza (Palestine)	2.24	30.00	150.00	n.a.	n.a.	180.00
Yemen	13.47	2,000.00	13,500.00	9.00	9.10	15,518.10

Sources: Compiled and provided by the United Nations Economic and Social Commission for Western Asia (ESCWA) Secretariat from Country Papers and International Sources, 1994 and 1995.

Notes:
a. Demographic and related Socio-Economic Data Sheets for the Countries of ESCWA, No. 8, 1995.
b. The flow of the Tigris and Euphrates rivers will be reduced by upstream abstraction in Turkey.
c. Shallow aquifer ground-water reserve with varying water quality.
n.a. = Information not available.

nization, and reclaimed wastewater are insufficient to meet expected demand.

On the basis of the past experiences of the moderately developed countries in arid zones, renewable fresh-water resources of 1,000 cubic metres per capita per year have been proposed as an approximate benchmark below which most countries are likely to experience chronic water scarcity on a scale sufficient to impede development and harm human health (WRI/UNEP/UNDP/WB, 1996). By this measure, many countries in West Asia suffer from water scarcity, with Bahrain having less than 18 per cent of the minimum threshold (WRI/UNEP/UNDP/WB, 1996). Jordan, Kuwait, Qatar, Saudi Arabia, the UAE, and Yemen all have water resources below 1,000 cubic metres per capita per year (WRI/UNEP/UNDP/WB, 1996).

Existing wastewater treatment facilities face difficulties in handling the ever-increasing volumes of wastewater generated by higher water consumption and urbanization. Wastewater discharge from major urban centres is polluting shallow alluvial aquifers and coastlines. The quality of drinking water and sanitation services in most West Asian countries is poor, although it is improving in some cases. Efforts to achieve water quality targets established for urban areas are encouraging, but rural communities remain inadequately serviced in terms of safe drinking water, sanitation facilities, and accessibility. (See Figure 2.23.)

Poor sanitation and sewage treatment systems, in addition to industrial wastes, are increasingly affecting water quality in the region. Access to safe drinking water and sanitation services in the cities of West Asia is relatively good. However, only 20 per cent of urban wastewater is treated (World Bank, 1994). Concentrated industrial development is leading to pollution problems for ground and surface waters in certain areas (UNEP/WHO, 1991).

In some areas, irrigation is resulting in salinization and degradation of soils. Overexploitation of ground-water resources is therefore a major concern in the region, causing a decline in ground-water levels as well as a deterioration of water quality.

Water salinity is also a concern throughout the region. With the dropping of water tables due to excess harvesting of ground water, salt-water intru-

Table 2.13
Water Demand for West Asia Region, 1990

Country	Sectoral Withdrawals (million cubic metres)			Total Demand (million cubic metres)
	Domestic	Agriculture	Industrial	
Bahrain	86	120	17	223
Iraq	3,800	40,000	5,600	49,400
Jordan	190	650	43	883
Kuwait	295	80	8	383
Lebanon	310	750	60	1,120
Oman	81	1,150	5	1,236
Qatar	76	109	9	194
Saudi Arabia	1,508	14,600	192	16,300
Syrian Arab Republic	650	6,930	146	7,726
United Arab Emirates	513	950	27	1,490
West Bank and Gaza (Palestine)	78	140	7	225
Yemen	168	2,700	31	2,899
Total	**7,755**	**68,179**	**6,145**	**82,079**

Sources: Compiled and provided by the United Nations Economic and Social Commission for Western Asia (ESCWA) Secretariat from Country Papers and International Sources, 1994 and 1995.

sion becomes a serious problem. Sea-water intrusion into the aquifers of Bahrain, Oman (Batenah Plain), and UAE is particularly severe. Total soluble salts measured in the ground water at different sites in the United Arab Emirates exceeded 10,000–20,000 milligrams per litre (UNEP/ESCWA, 1991b). It is estimated that the saline interface between sea and ground waters advances at the rate of 75–130 metres a year in Bahrain (UNEP/ESCWA, 1991a).

The region is thus characterized by the anomaly of high per capita consumption and very limited fresh-water resources (UNEP/WHO, 1991). The increasing pressure on all the water resources of the region, in terms of quality and quantity, combined with the increasing demand for water, will lead to serious water shortages in the near future.

Marine and Coastal Environments

Most of the GCC subregional population resides along the coast, with population densities ranging from 605 (Oman) to 5,700 (Kuwait) persons per square kilometre (UNDP, 1993). In addition, for many countries in West Asia, the marine environment is an important source of development. Besides offshore oil resources and fisheries, the coastal areas in some countries constitute important sites for industries and tourism. These areas and marine environments have come under increasing pressure, and the degradation of the ecosystem has adversely

affected both fisheries and tourism, one of the largest sources of foreign exchange revenue for several countries (LAS/UNEP, 1992; World Bank, 1994).

Oil pollution in the region is very pronounced. In addition to the danger of oil spills from ship and pipeline accidents, chronic pollution occurs from disposal at sea of oil-contaminated ballast water and dirty bilge, sludge, and slop oil. Some 1.2 million barrels of oil are spilled into the Persian Gulf annually (ROPME/IMO, 1996). The Gulf and Red Sea ecosystems are particularly vulnerable to oil pollution: the low rate at which sea water is flushed through these systems suggests that natural cleansing processes are slow (ESCWA, 1991). These problems are compounded in many countries by the lack of adequate port facilities for handling wastes from oil tanks and for cleaning up oil spills (ESCWA, 1991).

The Red Sea and the Kuwait/Oman areas probably receive more oil pollution than anywhere else in the world (GESAMP, 1990). At the same time, the Mediterranean accounts for 17 per cent of global marine oil pollution, even though it constitutes only 0.7 per cent of the global water surface (ESCWA, 1991). It has been estimated that in 1986 alone, nearly 3 billion tons of wastes (mostly ballast waters) were discharged into the Persian Gulf (ESCWA, 1991).

Fisheries are one of the most important resources in the GCC countries, particularly in the

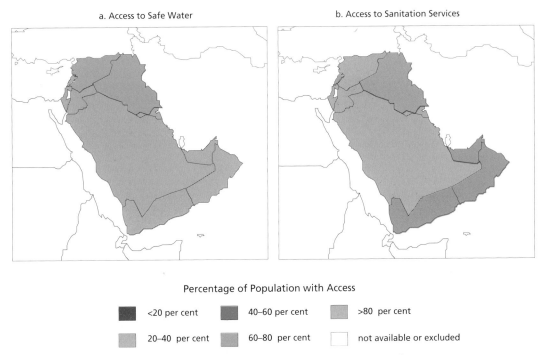

a. Access to Safe Water

b. Access to Sanitation Services

Percentage of Population with Access

<20 per cent

40–60 per cent

>80 per cent

20–40 per cent

60–80 per cent

not available or excluded

Figure 2.23. Access to safe water and sanitation services in West Asia.

Source: UNCHS (Habitat) (1996).

Notes: *Access to safe water:* Proportion of the population with access to an adequate amount of safe drinking water located within a convenient distance from the user's dwelling. *Access to sanitation services:* Proportion of the population with access to a sanitary facility for human extreta disposal in the dwelling or located within a convenient distance from the user's dwelling. *Access, sanitary facility,* and *convenient distance* are defined at the country level.

UAE and Oman, with annual fish production in the region of 298,000 tons in 1994 (LAS, 1995c). There has been a sharp decline in fish harvests in some countries over the past few years due to overexploitation and inadequate fisheries management, land reclamation and coastal dredging, excessive trawling, and increased marine pollution from waste discharge and oil pollution (UNEP, 1990; ROPME/IMO, 1996). (See Figure 2.24.) Mangroves and associated intertidal areas and marshes are under increasing threat in Bahrain and Saudi Arabia and are rapidly declining in other GCC countries as a result of infilling and reclamation. The geographic concentration of industrial complexes in coastal and estuarine areas around the Arabian Peninsula means that many pollutants are deposited directly into the sea (UNEP/WHO, 1991).

In summary, the coastal zone is an invaluable economic resource for development and tourism. It is regarded, however, as having one of the most fragile and endangered ecosystems in the world and is seriously affected by severe sources of pollution, by stress through deliberate and accidental oil spills, by sewage and industrial wastewater discharges, and by commercial shipping.

Urban and Industrial Environments

In the past two decades, the cities of West Asia have seen the most radical transformation ever experienced. The urban growth rate in the region was 4.2 per cent between 1990 and 1995 (UN, 1994b). The high rate of growth has been fuelled by massive rural to urban migration, prompted by rural poverty and degradation of agricultural land, itself a consequence of overcultivation and overgrazing and induced by a general increase in the region's population. Almost 70 per cent of the population is estimated to be living in urban areas (UN, 1994c). (See Table 2.14.) This unplanned migration has caused deterioration of the environment in urban areas (LAS/UNEP, 1992). It has also caused a marked deterioration of natural resources in rural areas due to increasing neglect of agricultural lands (LAS/UNEP, 1992).

Historically, cities have grown alongside the fertile lands that supported them and consequently

(per cent change in marine catch)

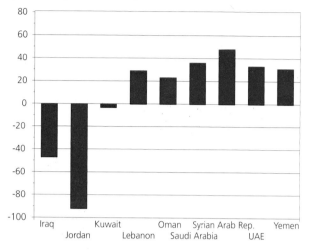

Figure 2.24. Percent change in average annual marine catch from 1981–83 to 1991–93.

Source: FAO (1995a).
Note: Marine catch data refer to marine and fresh-water fish killed, caught, trapped, collected, bred, or cultivated for commercial, industrial, and subsistence use. Crustaceans and molluscs are included. Base figures used to calculate percentages are national fish catch totals averaged over a three-year period.

have expanded onto them. Prime agricultural land has therefore had to support structures and road networks in a region where fertile agricultural land is very scarce.

The most pressing environmental problem facing big cities in the region relates to waste management. As populations grow at an unsustainable rate, sewerage and other waste disposal systems are unable to cope with the volume, and environmental degradation sets in. The crowding of the poor in communities lacking infrastructure and decent housing leads to an accumulation of waste, which leads to contamination and attendant health hazards.

The region also faces urban air pollution problems. Industries owned or subsidized by the public sector have little access or incentive to adopt cleaner technologies. Protective trade regimes and the lack of environmental regulations have permitted the survival of old, highly polluting industries. Obsolete vehicle engine technology, low fuel efficiency, leaded gasoline, and high sulphur fuels have exacerbated urban air pollution (World Bank, 1994). Changes, however, are occurring. In Oman, for example, new industries are obliged to comply with

environmental standards before they are established (UNEP, 1996).

Industry plays an increasing role in social and economic development in West Asia and also constitutes a major source of pollution in the region. Much of the industry is highly concentrated in few locations in most countries in the region and has led to areas of potentially severe industrial pollution of surface and ground-water bodies. Uncontrolled discharge of industrial effluents, undetected seepage of toxic substances into aquifers, and the unprotected dumping of hazardous wastes are increasing as rapidly as industry expands (UNEP/WHO, 1991).

There is serious potential environmental degradation arising from toxic chemicals and hazardous and radioactive wastes. The phosphate industry, for example, is associated with environmental problems such as the contamination of water as a result of wastewater from the washing of phosphates. This could potentially contaminate ground water. Gypsum, a by-product of the fertilizer industry, contains radioactive elements that affect ground water, as well as harmful heavy metals such as cadmium. In Jordan, phosphate residue is reported to cover up to 60 per cent of the total area (Tell, 1996).

The potential risks of radioactive waste resulting from armed conflict in the area cannot be underrated. Possible accidental radioactive leakage from nuclear reactors in the region, such as from the Daimora reactor in Jordan, could have serious regional environmental impacts (Tell, 1996).

Pesticide and herbicide use needs to be monitored because pesticide disposal is leading to edible-product contamination. Pesticide imports need to be controlled and should satisfy specified standards and meet the best technology standards.

Underlying Causes

Social

West Asia has one of the highest rates of population growth in the world, exceeding 3 per cent a year in most countries during the period 1990–95; the growth rate ranges from 2 per cent in Lebanon to

3.6 per cent in Oman (UN, 1994b). The limited arable land of the region is suffering from intense development due to population expansion. The human pressure on land is noticeable in Jordan, Iraq, the Syrian Arab Republic, and Yemen. Irrigated land is being cultivated all year round, with increasing applications of water, fertilizer, and pesticides. At the same time, large areas of fertile land are being taken out of production to meet urban, transport, and industrial needs, while land of low productivity is being overused as herds overgraze rangelands. Poorer farmers cultivate marginal land with low rainfall without adequate fallowing or fertilizer application. Forest products, particularly in Iraq, Lebanon, and Yemen, are harvested at rates that exceed the annual growth rate.

The increased population and agricultural activity have also raised water demand in the region, as noted earlier. This has prompted an overexploitation of ground water leading to salinization and destruction of habitats for plants and animals.

Political instability and armed conflict in the region have led to population movements, which introduce further pressures on cities and countries. The refugees and returnees in the aftermath of the Gulf War converged on the major cities of Jordan, for example, stressing the infrastructure and leading to environmental degradation.

Other direct environmental consequences are the air pollution arising from fires in the oil fields. In the Gulf areas, about 1.5 million barrels of oil were spilled during the conflict (ESCWA, 1991). The slow flushing process in the Persian Gulf greatly exacerbated cleanup problems, affecting the marine and coastal environment and the resources there.

Poverty plays a role in the region with regard to environmental degradation, especially in the cities where the poor are crowded in settlements on the periphery of cities with inadequate infrastructures.

Economic

Industrial development is progressively playing a key role in the economic development of West Asia. Highly mechanized and intensive agricultural production aimed at high economic returns means the

Table 2.14
Urban Growth Rates for West Asian Countries in 1980–85 and 1990–95

Country/Territory	1980–85	1990–95
Bahrain	82.30	83.60
Gaza Strip	91.25	77.95
Iraq	67.15	73.20
Jordan	62.00	69.75
Kuwait	92.00	96.40
Lebanon	76.25	85.50
Oman	8.40	12.10
Qatar	86.75	90.65
Saudi Arabia	69.90	78.75
Syria	47.55	51.30
United Arab Emirates	74.20	82.45
Yemen	22.30	31.25

Source: UN (1994).

use of pesticides and fertilizers that get into the food chain and also pollute rivers and marine and coastal areas.

Oil production is by far the most important industry in the Persian Gulf, with the economy of almost all countries being oil-based. Oil and gas exploration, refining, petrochemicals industries, and oil transportation all affect the environment. There are about 34 offshore oil and gas fields, and more than 800 producing offshore wells (ESCWA, 1991). Thousands of kilometres of underwater pipelines connect these wells to shore facilities and terminals. The hazards to marine and coastal environments are greatest from offshore activities, but land production of oil also poses a threat from the disposal of oily sludges, which are often deposited near or directly into the sea. By quantity, these sludges present the largest solid waste problem in the Persian Gulf (ESCWA, 1991).

Institutional

The development of policies and institutions to monitor and protect the environment has not kept pace with economic growth in the region. For example, most surface water comes from rivers shared among member and non-member countries. Lack of formal agreements for sharing the flow of the Euphrates and Tigris rivers could create conflict in the future. This is, however, now receiving appropriate attention at both the national and regional level.

References

ESCWA. 1991. Discussion paper on general planning, marine and coastal resources, and urbanisation and human settlements. United Nations Economic and Social Commission for Western Asia. Arab Ministerial Conference on Environment and Development. 10–12 September. Cairo.

ESCWA. 1995. Expert group meeting on the implications of Agenda 21 for integrated water management in the ESCWA region. 2–5 October. Amman.

El-Hinnawi, E. 1993. Population, Environment, and Development in the Arab World. Paper presented to the Arab Population Conference, Amman. United Nations Economic and Social Commission for Western Asia (ESCWA). 4–6 April.

FAO. 1995a. *FISHSTAT-PC*. Food and Agriculture Organization of the United Nations (FAO). Rome.

FAO. 1995b. *Forest Resource Assessment 1990*, Forestry Paper 124. Rome.

FAO/ESCWA. 1994. Analysis of recent developments in the agricultural sector of the ESCWA region (in Arabic).

GESAMP. 1990. *The State of the Marine Environment*. IMO/FAO/UNESCO/WMO/WHO/IAEA/UN/ UNEP Joint Group of Experts on the Scientific Aspects of Marine Pollution. Blackwell, London.

Government of Lebanon. 1996. Framework Environment Strategy for Lebanon.

LAS/AOAD. 1995a. Deteriorated rangelands in the Arab region and the projects recommended for development. League of Arab States (LAS) and Arab Organisation for Agricultural Development (AOAD). Khartoum (in Arabic).

LAS/AOAD. 1995b. Improvement of productivity of irrigated lands in Arab countries. Regional project document. Khartoum (in Arabic).

LAS/AOAD. 1995c. *Arab Agricultural Statistics Yearbook*. Khartoum.

LAS/UNEP. 1992. The Arab Programmes for Sustainable Development, adopted by the Council of Arab Ministers Responsible for the Environment (CAMRE). United Nations Environment Programme (UNEP). October.

ROPME and IMO. 1996. The effect of oil on the marine environment—An overview. Regional Organisation for the Protection of the Marine Environment (ROPME) and International Maritime Organization (IMO). Symposium on MARPOL 73/78, 28–29 February. Kuwait.

Tell, S. 1996. Personal Communication with UNEP.

UN. 1994a. *Interpolated National Populations (The 1994 Revision)*. United Nations (UN) Population Division. New York.

UN. 1994b. *The State of World Population 1994*. United Nations (UN) Population Fund. New York.

UN. 1994c. *World Urbanization Prospects (The 1994 Revision)*. United Nations (UN) Population Division. New York.

UNCHS (Habitat). 1996. Habitat Atlas: Graphic Presentation of Basic Human Settlement Statistics. UNCHS. Nairobi.

UNDP. 1993. *Human Development Report*. UNDP. New York.

UNEP. 1990. State of the Marine Environment in the ROPME Sea Area. UNEP Regional Seas Reports and Studies No. 112 (Rev. 1). Prepared with OIC and FAO by O. Linden *et al*. UNEP Nairobi.

UNEP. 1991. Status of Desertification and Implementation of the United Nations Plan of Action to Combat Desertification. Nairobi.

UNEP. 1996. Report of the Regional Consultations held for UNEP's first Global Environment Outlook. Nairobi.

UNEP/ESCWA. 1991a. The National Plan of Action to Combat Desertification in Bahrain. UNEP. Bahrain.

UNEP/ESCWA. 1991b. The National Plan to Combat Desertification in the United Arab Emirates. UNEP. Bahrain.

UNEP/ESCWA. 1992. The National Plan of Action to Combat Desertification in the Sultanate of Oman. UNEP. Bahrain.

UNEP/WHO. 1991. *Water Quality: Progress in the Implementation of the Mar del Plata Action Plan and a Strategy for the 1990s*. Earthwatch GEMS.UNEP and World Health Organization (WHO). Nairobi.

World Bank. 1994. Forging a partnership for environmental action: An environmental strategy toward sustainable development in the Middle East and North Africa. December.

WRI/UNEP/UNDP/WB. 1996. *World Resources 1996–97*. World Resources Institute (WRI)/UNEP/UNDP/World Bank. Oxford University Press. New York.

POLAR REGIONS

THE ARCTIC

There is no single definition for delineating the Arctic. Geographers often use the Arctic Circle at a latitude of 66°33'N. Climatologists define the Arctic as a climatic region often using the 10° July isotherm as the boundary. Ecologists use boundaries determined by differences in animal and plant communities, such as the treeline that marks the boundary between taiga forest and tundra (Stonehouse, 1989). The Arctic region typically includes the northern parts of Canada, Finland, Norway, Russia, Sweden, the United States (Alaska), and the whole of Greenland and Iceland. In contrast to the Antarctic, the most northern parts of the Arctic are dominated by the large and deep Arctic Ocean, surrounded by shallow shelves that border the continental masses of North America and Eurasia.

In total, the land mass amounts to 14.8 million square kilometres (CAFF, 1996a), and the Arctic marine area covers approximately 20 million square kilometres (AMAP, personal communication, 1996). Maximum sea ice covers an area of approximately 23 million square kilometres in March and a minimum area of 8 million square kilometres in September (EEA/NPI, 1996).

As with the Antarctic, the Arctic environment is inextricably linked with global climate and sea level. Change in the global climate could have a profound impact on Arctic terrestrial and marine systems. One possible scenario of the impact of climate change in the region is that global warming would decrease snow and ice cover and hence reduce albedo and increase solar energy absorption, leading to faster warming of the region. The ocean's ability to trap carbon dioxide from the atmosphere is reduced when the waters become warmer. In addition, methane and other greenhouse gases trapped in the permafrost may be re-

leased as ice melts. The melting of glaciers would also contribute to sea level rise; recent work suggests that the Greenland ice sheet has made a positive contribution to the sea level rise of 10–25 centimetres observed over the last 100 years (IPCC, 1996).

The relatively pristine Arctic region is threatened by human activities in a number of ways. This large area of sea and sparsely populated land has been perceived as an unlimited resource open for exploitation as well as for the dumping of waste. Arctic areas have been inhabited by humans since the end of the last Ice Age, but population densities have always been low (EEA/NPI, 1996). During most of history the human influence has been limited to local fishing, hunting and gathering, simple agriculture, and pastoralism—widespread but not extensively damaging. The more recent human activities in the region include exploiting ocean fisheries, the forest industry, mining, metallurgic industry, petroleum exploration, tourism, and military activity (EEA/NPI, 1996). Furthermore, the changing life-styles of the indigenous inhabitants, infrastructure development, urbanization, and local waste problems are creating additional pressures. These human activities, together with long-range transported pollutants, threaten many of the natural species and habitats of the Arctic.

Major Environmental Concerns

Land Degradation in the Tundra

The mainland of the Arctic is dominated by tundra with taiga, or boreal forest, in the southern parts of the region. Other major land cover types include alpine and high mountain areas, broad-leaved forests in coastal areas and valleys, as well as marshes and glaciers.

The tundra are the vast treeless plains of the Arctic. Due to low temperatures, permafrost, low bacterial activity, and almost complete lack of invertebrate soil fauna, biological material is decomposed slowly in tundra areas. Nutrients are thus not readily available for new plant growth. The result is low production, slow plant growth, and slow revegetation where vegetation has been damaged or removed (EEA/NPI, 1996).

The natural factor that most strongly determines the landscape character in the far north is permafrost. Where there is continuous permafrost, the ground is frozen up to a depth of 400 metres. During the summer, melting only occurs to a depth of about 1 metre, which creates a poorly drained often marshy landscape intersected by dry ridges (EEA/NPI 1996).

The low production of the terrestrial ecosystems makes the Arctic tundra particularly sensitive to land degradation and erosion. Annual melting of the topsoil above the permafrost layer combined with damage to the vegetation cover by human activities can lead to erosion. This process is further exacerbated by slow vegetation regrowth. In northern Scandinavia, herding of reindeers has also led to overgrazing and subsequent erosion. Sulphur dioxide emissions from nickel smelters have also led to vegetation damage and subsequent erosion, as, for example, on the western part of the Kola Peninsula (Tommervik *et al.,* 1995).

Forests

The taiga is a zone of coniferous forest encircling the northern hemisphere south of the permafrost line. It represents an important commercial resource in the Russian Federation, Finland, and Sweden. The plant and animal species composition is relatively uniform throughout the taiga. The taiga forest basically consists of one canopy layer with an undervegetation of dwarf shrubs, mainly of the heather family, crowberry, and mosses and lichens. Broad-leaved deciduous forests are found in the areas of warmer and more oceanic climates. A characteristic feature of the boreal zone is the formation of peatlands (bogs), which develop in wet areas due to poor drainage and incomplete decomposition of plant material. Iceland had large forests before the arrival of the first settlers in the early Middle Ages. Gradual but steady deforestation and extensive sheep and horse herding have since practically cleared the entire island of forests. In the Russian Federation, large-scale clear cutting and plantation forest monoculture are environmental concerns. Landscapes are altered, the local climate is affected, the natural diversity of the forests is disrupted, and bogs and marshes are often drained in the process of planting new forest stands. The new stands are usually single species of uniform age (EEA/NPI, 1996).

Biodiversity

A relatively small number of terrestrial species is able to survive the strong climatic contrasts of the Arctic year, characterized by long, cold, dark winters and short, light summers. Only a few species live in the tundra areas through the winter. Other species migrate into the region for the summer season only.

Arctic plants generally have reduced exposed leaf areas (needles or small narrow leaves) or shed their leaves during winter to increase survival when available moisture is very low. In the High Arctic, most plants have developed low and creeping structures more suitable for survival where cold, drying, and damaging winds are prevalent. Bowl-shaped flowers and hairy stems are also common because these features help to capture and retain heat from the sun. In general, the plants have low growth rates, low production capacities, inefficient sexual production, and simple distribution mechanisms. Growth and production decreases from south to north (EEA/NPI, 1996).

Animals face many of the same challenges for surviving in the Arctic. Whether living permanently in the region or visiting for parts of the year, the animals of the Arctic have special adaptations. Both marine and terrestrial mammals have large body-volume-to-surface ratios and store considerable amounts of fat (for example, as in seals, whales, and polar bears). The mammals, as well as birds, are quite mobile with some exceptions such as the Svalbard reindeer, which are extremely sedentary. Many of the animals are long-lived, reproducing often but having few young at a time. This increases the chances of successful reproduction in a situation of high mortality of the young (EEA/NPI, 1996).

Because of the harsh climatic conditions on land, the biodiversity of the region is relatively poor. However, several interesting and important species are endemic or strongly influence the terrestrial ecosystems. These include, for example, the lemming and other rodents, reindeer species, arctic fox, wolverine, wolf, lynx, and brown and polar bears. Some of these species are endangered. In addition, some of the world's largest populations of sea birds are found in the Arctic.

Although listings of Arctic species may appear substantial, the number of species in any given area is usually limited. The diversity and complexity of food webs increase as arctic ecosystems grade into more temperate ecosystems. Because of the relatively low diversity, some food chains are short and simple. An example is the lichen–caribou–wolf chain in Arctic Canada. This food chain is of particular concern as a potential pathway of contaminants because of the importance of caribou and reindeer as a traditional food source for Northerners.

By comparison, the marine environment is far more productive. The North Atlantic waters are among the most productive areas of the world due to the inflow of warmer, nutrient-rich water from the southern Atlantic, the influx of Arctic water bringing nutrient-rich water from ice-covered areas, and considerable vertical blending on the banks in the shallow waters (EEA/NPI, 1996). The nutrient-rich water masses, together with 24-hour sunlight in the summer, support a large production of biomass, such as algae, that are consumed by higher trophic animals and eventually by top predators, including humans.

The region's marine ecosystems are characterized by large stocks of a few key plankton, crustacean, and fish species as well as sea birds and large sea mammals. Capelin, cod, and herring are the largest fish stocks (EEA/NPI, 1996). High natural fluctuations in fish stocks and other species are typical of the region. The more stable benthic (sea bed) ecosystems are rich in species. For example, the Barents Sea and adjacent areas contain 2,000 species of benthic animals, constituting 80–90 per cent of the total number of marine animal species in the area (EEA/NPI, 1996).

Fishing, whaling, and other sea mammal hunting are well-known examples of overexploitation of Arctic resources. Massive hunting of the marine mammals started in the early 1600s. The bowhead whale was practically driven to extinction between 1600 and 1700; the blue whale, fin whale, humpback whale, and sei whale populations were drastically reduced between the mid-1800s and 1920; and the smaller minke whale has been exploited from the 1930s. Walrus and harp and hooded seals were hunted from the early 1800s up to the 1980s. By the 1900s, the survival of the popular polar bear was dangerously threatened throughout the European Arctic area. In the past three decades, overfishing and the decline of certain fish stocks have led to conflicts among nations regarding access and management of resources.

All countries in the region have established protected areas. As of 1995, there were 285 such areas. (See Figure 2.25.) They covered approximately 2.1 million square kilometres, or a little over 14 per cent of the Arctic area (CAFF, 1996b). Some of the first nature protection areas of the Arctic were established in Sweden and Alaska in 1909. The largest protected area is the Northeast Greenland National Park (972,000 square kilometres). This park, which is mainly ice cap, makes up about half of the protected area total. The majority of the protected areas cover terrestrial ecosystems; the marine areas are poorly represented.

Marine and Ice Edge Ecosystems

Ice edges and associated waters are key areas of productivity in all regions of the Arctic (Smith and Sakshaug, 1990). Melting ice causes an increase in the stability of the water column, which allows phytoplankton to be retained (phytoplankton bloom) in a defined active photosynthetic layer at the ice edge (Marshall, 1957). Contaminants that

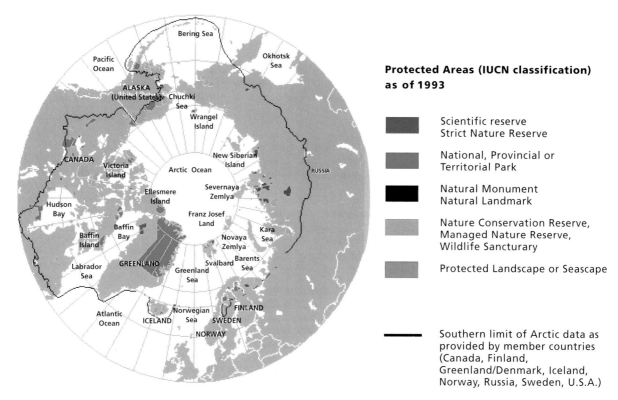

Protected Areas (IUCN classification) as of 1993

- Scientific reserve Strict Nature Reserve
- National, Provincial or Territorial Park
- Natural Monument Natural Landmark
- Nature Conservation Reserve, Managed Nature Reserve, Wildlife Sancturary
- Protected Landscape or Seascape

Southern limit of Arctic data as provided by member countries (Canada, Finland, Greenland/Denmark, Iceland, Norway, Russia, Sweden, U.S.A.)

Figure 2.25. Map of protected areas in the Arctic region.

Source: CAFF (1996b).

accumulate on the sea ice surface are released to sea surface waters when the ice melts. Most melting and subsequent particle/contaminant release occurs in the marginal ice zone where biological activity is concentrated in surface waters. Fauna associated with the ice edge form an important pathway for contaminants to enter the food web between primary producers and fish, sea birds, and mammals (Futsaeter *et al.*, 1991).

Ozone Depletion

Although the ozone layer over the Arctic has been depleted recently, there have been no "holes in the ozone layer" comparable to those over the Antarctic region. In the spring of 1995, however, stratospheric ozone concentrations over Europe were 10–12 per cent lower than in the mid-1970s, and over North America, 5–10 per cent lower. From January to March 1995, the ozone layer was reduced by as much as 35 per cent over Russian Siberia (SFT, 1996). The Arctic winter in 1994–95 was exceptionally cold, and ozone concentrations

were 20–30 per cent below normal. The winter of 1995–96 was even colder. This unexpected recurrence of cold winter temperatures may in itself be due to cumulative ozone destruction or possibly climate change; in either case, ozone losses over the northern hemisphere may be more severe than anticipated in the near future.

The intensity of ultraviolet-B radiation (UV-B) has increased accordingly; 1992–93 saw the first reported examples of persistent increases over densely populated regions in the northern hemisphere, posing a threat to primary plant and animal plankton productivity and human health in terms of increased risk of skin cancer and other health problems (UNEP, 1994).

Chemical Pollution in the Arctic Region

Measurements indicate that pollutants, such as persistent organic pollutants (POPs), heavy metals, radionuclides, and acidifying gases, are transported to the Arctic by the atmospheric, riverine, and ocean pathways. The Commonwealth of Independent

States countries, Europe, North America, and Japan are the main sources for these long-range transported pollutants. Trends in measurements of chemicals such as DDT and toxaphene in the region indicate that developing countries, where these chemicals are still in use, also contribute to the presence of these pollutants in the Arctic region (Canadian Dept. of Foreign Affairs and International Trade, personal communication, 1996).

Although the concentration of many pollutants tends to be low in the Arctic environment, there are notable exceptions. Elevated concentrations of certain heavy metals such as cadmium and mercury have been found in Arctic sea birds, fish, and marine mammals. The levels of POPs are also high in Arctic species like the polar bear, as well as in other marine mammals. Because fish and marine mammals are a major food source for indigenous peoples in the region, the toxic contaminants they contain pose a human health risk (PAME, 1996).

Radioactive contamination is considered one of the main threats to the Arctic environment in spite of low current levels of contamination and sharp falls in caesium-137 levels in both the North and the Barents seas since the 1980s (Strand and Cooke, 1995). The main sources of radioactivity are the French La Hague and British Sellafield reprocessing plants and global fallout from atmospheric tests in the 1950s and 1960s. There are additional inputs and risks from Russia, including contamination from the Chernobyl accident, earlier dumping of liquid and solid radioactive waste, minor leakages from installation and dumping sites, and improper storage and management of spent fuel from both civil and military sources. Waste management is also an issue in the Canadian north where, prior to land use regulations, waste was abandoned with little concern for the environment. Military installations, exploration camps, and mines were the main source of these wastes (Canadian Dept. of Foreign Affairs and International Trade, personal communication, 1996).

During the cold war, the Arctic Ocean represented one of the main frontiers between the West and East. The ice-covered Arctic Ocean was a superb area for hiding submarines with strategic nuclear weapons. The Kola region in north-west Russia, the only ice-free harbour to the Atlantic, still houses the largest concentration of nuclear vessels and weapons in the world. After the end of the cold war there was a lack of resources to manage these installations. Radioactive materials were released accidentally or through leakages from these installations as well as from plants further south (Tomsk and Mayak), draining northwards. These, together with solid waste dumped into shallow waters in the Kara Sea, all represent threats to the Arctic environment, its people, and its fisheries (EEA/NPI, 1996).

Onshore and offshore exploration of oil and gas, and their transportation through pipelines and by ships, represent a risk to the region's environment. The continued use of outdated technology in some areas exacerbates this risk. The expected large onshore and offshore oil reserves of Siberia are one key area for exploration both by western and Russian companies (PAME, 1996; EPPR, 1996). The *Exxon Valdez* accident in Alaska and the oil spill in the Komi Republic of Russia are examples of accidental damage caused by oil-related activities. Decomposition of hydrocarbons is slower in the cold Arctic climate compared with warmer areas. This provides extra time for released contaminants to spread and extends the time that they can have an impact on the environment.

Arctic Population

The total human population in the Arctic currently exceeds 3.5 million. The indigenous population constitutes approximately 80 per cent of the total population in Greenland, 50 per cent in Arctic Canada, 15 per cent in Alaska and Arctic Norway, and a smaller proportion in the rest of the Arctic countries (AMAP, 1996). Due to improving living conditions through socio-economic development, the population growth rates in many parts of the Arctic are rising and the population is generally young (AMAP, 1996). At the same time, a number of northern regions in Russia have lost 20–30 per cent of their population during the 1990s due to emigration, a decreased birth rate, and increased mortality (Goskomstat of Russia, 1995).

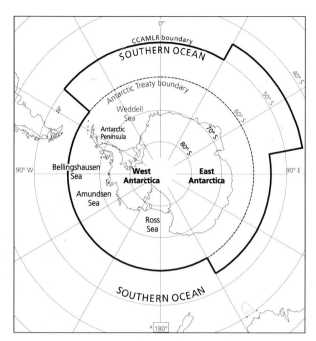

Figure 2.26. Antarctica and the Southern Ocean.

Source: UNEP/GRID-Christchurch (1996) based on SCAR-ADD (1993).

The indigenous peoples of the north have traditionally survived on a sustainable system of hunting and herding the local fauna. Today, many of the local inhabitants are increasing the level of resource exploitation to supplement their income and are involved in new and non-traditional activities, such as industrial processing and tourist services. Purely traditional life-styles are tending to disappear as indigenous people adopt "southern" life-styles to a greater or lesser extent. These are accompanied by changes in food and dwelling habits, education, and health care.

Differences between the local and introduced cultures are levelling out in some areas, most notably in the Nordic countries. In other areas, however, such as in the Arctic regions of the Russian Federation, there have been decreases or withdrawal of centralized subsidies for traditional economies. These economic changes are imposing hardships on the local populations and consequently on the environment on which they depend for much of their livelihood. Overall, there is a growing recognition of traditional values among the Arctic peoples themselves, among national Governments, and among international Arctic organizations. Increasingly, such

values are being addressed in various programmes, including those operating under the Arctic Environmental Protection Strategy.

THE ANTARCTIC

Antarctica is the coldest continent. It is also the driest, windiest, and cleanest. It is approximately 14 million square kilometres in area, about one tenth of the earth's land surface. The Antarctic continent is surrounded by one of the world's largest and stormiest oceans. (See Figure 2.26.) Less than 1 per cent of the land surface is ice-free (Fox and Cooper, 1994). During the winter, the area covered by ice is almost doubled as the sea freezes over. This fluctuation is the largest seasonal physical process on earth.

The Antarctic continent and the Southern Ocean play a critical role in the global environmental system. The interactions between atmosphere, oceans, ice, and biota that take place in the region affect the entire global system—influencing biogeochemical systems, atmospheric and oceanographic circulation patterns, the transport of energy and pollutants, and changes in sea level. The Antarctic is therefore a high priority for protection.

Antarctica is the least populated and least industrialized continent. For more than half the year, during winter, it is virtually devoid of any human activity. During summer, the only land-based activity is related to scientific research and a small amount of tourism. Both are highly localized. The continent is managed on a co-operative basis by the Consultative Parties to The Antarctic Treaty, which has been in force since 1961. Through the Treaty, the region south of latitude 60°S has been dedicated to science and peace.

In 1996, UNEP prepared a report entitled *The Question of Antarctica: State of the Environment in Antarctica* on behalf of the United Nations Secretary General. The report was presented to the 51st Session of the General Assembly in 1996 (General Assembly, 1996). Portions of this section are drawn from that report, with specific information and data sources individually cited and referenced. No comprehensive state of the Antarctic environment report has yet been written, although the preparation of such a report is currently being considered by the Scientific Committee for Antarctic Research.

Major Environmental Concerns

Currently, the principal environmental concerns in Antarctica are related to changes occurring at the global level rather than at any originating from human activities within Antarctica itself. Those considered of most significance relate to depletion of the ozone layer and climate change. It is only in the recent past, however, that the Antarctic marine environment was subjected to uncontrolled, unsustainable, and profound disturbances by commercial exploitation of whale and seal stocks, leading to near-extinction of some species. While commercial exploitation is now prohibited, the impacts from this overexploitation are still evident in the marine ecosystem today. In comparison to these changes and the global changes noted, the environmental impacts of human activities occurring within Antarctica today are relatively minor and localized. Yet even these remain of concern because of the high scientific and aesthetic value to be derived by maintaining Antarctica as far as possible in a relatively undisturbed state.

Ice Sheets and Ice Shelves

More than 87 per cent of the earth's fresh water exists in a frozen state. The Antarctic ice sheet, together with the fresh-water ice shelves that extend from the edges of the sheet over the sea surface, contain more than 90 per cent of this frozen water (Meier, 1983). If all of this water melted, it would be equivalent to a sea level rise of some 60–72 metres (Drewry and Morris, 1992).

Small changes in the mass of large ice sheets have widely recognized implications for the global climate system and for sea level. The most up-to-date evaluation suggests that the Antarctic ice mass is decreasing (Jacobs and Hartmut, 1996), although further investigation is needed before a reliable statement can be made. The breaking away of icebergs from the edges of the ice sheet is the largest single cause of the reduction (Jacobs et al., 1992),

followed by ice shelf melting (Jacobs and Hartmut, 1996).

Recent research on the Antarctic Peninsula has shown that steady ice shelf retreat has been occurring there over the past 50 years (Skvarca, 1993; Ward, 1995; Vaughan and Doake, 1996; Rott et al., 1996). Five northerly ice shelves on the Antarctic Peninsula have retreated dramatically during this period, perhaps in response to atmospheric warming (Vaughan and Doake, 1996). The recent dramatic collapse of the Larsen Ice Shelf implies that after an ice shelf retreats beyond a critical limit it may collapse rapidly (Rott et al., 1996). Ice shelves do appear to be sensitive indicators of climate change and, indeed, long-term warming trends on the Antarctic Peninsula are so large that they appear to be statistically significant (Stark, 1994; King, 1994).

Sea Ice

Winter temperatures in the Antarctic fall so low that huge areas of sea are frozen over. This sea ice varies in extent from 4 million square kilometres in late summer (February) to almost five times that area in late winter (September) (Fullard et al., 1990). (See Figure 2.27.) These large seasonal fluctuations, together with the fluctuations in Arctic sea ice, play an important role in global climate by affecting exchanges of energy and water vapour (Wadhams, 1991).

An analysis of global ice cover between 1978 and 1994 detected no statistically significant change in Antarctic sea ice while Arctic sea ice seems to have decreased by 5.5 per cent (Johannessen et al., 1995). However, significant reductions in summer sea ice in the late 1980s and early 1990s in the Amundsen and Bellinghausen seas are consistent with a warming climate west of the Antarctic Peninsula (Jacobs and Comiso, 1993).

Living Resources

The Antarctic is globally distinct in terms of biodiversity, although it is inhabited by a relatively small number of different species. Among the fauna are 120 species of fish, 72 cephalopod (mainly squid) species, and about 50 species of birds, 35 of which breed in the region. What the Antarctic lacks in variety, however, it often makes up for in sheer numbers. There are estimated to be 200 million individual birds, 65 per cent of which are penguins.

There are diverse communities of benthic flora where the bottom of the ocean is too deep to be disturbed by ice. However, few plant species can exist on land in the Antarctic. The terrestrial flora is dominated by lower plants, including 350 identified species of lichen and a green algae that grows on snow and ice, giving the surface a red appearance. Only two species of flowering plant grow south of latitude 60°S.

The marine ecosystem, which contains most of the Antarctic flora and fauna, is characterized by short food chains from phytoplankton through krill to large mammals or birds. These short food chains make the Antarctic marine ecosystem very fragile and susceptible to disruption.

The krill, which occupy a central position in the food chain, are crucial to the stability and sustainability of the Antarctic ecosystem. Krill are tiny, shrimp-like crustaceans found in Antarctic waters. Some 85 species have been identified, the most numerous being *Euphausia superba*. They form the main food for five species of whale, three species of seals, and 20 fish species as well as squid and bird species. Estimates of the Antarctic krill stock range from 500 million to 750 million metric tons.

Krill attract a large number of whales to the region. As a result, Antarctic waters support a more extensive stock of whales than any other part of the world's oceans. The state of Antarctic whale stocks is of major concern after an extensive period of whale hunting by humans. With the exception of a very few species, there is considerable uncertainty over the numbers of whales of different species and in different geographical stocks. Because of this uncertainty, the International Whaling Commission (IWC), established by the 1946 International Convention for the Regulation of Whaling, only publishes data on species for which there is high statistical probability. Estimates for the late 1980s put the total number of blue whales in the Southern Hemisphere at around 460 and minke whales at

around 760,000 (IWC, 1996). Seals, the other major mammalian group in the Antarctic, are estimated to number some 10 million individuals.

No estimates are currently available for Antarctic fish or cephalopod stocks.

Contamination

Many pollutants originating in the industrial and populated areas of the world are transported to the Antarctic by atmospheric and ocean circulations. They include chlorofluorocarbons, which cause ozone depletion (discussed later in this section), radioactive debris from past atmospheric nuclear bomb tests and accidents, heavy metals, and hydrocarbons. At present, contamination levels are generally extremely low, and the area therefore presents an ideal laboratory for monitoring background pollution in studies on long-range transport of pollutants (Wolff, 1990 and 1995; Cripps and Priddle, 1991). In addition, because the ice preserves a historical record of the atmosphere, ice core studies can reveal global changes in trace gases and in some pollutants such as lead. Studies have indicated, for example, a 10- to 20-fold increase in lead concentrations from pre-industrial times to 1980, followed by subsequent decreases that can be linked to the increasing use of lead-reduced fuels around the world (Wolff, 1990 and 1992; Wolff and Suttie, 1994).

There have also been incidents of local accidental release of pollutants. A case in point was the release of 600,000 litres of diesel fuel into Arthur Harbour, Antarctic Peninsula, as the ship *Bahia Paraiso* sank in 1989 (Kennicutt and Sweet, 1992). Although isolated to date, such incidents could increase as travel to the Antarctic becomes more popular.

Ozone Depletion

The discovery of the Antarctic ozone hole necessitated a major revision in theories of stratospheric chemistry. While stratospheric ozone loss had been predicted (Molina and Rowland, 1974), the magnitude of the ozone depletion over Antarctica, first

a. Mean minimum ice coverage

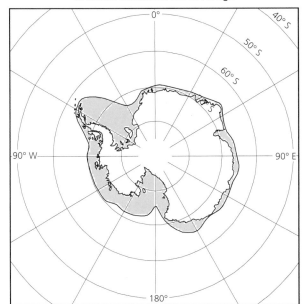

b. Mean maximum ice coverage

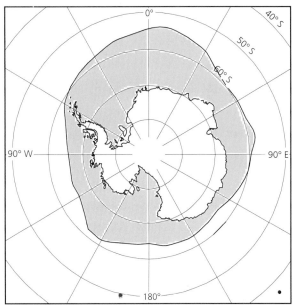

Figure 2.27. Seasonal variability of Antarctic sea ice, 1973–92.

Source: Adapted from Simmonds and Jacka (1995).

identified in 1985 (Farman *et al.*, 1985), was not. During 1978 to 1987, the ozone hole grew, both in depth (total ozone loss in a column) and in area. The growth was not linear but seemed to oscillate within a two-year period (Lait *et al.*, 1989). The hole shrank dramatically in 1988, but in 1989–91 was as large as in 1987. The Antarctic ozone holes of 1992 and 1993 were the largest ever, although this was due in part to natural causes, specifically enhanced ozone-destruction by sulphate aerosols from Mount Pinatubo (WMO, 1995a).

In 1995, the ozone decline started earlier than in any previous year, while the rate of decline was the most rapid on record (WMO, 1995b). Measurements over the South Pole during September and October 1995 showed that there was nearly complete destruction of ozone at altitudes between 15 and 20 kilometres. At the same time, total ozone values over Antarctica were extremely low.

Increased surface solar UV-B, attributable to the depletion of stratospheric ozone, poses a threat to Antarctic ecosystems. UV-B is detrimental not only for primary terrestrial colonizers such as cyanobacteria and algae but also for lichens and mosses, higher plants, invertebrates, and marine organisms

(Wynn-Williams, 1994). One study on productivity of phytoplankton in the marginal ice zone revealed an overall decrease of 6–12 per cent where phytoplankton were exposed to increased UV-B concentrations (Smith *et al.*, 1992). While this overall loss is not large, the cumulative effect on the marine community is not yet known. In terms of ecological consequences, the displacement of UV-sensitive species by UV-tolerant ones is likely to be more important than a decline in overall productivity (McMinn *et al.*, 1994).

The growth rates of several major ozone-depleting substances in the atmosphere have now slowed, demonstrating the expected impact of the 1987 Montreal Protocol and its subsequent amendments and adjustments (WMO, 1995a). (See also Box 2.4.) However, a substantial Antarctic ozone hole is expected to occur during every southern hemisphere spring for many more decades as stratospheric chlorine and bromine concentrations very slowly decline and begin to approach the levels of the late 1970s during the next century. Only if the restrictions controlling chlorine and bromine emissions are maintained can we expect the Antarctic ozone hole to disappear.

Box 2.4
The Ozone Success Story

The protection of the Earth's ozone layer is one of the most inspiring stories in the annals of international environmental diplomacy. The thinning of the protective ozone layer poses a great danger to the health and well-being of people and ecosystems around the world: it threatens human skin, eyes, and immune systems; damages plants and animals; and poses unknown hazards to the planet's climate. To halt this thinning, action against a range of highly diverse (and profitable) industrial chemicals is required, chemicals that have helped to bring what are now commonplace products into the homes of millions—refrigerators, aerosol sprays, insulating and furniture foams. The action has brought onto the global stage a vast array of players: scientists, industrialists, and diplomats, all working together in pursuit of a common goal—the protection of the ozone layer. It is a story of painstaking investigations, courageous decisions, hard-fought negotiations, and last-minute compromises. And it is not yet over.

This success story of international environmental diplomacy was possible because science and industry, stimulated by the clear objectives of the Montreal Protocol, have been able to develop and commercialise alternatives to ozone-depleting chemicals. The 1995 Vienna meeting marked the end of the initial phase of the ozone regime, which concentrated on identifying ozone-depleting substances, agreeing on control measures, and phasing out substances in industrialized countries. Attention is now turning increasingly to issues of implementation in developing countries and countries with economies in transition, and to dealing with new emerging problems such as the first cases of non-compliance and the growth in illegal trade.

Reference

UNEP. 1996. *Action on Ozone*. UNEP. Nairobi.

Human Activities

Science and Support Activities

Scientific investigation is the predominant human activity in this region that offers outstanding opportunities for fundamental research essential to understanding the global environment. Since regular scientific and support activities began, the number of people visiting the Antarctic has increased steadily through to 1989–90 (Beltramino, 1993). Exact data on person-days spent in the region are unavailable due to the way in which data are reported but, for obvious reasons, most activity occurs during the summer months. The United States has the largest Antarctic science programme. The size and nature of the scientific presence in Antarctica, coupled with more relaxed rules and practices of environmental management in the past, have resulted in localized impacts on the Antarctic environment. The effects of past activities, such as open burning and dumping of trash close to stations, may still be seen today,

although the Madrid Protocol (see Chapter 3) now bans these practices and calls for the cleanup of old dump sites. Aircraft, vehicular and boat traffic, travel by foot, and camp and station construction all inevitably still have some impacts, even under the more stringent rules of the Madrid Protocol.

Tourism

Antarctica has been a limited tourist destination for the past 40 years; around 60,000 tourists are estimated to have visited during that time (adapted from Enzenbacher, 1993). In addition to those arriving by sea and air, a number of tourists see Antarctica only by air, without landing.

However, commercial tourism has undergone a period of accelerated growth in the past 10 years. The number of tourists visiting Antarctica in 1995–96 was the highest ever recorded. There have also been associated increases in the number of vessels used to carry tourists and in the number of sites they visit. At least 12 ships are now in use for

Table 2.15

Changes in Total Fish Catch in the Antarctic Region from 1991–92 to 1995–96[a]

Species	Total Catch (metric tons)				
	1991–92	1992–93	1993–94	1994–95	1995–96
Krill	288,546	88,776	83,818	118,714	
Finfish[b]	11,062	5,751	1,853	12,933	
Antarctic crabs	—	299	0	0	79[c]

Sources: CCAMLR (1993, 1995); United Kingdom (1995).

Notes: a. Data are for the region as defined by the Convention for the Conservation of Antarctic Marine Living Resources (CCAMLR). b. Includes the main finfish species, *Dissostichus eleginoides, Champsocephalus gunnari,* and *Electrona carlsbergi.* c. Represents the catch between 1 September 1995, when the fishery started, and 10 October 1995.

tourism each season (United Kingdom, 1995), and landing sites have increased from 36 to more than 150 since the early 1990s (NSF, 1995; Ucha and Barrio, 1996).

The types of activities available to tourists have broadened to include skiing, climbing, camping, and sea kayaking. Although numbers are low, there is growing awareness of the importance of environmental issues arising from tourism (Enzenbacher, 1994). In response to the increase in tourism, the International Association of Antarctica Tour Operators was founded in August 1991. Antarctic Treaty Recommendation XVIII-1 (see Chapter 3) provides operational and environmental guidelines to tour operators in Antarctica.

Exploitation of Marine Living Resources

Exploitation of living marine resources in the Antarctic is focused on krill (*E. superba*) and Antarctic finfish species. Predominant target species are the Patagonian toothfish (*Dissostichus eleginoides*), mackerel icefish (*Champsocephalus gunnari*), and lanternfish (*Electrona carlsbergi*). The finfish fisheries have been active since 1969–70, with more than 3 million metric tons caught prior to 1995–96, though finfish catches have been very low since 1992. Krill harvesting began in 1972–73, and the current catch, which is the largest in Antarctic waters, is around 90,000 metric tons a year (Kock, 1994). (See Table 2.15.) Some new fisheries are being initiated and investigated, such as harvesting of stone crabs (*Lithodidae*) and squid (*Martialia hyadesi*), which may have potential for commercial exploitation (New Zealand Ministry of Foreign Affairs and Trade, 1995;

CCAMLR, 1996). Krill catches have declined since the early 1990s. However, this is primarily due to a reduction in the Russian and Ukrainian fishing activities rather than to a decline in the krill population (CCAMLR, 1993).

Total allowable catch limits have been set for targeted species under the Convention on the Conservation of Antarctic Marine Living Resources (CCAMLR). Current fishing levels are well below these limits, with the possible exception of the Patagonian toothfish, for which illegal fishing is believed to equal or exceed the allowable catch limit (ASOC, 1996). Many fisheries, including krill, are still considered to be in the exploratory stage of exploitation. Thus it is important to have accurate knowledge of the biology and ecology of the entire marine ecosystem to allow for informed management decisions leading to a sustainable fishery.

Most finfishing in the Southern Ocean has been conducted with bottom trawls—funnel-shaped nets towed behind a vessel (Kock, 1994). Trawl gear is reported to affect the environment by scraping and ploughing the seabed, resuspending sediments, and generally disturbing the benthos (seabed environment) (Jones, in Kock, 1994). Exact effects on the rich benthic flora and fauna of the Southern Ocean are largely unknown. It is speculated, however, that trawling could have serious, long-lasting impacts on the slow-growing, low-resilience benthic assemblages, with consequent effects on food chains and sustainable fisheries.

Incidental mortality of seabirds during longline fishing operations has been reported as a significant problem (Ashford and Croxall, 1994 and 1995). Mitigation measures, such as setting of longlines only at night, have now been adopted under the CCAMLR.

A 1982 decision of the IWC imposed a moratorium on whaling (except for indigenous subsistence and scientific purposes) from the 1985–86 season. The moratorium ended in 1994, the same year in which a Southern Ocean Whale Sanctuary was established by the IWC. There is presently no known commercial hunting of seals in Antarctica.

References

AMAP. 1996a. *Interim Report to the Third Ministerial Conference, Arctic Environmental Protection Strategy.* Arctic Monitoring and Assessment Programme (AMAP). Inuvik, Canada.

AMAP. 1996b. *AMAP Assessment Report.*

Ashford, J.R., and J.P. Croxall. 1994. Seabird interactions with longlining operations for *Dissostichus eleginoides* at the South Sandwich Islands and South Georgia. *CCAMLR Science.* 1:143–153.

Ashford, J.R., and J.P. Croxall. 1995. Seabird interactions with longlining operations for *Dissostichus eleginoides* around South Georgia, April to May 1994. *CCAMLR Science,* 2:111–121.

ASOC. 1996. Illegal fishing threatens CCAMLR's ability to manage Antarctica's fisheries. *The Antarctica Project* 5(2):2. Antarctic and Southern Ocean Coalition (ASOC).

Beltramino, J.C.M. 1993. *The Structure and Dynamics of Antarctic Population.* Vantage Press. New York.

CAFF. 1996a. Circumpolar Protected Areas Network (CPAN) - Strategy and Action Plan. Conservation of Arctic Flora and Fauna (CAFF). Habitat Conservation Report No. 6. Directorate for Nature Management. Trondheim, Norway.

CAFF. 1996b. Proposed Protected Areas in the Circumpolar Arctic. CAFF Habitat Conservation Report No. 2. Conservation of Flora and Fauna (CAFF). Directorate for Nature Management. Trondheim, Norway.

CCAMLR. 1993. *CCAMLR Newsletter No. 15.* November. Convention for the Conservation of Antarctic Marine Living Resources (CCAMLR).

CCAMLR. 1996. *Statistical Bulletin 1996 (1986–1995).* Hobart.

Cripps, G.C., and J. Priddle. 1991. Hydrocarbons in the Antarctic marine environment. *Antarctic Science* 3(3):233.

Drewry, D.J., and E.M. Morris. 1992. The response of large ice sheets to climatic change. *Philosophical Transactions of the Royal Society of London B.* 338:235–242.

EEA. 1995. Europe's Environment: The Dobříš Assessment. D. Stanners and P. Bourdeau (eds.). Office for Official Publications of the European Communities. Luxembourg.

EEA/NPI. 1996. *State of the European Arctic Environment.* J.R. Hansen, R. Hansson, and S. Norris (eds.). European Environment Agency/Norwegian Polar Institute (EEA/NPI). EEA Environmental Monograph No. 3. Norsk Polarinstitutt Meddelelser No. 141.

Enzenbacher, D.J. 1993. Tourists in Antarctica numbers and trends. *Polar Record* 28(164):17–22.

Enzenbacher, D.J. 1994. Antarctic tourism: an overview of 1992/3 season activity, recent developments, and emerging issues. *Polar Record* 30(173):105–116.

EPPR. 1996. *Emergency Prevention Preparedness and Response: Environmental Risk Analysis of Arctic Activities.* Report No. 1. AEPS Working Group on Emergency Prevention, Preparedness and Response (EPPR).

Farman, J.C., B.G. Gardiner, and J.D. Shanklin. 1985. Large losses of total ozone in Antarctica reveal seasonal CLO_x/NO_x Interaction. *Nature* 315:207–210.

Fox, A.J., and A.P.R. Cooper. 1994. Measured properties of the Antarctic ice sheet derived from the SCAR Antarctic digital database. *Polar Record* 30(174):204.

Fullard, C.K., T.R. Karl, and K. Ya. Vinnikov. 1990. Observed climate variations and change. In: J.T. Houghton, G.J. Jenkins, and J.J. Ephraums (eds.). *Climate Change: The IPCC Scientific Assessment.* Report prepared for the IPCC by Working Group 1. 195-238. Cambridge University Press. Cambridge.

Futsaeter, G., G. Eidnes, G. Halmo, S. Johansen, H.P. Mannvik, L.K. Sydnes, and U. Witte. 1991. Report on Oil Pollution. The State of the Arctic Environment Reports. Arctic Centre, University of Lapland.

General Assembly. 1996. *Question of Antarctica: State of the Environment in Antarctica.* Report of the Secretary General to the 51st Session of the United Nations General Assembly. A/51/390 Report prepared on behalf of the Secretary General by UNEP with the assistance of the International Centre for Antarctic Information and Research. Christchurch, New Zealand.

Goskomstat of Russia. 1995. *The Demographic Yearbook of Russia. Statistical Handbook.* State Committee of the Russian Federation for Statistics. Moscow.

IPCC. 1996. *Climate Change 1995. The Science of Climate Change*. Intergovernmental Panel on Climate Change. Cambridge University Press. Cambridge.

IWC. 1996. Data provided by the International Whaling Commission. 14 August 1996. Cambridge.

Jacobs, S.S., and J.C. Comiso. 1993. A recent sea-ice retreat west of the Antarctic Peninsula. *Geophysical Research Letters* 20(12):1171–1174.

Jacobs, S.S., and H.H. Hartmut. 1996. Antarctic ice sheet melting and the Southeast Pacific. *Geophysical Research Letters* 23(9):957–960.

Jacobs, S.S., H.H. Helmer, C.S.M. Doake, A. Jenkins, and R.M. Frolich. 1992. Melting of ice shelves and the mass balance of Antarctica. *Journal of Glaciology* 38:375–387.

Johannessen, O.M., M. Miles, and E. Bjorgo. 1995. The Arctic's shrinking sea ice. *Nature* 376:126–27.

Kennicutt, M.C., and S.T. Sweet. 1992. Hydrocarbon contamination on the Antarctic Peninsula: III. The *Bahia Paraiso* two years after the spill. *Marine Pollution Bulletin* 25 (9–12).

King, J.C. 1994. Recent climate variability in the vicinity of the Antarctic Peninsula. *International Journal of Climatology* 14:357–369.

Kock, K-H. 1994. Fishing and conservation in southern waters. *Polar Record* 30(172):3–22.

Lait, L.R., M.R. Schoeberl, and P.A. Newman. 1989. Quasi-biennial modulation of the antarctic ozone depletion. *Journal of Geophysical Research* 94:11559–11571.

Marshall, P.T. 1957. Primary production in the Arctic. *J. Cons. Perm. Int. Explor. Mer.* 23:173–177.

McMinn, A., H. Heijnis, and D. Hodgson. 1994. Minimal effects of UV-B radiation on Antarctic diatoms over the past 20 years. *Nature* 370:547.

Meier, M.F. 1983. Snow and ice in a changing hydrological world. *Hydrological Sciences Journal* 28(1):3–22.

Molina, M.J., and F.S. Rowland. 1974. Stratospheric sink for chlorofluoromethanes: chlorine atom-catalysed destruction of ozone. *Nature* 249:810–812.

New Zealand Ministry of Foreign Affairs and Trade. 1995. Commission for the Conservation of Antarctic Marine Living Resources: Fourteenth meeting. Report of the New Zealand Delegation. Hobart.

NSF. 1995. Reported at 7th Antarctic Tour Operators Meeting. National Science Foundation (NSF). July. Washington.

PAME. 1996. *Report to the Ministerial Conference on the Protection of The Arctic Environment*. AEPS Working Group on Protection of the Arctic Marine Environment. 20–21 March. Inuvik, Canada.

Rott, H., P. Skvarca, and T. Nagler. 1996. Rapid collapse of the Northern Larsen Ice Shelf, Antarctica. *Science* 271:788.

SFT. 1996. *Miljøtilstanden i Norge*. Statens forurensningstilsyn.

Skvarca, P. 1993. Fast Recession of the northern Larsen Ice Shelf monitored by space images. *Annals of Glaciology* 17:317–321.

Smith, R., B. Prezelin, K. Baker, R. Bidigare, N. Boucher, T. Coley, D. Karentz, S. MacIntyre, H. Matlick, D. Menzies, M. Ondrusck, Z. Wan, and K. Waters. 1992. Ozone depletion: ultraviolet radiation and phytoplankton biology in Antarctic waters. *Science* 255:952.

Smith, W.O. Jr., and E. Sakshaug. 1990. Polar phytoplankton. In: *Polar Oceanography, Part B: Chemistry, Biology, and Geology*. W.O. Smith, Jr. (ed.). Academic Press. New York.

Stark, P. 1994. Climatic warming in the central Antarctic Peninsula area. *Weather* 49:215–220.

Strand, P., and A. Cooke (eds). 1995. *Environmental Radioactivity in the Arctic*. Scientific Committee on Environmental Radioactivity in the Arctic. Norway.

Stonehouse, B. 1989. Polar Ecology. Blackie. London.

Tommervik, H., B.E. Johansen, and J.P. Pedersen. 1995. Monitoring the effects of air pollution on terrestrial ecosystems in Varanger (Norway) and Nikel-Pechanga (Russia) using remote sensing. In: *The Science of the Total Environment*. 160/161:753–767.

Ucha, S.B., and A.M. Barrio. 1996. *Report on Antarctic Tourism Numbers Through the Port of Ushuaia 1995–96*. Insituto Fueguino de Turismo. Ushuaia, Argentina.

UNEP. 1994. Environmental Effects of Ozone Depletion: 1994 Assessment. UNEP. Nairobi.

United Kingdom. 1995. *Recent Developments in Antarctic Tourism*. Information Paper 13, XIX Antarctic Treaty Consultative Meeting (ATCM). 8–19 May. Seoul.

UNEP/GRID-Christchurch. 1996. Map of Antarctica and the Southern Ocean. Based on SCAR Antarctic Digital Database (ADD), 1993. UNEP/GRID. Christchurch, New Zealand.

Vaughan, D.G., and C.S.M. Doake. 1996. Recent atmospheric warming and retreat of ice shelves on the Antarctic Peninsula. *Nature* 379:328–331.

Wadhams, P. 1991. Atmosphere-ice-ocean interactions in the Antarctic. In C.M. Harris and B. Stonehouse (eds.). *Antarctica and Global Climate Change*. Belhaven Press. London.

Ward, C.G. 1995. Mapping ice front changes of Muller Ice Shelf, Antarctic Peninsula. *Antarctic Science* 7:197–198.

WMO. 1995a. *Scientific Assessment of Ozone Depletion: 1994 Global Ozone Research and Monitoring Project.* Report No. 37.

WMO. 1995b. *Antarctic Ozone Bulletin 10/95.* World Meteorological Organization (WMO).

Wolff, E.W. 1990. Signals of atmospheric pollution in polar ice and snow. *Antarctic Science* 2(3):189–205.

Wolff, E.W. 1992. The influence of global and local atmospheric pollution on the chemistry of Antarctic snow and ice. *Marine Pollution Bulletin* 25(9-12):274.

Wolff, E.W. 1995. Environmental monitoring in Antarctica: atmospheric pollution. Unpublished paper presented at SCAR/COMNAP Antarctic Environmental Monitoring Workshops: Workshop 1—Prioritisation of impacts and the development of monitoring options. 17–20 October. Oslo.

Wolff, E.W., and E.D. Suttie. 1994. Antarctic snow record of southern hemisphere lead pollution. *Geophysical Research Letters* 21(9):781.

Wynn-Williams, D.D. 1994. Potential effects of UV radiation on Antarctic primary terrestrial colonizers: cyanobacteria, algae and cryptograms. In Weiler, C.S., and P.A. Penhale (eds.). Ultraviolet radiation in Antarctica: measurements and biological effects. *Antarctic Research Series.* American Geophysical Union. 62:243–257. Washington.

chapter 3

POLICY RESPONSES AND DIRECTIONS

egional and global State of the Environment (SOE) reports traditionally do not systematically document existing policy responses, let alone assess their impact and effectiveness or analyse factors contributing to their success or failure. This trend is changing, however, as national and sectoral SOE reports pay more attention to the policy side of the environmental situation. Improving our ability to produce overviews and assessments of societal responses to current and emerging environment issues is one of the aims of the GEO Report Series.

This chapter takes a first step in forging the link between environment assessment and policy-making by providing a brief overview of some major responses. First, some current changes in approaches to environmental management are briefly analysed. Second, a summary is provided of policy responses in the different regions to the priority environmental concerns described in Chapter 2. And third, a more detailed account of environmental responses in each region is given. Since it is impossible to report on all the environmental policy initiatives implemented at national, regional, and global levels, this chapter mainly draws on examples to illustrate overall trends.

CURRENT CHANGES IN APPROACHES TO ENVIRONMENTAL POLICY

Global Frameworks and Conventions and National Policy Initiatives

Since the 1972 Stockholm Conference, the number and scope of international environmental policy responses have increased significantly. Initially, the established global strategic planning frameworks usually had a sectoral nature. Examples of this include the United Nations Plan of Action to Combat Desertification (1977), the World Conference on Agrarian Reform and Rural Development (1979), the World Conservation Strategy (1980), the World Soil Policy (1982), and the Tropical Forest Action Plan (1984). Under these global programmatic frameworks, national action plans, strategies, and policies were prepared.

EFFECTIVE POLICY SETTING FOR SUSTAINABLE DEVELOPMENT REQUIRES A BLEND OF POLICY INSTRUMENTS THAT ADDRESSES THE SOCIAL FABRIC OF LIFE, ENSURES EFFECTIVE INSTITUTIONAL ARRANGEMENTS, IMPROVES THE ECONOMY, AND PROTECTS THE ENVIRONMENT.

Box 3.1
Some Ongoing International Negotiation Processes

- The Intergovernmental Negotiating Committee (INC) has made good progress on the development of an Internationally Legally Binding Instrument for the Application of Prior Informed Consent Procedure for Certain Hazardous Chemicals and Pesticides in International Trade. The final INC and Diplomatic Conference is expected to be held in Rotterdam in 1997.

- The Intergovernmental Forum on Chemical Safety has developed recommendations on international action on persistent organic pollutants for consideration by the 1997 sessions of the UNEP Governing Council and the World Health Assembly.

- An Open-Ended Ad-Hoc Working Group on Biosafety is negotiating a biosafety protocol under the Convention on Biological Diversity to be concluded in 1998.

- A 3rd Ministerial Round Table meeting in Geneva in October 1996 made a clear step ahead in developing supportive environment and trade policies, focusing on multilateral environmental agreements, market access, and trade liberalization.

- Institutional arrangements are under way for implementation of the Global Programme of Action for the Protection of the Marine Environment from Land-Based Activities.

- During the World Food Summit in Rome in November 1996, a Plan of Action was adopted by Heads of States and Governments stipulating concrete, practical actions to cut the number of people suffering from hunger in half by 2030.

- An open-ended ad hoc Intergovernmental Panel on Forests was established by the United Nations Commission on Sustainable Development (CSD) to enhance the political debate on forests while focusing on priority issues. Final conclusions and forest policy recommendations will be submitted to the CSD at its fifth session in April 1997.

For details on existing conventions and their amendments and protocols, see the references listed below.

References

Bergesen, H.O., and G. Parmann (eds.). 1994. Green Globe Yearbook of International Co-operation on Environment and Development. The Fridtjof Nansen Institute. Oxford University Press. Oxford.

CIESIN. 1996. Environmental Treaties and Resource Indicators (ENTRI) [on line]. Consortium for International Earth Science Information Network (CIESIN). University Center, Michigan. <http://sedac.ciesin.org/entri/>.

UNEP. 1993. Register of International Treaties and Other Agreements in the Field of the Environment. United Nations Environment Programme. Nairobi.

At the same time, multilateral agreements and conventions were negotiated, resulting in some 200 legal instruments that target regional and global action to protect the environment. Some of the new, currently negotiated legal instruments and action programmes are detailed in Box 3.1. Several of the global conventions call for national inventories, action programmes and reporting mechanisms, such as climate change country studies, biodiversity country studies on sources and sinks of greenhouse gases, and country programmes for the phaseout of ozone-depleting substances under the Montreal Protocol. Countries have adopted standards, limits, rules, and regulations to implement these international agreements at the national level. The main policy instruments used by Governments to translate international agreements into concrete action are based on command-and-control principles.

Although initial co-ordination of such national-level efforts may not have been very good, today national implementation of global programmes is better co-ordinated and often manifested in single overall environment action plans. The nature of national instruments has changed from a narrowly defined sectoral focus to a more comprehensive and anticipatory approach to protecting ecosystems. Increasingly, socio-economic factors are taken into consideration. Many countries have established SOE reporting programmes, which attempt to report on the status and trends of various sectors in an integrated way. As part of the strategic planning processes and reporting programmes, national institutions (Ministries, Secretariats, Departments, Committees, Commissions, and so on), non-governmental organizations (NGOs), advocacy groups, and private-sector institutions have been established or strengthened to deal specifically with environmental issues.

In addition, national legislation has been developed at a rapid pace in the past decades. Governments of many countries, for example, undertook significant amendments to existing natural resources legislation in order to deal with environmental problems arising from overexploitation by commercial and industrial sectors. The evolution of environmental legislation, especially in developing countries, can be divided into two distinct periods (UNEP, 1996c). In the pre-Stockholm era, largely characterized by "use-oriented" natural resource laws and legislation to address environmental pollution as a local problem, legislation was primarily concerned with the allocation and exploitation of natural resources. The post-Stockholm period is characterized by the emergence of "resource-oriented" legislation and, ultimately, system-oriented and integrated legal regimes aimed at long-term management and more sustainable use of natural resources. In industrial countries, some of these already existed before Stockholm. Wildlife legislation, for instance, gradually incorporated the concept of maintenance of a safe minimum stock through protection of vulnerable species.

Changing Environmental Policy Perceptions and Concepts

Many parts of the industrial world achieved economic growth and wealth in the past by having unlimited access to environmental resources (air, water, land, soils, and so on), and little thought was given to the impacts of growth on the environment. They then sought to improve and protect their quality of life from the environmental impacts of their development—initially from the effects of pollution on air and water, and more recently from hazardous waste, biodiversity loss, ozone layer destruction, and global climate change. This protection was largely achieved through Government-regulated command-and-control policies and end-of-pipe solutions that relied on legislation and measures such as emission standards and limits and on maximum permitted rates of resource use.

Significant improvements in environmental protection have been made in many parts of the world through such strategies and action (see below). Yet the state of the ecosphere as a whole continues to deteriorate. Developments in the different regions (Chapter 2) and explorations of the future (Chapter 4) show that an increasing number of environmental constraints will be encountered in the next few decades. Although command-and-control standards are effective in many cases in terms of short-term environmental improvements, the costs of implementation, enforcement, and compliance are high and may hinder long-term economic development. Furthermore, although such policies have proved to be efficient for pollution control, they are less effective for problems associated with the management, protection, and conservation of natural resources, particularly when a large number of different groups and people use these resources. Environmental issues have developed from simple (local, attributable, quantifiable, easy-to-solve, low-risk, and with short time horizons) to complex (global, non-attributable, non-quantifiable, difficult-to-solve, high-risk, and with long time frames). Complex environmental problems demand a combination of policy instruments to achieve environmental goals without constraining economic growth, development, and human well-being. Effective policy setting in support of sustainable development indeed requires a more diverse mix of policies that address the social fabric of life, ensure effective institutional arrangements, improve the economy in all its sectors, protect the environment, and so on. Consequently, countries are complementing command-and-control policies with, among other things, market-based economic instruments, methods to achieve cleaner and more resource-efficient production systems, and efforts to change consumer attitudes.

Economic instruments are increasingly applied world-wide. They aim at changing behaviour by offering incentives rather than by imposing standards or regulating specific technical improvements. Many of them seek to internalize external costs (both resource depletion and pollution costs), so that the producers, transporters, and consumers of various commodities face the full social costs of their activities (the "polluter pays" principle—PPP). A simple example is a carbon tax applied to motor fuel: this makes the producer pay the full social costs of depletion of the resource and makes the consumer absorb the full social costs of environmental damage, thus creating incentives to use fuel and vehicles more efficiently.

Few, if any, economic incentives have actually replaced regulations because most have been introduced with the primary objective of increasing Government revenues rather than altering behaviour towards more environmentally friendly activities. Also, some examples are available whereby economic instruments have been used "for short-term economic gains," which resulted in degradation of the environment. The issue at hand is how to get the best out of market forces, while at the same time moving towards environmental protection and equitable opportunity, and how to determine the appropriate level and type of regulation by Government to achieve this. In countries with strong institutional frameworks, it appears to be mostly a question of fine-tuning existing policies. For countries with weak and transforming institutions, it will entail an extensive and lengthy process of capacity building at all levels.

As detailed in the following sections, the trend is definitely toward using economic instruments to modify behaviour in a positive way. A summary of different groups of economic instruments is given in Box 3.2. In Box 3.3, positive experiences with economic instruments are described briefly.

In this context, clear interest in environmental impact assessments (EIA) has also developed. An EIA is the analysis of the likely environmental consequences of a proposed human activity. Although generally project-specific, EIAs have increasingly been applied to policies, plans, and programmes as well (UNEP, 1996d). The principle objective is to ensure that environmental considerations are incorporated into the planning for, decisions on, and implementation of development activities. EIAs increasingly assist in preventing or minimizing an activity's adverse impacts, while maximizing its beneficial effects.

Experience demonstrates that an effective EIA depends on three fundamental mechanisms: public participation (effectiveness is determined largely by how successfully the community has been involved), inter-sectoral co-ordination, and a consideration of alternatives. Through these mechanisms, EIAs serve an increasingly integrative and preventive role in development policy and planning.

A perceptional change is also manifested in structural adjustment programmes that are being implemented in developing countries. A combination of long-standing domestic policy distortion and the adverse external conditions of the 1970s (such as oil shocks, debt crisis, and world recession) created severe macro-economic and structural problems for developing countries. In response, stabilization and structural adjustment programmes were implemented. Structural adjustment policies predated the concept of sustainable development and focused on the objective of development assistance and economy-wide policies. They have now evolved to realign with the concept of sustainable development through integration with social and environmental policies.

A 1996 UNEP study explored the question of the environmental effects of stabilization and structural adjustment programmes (UNEP, 1996a). Understandably, the answer depended on a large number of interrelated factors, implying that economic policy-makers cannot apply a simple, standardized set of reforms to any given economy and expect predictable, consistent, or even beneficial results. Macro-economic reforms may even have unpredictable and mixed effects, depending on the situation in a country, or threaten economic growth and environmental integrity for the future in certain cases.

Box 3.2

Economic Instruments for Environmental Protection and Natural Resource Management

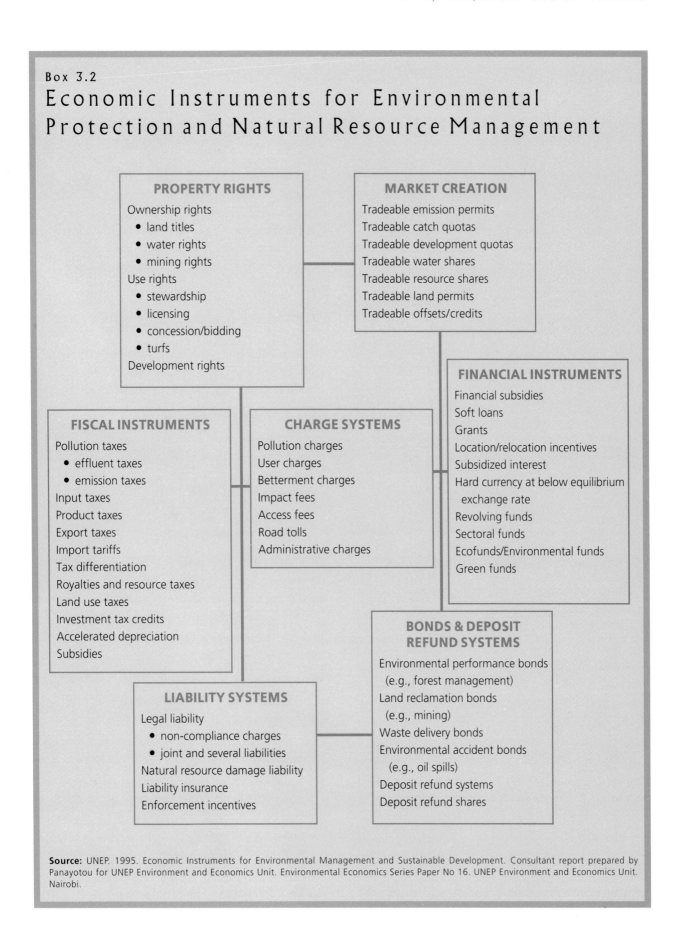

PROPERTY RIGHTS

Ownership rights
- land titles
- water rights
- mining rights

Use rights
- stewardship
- licensing
- concession/bidding
- turfs

Development rights

MARKET CREATION

Tradeable emission permits
Tradeable catch quotas
Tradeable development quotas
Tradeable water shares
Tradeable resource shares
Tradeable land permits
Tradeable offsets/credits

FISCAL INSTRUMENTS

Pollution taxes
- effluent taxes
- emission taxes

Input taxes
Product taxes
Export taxes
Import tariffs
Tax differentiation
Royalties and resource taxes
Land use taxes
Investment tax credits
Accelerated depreciation
Subsidies

CHARGE SYSTEMS

Pollution charges
User charges
Betterment charges
Impact fees
Access fees
Road tolls
Administrative charges

FINANCIAL INSTRUMENTS

Financial subsidies
Soft loans
Grants
Location/relocation incentives
Subsidized interest
Hard currency at below equilibrium
    exchange rate
Revolving funds
Sectoral funds
Ecofunds/Environmental funds
Green funds

BONDS & DEPOSIT REFUND SYSTEMS

Environmental performance bonds
    (e.g., forest management)
Land reclamation bonds
    (e.g., mining)
Waste delivery bonds
Environmental accident bonds
    (e.g., oil spills)
Deposit refund systems
Deposit refund shares

LIABILITY SYSTEMS

Legal liability
- non-compliance charges
- joint and several liabilities

Natural resource damage liability
Liability insurance
Enforcement incentives

Source: UNEP. 1995. Economic Instruments for Environmental Management and Sustainable Development. Consultant report prepared by Panayotou for UNEP Environment and Economics Unit. Environmental Economics Series Paper No 16. UNEP Environment and Economics Unit. Nairobi.

Box 3.3
Experience with Economic Instruments

A recent survey showed that 14 members of the Organisation for Economic Co-operation and Development used between 1 and 20 economic instruments for environmental protection. Germany, Sweden, and the Netherlands were the most progressive in this respect. Of the 151 instruments in use, approximately half were charges and one third were subsidies. Others were such instruments as deposit-refund systems, market creation, and enforcement incentives.

In the developing world, there is considerable emphasis on communal management systems. Property rights can play a particularly important role in conservation and biodiversity protection. It all relates to the conversion of non-domesticated land to other uses, such as agriculture or industry, as detailed in Chapter 4. Transferring the responsibility of resource management to local communities and allowing them a fair share of the benefits arising from economic activities associated with non-cultivated biological resources helps reduce the pressure to convert such areas.

An example of retention of customary rights over land is found in Papua New Guinea, where more than 90 per cent of the land remains communal. In contrast with other developing countries, only 13 per cent of the forestland in Papua New Guinea has been converted to other uses.

Other economic instruments are also widely used. Private water rights in India provide incentives for the efficient management of an increasingly scarce resource. Concession bidding, forest fees, timber taxes, and environment bonds are used throughout West and Central Africa to promote sustainable management. China has introduced industrial discharge permits and emission charges that double or even triple if the allowable discharge standard is exceeded. Turkey has found relocation incentives to be effective for urban-based industry, while Chile has introduced both tradeable emission permits and tradeable water rights. Puerto Rico uses transferable development rights to promote coastal conservation. Costa Rica introduced biodiversity prospecting rights and tradeable reforestation tax credits, and is currently experimenting with internationally tradeable development rights and carbon offsets. Kenya has introduced differential pricing for entry into National Parks to combat congestion in the most popular eco-tourism destinations.

Cleaner and Leaner Production

As illustrated in the regional policy sections, countries are moving towards cleaner production and eco-efficiency, and a shift can be seen from cleaner processes to cleaner products and/or services. Government environmental policies to stimulate market partners to move from end-of-pipe solutions to more integral approaches and accounting on a "cradle-to-grave" basis are being tested in a number of countries. Cleaner, more resource-efficient production applies not only to industrial production processes, but also to agriculture, fisheries, forestry, transportation, and so on. There is an obvious and urgent need to distribute this knowledge and expertise world-wide.

Cleaner production is "the continuous improvement of industrial processes and products to reduce the use of resources and energy; to prevent the pollution of air, water, and land; to reduce wastes at source; and to minimize risks to the human population and the environment" (UNEP, 1994a). Increasing the sustainability of products and services can be achieved by such measures as (UNEP/IE, RIVM, ILO, and Wuppertal Institute, personal communication, 1996):

- *input substitution*: using less toxic material; using materials with a longer service lifetime;

- *technology change*: replacing technology or process sequence to increase resource efficiency and to minimize waste and emission rates;

- *equipment modification*: changing existing equipment and utilities to run processes at higher resource efficiency and at lower waste and emission rates;

- *better process control*: using working procedures, machine instructions, and process record keeping to run processes at higher efficiency and at lower waste and emission rates;

Box 3.3 continued

Removal of timber from forests is being controlled in several countries by tradeable extraction permits, as, for example, in Côte d'Ivoire.

In offshore fisheries, for example, several countries are using tradeable quotas when conventional property rights cannot be assigned but an aggregate catch quota can be set, monitored, and enforced. Similar approaches are being used to optimize the numbers of visitors to national parks in Africa (through tradeable visitor permits), the numbers of hotels built in tourist development areas (through tradeable development permits), and the use of irrigation water (through tradeable water shares). Some economies in transition are experimenting with tradeable emission permits.

Urban pollution and congestion are being controlled by restricting the number of certain vehicles with access to urban areas. In New York City, for example, the number of taxis is controlled with tradeable licenses. In Santiago, Chile, the right of access to certain key city roads for buses and taxis has been auctioned.

Charge systems have typically been applied to the protection of resources from waste discharges and emissions. In Malaysia, for instance, effluent charges have been

in operation for 20 years to protect water quality from effluents arising from the palm oil and rubber industries. In Singapore, a scheme that charged drivers for using roads in the city centre during peak hours resulted in a 73-percent reduction in traffic in the restricted zone (and less carbon monoxide). Virtually all the economies in transition have introduced pollution charges.

Throughout the developing world, traditional societies maintain a wealth of customary use rights and communal management systems that provide incentives for the efficient use and conservation of natural resources. Although many have come under intense pressure from population growth, from new markets, and from technology, these systems contain valuable lessons and experiences for the design of effective, modern resource management systems that are attuned to local customs.

Reference

UNEP. 1995. Economic Instruments for Environmental Management and Sustainable Development. Consultant report prepared by Th. Panayotou for UNEP Environment and Economics Unit. Environmental Economics Series Paper No. 16. UNEP Environment and Economics Unit. Nairobi.

- *good housekeeping*: preventing leaks and spills, and enforcing existing working instructions;

- *on-site re-use*: using waste in the same process or for other useful applications within the company;

- *production of useful by-products*: modifying waste generation processes in order to promote re-use outside the company;

- *changes in product design*: reducing resource use and waste and emission rates; and

- *improved management*: ensuring a safe and healthy working environment, with good collaboration between management and workers, effective training, and development of partnerships among stakeholders in the enterprise and the community.

The key difference between pollution control and cleaner and leaner production is one of timing: from "notice and treat" to "anticipate and prevent"

or from "cure" to "prevention." Cleaner production leads to reductions of resource use and in amounts of waste and emissions generated. Achievable reductions of 50 per cent to 75 per cent are more and more the rule rather than the exception; reductions of 90 per cent are no longer uncommon either. (See Box 3.4.) The challenge is to achieve increases in efficiency and reductions in pollution and other forms of degradation by about one order of magnitude, as several prominent figures from different countries are advocating through the international Factor 10 Club they established in 1995 (Factor 10 Club, 1995).

On a macro-economic level, resource productivity refers to the total quantity of resources consumed to provide services and goods such as housing, transport, medical care, higher education, and export products for a given number of people (or within certain geographical or political boundaries)

Box 3.4
Examples of Possible Resource Efficiencies

In "Factor Four" (Weizsäcker *et al.*, 1996), an impressive number of examples is presented to support the message of the Factor Ten Club. These examples combine changes in thinking, systems, and technologies that lead to reductions in resource efficiency of a factor of four or more. All these examples are combinations of available technologies:

- super windows (factor 4),

- super refrigerators (factor 10),

- user-oriented and least-cost power plant management (factor 4),

- CD-ROM versus paper (factor 50),

- water use in paper manufacturing (factor 40), and

- marketing of low-transport products (factor 4 to 100).

The UNEP Industry and Environment Office has compiled concrete examples of cleaner production applied by companies in different regions of the world. They illustrate real achievements in waste and emission reduction and in raw material and energy use with factors ranging from 2 to 10. All examples given have an attractive payback time and were beneficial for the companies from various perspectives. They include:

- enzymatic bleach cleanup in cotton dying versus rinsing (factor 2 in water use, factor 5 in energy use), Denmark;

- waste generation in sugar milling and refining (factor 10 in wastewater, factor 2 in lead subacetate), the Philippines;

for a certain period of time. A country's total resource productivity can be accounted for by adding all resource inputs generated within the borders and those that were imported, and then subtracting the resource inputs exported. These material intensity and flow accounts aim to quantify the efficiency of economic operations; to consider how much material and energy is used, by whom, and how it is distributed; and to establish global patterns in the origin and movement of materials and energy.

Currently several initiatives are under way to calculate the material intensity of production processes and the flows of materials within and between nations. Their goal is to draw attention to the wasteful use of resources and promote resource efficiency. Such accounts can highlight policy opportunities for increasing resource productivity and can provide a way to assess the ecological quality of products and services, expressed in resource intensity throughout life cycles. (See Box 3.5.)

Although these attempts to look at macro-economic performance in an alternative way are currently limited and anecdotal, they hold the promise of providing different insights in how society operates, thus opening new avenues of dealing with environmental management.

Population and Poverty

The global concern for the issues addressed in the *GEO Report* emerges from the recognition that the environment affects all people and future generations. Many people are living in absolute poverty without security of food, shelter, health care, education, or other basic survival supplies. Unsustainable consumption in the North and rampant poverty in the South are great threats to the achievement of sustainable global development. Poor people are very vulnerable and the primary victims of environmental degradation and ecological disasters. Few issues have aroused more controversy and political, social, and moral divisiveness than that of population growth. The dual concerns of population growth and the increasing number of poor people worldwide, despite all development efforts, offer a great challenge to planners everywhere.

The growth rate in the world population as a whole passed its peak in the mid-1960s, when it was more than 2 per cent a year. The rate slowed to 1.54 per cent in the early 1990s. A large absolute increase is however still to be expected in the coming decades, due to the momentum of population growth. (See also Chapter 4.)

Box 3.4 continued

- emission abatement in coking works (factor 10 in hydrogen cyanide, toluene, benzene, xylene, and hydrogen sulphide), Poland;

- zero wastewater in metal finishing (factor 10 and more in water, chemicals, and sludge), Spain;

- fewer toxic wastes in leather tanning (zero production of sulfides and foul smells, factor 4 in consumption of chromium sulfate), Tunisia;

- treatment of wastewater in the rubber industry (factor 10 in BOD and COD reduction, factor 9 in water use), Malaysia;

- automating the bicycle wheel plating process (factor 1.5 in wastewater reduction; factor 10 in chrome discharge), China.

References

UNEP. 1993. Cleaner Production Worldwide. UNEP Industry and Environment Office. Paris.

UNEP. 1994. Cleaner Production in the Asia Pacific Economic Cooperation Region. UNEP Industry and Environment Office. Paris.

UNEP. 1995a. Cleaner Production in the Mediterranean Region. Ecomed, UNEP and Impressa Ambiente. Rome.

UNEP. 1995b. Cleaner Production Worldwide. Vol. II. UNEP Industry and Environment Office. Paris.

Weizsäcker, E.U. von, B. Lovins, and L. Hunter Lovins. 1996. "Factor Four: Doubling Wealth–Halving Resource Use," A Report to the Club of Rome. Wuppertal Institute. Wuppertal, Germany.

The demand that this burgeoning population places on global resources is a function of both the numbers and their per capita consumption. Poor people often eke out a living based on natural resources and they are often forced to live in areas that are environmentally vulnerable or fragile and prone to risk. Policy responses vary and depend on the region, culture, and economic status. It is increasingly acknowledged that social investment such as female education, better nutrition, and employment generation for women will have direct impacts on the rate of population growth and the degree of poverty. (See also the Health section of Chapter 4).

Policy responses addressing the dual and complementary targets of stabilizing population growth and reducing poverty, in addition to the traditional approaches of employment generation and macro-economic stabilization, include the following (Bangladesh Centre for Advanced Studies, personal communication, 1996):

- *Pro-poor planning*: Central planning has often worked against the interest of poor people and its macro-economic thrust and control has seldom been pro-poor or pro-environment. Pro-poor planning means "make bene-fiting poor people the main objective of planning;" if not, poor people will remain peripheral to the planning and development processes.

- *Social mobilization*: This involves making development itself more participatory and equitable, among other things through education and empowerment, particularly of women. An educated mother with some resources is the best insurance for a sustainable future in any culture. Children are good agents of change too: they raise awareness among their parents. Child education can create awareness of environmental realities along with economic opportunities.

- *Using indigenous knowledge and local coping and risk minimization strategies*: Poor people have survived in specific ecosystems for many centuries while developing their own indigenous knowledge, technologies, institutions, and support systems. The lessons to be learned here have true value in developing new intervention strategies.

- *Ensuring people's participation in decision making*: This entails involving all stakeholders in decision-making at the local level, particularly in natural resources management. Dialogue, the

> **Box 3.5**
> # Material Intensity and Flow Accounts
>
> In Germany, the Wuppertal Institute, in co-operation with the German Federal Statistical Office, developed an overall material flow account that provides a physical mass balance—domestic extraction from the environment, domestic deposition and release to the environment, imports, and exports. The account includes elements such as water, abiotic (non-renewable) and biotic (renewable) raw materials, soil and its erosion, emissions into the atmosphere (such as carbon dioxide, nitrogen oxide, and sulphur dioxide), and oxygen for combustion. The total material input indicator derived from these accounts can be regarded as a highly aggregated measure that relates pressures from the physical basis of the German economy to the global environment.
>
> The analysis carried out in Germany found that the relative dependence on a material-intensive supply is greatest for the energy sector, the iron and steel industry, and the construction sector. The energy sector was also found to be responsible for a high level of direct extraction of domestic primary material. The construction sector was found to be the most material-intensive. As a result, these two industrial sectors in Germany will be primary targets for dematerialization policies, which aim at reducing both material and energy intensity.
>
> Source: Wuppertal Institute. Personal communication. 1996.

participation of local poor populations, and conflict resolution among stakeholders strengthens the acceptablility and adaptability of concepts, projects, and programmes and makes interventions more cost-effective and culturally appropriate.

- *Linking informal to formal economic systems*: Most of the large contribution that poor people make to a national economy is informal and never enters national economic accounts (such as domestic and agricultural work by women). Formal micro-credit has proved to be one of the few tools to fight poverty and to enter the formal economy. Adapted technology also offers opportunities for poor people to enter the more formal, assured markets (such as better preservation of local agricultural products, so that goods can be sold when the market is favourable).

- *Enhancing resource availability*: Usually landless poor people need access to common or state-owned property, from which they extract resources for survival or economic development. The resource base can be made more secure by planting trees for construction material, firewood, and organic soil fertilization, by increasing fish productivity, and by installing hand pumps to ensure a nearby supply of clean drinking water.

- *Involving poor people in eco-specific interventions*: This involves developing local-level participatory eco-specific plans, managed and implemented by poor communities themselves, thereby creating employment and supporting livelihood systems. It can mean offering opportunities to regenerate areas and parts of degraded ecosystems to improve environmental conditions and productive potentials.

- *Information technology as an aid to awareness raising and local issue debate*: Though many poor people are illiterate, this need not be a hindrance to the use of modern technology. It can be effectively used for human resource development and empowerment. For instance, computer technology with interactive graphics is more and more used directly in the field to demonstrate impacts of projects or programmes to the local poor involved.

Changing Consumer Attitudes and Patterns

The policy initiatives described so far are, however, not sufficient by themselves to prevent further environmental damage or reverse existing destruction. They do not sufficiently address the fundamental issue of unsustainable consumption patterns, do little to encourage more environmentally sound industrial processes all over the world, and do not pursue vigorously the permeation of sound environmental knowledge and technology to all sectors of the global society.

For example, a major cause of global and regional environmental problems such as climate change and acidification continues to be the unsustainable consumption of natural resources in industrial countries and by more affluent groups within developing countries. If the number of cars per person in the United States were ever matched in China, some 20 per cent of the nation's arable land would be covered by roads and parking spaces (Wuppertal Institute, personal communication, 1996). If the world's 5 billion people emulated what the advanced industrial nations have reached, rapid ecological collapse would be the inescapable consequence.

What is needed is a fundamental change in the hearts and minds of everyone. As Maurice Strong, Secretary General of the 1992 United Nations Conference on Environment and Development, said in Singapore in early October 1996: "Greater co-operation between developing and industrialized countries is needed, with the rich prepared to share in solving environmental problems of the poor. We really need a change in ethos and culture. We need to move from a culture of greed and competition to one of co-operation and stewardship, a culture of sharing." This requires more than Governments providing an environment that will accelerate the process. All major groups need to feel responsible: women, children and youth, indigenous people, NGOs, local administrators, workers and trade unions, business and industry, scientists and academics, and farmers, including all rural people who derive their livelihood from activities such as farming, fishing, and harvesting the forest (UNEP, 1996b).

SUMMARY OF REGIONAL POLICY RESPONSES

From the reports on regional policy responses detailed below, a pattern emerges that reflects the state of development of the machinery for managing the environment in each Region. Identified responses range from institutional strengthening and the establishment of appropriate policies and legislation, to supplementing command-and-control strategies using market-based incentives. Other responses stimulate changes in production and consumption processes, emphasize environmentally friendly technologies, or encourage increased popular participation in policy development and implementation.

Getting Started

The most widespread response in all regions to the needs expressed in Stockholm and Rio de Janeiro has been the establishment of national environment-related ministries and specialist agencies dealing with sectoral environmental concerns. In Europe and North America, this process had already begun at the time of the Stockholm conference. The lead-up to UNCED provided the additional stimulus for all regions to further develop an institutional and constitutional basis for sustainable development. The recent inclusion of environment in constitutional reform in many developing and rapidly industrializing countries is another important development in this regard. Complementing these institutional and constitutional changes, an almost universal interest in sustainable development has emerged in the latter half of this decade among governmental and non-governmental stakeholders alike. The "hearts and minds" of stakeholders are changing, raising hopes that environmentally sustainable development can be achieved.

Basic Policy Instruments

Most countries in the different regions have established command-and-control policies as logical steps in the pursuit of better environmental management. The tools for implementing these policies are primarily legislation, compliance monitoring, and litigation. However, the effectiveness of implementation depends on the presence of appropriate environmental agencies, the comprehensive scope of legislation, availability of adequate human and financial resources to monitor compliance, and an effective legal system. As a consequence, environmental policy implementation varies greatly between regions and nations.

In Asia and the Pacific, umbrella environmental legislation and comprehensive environmental policies increasingly provide an overall framework for regulating most forms of pollution and enhancing environmental management in general. Specific command-and-control policies are firmly in place. Implementation of umbrella policies has unfortunately been hampered in a number of countries by institutional weaknesses and a lack of human and financial resources.

Many African countries have also enacted umbrella legislation, mainly within the framework of national environment action plans (NEAPs) stimulated by international financial institutions and conventions. Monitoring and regulatory systems have been set up in several states in the region to implement the legal provisions of new or revised environmental legislation. Unfortunately, institutional weaknesses, lack of skilled manpower, and inadequate training facilities still hamper monitoring and enforcement of environmental policies and regulations in a large number of African countries. Limited financial resources are partly to blame, but lack of coordination between involved authorities and counterproductive government policies also contribute in many instances to further restraint of policy implementation.

In countries of the EU, environmental legislation, and environmental considerations now impact on every individual, sector of society and governance structure. North America also relies strongly on legislative measures to combat environmental deterioration. While economic reform offers the key to solving certain environmental problems in countries of Central and Eastern Europe, environmental legislation needs further development, harmonization and enforcement to achieve maximum effectiveness.

In Latin America and the Caribbean most national initiatives concerning the environment revolve around command-and-control mechanisms, particularly legislation. While new institutions established to deal with the environment greatly assist implementation of legislative reforms throughout

the Region, institutional weaknesses remain and are often aggravated by limited finances. Structural adjustment programmes have also led some governments to cut social and environmental spending in this region, as well as in Africa, causing the temporary abandonment of environmental planning in a number of affected countries.

Environmental programmes, institutions, and laws in West Asia have sometimes been created haphazardly and not in the context of an over-arching strategic plan for the environment. This has resulted in dominantly sectoral approaches to environmental planning without due consideration of the need for cross-cutting policies and institutional requirements. Recently, attempts to harmonize environmental legislation and the role of institutions in developing strategic frameworks for environmental planning have taken place in a number of countries in West Asia.

Overall, in the developing regions compliance monitoring is still constrained by a lack of financial resources and inadequate availability of skilled manpower.

Refining Environmental Policy

Command-and-control systems tend to function more effectively when addressing sectoral environmental problems. The sectoral nature of much environmental legislation and the short-term success of end-of-pipe solutions when treating site-specific environmental problems have historically reinforced the application of command-and-control mechanisms in isolation. As most countries are now aware, sustainable development and general environmental well-being are complex, integrated problems requiring cradle-to-grave solutions and public participation. Comprehensive environmental policies that take account of this are therefore gaining favour in many regions. Greater co-ordination of effort between national environment-related authorities is also becoming evident world-wide.

With command and control policies firmly in place, and long experience in their use, a number of regions are exploring alternative and supplementary strategies to augment environmental quality and further protect the health and well-being of their citizens. Alternative strategies are projected to be more cost effective than the further expansion and reliance on command and control approaches.

Innovative approaches to environmental policy formulation are now evident in North America and Europe, and emerging in Asia and the Pacific and certain countries in Latin America and the Caribbean. In North America, the creation of better environments for voluntary action has resulted in a multitude of alternative policy responses. Concepts founded on common sense, innovation and flexibility are leading to creative partnerships between government authorities and society. These partnerships to environmental problem-solving rely on the use of market incentives and encourage the application of innovative, cost-effective, cleaner production technologies and processes.

In Europe, for example, industrial groupings have adopted responsible care programmes, and public participation is now firmly embedded in policy and decision-making processes. Pan-European capacity building programmes also operate to forward environmental management and economic development, including the development of regulatory frameworks and restructuring of higher education.

Environmental Citizenship

The past five years has witnessed the emergence of democratization in several regions and with it, a growth in the intertwining of politics and the environment. Many of the mechanisms required to successfully implement sustainable development rely on accountable partnerships between government, industry, business, and the community at large. The value of popular participation by both individuals and interest groups in the development of environmental policy is increasingly being recognized by formerly centralized governments; thus, opening the way for greater environmental citizenship in the future.

In Africa, decentralization of government authorities offers potential for increased grass-roots participation in policy development and implemen-

tation in the future. Individual rights to a clean and healthy environment are clearly acknowledged in the constitutions of several African countries and care for the environment considered a duty of all citizens. In specific instances, the role of NGOs in Latin America and the Caribbean in policy development and implementation has grown in recent years. Continued involvement of NGOs and other responsible interest groups is important for the future of environmental management in the Region. The role of environmental NGOs in West Asia in policy development and environmental management is still minimal. Community based action programmes are evident in a number of countries in Asia and the Pacific, with people-oriented environmental restoration programmes and involvement of women notable in south Asia.

Significant popular mobilization has created networks of environmental organizations in civil society in both North America and Europe. A plethora of environmental NGOs contributes vigorously to policy evolution, and implementation and monitoring of programmes in both regions. Increased participation of the private sector in policy development and environmental management is significant. Voluntary codes of conduct, guidelines on environmental management and similar initiatives contribute increasingly to sound stewardship of the environment and economic development.

Political reform in many countries has also improved access to information for environmentalists. Additional opportunities are growing rapidly where national telecommunications supporting the global information highway are adequate and affordable.

Regional Cooperation

Regional cooperation concerning the environment has grown significantly in all regions during the past decade. In most regions, there are active programmes to establish regional environmental databases, to strengthen policy making capacities and to develop regional institutional and legislative frameworks, regional environmental networks and high-level policy forums. In Asia and the Pacific for example, considerable emphasis is now placed on regional cooperative mechanisms to strengthen state of environment reporting. A range of regional agreements designed to tackle transboundary environmental problems and to support Pan-European capacity building in CIS countries has been instituted with high-level policy support in Europe.

In Africa regional agreements have recently been drawn up to address the negative effects of conflicts, with consequent benefits for the environment. Other regional policy negotiations deal with land-related issues such as desertification. In North America transboundary environmental issues are among the key concerns of the Region. A number of regional agreements have consequently been put in place to deal with issues such as the Great Lakes ecosystem and joint action on acid rain. The last years have also witnessed the growth and strengthening of sub-regional agreements in Latin America and the Caribbean that address environmental issues as well as economic and social issues, which at the same time recognize attendant environmental and sustainability issues. Specific environmental treaties, conventions, and agreements have been signed in Latin America and the Caribbean that deal with regional resources such as the Amazon and sustainable development of island states. The focus of the many regional groups guiding environmental management in West Asia is on the four regional seas surrounding the countries of the Region, or sub-regional groupings of these countries such as those adjacent to the Mediterranean or comprising the Arabian Peninsula.

References

Factor 10 Club. 1995. Carnoules Declarations 1994/1995 of the Factor 10 Club. Wuppertal Institute. Wuppertal, Germany.

UNEP. 1994a. Government Strategies and Policies for Cleaner Production. UNEP Industry and Environment Office. Paris.

UNEP. 1996a. Environmental Impacts of Structural Adjustment Programmes: Synthesis and Recommendations. Environmental Economics Series Paper No. 21. UNEP Environment and Economics Unit. Nairobi.

UNEP. 1996b. Taking Action. An environmental guide for you and your community. UNEP and UN Non-governmental Liaison Service (NGLS). Nairobi.

UNEP. 1996c. UNEP's New Way Forward: Environmental Law and Sustainable Development. Chapter 12: Emerging Trends in National Environmental Legislation in Developing Countries. UNEP Environmental Law Unit. Nairobi.

UNEP. 1996d. UNEP's New Way Forward: Environmental Law and Sustainable Development. Chapter 16: Environmental Impact Assessment Legislation in Developing Countries. UNEP Environmental Law Unit. Nairobi.

AFRICA

National Initiatives

In recent years, nearly all countries in Africa have been engaged in strategic planning processes, either along with macro-economic reform policies or to implement international conventions and programmes. National Environment Action Plans (NEAPs), National Conservation Strategies (NCSs), National Plans of Action to Combat Desertification (NPACD), National Tropical Forestry Action Plans (TFPAs), Country Environmental Strategy Papers (CESPs), National Energy Assessments, and Country Programmes for the Phase Out of Ozone-Depleting Substances under the Montreal Protocol are playing significant roles in integrating environment and development in the countries. Among the more prominent of these activities in the 1970s were the preparation of desertification-control plans throughout western Africa and NCSs elsewhere on the continent (Dorm-Adzobu, 1995). At present, about 80 per cent of the countries in sub-Saharan Africa are involved in the NEAP process and other countries are preparing or implementing similar kinds of environmental strategies (World Bank, 1995). Egypt, Tunisia, and Morocco have each completed a NEAP [Centre for Environment and Development for the Arab Region and Europe (CEDARE), personal communication, 1996].

One major imperative addressed by all strategic planning processes, particularly the NEAPs, is the need for institutional mechanisms: organizational structures, both Government and non-governmental, at national and subnational levels that have responsibility for general planning. As part of the strategic planning processes, countries are implementing institutional reforms: national environmental institutions (ministries, departments, commissions, and so on), non-governmental organizations (NGOs), advocacy groups, and private-sector insti-

tutions have been strengthened or established to take responsibility for the environment and to promote sustainable development policies and programmes.

In many countries, high-level co-ordination agencies for environmental management have been created. Decentralization of central Government functions is taking place, especially with respect to environmental planning. This has created opportunities for NGOs and grassroots participation in identification, planning, and implementation of environmental projects. Examples of the institutionalization of these measures can be found in Benin, Madagascar, Ethiopia, The Gambia, Uganda, and Ghana (Benin, 1993b; Ethiopia, 1995; Madagascar, 1993; The Gambia, 1995b; Uganda, 1995; Ghana, 1995).

In many countries, however, institutions are still weak and not adequately equipped to implement their functions. These shortcomings stem from many factors, including a serious shortage of skilled staff, the absence of adequate training facilities, lack of integration and co-operation among major institutions, and counterproductive Government policies and legislation. (Ethiopia, 1995b).

Important changes are also being made to the national constitutions of African countries, in order to incorporate the basic principles of environmental management. The individual's right to a clean and healthy environment and the State's duty to protect and conserve environmental and natural resources are recurrent themes in the new constitutions (Ogolla, 1995). For example, the Constitution of Mali (1992) notes: "Every person has a right to a healthy environment. The protection and defence of the environment and the promotion of the quality of life are the duty of all and for the State."

Another example where the concept of sustainable development and intergenerational equity has been expressed is in the Constitution of Namibia (1990), which stipulates that the State shall actively promote and maintain the welfare of the people by adopting policies aimed at, among other matters, "the maintenance of ecosystems, essential ecological processes and biological diversity of Namibia and utilization of living natural resources on a sustainable basis for the benefit of all Namibians, both present and future."

The elevation of environmental concerns to constitutional status has no doubt enhanced the priority conferred by Governments on sound environmental management and sustainable development (Ogolla, 1995). Some of the other countries whose constitutions also provide for environment, natural resources, and sustainable development are Ghana, Kenya, and Uganda. (NESDA, personal communication, 1996).

Some of the general policies and directions being planned and implemented, often within the strategic planning framework, include the formulation and enactment of new umbrella legislation on environment and natural resources management and the establishment of monitoring and regulatory systems (Côte d'Ivoire, 1996; Burkina Faso, 1994; The Gambia, 1995a; Ghana, 1994; Kenya, 1994; and Benin, 1993a). Increasingly, countries are preparing Environment Impact Assessment (EIA) guidelines and procedures as a followup to EIA legislation as found in Ghana and Kenya, for example (Ghana, 1992; Kenya, 1994).

In order to strengthen capacity in terms of human resources, African countries are emphasizing the need for environmental education, training, and information; the role of NGOs and the media; development and implementation of natural resource management projects; and the active participation of grassroots groups in the environmental management process. For example, The Gambia, Senegal, and Ghana have introduced environmental studies into school curricula, as well as population control programmes (The Gambia 1992; Senegal 1995; Ghana 1995). Countries are also establishing Environmental Information Systems (EIS) programmes and acquiring electronic mail systems to facilitate information exchange within and outside

the region (Cameroon, 1996; NESDA, personal communication, 1996).

Several sectoral policy responses have been formulated and applied, many of which come up under NEAPs, macro-economic policy frameworks [such as Economic Recovery Programmes (ERPs)], and similar plans. It is impossible to report in detail on the plethora of environmental initiatives that have occurred, particularly given the diverse social, institutional, and environmental conditions of the region and even within each country. These differences are reflected in the focus and priorities as well as policy formulation and action implementation occurring in the region to address environmental problems. Only a brief account of some of the more common directions in and examples of policy responses and actions on some of the priority environmental concerns is provided here.

The environmental problems related to land are some of the most compelling issues in Africa. The need to reduce pressure on already overstressed land resources is one of the main challenges. Some of the policies and actions planned or implemented include review of tenurial rights, land classification, establishment of land resource information systems, soil conservation and improved farming practices, eco-farming, agro-forestry, and afforestation programmes. Examples of countries where these measures are implemented include Ghana and Senegal (Ghana, 1992; Senegal, 1995).

Traditional rights on land and access to land vary greatly from country to country. In some, these rights facilitate access to land for small farmers; in others, the opposite occurs. Relationships between the State and rural communities about landownership is also variable, from situations where most of the lands belong to the State to situations where most belong to traditional chiefs. The strong trend on the continent towards democracy and decentralization of civil powers apply particularly in the areas of land resources management and rural development.

Since the modest initiative of pilot villages at the time of the Cairo Conference in 1985, the concept of giving back to villagers full authority for their land has gained ground. Not only were the few pilot villages of the AMCEN programme a success (for example, in Senegal), but many bilateral and multilateral donors and African Governments adopted this grassroots approach (for example, Germany in Burkina Faso; the World Bank, with Natural Resources Management Projects in many countries; and the United Nations Development Programme [UNDP] in Senegal).

Research on traditional rural systems has been strengthened and the complex relationship between rural populations and their environments is better understood. Integrated plant nutrition systems, integrated pest management, and agroforestry are providing new packages for land rehabilitation and productivity increase. The Organization of African Unity (OAU) programme on the use of local minerals and organic resources as low-cost fertilizers and soil ameliorants (implemented by the International Fertilizers Development Centre) is bringing new solutions to soil fertility depletion (UNEP, 1996).

One important reason for the continued land-related environmental problems is that there are limited alternative industrial activities to reduce pressure on land. Furthermore, the declining terms of trade on agricultural commodities add pressure on land and contribute to continuing poverty. (See Box 3.6 on Trade Issues.) Governments have tried to expand and diversify the production structure throughout the industry sector. These efforts have focused on policies for developing institutional infrastructures that enable change. They include provision of the right atmosphere to do business involving fiscal, monetary, import-export regulations, and investment codes. They also aim at improving the education system to enable it to respond to the complex skill and staffing needs. Support to industry also includes establishing and strengthening industrial research and development institutions and other institutions that support small- and medium-sized industries as well as improving financing conditions for industrial projects by creating financial institutions, and so on.

Because of the pressure to develop fast, however, investments are often being made without due consideration to their impact on the environment. At the national level, there are also problems in reaching agreements among various stake-holders (Government, the local community, foreign investors, and international financing agencies) on investment activities. The means to appraise the degree of success of various actions and their accountability are urgently needed (UNEP, 1996).

Solving water-related issues is an important priority and includes providing sustained water and sanitation services to all people. Programmes for water supply and sanitation increasingly incorporate new ideas that focus on the assessment of needs and requirements of the beneficiaries and their participation. There has been a gradual move towards community participation and management, with the community itself setting priorities and assuming responsibility, authority, and control over improvements in and operation of services. Some examples of successful rural water supply and sanitation projects are found in Burkina Faso, Mali, and Togo, featuring drilled wells with handpumps. Two examples of the most successful rural sanitation programmes in the region can be found in Lesotho and Zimbabwe.

Under these programmes, the needs of the population and the constraints within the community to widespread adoption of improved sanitation and hygiene were first identified. Public awareness raising, promotion, and marketing resulted in successful provision of sanitation, the costs of which were met by receiving families. The Lesotho Sanitation Programme also maximized the private-sector involvement in planning, financing, and implementation, including involvement of local latrine builders, credit unions, and building materials suppliers (World Bank, 1996).

Countries such as Botswana and Namibia have developed master plans for effective use of available water, the provision of safe water, and treatment of wastewater. The Botswana National Water Master Plan is one of Africa's most realistic plans for sustainable use of water resources. It recognizes the limitations in water availability in the country and hence the inability to establish large-scale irrigation schemes. This has led to the adoption of a policy on "food security" instead of "food self-sufficiency" (Ohlsson, 1995).

Box 3.6
Trade: Some Problems, Some Policy Responses

International trade is often a magnifier of existing environmental problems, with adverse local and regional impacts. Some of the major existing problems related to trade and environment are:

Market Distortions

1. Import restrictions (e.g., escalating tariffs that rise with the degree of processing involved, tariff rate quotas, voluntary import restrictions, and other non-tariff barriers) are widely used by developed countries, often with the intention of benefitting domestic industries. They impact the environment in two ways: (i) they protect inefficient industries whose overproduction leads to excess pollution and resource degradation; (ii) when these restrictions are aimed at developing country exports, they perpetuate poverty in those countries by reducing options for employment and income generation—this in turn leads to environmental and health impacts that result directly from poverty.

2. Use of subsidies for energy, water, pesticides, fertilizer, etc., distorts the price of traded goods and contributes, indirectly, to environmental problems. For example, the widespread and liberal use of energy subsidies encourages overuse of energy resources, discourages innovation and supports economically unviable energy-intensive industries. The energy overuse contributes to climate change. Removing such subsidies becomes difficult when imported goods (subsidized by exporting countries) compete directly with domestically produced goods.

Uninternalized Environmental and Social Costs

Traded goods usually do not include environmental and social costs in their prices. This results in the manufacture and sale of excessive quantities of under-priced goods and a lack of encouragement to develop and market environmentally preferable substitutes. It also leads to over-intensive exploitation of natural resources and production of wastes.

Fierce international competition in commodity markets means that producers cannot easily internalize costs unilaterally, for fear of losing market share, particularly for unprocessed commodities such as agricultural products, forest products and minerals. The buyers of their products will deal with whoever can offer the lowest price. Many developing countries depend on such primary commodities for export income and are trapped in a vicious cycle: poverty and debt force them to increase natural resource-based exports, without internalizing environmental costs; these exports then face barriers in developed countries and increased competition from other exporters following the same strategy. The resulting low revenues result in yet further exports and further environmental degradation, as well as continuing poverty and poverty-related environmental problems.

Policy Responses and Directions

To address trade-related hindrances to improved environmental stewardship, some examples of possible policies to be considered at the national level by all countries include:

The need for appropriate technology, facilities, and management to harness available water is an important issue in Africa, particularly because of the uneven distribution of freshwater resources and increasing demand for water for various activities such as agriculture, fisheries, mining, industry, and tourism. The rapidly growing demand for food, coupled with seasonal variations and unreliability of precipitation, make irrigation an important means to ensure sustenance of food supply. Experiences in Africa show that large-scale irrigation schemes are not always the most appropriate. Small- and medium-scale ones, involving water user associations in project planning and implementation, use of low-cost technologies, and less costly infrastructure and distribution schemes, have been suc-

Box 3.6 continued

- Dismantling escalating tariffs that discourage processing and diversification in developing country export sectors.

- Accelerating the dismantling of import quotas and other non-tariff barriers to developing country exports, including multilateral protectionist deals.

- Reducing subsidies for exports, or to export-competing goods, particularly in areas such as the agricultural sector;

- Developing and applying economic instruments to promote internalization of external environmental and social costs in order for goods and services to be traded at prices that reflect their true costs, and at the same time, strengthening capacity in developing countries through, inter alia, bilateral aid programmes.

Given the international nature of trade and environment issues, the most urgent need for action is at the international level. Some examples of actions to be considered at the international level include:

- Making concerted efforts to create new types of international environmental agreements, e.g., on minimum standards for certain types of processes, or in the harvest of certain types of resources, allowing for legitimate diversities of approaches to common problems. Convergence of disparate approaches can be assisted by equity improving measures.

- Seeking agreements that also involve producers, consumer interests and specialized environment and development organizations. Voluntary sectoral agreements are increasingly used in various fields, and the sentiment that propels them could be harnessed in an effort to create international agreements that are

between industry-driven voluntary measures and government-negotiated agreements.

- Developing new types of commodity agreements. Traditionally, making commodity agreements more efficient contributed to lower consumer prices and more production, but could, under different circumstances, be used to fund cost internalization measures at the producer level.

- Implementing measures to better integrate policy making across the trade and environment spheres, for example:

  - developing formal instruments to engage the international trade and environment regimes in cooperation and consultation;

  - establishing an intergovernmental panel on trade and sustainable development, so that experts from the trade, environment, and development communities can define, prioritize, and research the relevant issues; and

  - creating a high-level international forum responsible to both trade and environment concerns, with the mandate and authority to hammer out deals on cross-cutting issues.

- Multilateral environmental agreements (MEAs) are becoming increasingly important in international environmental management and they evoke trade and sustainable development principles. There is consequently a need to strengthen them as an effective means of cost internalization and protection of environmental integrity.

cessful overall. Examples can be found in Ethiopia, Madagascar, and Nigeria.

The Fadama Irrigation in Nigeria consisted of individually owned and maintained pump-tubewell systems to irrigate 1–2 hectares. The result was increased market crop production and widespread use of pumps, leading to the rise of a service industry to maintain the pumps. In Ethiopia, more than 40 water user groups were voluntarily formed for rehabilitation and construction schemes covering

4,400 hectares in total. These user groups are now fully responsible for operation and maintenance of the schemes that can ensure subsistence during droughts, and marketable surplus during normal rainfall years. In Madagascar, 116 medium-sized schemes of approximately 1,000 hectares each were established. This required regulatory changes to create an enabling environment that encourages production. Schemes that performed unsatisfactorily were located in areas with adverse environmental conditions or areas that lacked social cohesiveness (World Bank, 1996).

There are also examples of successful watershed protection and management programmes, including measures to enhance and control land use through water and soil conservation as well as afforestation. For example, a watershed protection programme in the Fouata Djallon Mountains of Guinea involved detailed studies and mapping of human and live-stock densities, climate, land use, and susceptibility to soil erosion. With full participation of farmers and their confidence, afforestation was undertaken to rehabilitate the watershed (World Bank, 1996). Other examples can be found in the Zambezi and Nile river basins (UNEP, 1996).

Successful measures to prevent deforestation and to meet the need for fuelwood and other wood-land products have been achieved through large-scale planting managed by Governments or compa-nies for commercial timber production. Smaller, community-level forest management and tree plant-ing schemes, often operated by forestry departments or municipal and village organizations, have also played an important role in some areas. For example, in Swaziland, one village that was given a plantation by the Government sold the timber with consider-able returns. The village, now interested in tree plant-ing, has reinvested in the woodlot (SARDC, 1994).

Tanzania has built on traditional views regard-ing tree rights to install legal instruments to protect tree ownership. Planting trees strengthens the rights to land. In Mamire village, for example, a law states that a person who deliberately destroys an-other person's tree will be fined and has to buy, care for, and plant 20 new seedlings wherever the injured party wishes. On the strength of this law, virtually every small-holder in the village planted trees along field boundaries, tempering escalating local con-flicts over land access (SARDC, 1994).

Better management of natural forests is also being achieved in countries such as Namibia and Zimbabwe through "annexing" of as much as 2 hectares of common woodland to private home-steads. Villagers with such private woodlands usually manage them efficiently and are self-sufficient in poles and fuelwood (SARDC, 1994).

Attempts to reduce deforestation problems with fuel-saving stoves have, in general, not been success-ful in the sub-Saharan region. This is primarily because fuelwood use is not the major cause of deforestation and also because the stoves were not appropriately designed or promoted. In rural set-tings, the actual consumption of fuelwood was not significantly reduced because the stoves could not be used for other purposes, such as heating and lighting. In addition, the stoves were often promoted in areas where people were already using fuelwood as con-servatively as possible (SARDC, 1994).

The region has several innovative wildlife man-agement strategies, such as game ranching and community-based management schemes, offering promising and practical alternatives to the standard approaches to wildlife conservation. Many of these are pioneered in southern Africa, such as the Com-munal Areas Management Programme For Indige-nous Resources (CAMPFIRE) in Zimbabwe, launched in 1987; the Administrative Management Design for Game Management Areas (ADMADE) in Zambia; and the Selous Conservation Programme in Tanzania (Makombe, 1993). Under these pro-grammes, communities raise revenues through sport hunting management, for example. Hence less habi-tat is converted to agricultural land and poaching is prevented. The establishment of natural history mu-seums and botanic gardens is also significant in conserving and documenting biodiversity.

With regard to coastal and marine areas, coun-tries have various regulations in place to control activities in the areas of investments, fishing prac-tices, oil spills, and withdrawal of coastal ground water. EIAs are mandatory for development proj-ects in coastal zones. In general, implementation of these regulatory measures has not been all that successful because of a lack of co-ordination among various authorities; overlapping mandates of various institutions; and a lack of resources, including skilled staff and financial and technical resources, to enforce the laws. Existing local and national environmental policies are often compromised for the sake of short-term economic benefits, resulting in the im-plementation of development projects without ade-quate environmental consideration (UNEP, 1996).

Conservation of marine environments has been lagging behind efforts on the land, for example, in southern Africa (SARDC, 1994), resulting in the proliferation of illegal fishing and the overexploitation of mangroves. However, there have been some successful efforts. In Namibia, for example, the conservation of marine resources has been brought about in part through quota systems, the prohibition of fishing in some areas during certain times of the year, and bans on the use of destructive fishing methods. This has been successful in Namibia because capacities exist to enforce the regulations (SARDC, 1994).

In the island States of Africa, an Integrated Coastal Zone Management (ICZM) Programme, a five-year project funded by the European Union, is being implemented. The goal of the programme is to enable sustainable development of coastal zones. Policies and actions under the ICZM include better land use planning and zoning, control of wastewater, control of fertilizer use, protection of dunes from sand mining, protection of aquifers from salinization through controlled pumping, monitoring of water quality in lagoons, conservation of a large variety of endemic plant species, and a complete environmental audit (UNEP, 1996). Also, appropriate inland measures are taken, such as anti-erosional measures using silt traps, controlling activities on slopes, vegetation planting on areas that are likely to be eroded, and prevention of land-based pollution (UNEP, 1996). Similarly, projects for solid waste management, embodying recycling of inorganic waste as well as composting of organic waste, are being prepared for implementation within the framework of the ICZM, in conformity with the Barbados Action Programme (UNEP, 1996).

Climate change and its potential to cause sea level rise is a serious concern, particularly in the coastal countries and the island States. At national and subregional levels, individual Governments have developed policy instruments and institutions to address climate issues (UNEP, 1996). Much of the action taken comes under the United Nations Framework Convention on Climate Change (UNFCCC), including public awareness raising and preparing national inventories of the sources and sinks of greenhouse gases. It is expected that climate change would cause arid and semi-arid areas to become drier and prone to frequent and severe extreme weather events, like droughts and storms. Although Africa's contribution to the emission of greenhouse gases is relatively small, Governments there are combining their endeavours to secure greater energy self-sufficiency with an emphasis on energy efficiency and broader use of renewable energy sources (UNECA, 1992). Energy efficiency and conservation are the most efficient ways to combat energy-related pollution.

There are a series of brown environmental issues, such as ambient air pollution issues, workplace exposure, deposition of agrochemicals, and household exposure to particulates, that are known to occur in Africa but that have not been studied in sufficient detail to assess their magnitude and severity. There is a clear need to address these issues within strategic frameworks for action (IMERCSA, personal communication, 1996).

Regional Initiatives

The institutional arrangements to facilitate and coordinate regional actions on environment and development include subregional organizations such as the Arab Magreb Union (AMU); the Permanent Inter-State Committee for Drought Control (CILSS); the Economic Community of Central African States (ECCAS); the Economic Community of West African States (ECOWAS); the Inter-governmental Authority on Development (IGAD), formerly known as the Inter-governmental Authority on Drought and Development (IGADD); and the Southern African Development Community (SADC).

High-level regional forums have also been established to formulate regional policies and programmes dealing with environment and sustainable development issues. These forums include the African Ministerial Conferences on the Environment (AMCEN), established under the auspices of UNEP in 1985; the African Economic Community (AEC), established within the framework of the OAU and the Abuja Treaty in June 1992; and the Council of Arab Ministers Responsible for the Environment

(CAMRE), established as the special body of the League of Arab States, consisting of 11 North African States and 12 West Asian States. Under CAMRE, a Joint Committee on Environment and Development in the Arab Region (JCEDAR) was established in 1993 to facilitate co-ordination and co-operation among member states (CEDARE, personal communication, 1996).

In various regional forums of African Government leaders, priority actions have been identified in order to achieve progress towards sustainable development. At the Earth Summit in 1992, the Africa region, through the OAU, submitted a comprehensive report entitled the "African Common Position on Environment and Development" as its contribution to Agenda 21. This report clearly addresses the regional constraints, concerns, and opportunities for sustainable development. Some of the most important programmes for action developed since Rio include:

- "African Strategies for the Implementation of the United Nations Conference on Environment and Development," adopted by the Conference of Ministers of Economic Planning and Development at its 19th Session, 3–6 May 1993;

- "Proposals for the Implementation of the Abuja Treaty Establishing the African Economic Community," the 14th Meeting of the Technical Preparatory Committee of the Whole, 12–16 April 1993, and the 28th Session of the Commission/19th Meeting of the Conference of the Ministers, 19–22 April 1993;

- "Relaunching Africa's Economic and Social Development: the Cairo Agenda of Action," adopted at the Extraordinary Session of the OAU Council of Ministers on 28 March 1995, subsequently endorsed by the June 1995 Summit of the African Heads of State and Government in Addis Ababa; and

- the 1996–97 Programme of Work, adopted by AMCEN at its 6th Ministerial Session in Nairobi, 14–15 December 1995.

In 1996, the United Nations System-wide Special Initiative on Africa was launched to reinforce previous United Nations initiatives, such as the United Nations Programme of Action for African Economic Recovery and Development (UN-PAAERD) and its successor, the United Nations New Agenda for the Development of Africa (UN-NADAF) in the 1990s. The System-wide Special Initiative reflects the priorities enunciated by Africa's leaders and was formulated in consultation with African leaders. The challenges of the Initiative are twofold: to carry out the best supportive actions congruent with Africa's priorities to stimulate development, and to mobilize international political support for action to remove some of the obstacles to Africa's development.

It is recognized in the African region that conflicts present a grave threat to environmental security. The impacts of conflicts are more openly discussed these days, and the importance of developing institutional structures and mechanisms to manage them is recognized. Examples of this are the OAU mechanism for the prevention, management, and resolution of conflicts and the wide range of civil society organizations engaged in conflict management efforts (UNDP, 1996).

In addition to the initiatives at the political level, collaboration with and participation of NGOs, women's and youth organizations, and the private sector are considered important for environmental protection and sustainable development. The creation of an enabling environment for the implementation of relevant actions in Africa involves the full democratization of political systems and the decision-making process, as detailed in the African Charter for Popular Participation in Development Transformation (UNECA, 1993).

Examples of regional NGOs active in strengthening regional co-operation and co-ordination in the field of environment include the Network for Environment and Sustainable Development for Africa (NESDA) and CEDARE. NESDA was established to bring together African experts, public- and private-sector institutions, and NGOs involved in sustainable development initiatives. It provides, among other things, expertise for capacity development and for environmental information. CEDARE was established in 1992 as an independent, non-profit organization to assist member countries in building capacity to enhance environmental management and to accelerate development. It has five priority programmes: freshwater resources, land, urbanization and human settlements, marine and coastal management, and industrialization. It also operates an active Information Service Unit.

Several sectoral action programmes have been developed and are implemented under regional environmental initiatives to enhance the implementation of global environmental conventions. For example, in combatting land degradation, implementation of the United Nations Convention to Combat Desertification is of prime importance to Africa, and one of the key initiatives of the region to implement the convention is the "International Convention to Combat Desertification and Urgent Action for Africa." Most African countries have signed the Convention, although ratification has been very slow. Even more important in terms of an action-oriented common framework is the Sustainable Agriculture and Rural Development (SARD) programme, which was prepared by the United Nations Food and Agriculture Organization (FAO) with the full participation of African ministries of agriculture and African experts and approved at an international level by the Rio conference in Agenda 21.

Regional co-operation in the field of land degradation has also been strengthened either directly through subregional institutions such as IGAD (see Box 3.7), SADC, and CILSS, and the African Development Bank (ADB), or indirectly through the institutes for applied research within the Consultative Group on International Agricultural Research (CGIAR) (UNEP, 1996). For example, under SADC, the Environment and Land Management Sector (ELMS) has developed an environment and sustainable development policy and strategy that deals with land degradation issues, and the Southern African Centre for Cooperation in Agricultural and Natural Resources Research (SACCAR) and Training, established in 1984, co-ordinates and promotes co-operation in agricultural research and natural resources and training activities.

The World Bank has also reinforced its activities on some of the major causes of land degradation and low food production growth (such as water, soil fertility, and technologies) (UNEP, 1996).

Other examples of regional activities on land issues include the Desert Margins Initiative (DMI) for Sub-Saharan Africa, a project in its early stages led by a consortium of six research centres within the CGIAR, UNEP, and other international, regional, and national institutes, and coordinated by the International Crops Research Institute for the Semi-Arid Tropics (ICRISAT). The main aim of the project is to address problems of food security, poverty, and the sustainable management of natural resources and to promote innovative and action-oriented dryland management research to arrest land degradation in sub-Saharan Africa. The initiative will first be implemented in the affected areas of Botswana, Burkina Faso, Kenya, Mali, Namibia, and Niger (Sivakumar and Willis, 1995).

The AMCEN also has a special role in the implementation of the Convention to Combat Desertification, through its Committee on Deserts and Arid Lands (ADALCO). In Zimbabwe, for example, it initiated five pilot projects in 1995 that address desertification problems through improved land management practices (IMERCSA, personal communication, 1996). In 1994, African NGOs established an international network on desertification—Reseau International ONG sur Desertification (RIOD)—including community-based organizations. RIOD will promote action to combat desertification and will give community-based organizations and NGOs an effective role in the preparation, implementation, and review of national action programmes (Mpande, 1995).

An important regional agreement that deals with hazardous waste problems in Africa is the 1991 Bamako Convention on the Banning of Transboundary Movement of Toxic Waste. Importation of any hazardous wastes into Africa is outlawed under the Convention. Twenty-two countries are signatories and at least 10 countries are Parties to the Convention.

In the field of drought monitoring and early warning, as well as of climate in general, regional

Box 3.7

IGAD Experience in Implementing Its Programmes

The Inter-governmental Authority on Development (IGAD), comprises presently Djibouti, Eritrea, Ethiopia, Kenya, Somalia, Sudan, and Uganda and has its seat in Djibouti. Most of the subregion is arid and semi-arid, and can be characterized by a vulnerable ecosystem with recurrent drought and rainfall variability both in space and time. IGAD was created to co-ordinate efforts of Member States in controlling drought and desertification. IGAD focuses on food security, the proper management of the environment, and desertification problems. A substantial number of programmes and projects were identified and developed through a consultative process with the Member States and donors.

Successful implementation of projects was mainly in the food security sector. One of the major projects in the sector, implemented with funds from Italy, was the Early Warning and Food Information System (EWFIS) with a Remote Sensing component. The project has created national early warning units, trained manpower, and developed standard methodologies and software, databases and networking both at subregional and national levels except in Djibouti.

The major constraints faced in implementing the agreed programmes and projects include the following:

- Lack of resources, at national and donor levels. Some Member States are unable to pay their annual contribution regularly, which, in turn, has an impact on donors' support.

- Lack of capacity both at the subregional and national levels as well as at the IGAD secretariat. The secretariat is faced with financial constraints, making hiring consultants to assist the core staff difficult. The Member States often do not have the capacity to implement subregional, regional, and international activities parallel to the national activities.

- Lack of coordination and transparency, complicated by overlapping policies and institutions both at the regional, sub-regional, and national levels.

- Lack of democratization and grassroots-level participation in project formulation and implementation. In many countries, local communities are not empowered to deal with environmental concerns and share benefits from natural resources projects.

- Lack of peace and security in the subregion greatly affected food security, environment protection, and the overall sustainable development of the subregion.

A Special Summit of the Heads of State and Government of IGAD was held on 21 March 1996, to deliberate on the revitalization of IGAD and other matters of interest to the subregion. The Summit approved extensive amendments to the 1986 Agreement establishing IGAD. The amendments included changes to the organizational structures as well as the strengthening of programmes. The meetings of the Council of Ministers and Technical Experts decided on the new priority areas of IGAD (Food Security and Environment, Infrastructure Development and Conflict Prevention, Management and Resolution) and a package of projects in the priority areas. A total of 31 projects selected from 105 subregional projects proposed by the Member States was submitted to the international community for consideration, three in the area of Conflict Prevention, Management, Resolution, and Humanitarian Affairs; 15 in the Infrastructure Development, and 13 in the Food Security and Environment Protection area.

The international community deliberated on the project profiles and expressed support noting the need for improved donor coordination and harmonization and the need for an improved mechanism for IGAD's cooperation with donors. The priority project profiles were presented to donors at the launching of the revitalized IGAD in November 1996.

Reference

UNEP. 1996. Report of the Regional Consultations held for the first Global Environment Outlook. UNEP. Nairobi.

initiatives include the establishment of a Climatology Network under AMCEN to provide a framework for action on issues related to climate. In light of the climate-related disasters experienced in the African region, it has become important, especially for countries affected by drought, to adopt policies and programmes to minimize the impacts of these disasters. As a part of the Climatology Network and under the World Climate Impacts and Response Strategies Programme (WCIRP), UNEP established a Climate Impacts and Response Strategy Network for Africa (CIRSNet/Africa) to share information and experiences to facilitate the development and implementation of climate-related activities, particularly climate change-related activities in the region. In addition, the need for strengthening early warning systems for floods and droughts through existing institutions dealing with climate-related issues, such as Agrymet, African Centre for Meteorological Application for Development (ACMAD), and subregional drought monitoring centres (for example, in Harare and Nairobi) is recognized (UNEP, 1996).

Research activities are particularly strong on land degradation issues. These include the FAO Programme of Action for Africa initiated in 1986, targeting soil conservation techniques, communal grazing, fuelwood problems, and conservation-based resource development; Agroforestry Research Networks for Africa promoting, in collaboration with the International Council for Research on Agroforestry (ICRAF), research on soil fertility conservation; the four ICRISAT centres in Africa, specializing in drought-tolerant crop research; and the FAO Erosion-Productivity Research Network, looking at the link between land degradation and crop yields (Stocking, 1992).

In Africa, there is growing recognition that indigenous knowledge and systems make a valuable contribution to land and agricultural systems as well as other natural resource management, and these are increasingly being applied (IMERCSA, personal communication, 1996). For example, with regard to forestry, SADC has initiated a project on community-based management of indigenous forests to enable village communities in southern Af-

rica to manage the surrounding natural forests in a sustainable way and to create income-generating activities through the sustainable use of wood and non-wood forest products (SADC-IFFWS, 1996).

Africa's strategy on biological diversity is clearly stipulated in the African Common Perspective and Position of the Convention on Biological Diversity (AMCEN, 1994). Policy directions emphasized for regional-level action are in the field of human resource and institutional capacity development:

- strengthening or establishing African biological diversity institutions;

- establishment of African subregional technology research institutes, including strengthening of the AMCEN Network on Biological Diversity as well as other institutions active in this area under the aegis of the ECA and OAU; and

- development of expertise in biological diversity.

In southern Africa, the SADC Plant Genetic Resource Centre (SPGRC), an autonomous regional organization, collects, conserves, documents, evaluates, and uses regional plant germplasm as part of Southern Africa's efforts to conserve biodiversity (IMERCSA, personal communication, 1996). A Seed Bank of the SPGRC was recently established, based in Lusaka. Another regional policy that provides a concrete basis for enforcing measures to protect biological diversity and to implement the Convention on International Trade Endangered Species (CITES) is the Lusaka Agreement of 1994. This was reached after the African States realized the wide scope for illegal trade in precious fauna and flora, resulting in large-scale poaching and depletion of the continent's biological diversity to a level that is gravely prejudicial to sustainable development. The agreement was signed by Kenya, South Africa, Swaziland, Uganda, Tanzania, and Zambia, which are establishing a Task Force to investigate and fight the lucrative business of poaching and smuggling (IMERCSA, personal communication, 1996).

Actions are also being taken at subregional levels in the management and use of international waters and their basins. Only a few international river basins have been managed effectively through co-operation among riparian countries. One example of an important initiative is the Nile Basin Action Plan, which has five main components (integrated water resources planning and management; capacity building; training and assessment; regional co-operation, including harmonization of legislation and joint projects; and environmental protection and enhancement) and which promotes a comprehensive and co-operative framework for the basin. Another is the SADC Protocol on Shared Watercourses Systems negotiated by 11 of the 12 members of SADC and signed so far by nine countries. Member states are also working on establishing an SADC Water Sector, an intergovernmental organization whose responsibilities will include planning water issues (IMERCSA, personal communication, 1996; World Bank, 1996).

The FRIEND project of southern Africa is a well-functioning network of professional hydrologists and water resources institutions sharing hydrological information for effective water resources management (World Bank, 1996). Action plans for co-operation also exist for the Zambezi River Basin, Lake Chad Basin, and the Okavango (IMERCSA, personal communication, 1996).

While most countries have developed their own energy policies, regional co-operation in the energy sector is being developed through the creation of an African Energy Commission at the Ministerial level backed by the ADB, ECA, and OAU, with a goal to harmonize and co-ordinate the development of the energy sector in the region (UNEP, 1996). There are also ongoing activities to develop hydroelectric power for common river basins through regional co-operation. Examples are the Gambia, Mano, Niger, Nile, Senegal, and Zambezi rivers.

The policy direction of Africa is to promote environmentally sound energy systems by ensuring that policies and policy instruments support and stimulate effective actions. These include developing and strengthening regional, subregional, and national legislative instruments on energy within the context of national environmental conservation programmes. Some of the most important issues to be addressed

through regional policies and co-operation include reducing the pressure on natural vegetation cover through the development and use of alternative sources of energy; developing the energy potential of common river basins through systematic co-operation between riparian states to speed up sustainable development and economic integration, including regional electricity grids; using African fossil fuels and renewable energies on a sustainable basis through co-operation agreements between producer and non-producer countries; mobilizing both human and financial resources to develop the energy sector; and improving the efficiency of existing energy use (UNEP, 1996).

Some examples of regional initiatives on coastal and marine areas include the Regional Seas Programmes, such as for the West and Central African (WACAF) region and for the Eastern African (EAF) region; various agreements for management of coastal resources, such as the Eastern African Convention on the Protection of Coastal and Marine Environment and the Indian Ocean Fisheries Commission; and Technical Assistance programmes, such as the Mediterranean Environmental Technical Assistance Programme (METAP) and similar programmes under CEDARE and SARDC. Constraints on the implementation of these regional programmes include a lack of adequate financial resources; weak co-ordination, resulting in duplication of efforts and waste of scarce resources; and lack of incentives and commitments of countries to participate fully in regional initiatives or programmes. A key action to address the constraints is to develop mechanisms for mobilizing the financial resources.

There are also several co-ordinated efforts in regional information sharing. The major international players are CILSS, IGAD, SADC-ELMS, the Sahara and Sahel Observatory (SSO), the United Nations Sahelian Office in UNDP (UNDP/UNSO), UNEP, the United Nations Institute for Training and Research (UNITAR), the World Conservation Monitoring Centre (WCMC), the World Bank, and the World Resources Institute (WRI), along with bilateral donors such as the German and U.S. development assistance agencies (GTZ and USAID).

The World Bank Programme for Environmental Information Systems in sub-Saharan Africa aims to bring together the major players involved in setting up environmental information systems. WRI supports the use of environmental information in the development and implementation of policy through its Natural Resources Information Management Programme, which has three main components: institutional development; statistics, indicators, and digitial data for policy-makers; and information access through guides, directories, and electronic communications. WCMC has created a capacity-building programme to provide services that empower institutions and individuals to assess their own information needs, set their own priorities, and build their own information systems.

UNDP/UNSO actively supports countries to develop programmes on Environmental Information Systems. They, for example, support case studies to better understand technical problems hindering EIS development in Africa. UNITAR, together with the SSO, also aims to reinforce African capacities in the domain of Integrated Information Systems for Environment.

The Environmental and Natural Resources Information Network (ENRIN) Programme of UNEP focuses on institutional and policy frameworks for data and information management to support environmental assessment and reporting, as well as networking and standardization. It undertakes liaison and joint activities with all the players and programmes mentioned. The SADC region has established a Regional Environment Information System Programme, a process that has been co-ordinated by SADC's Environment and Land Management Sector with the support of GTZ, USAID, and UNEP.

In the CILSS and IGAD subregions, EIS programmes are under development. As a start, the status of EIS in the member states has been assessed. In northern Africa, CEDARE is helping countries create national EIS networks. These are to be co-ordinated into a regional EIS network that is organized into a distributed, integrated environmental information network that links databases located at various institutions in the region. The system will also carry out monitoring functions that support decision-making on regional and national scales.

References

AMCEN. 1994. African Common Perspectives and Position on the Convention on Biological Diversity. AMCEN/Conventions/CBD/1. UNEP. Nairobi.

Benin. 1993a. Les Aspects Législatifs et le Cadre Juridique de l'Environnement du Benin. Samuel Ogoumma, Proceedings of the 4th Regional Workshop on National Strategies for Environment and Sustainable Development. NESDA. Abidjan. mai 1993.

Benin. 1993b. Plan d'Action Environnemental du Benin. juin 1993.

Burkina Faso. 1994. National Environment Code. 1994.

Cameroon. 1996. Plan National de Gestion de l'Environnement PNGE, Volume I, Rapport Principal. Ministère de l'Environnement et des forêts (Cellule de Coordination du PNGE). février 1996.

CEDARE, NESDA, IMERCSA (SARDC). 1996. Input provided, in coordination with other institutions in the region, through reviews of the drafts.

Côte d'Ivoire. 1996. Project de loi-cadre portant code de l'environnement, 15 juin 1996.

Dorm-Adzobu, C. 1995. New Roots: Institutionalizing Environmental Management in Africa. World Resources Institute. Washington.

Ethiopia. 1995. Ethiopia National Conservation Strategy. *Institutional Mechanisms for Environmental Management in Africa*. By C. Dorm-Adzobu & Allan Hoben. NESDA. Abidjan.

The Gambia. 1992. The Gambia Environmental Action Plan, 1992–2001. Coordinated by the Environment Unit of the Ministry of Natural Resources and the Environment. July. Banjui, the Gambia.

The Gambia. 1995a. National Environment Management Act (1994), National Environment Agency, Banjul. Country Environment Profile, ESP No.7 of the African Development Bank. Abidjan.

The Gambia. 1995b. The Gambia National Environmental Action Plan (GEAP). Institutional Mechanisms for Environmental Management in Africa. NESDA. Abidjan, Côte d'Ivoire.

Ghana. 1992. Seminar Report on the Effect of Mining on Ghana's Environment with Particular Reference to Proposed Mining Environmental Guidelines. Edited by Dr. Peter C. Acquah, Minerals Commission. June 24-26. Accra, Ghana.

Ghana. 1994. Environmental Protection Agency Act, 1994. Government Printer. Accra.

Ghana. 1995. The Ghana Environmental Action Plan. Institutional Mechanisms for Environmental Management in Africa. NESDA. Côte d'Ivoire.

Kenya. 1994. The Kenya National Environment Action (NEAP) Report. Ministry of Environment and Natural Resources. June. Nairobi, Kenya.

Madagascar. 1993. Plan d'Action Environmental de Madagascar: Perspective de Misc en Oeuvre de la Politique. Présenté par AID/AFR/ARTS/FARA, novembre 1993.

Makombe, K., ed. 1993. *Sharing the Land: Wildlife, People and Development in Africa.* IUCN/ROSA. Harare, Zimbabwe.

Mpande, R. 1995. The Role of Community-Based Organisations (CBOs)/Non-Governmental Organisations (NGOs) in the Implementation of the Desertification Convention: Workshop Report. 3-4 August 1995. ZERO. Harare.

Ogolla, B.D. 1995. *Environmental Law in Africa: Status and Trends.* International Business Lawyer, Vol. 23, No. 9, pp. 397-444, October.

Ohlsson, L. 1995. *Water and Security in Southern Africa,* Publications on Water Resources No. 1, Department for Natural Resources and the Environment. Stockholm, Sweden.

SADC-IFFWS. 1996. Managing of indigenous forests. Natural Resources Newsletter for the SADC Inland Fisheries, Forestry and Wildlife Sectors. No.6. April 1996. Lilongwe, Malawi.

SARDC. 1994. The State of the Environment in Southern Africa. Southern African Research and Documentation Centre (SARDC), the World Conservation Union (IUCN), Southern African Development Community (SADC). Penrose Press. Johannesburg.

Senegal. 1995. Processus d'élaboration du plan national d'actions pour l'environnement. CONSERE. Ministère de l'Environnement et de la Protection de la Nature. 13-16 février. Dakar.

Sivakumar, M.V.K., and J.B. Wills (eds.). 1995. Combating Land Degradation in Sub-Saharan Africa: Summary Proceedings of the International Planning Workshop for a Desert Margins Initiative, 23-26 Jan. 1995, Nairobi, Kenya. ICRISAT. Andhra Pradesh, India.

Stocking, M. 1992. Land Degradation and Rehabilitation Research in Africa, 1980–90: Retrospect and Prospect. IIED. London.

Uganda. 1995. The Uganda National Environmental Action Plan. Institutional Mechanisms for Environmental Management in Africa. NESDA. Abidjan, Côte d'Ivoire.

UNDP. 1996. The United Nations System-wide Special Initiative on Africa. UNDP.

UNECA. 1992. African Common Position on Environment and Development. UNECA. June.

UNECA. 1993. African Strategies for the Implementation of the United Nations Conference on Environment and Development Agenda 21. Conference of Ministers of Economic Planning and Development at its 19th Session, 3–6 May 1993. ECA. Addis Ababa, Ethiopia.

UNEP. 1996. Report of the Regional Consultations on the first Global Environment Outlook. UNEP. Nairobi.

World Bank. 1995. Toward Environmentally Sustainable Development in Sub-Saharan Africa. World Bank.

World Bank. 1996. African Water Resources: Challenges and Opportunities for Sustainable Development (Draft). January.

ASIA AND THE PACIFIC

National Initiatives

A recent trend in many countries in Asia and the Pacific has been the strengthening of governance structures for environmental protection. A large number of environmental institutions have been established in the public sector, including environment ministries and independent environment agencies created to assist the environment ministries. These bodies need to be strengthened if they are to fulfil their mandated roles.

The environmental policy instruments applied in the region are mainly command-and-control policies and strategic environmental planning (ESCAP, 1995). Legislation, regulatory standards, and environmental planning procedures related to public works, particularly environmental impact assessments, are the most common instruments of environmental management. Serious efforts are also being made by industries and research institutes to develop new environmentally friendly technologies and to incorporate environmental considerations into production processes.

Umbrella environmental legislation and comprehensive environmental policies are commonly found in the region. Good examples are found in China (see Box 3.8) and Malaysia. In Malaysia, the Malaysian Environmental Quality Act (EQA) provides a framework for regulating most forms of pollution and enhancing environmental quality and management. The sectoral acts under the EQA of Malaysia include a Water Enactment act (control of river pollution); a Street, Drainage, and Building Act (control of effluent discharges into rivers); a Local Government act (control of pollution of streams within areas under local authorities); guidelines for air pollution control measures; and a motor vehicles act (control of smoke and gas emissions) (Malaysia, 1992 and 1993).

Another comprehensive policy has been implemented in Singapore. The Singapore Green Plan of 1992 set in place a mechanism to establish a city with high standards of public health, clean air, clean water, and clean land by the year 2000. The plan also addresses environmental education, environmental technology, resource conservation, clean technology, nature conservation, and environmental noise. It further calls for reducing carbon dioxide emissions, improving energy efficiency, and keeping daily garbage production at one kilogram per person (Singapore, 1993).

Appropriate policies and associated programmes and projects have been implemented to combat land degradation in the region. These include watershed management, soil and water conservation, sand dune stabilization, reclamation of waterlogged and saline land, forest and range management, and replenishment of soil fertility in croplands by use of green manures and cultivation of appropriate crops. In Nepal, for example, various watershed management projects operate in critically affected or degraded areas, such as the Kulekhani and Phewa Tal watersheds. Considerable success has been achieved in reducing the extent of land degradation in targetted areas. Involvement of the local communities at every stage in the projects' implementations ensured sustainability of the measures introduced (ESCAP, 1995).

Integrated watershed management programmes in many other countries, including India, Pakistan, Bangladesh, and Bhutan, have been instrumental in rehabilitating degraded land and preventing further degradation. In India, 86 million hectares are affected by degradation, 26 million of which are in highly critical areas being addressed on a priority basis under 35 centrally sponsored projects

Box 3.8

An Example: China's Environmental Policy Framework

Management Framework, Policies, and Measures

The main emphasis of the environmental policies in China is to bring environmental protection in line with national economic development and social advancement, maximizing the economic, social, and environmental benefits. The Environmental Protection Laws of the People's Republic of China were adopted in 1979, under which a comprehensive environmental regulatory system was established. It comprises provisions in the nation's Constitution and laws and regulations that cover various aspects of environmental protection, including administrative aspects and the implementation of international conventions and agreements on the environment. In addition, eight national environmental programmes have been developed and implemented. These include both market-based and command-and-control instruments including:

- *The Three Synchronization Policy*—requires the design, construction, and operation of pollution treatment facilities along with any development projects involving new construction, renovation, or reconstruction;

- *Environmental Impact Assessment (EIA);*

- *Pollution Charges System;*

- *Responsibility System for Environmental Protection Targeting*—defines the distribution of responsibility for ensuring environmental quality to a locality, a department, or a work unit;

- *Quantitative Assessment of Urban Comprehensive Environmental Control*—provides a mechanism for co-ordinating economic, urban, and environmental construction activities under municipal governments to attain maximum cost effectiveness and to protect and shape the urban environment through appropriate policy adjustment;

(UNEP/UNDP/FAO, 1994). More than 30,000 hectares of shifting and semi-stable sand dunes have been stabilized (ESCAP, 1995). In Pakistan, too, rehabilitation of desertified lands through plantations and fixation of mobile sand dunes by shelter belts and checker barrier fences has been successful (ESCAP, 1995).

China has also achieved remarkable success in some areas in controlling soil erosion since the State Council initiated a soil erosion control scheme in 1983. This involves soil and water conservation measures in eight different areas. After 10 years of conservation efforts, the erosion has been brought under control in 2 million hectares, a third of the total affected area. Improved land productivity doubled the total grain output in these areas. The second phase of the programme, covering 1993–2002, aims to introduce higher quality and efficiency in crop production (NEPA, 1993). About 10 per cent of China's desertified land has been rehabilitated in the

past few decades, and the deterioration of another 12 per cent, mainly in northern China, has been halted by successful policy implementation. Afforestation in the Shaanxi province—on the southern edge of the Muus Sandland—has brought more than 330,000 hectares of shifting sand dunes under control and protected 100,000 hectares of farmland; vegetation coverage increased more than nine times from 1978 to 1987. (Up to 18 million hectares of land have been afforested through the "Three North" Shelter System, the Upper Yangtze River Shelter System, and the Coastal Shelter System).

Combating desertification features high in China's Agenda 21, approved by the Central Government in April 1994. Nationwide mapping and assessment of sandy desertification and water erosion have been carried out, and field experimental stations for the study and control of sandy desertification have been established. National and regional maps of geomorphology, land resources, and

Box 3.8 continued

- *Centralized Control of Pollution;*

- *Pollution Discharge Registration Application and Discharge Permit Systems (DPS);* and

- *System for Pollution Control within Deadlines*—requires pollution-discharging enterprises and projects to reach a discharge standard set by the government within a given time period.

Efforts are being made to continuously improve the system of environmental laws and to establish and strengthen the institutional framework to ensure effective environmental management. The role of science and technology in environmental protection along with environmental education and awareness-raising activities are receiving increasing attention.

International Cooperation

International cooperation in the fields of regional and global environmental protection is being promoted. Bilateral agreements on cooperation have been signed with countries including the United States, Korea, Canada, India, South Korea, Japan, Mongolia, Russia, Germany,

Australia, Ukraine, Finland, Norway, Denmark and the Netherlands, covering topics such as environmental planning and management, global environmental problems, pollution control and prevention, protection of forest and wildlife, oceanic environment, climate change, atmospheric pollution, acid rain, and treatment of sewage. Close cooperation is maintained with organizations like the United Nations Economic and Social Council for Asia and Pacific (ESCAP), and contributions are made towards environmental development in the Asian and Pacific regions by way of participation in various regional and subregional environmental activities such as in the North-West Pacific Action Plan and East-Asian Seas Action Plan under the Regional Seas Programme. China is a Party to most of the global environmental conventions and agreements and an active participant in several international programmes such as the International Register of Potentially Toxic Chemicals (IRPTC), and INFOTERRA.

Reference

National Environmental Protection Agency of China (NEPA), personal communication. 1996.

---

land use were completed in 1980, providing a basis for combating desertification and for rational land reclamation. A further 20 per cent of desertified land in the arid and semi-arid zones are targetted for rehabilitation by 2000, while another 32 million hectares severely affected by water erosion will be brought under control (Jinfa, 1994; UNEP, 1994).

In Australia, which has learned from past mistakes in land use management, restrictions have been placed on land clearing in most areas, and much of the native fauna is now protected. A taxation system is imposed to promote better land management, and soil conservation works are tax-deductible. Community-based action programmes are seen as crucial in dealing with land degradation and make up a major part of the National Landcare Programme. A joint effort of the National Farmers' Federation and the Australian Conservation Foundation resulted in a nationwide programme involving one third of all farm families in 2,200 land-care groups (Australia, 1994).

China, Indonesia, Malaysia, Myanmar, Nepal, Papua New Guinea, the Philippines, Sri Lanka, and Thailand have all enacted laws to minimize the impact of mining activities on land degradation and to ensure proper utilization of underground resources with minimum impact on the environment (ESCAP, 1995).

To tackle the problem of deforestation, national Governments have taken steps to protect forested areas, such as establishing forest parks and wildlife conservation areas, and afforestation. According to the United Nations Food and Agriculture Organization (FAO) 1990 Assessment, the rate of afforestation was higher in Asia and the Pacific in the 1980–90 period than in any other region of the world for which estimates are available. For example, from 1981 to 1990, an average of 525,000 hectares of forest was planted each year throughout the Association of South-East Asian Nations (ASEAN) region. The annual percentage increase in plantation in South Asia during the same period was close to 30 per cent. As a result of a massive tree-planting programme in China, nearly 32 million hectares of forest had been established by 1990. The Pakistan Environmental Protection Council also launched a massive afforestation programme in 1995, aimed at increasing the country's forested area from 5 per cent to 10 per cent.

The Chipko movement has been active in parts of the Himalayan region of India since 1973. It is one of the most successful examples of people-oriented environmental restoration. The main aim of this movement, in which women play a key role, is tree protection and plantation. Similarly, the Appiko movement was launched to save the tropical forests of the Western Ghats. Since the National Forest Policy was established in India in 1988, considerable achievements have been registered, and net deforestation has been arrested (India, 1992b). In the Republic of Korea, the First 10-Year Forest Development Plan initiated in 1973 had a target of 1 million hectares of new plantations. The target was achieved ahead of schedule. At present, the Third National Forest Plan (1988–97) is under implementation and has proved very successful (Republic of Korea, 1992). In Malaysia, the National Forest Policy enacted in 1977 has been a major breakthrough in strengthening the institutional base for forest management and the co-operation between the Federal and State Governments (ESCAP, 1995).

Other examples of forest-related policies include the establishment of the Bhutan Trust Fund in March 1991 to ensure sustainable financing for the preservation of Bhutan's forestry and rich biological diversity (World Bank, 1992) and, in Nepal, the introduction of the National Forestry Plan in 1976 and a Master Plan (1986–89) to achieve the national policy goals of rehabilitating degraded forest resources through people's participation (Nepal, 1992). Indonesia's forest policy focuses mainly on improving the harvesting and regeneration of natural forests and on establishing industrial forest plantations in denuded and unproductive forestland. In Myanmar, the basic forest policy features sustainable timber production without depleting existing forest resources (ESCAP, 1995).

Despite all these programmes, rapid population growth has contributed to destruction of forest through land clearing for cultivation and the over-harvesting of forest for fuelwood, roundwood, and fodder. At the current rate of harvesting, the remaining timber reserves in Asia will not last more than 40 years. Forest policies, therefore, still need to be strengthened and rigorously enforced, trade in forestry products needs to be controlled, and afforestation programmes need to expand to match deforestation rates. Agricultural productivity needs to be increased without further sacrificing the forested area—for example, through adoption of high-yielding crop varieties and improved management of water and agro-chemicals.

Governments in the region have responded actively to the issue of biodiversity by participating in biodiversity conventions and taking measures to protect biologically rich areas. Twenty-nine Asia-Pacific countries had ratified the Convention on Biological Diversity as of 1 May 1996. Progress in designating protected areas is widespread, with almost all countries in the region having established natural terrestrial and aquatic reserves in the form of national parks, wildlife sanctuaries, gene pool reserves, and so on. A dramatic rise in the number and total area of protected areas in both South and South-East Asia has occurred. The Pacific region has also shown a major increase in the number of protected areas, although the development in this subregion has been less dramatic.

One example of a Government response to the Convention on Biological Diversity is the formulation of the National Action Plan on Biodiversity in India, led by the Ministry of Environment and Forests (India, 1994). India is also implementing various projects for ensuring the protection of animals and their habitats. Project Tiger, launched in 1973 in 23 Tiger Reserves and covering a total area of 3,049,700 hectares, succeeded in increasing the tiger population to 3,750 by 1993. Project Elephant, launched in 1991–92 to ensure the long-term survival of elephant populations, focuses on restoring lost and degraded habitats, mitigating human-elephant conflicts, and establishing a database of the migration and population dynamics of elephants.

Project Crocodile was begun in 1976 to help save the three endangered crocodile species—fresh- and salt-water crocodiles and the rare gharial (*Gavialis gangeticus*) (India, 1992b and 1993).

Biotechnology research programmes (development of germplasm facilities, tissue culture pilot plants, biocontrol agents, biofertilizers, clean technologies, bioinformatics, and so on) have also become operational in India. Sacred groves, areas usually within temple compounds containing original flora and fauna, are being enhanced and preserved; these are commonly found in Western Ghats and north-eastern parts of India.

Different measures are being taken by many countries to meet the growing demands for clean and safe water and to safeguard water quality. These include water reuse/recycling, sea-water desalinization, demand-side management, interbasin transfers, leak detection programmes, differential payment rates, legislation, environmental impact assessment, establishment and enforcement of water and effluent standards, protection of wetlands, and use of economic incentives. Integrated watershed management programmes are also being implemented extensively.

Many countries in the region, including Japan, Malaysia, New Zealand, the Republic of Korea, and Singapore, use economic incentives and instruments, such as the "polluter pays" principle, tax rebates, tax write-offs, and other preventive measures, to encourage industries to reduce water pollution. Curative measures include river cleaning programmes. A notable example is the 10-year "clean river" programme initiated by the Singapore Government in 1977. The programme, costing US$200 million, has brought life back to the Singapore River and the Kallang Basin. Singapore's rivers today support aquatic life again with dissolved oxygen levels ranging from 2 to 4 milligrams per litre. The Government's goal is to reduce pollution further and to raise the dissolved oxygen level in all streams to 4 milligrams per litre by 2000 (Singapore, 1992). The cleanup of rivers has been made possible through improvements in wastewater treatment and the enforcement of stringent standards (ASEAN, 1995).

Since 1988, Hong Kong has undertaken river cleaning efforts, and river and stream water quality has shown steady improvement. Compared with the early 1980s, when only 35 per cent of rivers were rated "fair quality" or better, 74 per cent were in these categories by 1994 (ESCAP, 1995). Similarly, in Surabaya, Indonesia's second largest city, a clean river campaign programme called PROKASIH has been instrumental in bringing greater public and political pressure to bear on industrial polluters. As a result, most industries have installed treatment facilities, and in some cases pollution loads have fallen by more than 50 per cent (ESCAP, 1995).

Other successful examples of cleanup programmes include the Ganga River Action Plan (GAP), launched in 1986, and the National River Action Plan (NRAP) in India. The first phase of GAP aimed to intercept, divert, and treat 870 million litres of sewage per day; 405 million litres per day had been diverted as of December 1991. The second phase of GAP covers sewage-related works as well as pollution abatement in additional towns on the main river Ganga. The Central Ganga Authority identified 68 industrial units as heavy polluters; by 1992, 43 had installed effluent plants and seven were in the process of doing so, while 10 units were closed down. The NRAP will involve cleanup projects for 14 grossly polluted stretches in nine rivers and 14 less polluted stretches in another eight rivers. Furthermore, the Survey of India has prepared a Water Quality Atlas, based on the data provided by the Central Pollution Control Board (India, 1992b).

A number of countries in the region have emphasized demand-side management for their water conservation policies. This includes rationalizing water prices, involving local communities in decentralized water management, and promoting public participation in water conservation. For instance, applying water conservation strategies has become popular in Beijing in both domestic and industrial sectors and has contributed savings of up to 30 per cent in overall consumption. Sea water is also increasingly replacing fresh water where appropriate for domestic purposes in Hong Kong (ESCAP, 1995).

The potential for the Asia-Pacific region to be affected by acid rain is significant. A strong scientific or public constituency to mitigate the potentially serious effects of acidification, such as damage to ecosystems and materials, does not exist. There is a need to intensify research on the emissions of air pollutants and their transboundary effects, to assess damage to ecosystems, and to install mitigation strategies (such as a sulphur protocol).

Numerous initiatives do exist in the region, however, to bring air pollution problems under control. (See Box 3.9.) Vehicular emissions are a significant problem in all major cities. The Government of the Philippines addresses this issue through plans to limit the number of vehicles on the road. Similar measures are being taken in Thailand.

India has implemented programmes setting emissions standards for vehicles, as well as requiring manufacturers to meet strict standards for all new vehicles. Significant penalties are imposed on violators. Since 1993, all new cars assembled by some companies in Malaysia contain catalytic converters to minimize vehicular emissions. In several countries, including the Philippines, unleaded gasoline has been widely introduced, and new vehicles are required to run on this fuel. Research on the use of gasohol (and other petroleum substitutes) and electric cars continues in many countries.

Other technological advances have also been made. In Japan, a new method to remove up to 95 per cent of sulphur dioxide and 80 per cent of nitrogen oxide from the combustion emissions of flue gas has been developed (ESCAP, 1995). Fly ash problems in India resulting from the burning of certain varieties of coal have been addressed through better washing techniques and use of the ash as fertilizer, bricks, material for road construction, and a replacement for sand to refill mines.

Indonesia's Environmental Impact Management Agency (BAPEDAL), a non-departmental Government Agency, has developed a marine and coastal pollution control programme to address problems of this type. It includes pollution control in seaports and tourist beaches, and tanker service zones in the Malaya, Macassar, and Lombok straits (Indonesia, 1995). In India, the National Environmental Engineering Research Institute (NEERI) conducts research on biotechnological methods to clean up oil spills and protect marine resources (ESCAP, 1995).

India's renewable energy programme is a good example of the region's efforts to develop alternative energy sources. Both biogas electricity and wind power have emerged as significant and dependable renewable energy sources. The Indian Government is helping to finance both capital and maintenance costs of the early stages of operation of community biogas plants (India, 1992a). A comprehensive survey of its wind energy resources and environmental audits has also been carried out at all refineries as part of India's energy conservation programmes (TERI, 1992).

Participation of the private sector in environmental management is increasing throughout the region. In Japan, businesses are among the most active players in the region's environmental technology research and development (R&D) activities, accounting for more than 60 per cent of national R&D spending. A 1991 survey by Nihon Keizai Shimbun found that 88 per cent of the 144 major firms covered had established environmental divisions. Japanese industry is a world leader in the growing market for flue-gas desulphurization and denitrification equipment, as well as clean motor vehicle technology. Japan also puts major effort into the field of clean energy, including photovoltaic power and fuel cells, and the development of new technologies such as carbon dioxide recovery facilities and chlorofluorocarbon-free production processes (ESCAP, 1995).

Japan's private agencies have also been heavily involved in funding Government research agencies such as the New Energy and Industrial Technology Development Organization (NEDO) and the Research Institute of Innovative Technology for Earth (RITE), which mainly funds and conducts R&D related to global warming. Nine of Japan's largest steelmakers are involved in a project to increase the use of scrap in steel making, and the Japan Automobile Manufacturers Association (JAMA) has set standards for making vehicle plastic parts to promote easy recycling. Operations known as "consumer co-operatives" have become a powerful force in Japan to popularize "green products," including

Box 3.9

Thailand: Air Pollution from a Lignite Power Plant

Thailand's largest lignite-fired power plant is located in the Mae Moh district, Lam Pang province, north of Bangkok. With 11 generating units and a total production capacity of 2,625 megawatts, approximately 15 million tons of lignite are needed to run the machines. Prior to 1992, the plant emitted considerable amounts of air pollutants through high smoke stacks and discharged wastewater into its immediate surroundings.

High atmospheric pressure in October 1992 caused sulphur dioxide (SO_2) generated from the plant to drift above Mae Moh district. Analysis showed that rainwater had 50 per cent higher sulphate concentration levels as compared with acceptable international standards, and at peak pollution levels, more than 2,000 micrograms per cubic metre of SO_2 were found in the air. High levels of toxic acid rain continued in the locality until January 1993.

The October 1992 pollution episode caused widespread damage. More than 900 people had difficulty breathing and experienced sore throats and other related illnesses. Domestic livestock also suffered, some becoming ill or dying. Cash crops and trees were destroyed or experienced subsequent growth problems. The Electricity Generating Authority of Thailand (EGAT) had to compensate rural households for losses, and affected persons were resettled in safer areas. EGAT had to reduce production by almost 60 per cent (to 800 megawatts) while negotiations with affected parties went on.

Several measures were implemented to avoid future problems: approximately US$280 million was invested in pollution control, a limit was imposed on the scale of operation, and the quality of coal was improved by mixing it with high-quality coal. Due to the implementation of prompt control measures, air quality in the vicinity of the plant was under control by late 1993 to early 1994. The SO_2 concentration had been reduced to within 300 micrograms per cubic metre by then.

This case illustrates the need for thorough environmental impact assessments of large investment projects. It shows that good management can effectively reduce potential environmental hazards. It also illustrates the high costs associated with combating the adverse environmental effects of improperly planned operations.

Reference

Office of Environmental Protection and Planning (OEPP)—Thailand. Personal communication. 1996.

---

recyclable, biodegradable, rechargeable, ozone-friendly, and unleaded products (ESCAP, 1995).

Region-wide efforts also exist on eco-labelling. Singapore launched a Green Label scheme in May 1992 to help consumers identify products that are environment-friendly. The scheme sets specific guidelines for the manufacturing, distribution, usage, and disposal of products. When these are met, a Green Label logo is awarded by the Advisory Committee, which includes representatives from the private sector, academic institutions, and statutory organizations (ESCAP, 1995).

China and India adopted a system of environmental labels in 1993. To date, China has drafted standards for seven types of products and plans to launch the environmental label system for such products as household refrigeration appliances, aerosol products, degradable plastic film, non-leaded gasoline for cars, and water-solvent paints in the near future. India has so far prepared ECO-MARK criteria for 14 product categories: soap and detergents, paper, paints, plastics, lubricating oil, aerosols, food items, packaging materials, wood substitutes, textiles, cosmetics, electrical and electronic goods, food additives, and batteries (India, 1992b).

There has been growing recognition of the significance of disaster preparedness, prevention, and mitigation measures. Initiatives have already been taken in many countries to address the issue through a comprehensive framework of institutions, plans, programmes, and legislation (ESCAP, 1995). Over the years, Japan has developed a very efficient organizational framework to reduce the effects of natural disasters; relevant activities are overseen by a high-level committee under the chairmanship of the Prime Minister.

Several other countries have similarly set up committees and councils to co-ordinate, plan, and formulate policies and actions, such as natural disaster forecasts, management, and post-disaster relief and rehabilitation work: India has constituted a Cabinet Committee on Natural Calamities; Bangladesh has set up the Natural Disaster Prevention Council, chaired by the President; Sri Lanka has appointed a Cabinet Sub-committee; Myanmar has set up the Relief and Resettlement Department under the Ministry of Social Welfare; Indonesia has established a National Coordination Board for Natural Disaster Preparedness and Relief; China has constituted an interministerial co-ordination committee; Papua New Guinea has a National Disaster and Emergency Services Department; and the Philippines has formed the National Disaster Coordination Council, consisting of several ministries, Governments, and non-governmental groups (ESCAP, 1995).

With regard to forecasting, early warning, risk assessment, and mapping of climatic and water-related hazards, substantial progress has been made. China in recent years has made remarkable achievements in monitoring a wide range of natural disasters through application of aviation and satellite remote sensing and terrestrial sensing technologies (ESCAP, 1995). In India, 10 high-power cyclone detection radar stations have been installed along the east and west coasts of the country, and plans exist to extend cyclone warning systems to all vulnerable areas. The Republic of Korea also has a well-established disaster-related forecasting and warning network (ESCAP, 1995).

In Thailand, flood and landslide risk maps are being prepared for the vulnerable southern part of the country, and a flood modelling programme is being implemented for southern and north-eastern areas. Malaysia has initiated programmes on flood forecasting, warning, preparedness, and relief. It has also developed flood-proof structures as well as catchment development and floodplain management strategies. A project has recently been com-

pleted under which 20 river basins in the country have been equipped with telemetric systems for flood monitoring and warning (ESCAP, 1995).

Japan constantly observes, predicts, and issues warnings of potential earthquakes, volcanic eruptions, storm events, tsunamis, typhoons, and flood-related disasters. Earthquake prediction has been systematically carried out since 1964, and the country is implementing its 7th Earthquake Prediction Plan (1994–98). As a result, it has designated certain areas for intensified observation (Japan, 1987). In Australia, a comprehensive personal computer-based cyclone warning system was introduced in Perth, Darwin, and Brisbane in November 1990. To cope with the exceptional droughts in Australia, the National Drought Policy was formulated in 1992; it includes a range of measures such as the introduction of sustainable agriculture, drought preparedness, financial assistance for farmers exposed to exceptional drought circumstances, and drought-related research with an emphasis on drought prediction, monitoring, and management (IDIC, 1995).

Regional Initiatives

Since the Earth Summit in 1992, there has been great emphasis on regional environmental co-operation. (See Box 3.10.) Every five years, a State of the Environment Report of Asia and the Pacific is prepared by ESCAP, with assistance from members of the Interagency Committee on Environment and Sustainable Development.

Several regional networks and joint programmes address land degradation. An Asian Network on Problem Soils was established in 1989, involving 13 countries and supported by FAO. FAO, in co-operation with the Asia Soil Conservation Network for the Humid Tropics (ASOCON), is developing a Framework for Action on Land Conservation in Asia and the Pacific (FALCAP). It has commissioned a study on land degradation in eight countries of South Asia funded by the United Nations Development Programme (UNDP) and UNEP in 1993 (ESCAP, 1995). The Fertilizer and Development Network for Asia and the Pacific (FADINAP) is concerned with fertilizer production, trade, and use in the region.

Box 3.10
Regional Mechanisms of Co-operation

In July 1993, the ASEAN Senior Officials on the Environment (ASOEN) agreed on the development of a new Strategic Plan of Action on the Environment (1994–98). Environmental co-operation in this region is thorough and may provide a model for other regional organizations. (ASEAN encompasses Brunei Darussalam, Indonesia, Malaysia, the Philippines, Singapore, and Thailand.)

Countries of the South Asia Co-operative Environment Programme (SACEP)—Afghanistan, Bangladesh, Bhutan, India, Iran, Maldives, Nepal, Pakistan, and Sri Lanka—implement an Action Plan called SACEP's Strategy and Programme (1992–96). Key areas of activity include capacity building and awareness raising; systematic information exchange and intraregional technology transfer; training on environmental management and institutional development; management of mountain ecosystems, watersheds, and coastal resources; and wildlife and wildlife habitat conservation.

The South Pacific Regional Environmental Programme (SPREP), established in 1993 and covering 22 Pacific Island countries and territories, aims at enhancing the institutional capacity of its members. It has also initiated an Action Plan (1991–95)—a regional strategy covering many aspects of environmental assessment, management, and law in the subregion.

The Mekong River Commission (MRC), consisting of Cambodia, China, Lao PDR, Myanmar, Vietnam, and Thailand, is an intergovernmental organization responsible for co-operation and co-ordination in the use and development of water resources of the Lower Mekong Basin. In 1991, an Environment Unit was established within the Technical Support Division to deal with the environmental issues in this subregion.

The International Centre for Integrated Mountain Development (ICIMD), established in 1983 in Nepal, implements programmes to attain environmental stability, sustainability of mountain ecosystems, and poverty eradication in the Hindu Kush–Himalayas. The members are Afghanistan, Bangladesh, Bhutan, China, India, Myanmar, Nepal, and Pakistan.

A Regional Network of Research and Training Centres on Desertification Control in Asia and the Pacific (DESCONAP) was established in 1988. It includes 19 Governments, international organizations, and non-government agencies. More recently, ESCAP has helped develop National Plans of Action on Combating Desertification for Mongolia and Pakistan. Similar plans are being developed for China and Iran (ESCAP, 1995).

A Forestry Research Support Programme for Asia and the Pacific (FORSPA), organized by FAO's Regional Office for Asia and the Pacific (RAPA), includes work of relevance to combating land degradation. The programme supports research on tropical deforestation, forestry's role in sustaining agricultural productivity, management of fragile tropical soils, fuelwood, and forestry and the environment.

Regional initiatives on forestry include SACEP's Strategy and Programme (SPR-1, 1992–96), promoting regional co-operation in social forestry as one of 15 Priority Subject Matter Areas (SACEP, 1992), and UNEP's ongoing Land Cover Assessment and Monitoring project in Asia and the Pacific, primarily focusing on the assessment of major land cover types and detection of the land and forest cover changes for countries in the region.

Several regional conventions, covering parts of the Asia-Pacific region, deal with aspects of biological diversity. The most significant are the Convention on Conservation of Nature in the South Pacific (Apia Convention), the ASEAN Agreement on the Conservation of Nature and Natural Resources (ASEAN Agreement), and the Convention on the Protection of the Natural Resources and the Environment of the South Pacific (SPREP Convention). The ASEAN Strategic Plan of Action on the Environment, under Strategy 5, establishes a regional framework on biological diversity conservation and sustainable use. This strategy promotes the development of a framework for the protection and conservation of heritage areas and endangered species, to strengthen capacities for R&D, and to enhance biodiversity conservation in the region (ASEAN, 1994).

In line with the spirit of the Convention on Biodiversity, the Asian Development Bank (ADB) has initiated efforts to translate its recommendations into concrete actions through provision of financial assistance to developing member countries. For example, in 1992, the ADB approved a loan and technical assistance to Indonesia for biodiversity conservation covering an area of about 500,000 hectares using the integrated protected area system approach. The ADB also initiated a dialogue with the World Conservation Union (IUCN) to identify the issues and the constraints affecting implementation of the convention in the region (ADB/IUCN, 1994).

SACEP's Strategy and Programme includes regional co-operation in wildlife conservation and genetic resources and regional co-operation in conservation of corals, mangroves, deltas, and coastal areas as part of 15 Priority Subject Matter Areas (SACEP, 1992). In 1990, IUCN's Asian Elephant Specialist Group (AESG) completed the Asian Elephant Action Plan in collaboration with the 13 Asian countries where elephants still exist in the wild. The Action Plan provided both a status report and an outline of conservation priorities. Its implementation is the responsibility of the Asian Elephant Conservation Centre based at the Indian Institute of Science in Bangalore, India.

In the field of fresh-water resources, examples of regional co-operation include activities under the Mekong River Commission. The Mekong is the largest river in South-East Asia, flowing through China, Myanmar, Lao PDR, Thailand, Cambodia, and Vietnam. The lower Mekong is the focus of international co-operation in water quality and pollution control. Basic networks for water quality monitoring of surface water have been established with funding from the Swedish International Development Agency (SIDA), and a Ground Water Investigation Programme formulated for 1989–92. One of the main achievements of the project has been the establishment of a hydrogeological network for observation of water table variations, re-

gional hydraulic variations, and water quality variations in the Mekong countries (ESCAP, 1991).

Regional progress has also been made in training and information exchange. With financial and technical assistance from the ADB and other donors, projects have been developed that focus on Subregional Environmental Training and Institutional Strengthening in Selected Priority Areas and on Subregional Environmental Monitoring and Information Systems. The former addresses, among other issues, the standardization of national environmental legislation, particularly with regard to environmental standards; water quality management and industrial pollution; and appropriate technology transfer within the subregion.

Transboundary issues are complicated scientifically as well as politically. Very few regional scientific studies have been conducted in the past on trans-boundary pollution problems. But this is changing. Considerable effort has gone into studying the creation and flow of acid rain, such as in the RAINS-ASIA programme.

Climate change is also an issue of concern; one regional programme in the field is the Asia Least-Cost Greenhouse Gas Abatement Strategy (ALGAS) project under the Global Environment Facility (GEF), co-ordinated by ADB and UNDP. This project assists 12 developing states to formulate least-cost greenhouse gas abatement strategies and to develop the capabilities for a greenhouse gas inventory, including the scientific infrastructure to develop emission factors necessary in the inventory methodologies.

ESCAP, in a 1993 seminar on climate change co-sponsored by ADB and the Environment Agency of Japan, outlined the elements of a regional strategy for combating climate change. The strategy includes the establishment of a Regional Network on Climate Change (ESCAP, 1995). ADB also funded a pioneering Regional Study on Global Environmental Issues that produced an integrated assessment of climate change impacts and analysis of policy options for mitigation and adaptation. Bangladesh, India, Indonesia, Malaysia, Pakistan, the Philippines, Sri Lanka, and Vietnam were included in the study. SPREP has developed and imple-

mented a climate change programme with bilateral and multilateral support mainly focused on the assessment of sea level rise, climate monitoring, and development of national response strategies.

Regional co-operation in the field of coastal and marine resources is far advanced. The Coastal and Marine Environment Management Information System (COMEMIS), a collaborative project of UNEP and ADB, aims to develop and improve the capacities of all countries in the South China Sea region to engage in multisectoral analysis and apply geographic information systems for environmental impact assessment and management.

The ASEAN Strategic Plan of Action on the Environment, under Strategy 6, promotes the protection and management of coastal zones and marine resources (ASEAN, 1994). It aims to improve regional marine and coastal environmental co-ordination and to develop a framework for the integrated management of regional coastal zones. The SACEP Strategy and Programme focuses on regional co-operation in the conservation of corals, mangroves, deltas, and coastal areas and on co-operation in the regional sea programme as part of the 15 Priority Subject Matter Areas. Other regional co-operation programmes for coastal and marine environment protection include action plans under the Regional Seas Programme initiated by UNEP. These include the South Asian Seas (SAS) Action Plan; the East Asian Seas (EAS) Action Plan; the South Pacific Regional Environment Programme (SPREP); the North West Pacific Action Plan (NOWPAP); the ASEAN's Working Group on ASEAN Seas and Environment; the ASEAN Senior Officials on the Environment (ASOEN); the Council of Petroleum's Plan for the Control and Mitigation of Marine Pollution.

Bilateral and multilateral projects that have contributed towards the management and protection of the marine environment are the ASEAN/U.S. Agency for International Development (USAID) Coastal Resources Management Project; the ASEAN Australian International Development Assistance Bureau (AIDAB) Projects on "Red Tides and Tidal Phenomena" and on "Living Coastal Resources Management"; the ASEAN/Canada Project on as-

sessment of marine pollution by heavy metals; and the GEF project on the prevention and management of marine pollution covering nine countries (Brunei Darussalam, China, Indonesia, Korea DPR, Malaysia, Philippines, Singapore, Thailand, and Vietnam).

Regional co-operation in energy and environment is a priority under the SACEP Strategy and Programme. The promotion of environmentally sound management of toxic chemicals and hazardous wastes and the control of the transboundary movement of hazardous wastes are priorities under the ASEAN Strategic Plan of Action on the Environment, Strategy 7 (ASEAN, 1994). This involves the establishment of regional guidelines for assessing highly polluting industries and for safe handling of potentially harmful chemicals entering the ASEAN region. In addition, it addresses the strengthening of an information network on the transboundary movement of toxic chemicals and hazardous waste. Efforts, particularly by ASEAN, to improve trade arrangements that support environment and development are further examples of regional co-operation. This also aims to strengthen capacity in trade-environment policy analysis, planning, and evaluation, consistent with the principles of the General Agreement on Tariffs and Trade (GATT).

In the field of environmental economics, ADB, the Government of Norway, and Harvard University have developed a set of environmental indices for monitoring environmental change. This involves a systematic evaluation of the cost of impacts on the environment by calculating how much it would cost to restore an environmental situation. The study resulted in the development of a Cost-of-Remediation (COR) index for ADB's developing member countries. An Environmental Elasticity (EE) index, which aims to measure changes in the environmental quality relative to change in the economy over time, has also been developed by this consortium (ADB, 1996). Regional co-operation in environmental impact assessment and cost-benefit analysis is among the priority subject areas under the SACEP Strategy and Programme.

Progress is being made in information exchange for environmentally sustainable development planning and management—an area of major concern in developing countries in Asia and the Pacific. UNEP, through its Environment Information and Assessment Programme in Asia and the Pacific, provides assistance to developing countries in improving the availability of reliable environmental data for assessments and decision-making for sustainable development. Formulation of assessment frameworks and laying the foundation for standard State of the Environment databases supports national and regional reporting, policy formulation, priority setting, and action planning. In addition, environment and natural resource information networks for co-operative international assessments of shared resources are being co-ordinated by UNEP in the South Asia, South-East Asia, the South Pacific and Greater Mekong subregions.

References

ADB. 1996. Environmental Indicators (draft).

ADB/IUCN. 1994. *Biodiversity Conservation in the Asia and Pacific Region: Constraints and Opportunities.* Proceedings of a Regional Conference. 6–8 June 1994. Manila.

ASEAN. 1994. ASEAN Strategic Plan of Action on the Environment. ASEAN Semelanat. Association of South-East Asian Nations (ASEAN). Jakarta, Indonesia.

ASEAN. 1995. *State of the Environment Report* (draft).

Australia. 1994. Department of the Environment, Sport and Territories, Australia. Australian Initiatives to Combat Desertification.

ESCAP. 1991. "Groundwater Quality and Monitoring in Asia and the Pacific." Water Resources Series, No. 70. Economic and Social Council for Asia and the Pacific (ESCAP). Bangkok.

ESCAP. 1995. *The State of the Environment in Asia and the Pacific 1995.* ESCAP. Bangkok.

IDIC. 1995. *Drought Network News.* Vol. 7, No. 2, June 1995. International Drought Information Centre. USA.

India. 1992a. *Annual Report, 1991–92.* Ministry of Environment and Forests, India. New Delhi.

India. 1992b. *National Report to UNCED.* Ministry of Environment and Forests. India.

India. 1993. *Environment Action Program India.* Ministry of Environment and Forests. India.

India. 1994. *Conservation of Biological Diversity in India: An Approach.* Ministry of Environment and Forests. India.

Indonesia. 1995. BAPEDAL—The Environmental Impact Management Agency. Indonesia.

Japan. 1987. Earthquake Disaster Countermeasures in Japan. Government of Japan. Tokyo.

Jinfa, L. 1994. China Combats Desertification. In: *Our Planet.* Vol. 6, No. 5. UNEP. Nairobi.

Malaysia. 1992. *Environmental Quality Report 1992.* Ministry of Science, Technology and the Environment (MOSTE). Malaysia.

Malaysia. 1993. *Environmental Quality Report.* Ministry of Science, Technology and Environment (MOSTE). Malaysia.

NEPA. 1993. China Environment News. 8 December 1993. National Environmental Protection Agency (NEPA).

Nepal. 1992. National Report to UNCED. Government of Nepal. Katmandu.

Republic of Korea. 1992. Forests in Korea. Forestry Administration. Seoul.

SACEP. 1992. SACEP Strategy and Programme 1, 1992–96.

Singapore. 1992. *The Singapore Green Plan: Towards a Model Green City.* Ministry of the Environment Singapore.

Singapore. 1993. *Annual Report 1993.* Ministry of the Environment. Singapore.

TERI. 1992. Environmental Considerations in Energy Development. Final report submitted to the Asian Development Bank. Tata Energy Research Institute (TERI). New Delhi.

UNEP. 1994. *Our Planet.* Vol. 6, No. 5. UNEP. Nairobi.

UNEP. 1996. Report of the Regional Consultations held for the first Global Environment Outlook. UNEP. Nairobi.

UNEP/UNDP/FAO. 1994. *Land Degradation in South Asia: Its Severity, Causes, and Effects Upon the People.* World Soil Resources Reports 78. FAO. Rome.

World Bank. 1992. Bhutan Trust Fund for Environmental Conservation. Project Document.

EUROPE AND CIS COUNTRIES

National Initiatives

The multitude and magnitude of national and local policy responses to environmental problems in Europe and the Commonwealth of Independent States (CIS) preclude a comprehensive compilation and overview in this report. But there are some distinct subregional trends.

Awareness of the extent of and impacts of human activity on the environment developed unevenly across Europe after the United Nations Conference on the Human Environment in Stockholm in 1972. Most west European countries soon pursued strategies to tackle environmental problems, but these issues were given little priority elsewhere in the region until the end of the 1980s (EEA, 1995). Since then, wide subregional differences have emerged among the countries with economies in transition. In Bulgaria, the Czech Republic, Hungary, Poland, Romania, and the Slovak Republic, the desire to join the European Union (EU) acts as a powerful impetus for environmental improvement, since the Union's strict environmental standards will have to be met first. On the other hand, many CIS countries, particularly the Asian Republics, still face unprecedented environmental problems.

In the EU, environmental legislation now affects everyone's life, and environmental considerations have penetrated every sector of society and governance structure. Countries in this part of the region have a range of national and local programmes, legislation, and institutional arrangements to address environmental concerns and to implement Agenda 21. Several groups of industrial companies have adopted responsible care programmes. There is also emphasis on capacity building, interdepartmental co-operation, integrated approaches to problem solving, and compliance and enforcement of environmental legislation. Box 3.11 describes the situation for the former German Democratic Republic (GDR).

In Central and Eastern Europe (CEE), while economic restructuring offers the key to solving many environmental problems, environmental legislation needs further development and harmonization to be effective. Proper enforcement of existing legislation and standards and of appropriate economic instruments also constitutes a major obstacle to environmental improvement. Box 3.12 describes a modelling exercise on the impact of introducing cleaner production technologies on atmospheric pollutant levels in the CEE region.

Comprehensive Environmental Funds have become an increasingly important interim means of financing environmental expenditures in many CEE countries. In Poland and the Czech Republic, for example, such funds have become quite substantial, with annual budgets of US$100–300 million. (See Table 3.1). Environmental funds derive revenues mainly from pollution charges and taxes. These are set aside for environmental purposes only and cannot be used for the general Government budget. The revenues provide financial assistance to the private or public sector for investments and other projects designed to achieve environmental objectives (OECD, 1995). This contrasts strongly with the situation in the former Soviet Union, where, in terms of per capita gross domestic product, only negligible amounts are being spent on the environment.

National State of the Environment reporting is done throughout the region, often on a regular basis. Since 1990, at least 15 new national State of the Environment reports have been published (UNEP/DEIA, 1996).

Public participation is generally firmly embedded in environmental policy and decision-making processes at various levels in west European coun-

Global Environment Outlook **169**

Box 3.11

Environmental Management in Germany Since Reunification

German unity represented an unprecedented challenge for environmental management in Germany. Four decades of mismanagement of the environment and nature in the former GDR left behind a pollution legacy in many places: landscapes devastated by lignite mining; a highly ineffective waste disposal sector; an agricultural sector characterized by high levels of fertilizer and pesticide use; wasteful land use and contaminated sites left by the manufacturing and mining industries.

The environmental situation in the newly created federal states (*Länder*) on the territory of the former GDR has substantially improved since reunification. In particular, a host of emergency measures have helped protect the people living in the most affected areas from immediate health hazards. Inputs of pollutants into soil, water, and air have decreased considerably.

The guiding principle behind the Federal Government's ecological cleanup and development strategy has been, and continues to be, not only the restoration and safeguarding of a sound environment, but also the role of sound environmental management within integrated policies designed to make eastern Germany attractive for business investors. This strategy centres around the goal of reconciling improvement of the environment—in particular by removing the two major barriers to investment, a serious pollution legacy and an inadequate infrastructure—with economic development.

In December 1992 the Federal Government and the eastern German *Länder* signed an Administrative Agreement to cover the financing of contaminated site rehabilitation. Annual funds of DM 1 billion have been earmarked for a period of ten years for the so-called "site projects." In addition, 23 large projects for contaminated site rehabilitation, costing approximately DM 6 billion, have been set up. The Federal Government and the new *Länder* are defraying 75 and 25 per cent of the cost, respectively. These large projects include sites used by the chemical, shipbuilding and steel industries as well as by the potassium mining industry.

Another core element of the Administrative Agreement is the cleanup of eastern German lignite mining districts. Around DM 7.5 billion have been earmarked for the period 1993–97, making this the largest single environmental project in Germany. These cleanup measures have had a favourable impact on the employment situation as many contracts have been awarded to small- and medium-sized firms, helping to secure some 3,450 jobs in these firms.

Favourable results have been achieved, particularly in the areas of wastewater treatment and waste disposal. Between 1990 and 1995, some 550 sewage plants were built or modernized in the new *Länder*. In addition a large number of illegal waste dumps were closed down, and the construction of waste treatment and recycling installations got off to a speedy start. The process of reorganization within the waste management sector has seen substantial progress as a result of local authorities setting up high-performing cooperatives. The number of landfill sites in operation fell from 11,120 in 1990 to 274 in 1994.

Setting up a modern environmental protection infrastructure requires an enormous volume of investment. According to expert estimates, the building or modernization of wastewater treatment installations in eastern Germany alone will require investment amounting to DM 100 billion over the next 10 to 15 years; a similar volume of investment is likely to be required for the building of new landfill sites for wastes from human settlements and toxic wastes. An increased involvement of the private sector in the future may not only help accelerate the building process but also bring a reduction in costs as a result of an increase in competition, thus helping to keep waste disposal charges in check.

Reference

Information supplied by The German Federal Ministry for the Environment, Nature Conservation and Nuclear Safety, Division G II 4. (Cooperation with Developing Countries and with UN bodies).

Box 3.12

Getting the Priorities Right: Investing in Pollution Control in Central and Eastern Europe

In 1990, the energy intensity of economies in Central and Eastern Europe (CEE) was estimated to be about 3 times higher than in western Europe; emissions of NO_x and SO_2 were estimated at more than 4 times higher; and emissions of particulates, cadmium, and volatile organic compounds (VOCs) were estimated considerably higher per unit of GDP.

Within the framework of the European Action Plan for Central and Eastern Europe a study was conducted, jointly by the World Bank, RIVM, and Resources for the Future, on the impact of introducing different levels of cleaner production technologies on atmospheric pollutant levels in the CEE region. The following scenarios were analysed:

- *Base Case*—only new installations in CEE are equipped with current Western European technology.

- *Accelerated Substitution*—old as well as new installations in CEE are equipped with current Western European technologies by 2010 and fuel is switched from coal to gas.

- *BAT Policy*—old and new installations in CEE are equipped with the best available technology (BAT). Only gas and non-fossil fuels are used.

- *Worst Case*—old equipment remains operational and no switch is made from coal to gas.

Table 1 gives the results of the analysis, showing average reductions in emissions in CEE countries compared to 1990.

The analysis shows that retrofitting (or replacement) of the old capital stock (installations) could reduce emissions to a level that is sufficient to meet most environmental quality goals and standards such as the WHO standard for particulate matter and sulphur, the acidification targets in the framework of UN-ECE and the goals for greenhouse gases of IPCC.

In the Base Case scenario, investments are assumed to be US$175 billion per year. Accelerated substitution would bring the sulphur dioxide emissions down to acceptable levels. This would require an additional US$50 billion per year, raising the total to US$225 billion (60 per cent in Eastern Europe; 15 per cent in Central Europe and 25 per cent in the Balkan region). However, the worst pollution from the point of view of human health can be reduced by addressing local sources of sulphur dioxide, at about 10 per cent of the additional investment level (US$5 billion per year). This is an obvious starting point.

Source: RIVM. 1993. *Scenarios for Economy and Environment in Central and Eastern Europe.* Document prepared for the World Bank in the framework of the Environmental Action Plan of Central and Eastern Europe. National Institute of Public Health and the Environment (RIVM). Bilthoven, the Netherlands.

Projected Reductions in Emissions in Central and Eastern European Countries with Varying Levels of Cleaner Production Technologies

	Per Cent Reduction from 1990 to 2010			
	Base Case	Accelerated Substitution	Best Available Technology Policy	Worst Case
Carbon dioxide	25	55	65	5
Sulphur dioxide	60	95	98	30
Nitrogen oxides	55	85	90	35
Volatile organic compounds	35	60	75	25
Particulate matter	55	97	99	35
Cadmium	15	65	90	2
Landfills[a]	5	50	60	-10

Source: RIVM (1993).
Note: a. Municipal waste.

Table 3.1

Key Characteristics of Five National Environmental Protection Funds in Central and Eastern Europe

Key Characteristics	Bulgaria	Czech Republic	Hungary	Poland	Slovak Republic
Operational (in current form) since	1993	1991	1993	1989	1991
Institutional status	Part of MoE	Part of MoE	Part of MoE	Independent	Part of MoE
Number of full-time staff	2	34	13	95	22
Final decision-making authority	Minister of the Environment	Minister of the Environment	Minister of the Environment	Fund Directors or Supervisory Board[a]	Minister of the Environment
Public participation opportunities in decision-making	Included in the work of the Supreme Board; public hearings twice a year	During environmental impact assessments	NGOs consulted during formulation of Annual Program for Support	Membership on the Supervisory Board	Through the Fund Council
1993 National Fund environmental expenditures (as a per cent of total national environmental expenditures)	US$2.3 million (7 per cent)	US$107 million[b] (10 per cent)	US$27.7 million (11 per cent)	US$198.5 million (22 per cent)	US$34.7 million[b] (20 per cent)
1993 revenues	US$3.6 million	US$101.0 million	US$36.3 million	US$284.0 million	US$30.8 million
Major revenue sources (with per cent of total value)	-pollution fines (58 per cent) -import tax on used cars (33 per cent)	-water charges (41 per cent) -air charges (30 per cent) -waste charges (13 per cent) -land charges (12 per cent)	-fuel tax (44 per cent) -traffic transit fee (20 per cent) -PHARE support (19 per cent) -pollution fines (17 per cent)	-air emission charges -wastewater charges -water use charges -waste charges	-State budget (37 per cent) -wastewater charges (30 per cent) -air emission charges (25 per cent)
1993 primary disbursement mechanisms (with per cent of total expenditures)	-grants (68 per cent) -interest-free loans (32 per cent)	-grants (71 per cent) -loans (29 per cent)	-grants -interest-free loans	-soft loans (77 per cent) -grants (17 per cent) -interest subsidies (6 per cent)	-grants
Major fields of 1993 expenditures (with per cent of total value)	-monitoring system (40 per cent) -loans to companies (32 per cent) -subsidies to municipalities (19 per cent).	-water (58 per cent) -air (33 per cent)	-air (70 per cent) -waste (15 per cent) -water (11 per cent)	-air (47 per cent) -water (35 per cent) -other[c] (18 per cent)	-water (48 per cent) -air (27 per cent) -waste (8 per cent)

Source: Adapted from REC, 1994, p. 8.

Note: a. Fund Directors approve all expenditures except those greater than US$225,000. These are approved by the Supervisory Board.
b. For the Czech and Slovak Funds, the 1993 expenditures actually exceeded revenues. The matrix shown above does not include data for 1992, however, in which revenues exceeded expenditures, thus leaving a potential surplus for 1993. c. Includes soil, nature protection, monitoring, education, and emergencies.

tries. In CEE countries, according to a September 1995 survey, there has been substantial progress by Government officials, citizens, and non-governmental organizations (NGOs) in understanding the benefits of public participation in environmental matters. The basic groundwork for public participation, such as constitutional rights, environmental protection laws, and specific public participation procedures, has now been laid in most countries. In some CEE countries, however, basic legislative reforms have yet to be carried out in practice. There is still a lack of openness and transparency in decision-making processes, a lack of trust in public authorities, and a lack of participatory transition (REC, 1995a).

International organizations are involved with strengthening the capacities of Government environment agencies and NGOs in countries with economies in transition. For instance, 17 CEE countries actively participate in UNEP's Environment and Natural Resource Information Network (ENRIN) programme, designed to strengthen national environment information systems and State of the Environment reporting capabilities.

Regional Initiatives

The first European environment programme of the European Union, the Environmental Action Programme (EAP), was adopted in November 1973 as a follow-up to the 1972 Stockholm Conference. Its main principles were incorporated into the 1987 amendments to the 1957 Treaty of Rome (the 1987 Single European Act). The EAP was updated and extended in 1977, 1983, 1987, and 1992, and implementation of the Fifth EAP for the EU is still ongoing. It emphasizes a dual and co-ordinated approach in which high environmental standards set through regulations for almost all pollutant emissions, discharges, and wastes are combined with positive incentives for industry. The latter aim to further improve performance through development of new processes, products, and techniques. The Maastricht Treaty, adopted in 1994, spells out a comprehensive agenda for sustainable, non-inflationary growth in ways that demonstrate respect for the environment. More than 200 instruments, regulations, and directives have been called into play to improve environmental quality throughout Europe and to counter transnational and global ills.

After the changeover from centrally planned economies, and in order to create a framework for expanded co-operation, steps were taken to pave the way for the "Environment for Europe" process. The first pan-European Conference of Environmental Ministers took place at Dobříš Castle, then in Czechoslovakia, in 1991, attended by 36 ministers. The Dobříš Conference requested the preparation of the pan-European Dobříš Assessment and the development of an environmental programme for the whole of Europe. Further conferences in this process took place in Lucerne, Switzerland, in 1993 and in Sofia, Bulgaria, in 1995. The next conference will take place in Aarhus, Denmark, in 1998.

At the Lucerne Conference, environmental ministers from 50 countries endorsed the short-term Environmental Action Programme for Central and Eastern Europe (EAP/CEE). The programme—developed by an international task force composed of the European Commission, the World Bank, the Organisation for Economic Co-operation and Development (OECD), and the EU—provides a methodology for integrating environmental concerns into the economic transition in the CEE region. There are three major programme components: setting priorities, strengthening institutional capacity, and developing cost-effective financing for environmental action. International mechanisms for environmental cost-sharing and the effective co-ordination of assistance under this programme have yet to be developed.

The EAP/CEE places considerable emphasis on the human health consequences of environmental degradation. In particular, drinking-water contamination and lead and particulate pollution are key short-term concerns. Opportunities for implementing low-cost measures to address these concerns have been identified. Based on an assessment of a number of "hot spots" in the CEE countries, the EAP/CEE recommended specific "win-win" investments that would benefit both the economy and the environment. For example, phasing out subsidies on energy, raw materials, and water can encourage conservation, thereby reducing waste and pollution.

Since the Lucerne Conference, national environmental policy documents have been prepared in 13 CEE countries, some of which are national environmental action plans that adopt the EAP/CEE methodology. Institution-strengthening is considered the weakest component in most countries. The environmental priorities identified are drinking-water supply, air pollution control, and wastewater treatment (REC, 1995b). Regional Environment Centres (RECs) are now assisting with the implementation of the EAP/CEE. The REC in Hungary, for instance, is working with 15 CEE countries. Since its establishment in 1990, it has awarded more than 2,000 grants to environmental NGOs in CEE to increase public participation in environmental issues. Since the Sofia Conference, the REC network is being expanded to the CIS.

The Sofia Conference issued the Sofia Declaration, reaffirming Governments' commitment to co-operate in the field of environmental protection in Europe (UN-ECE, 1995). It acknowledged that, although progress is being made in a number of areas, many serious problems remain, and it stressed the urgent need for further integration of environmental considerations into all sectoral policies. The Conference endorsed the Environmental Programme for Europe (EPE), based on the Dobříš Assessment. The EPE is linked to Agenda 21 and regional environmental treaties and conventions, and describes the actions required to address, at the European level, the following major sets of issues:

- general issues (including information, public participation, and capacity building);

- cleaner production and efficient use of energy and materials;

- sustainable consumption and production patterns;

- sustainable management of natural resources;

- biological and landscape diversity; and

- sustainable agriculture, forestry, and fisheries.

Thus the EPE encompasses all the environmental issues of concern to Europe in a long-term perspective, constituting the first set of general ob-

jectives in the environment field adopted at the pan-European level.

A number of East-West initiatives are under way to assist countries undergoing economic transition with their environmental agendas. The United Nations Economic Commission for Europe (UN-ECE) is active in fostering East-West dialogue and co-operation on environmental matters. It has developed a number of regional environmental conventions in the fields of transboundary water, industrial accidents, and air pollution as well as being active in the preparation of ministerial conferences. The EU has a range of co-operative programmes, including PHARE and TACIS. PHARE (initially Poland, Hungary–EU Assistance for the Reforms of the Economies) now assists 11 CEE countries in the development of regulatory frameworks for the environment, pollution monitoring and assessment, and installation of corrective action and abatement strategies for priority pollution concerns.

The TACIS (Technical Assistance for the CIS Countries) programme helps CIS countries to move away from centrally planned to market economies and to strengthen their democratic societies. Environment ranks among the priority sectors of this programme (EC, 1994).

In addition to the broad-brush processes, a large number of policies and programmes are specifically targeted. Many focus on sectoral areas:

- The 1993 Helsinki Ministerial Conference on forests gave a common political commitment that the increasing demands on European forests for multiple goods and services should be met in a manner consistent with their sustainable management and conservation and appropriate enhancement of their biodiversity.

- At the Sofia Ministerial Conference, the environment ministers of 55 countries endorsed the Pan-European Biological and Landscape Diversity Strategy. This proactive strategy aims to stop and reverse the degradation of biological and landscape diversity values in Europe. It addresses all biological and landscape initiatives under a common European approach and promotes the integration of biological and landscape diversity considerations

Box 3.13

Selected Regional and Subregional Environmental Agreements: Europe and the CIS Countries[a]

Regional

1957 European Agreement concerning the International Carriage of Dangerous Goods by Road

1968 European Agreement on the Restriction of the Use of Certain Detergents in Washing and Cleaning Products (as amended), Strasbourg

1979 Convention on Long-Range Transboundary Air Pollution, Geneva, and its protocols

1979 Convention on the Conservation of European Wildlife and Natural Habitats, Berne

1991 Convention on Environmental Impact Assessment in a Transboundary Context, Espoo

1991 Agreement on the Conservation of Bats in Europe, London

1992 Convention on the Transboundary Effects of Industrial Accidents, Helsinki

1992 Convention on the Protection and Use of Transboundary Watercourses and International Lakes, Helsinki

1993 Convention on Civil Liability for Damage Resulting from Activities Dangerous to the Environment, Lugano

Subregional

1958 Convention Concerning Fishing in the Waters of the Danube, Bucharest

1959 Convention Concerning Fishing in the Black Sea (as amended), Varna

1963 Agreement Concerning the International Commission for the Protection of the Rhine Against Pollution (as amended), Berne

1973 Convention on Fishing and Conservation of the Living Resources in the Baltic Sea and Belts, Gdánsk

1974 Convention on the Protection of the Marine Environment of the Baltic Sea Area, Helsinki, and its 1992 revision

1974 Convention on the Protection of the Environment Between Denmark, Finland, Norway, and Sweden, Stockholm

1976 Convention for the Protection of the Mediterranean Sea Against Pollution, Barcelona, and its protocols

1976 Conventions on the Protection of the Rhine Against Chemical Pollution and Against Pollution by Chlorides, Bonn

1982 Benelux Convention on Nature Conservation and Landscape Protection, Brussels

1990 Agreement on the Conservation of Seals in the Wadden Sea, Bonn

1992 Agreement on the Conservation of Small Cetaceans of the Baltic and North seas, New York

1992 Convention for the Protection of the Marine Environment of the North-East Atlantic

1992 Convention on the Protection of the Black Sea Against Pollution, Bucharest, and its protocols

1994 Convention on Cooperation for the Protection and Sustainable Use of the Danube River, Sofia

Note: a. Some agreements have not yet entered into force.

into policies for social and economic sectors. The strategy also reinforces existing measures and identifies a number of additional actions to be taken over the next two decades. It also promotes a consistent approach and common objectives for national and regional action to implement the Convention on Biological Diversity.

- In the field of environmental health, the World Health Organization's European Office (WHO/EURO) convened a Ministerial Conference on Health and the Environment in 1994 that resulted in a Declaration and the development of National Environment Health Action Plans. Under this process, a Committee on Environment and Health was

Box 3.14

Regional Agreements for Air Quality: Some Impacts of the 1979 Convention on Long-Range Transboundary Air Pollution

Within the framework of the 1979 Convention on Long-Range Transboundary Air Pollution (CLRTAP), Parties to the 1985 Helsinki Protocol undertook to reduce sulphur emissions by the end of 1993 to at least 30 per cent below 1980 levels. Under the 1988 Sofia Protocol, Parties were obliged to stabilize nitrogen oxide (NO_x) emissions at 1987 levels (1978 levels for the United States) by the end of 1994.

A major review carried out in 1994 showed that countries have used a range of national policy measures to try and achieve these targets:

- *Regulatory Provisions*—standards for fuel and ambient air quality; emission and deposition standards; licensing of potentially polluting activities; etc.

- *Economic Instruments*—emissions and product charges and taxes; user charges; emissions trading; subsidies and other forms of financial assistance; etc.

- *Measures Related to Emission Control Technologies*—legislative requirements to use "best available technologies"; wide availability of unleaded fuel; etc.

- *Monitoring and Assessment of Air Pollution Effects*—monitoring of air quality and environmental effects; research into effects and assessment of critical loads and levels.

What Has Been Achieved?

By 1993, all 21 Parties had reached the sulphur reduction targets of the Helsinki Protocol. Together, they had reduced 1980 sulphur emissions by 48 per cent.

By 1993, 18 of the 25 Parties had reached the NO_x emissions target of the Sofia Protocol; 4 Parties had emissions 4–41 per cent above the 1987 levels; and 3 Parties had not submitted data. Total NO_x emissions by the 25 Parties were down 4 per cent on 1987 levels. Increases in urban traffic make it very difficult for countries to meet targets.

What Has Happened to Air Quality?

In general, concentrations of sulphur dioxide (SO_2) have improved but NO_2 concentrations and related health problems in urban areas have not been significantly reduced.

- Belgium reports major reductions in urban SO_2 concentrations and, since 1985, stabilization of SO_2 levels in ambient air. There has been no significant reduction in NO_2 levels and short-term health guidelines are not met.

- Bulgaria reports that 40 per cent of the population live in areas where sulphur and nitrogen emissions still lead to harmful effects.

- Finland reports significant reductions in sulphur depositions from domestic sources.

- Germany reports that mean annual SO_2 concentrations have decreased considerably in conurbations. In rural areas, SO_2 concentrations have nearly halved whereas NO_2 concentrations have remained stable.

- The Netherlands reports that acidifying depositions decreased by about 60 per cent between the early 1980s and early 1990s.

- Norway reports that sulphur concentrations in air and precipitation decreased by 30–40 per cent since 1979, but critical loads are still exceeded in more than 30 per cent of the country. Nitrate concentrations in the lakes of southern Norway almost doubled between 1974 and 1986, and the high levels have since been maintained.

Reference

UN-ECE. 1995. *Strategies and Policies for Air Pollution Abatement: 1994 Major Review Prepared under the Convention on Long-Range Transboundary Air Pollution.* ECE/EBAIR/44.UN- ECE. New York and Geneva.

set up under the auspices of WHO to foster a co-ordinated European approach in this area.

Other initiatives are specifically designed to tackle environmental problems affecting a defined geographical area. Many of the seas, including the Aral, Baltic, Black, and Mediterranean, and some major river basins, including the Danube and Rhine, have such programmes or action plans. The "Green Lungs of Europe" is another collaborative effort involving seven countries (Belarus, Estonia, Latvia, Lithuania, Poland, Russia, and the Ukraine). It is designed to create sustainable development zones through integrated ecosystem and economic management.

There are a range of regional and subregional agreements that relate specifically to the environment (See Box 3.13.) and form a common basis for policy setting. Some agreements focus on sectoral issues; others, on geographical areas; and a few focus on both. Where commitments have been implemented by countries and sufficient time has elapsed for the agreement to have had an impact, results have demonstrated the beneficial role of multilateral policy options approaches. (See Box 3.14.)

In addition to Government-level initiatives, numerous international organizations and institutions provide vital support for the environmental movement and for NGOs in the region, as well as providing funds for nature protection, environmental education, and research.

Regional Information Sharing

The region has a clear policy towards promoting access to and sharing of environmental information. At the Sofia Ministerial Conference, the ministers adopted the UN-ECE Guidelines on Access to Environmental Information and Public Participation in Environmental Decision-Making and recommended that it should be developed into a convention (UN-ECE, 1995). EU members have already been instructed to implement Directive 90/313 on the freedom of access to environmental information, giving any person anywhere in the world the right of access to any information on the environment held by public authorities (Stichting Natuur en Milieu & FIELD, 1994).

International organizations have established programmes to make environmental information more generally accessible through environmental information networks in support of such policies. These include the European Information and Observation Network of the European Environment Agency (EEA), UNEP's ENRIN programme, OECD, and UN-ECE. All these activities extend into countries with economies in transition. UNEP has set a priority in strengthening the information networks in the countries with economies in transition, and EEA's CORINE inventories are being expanded to the PHARE countries.

The EEA, established in 1993, implements a co-ordinated approach to environmental information, monitoring, and assessment. In addition to incorporating many of the integrated and sectoral monitoring and assessment programmes, the activities of the agency are expected to improve the co-ordination of European and global data systems, thereby strengthening the European partnership towards the solution of global problems (EEA, 1995).

UNEP is working with and through a number of internationally supported, regionally based programmes to build or increase capacities for handling environmental data and information. These include the GEF-funded Black Sea and Danube River Basin Programme Co-ordination Units in, respectively, Istanbul and Vienna.

NGOs and NGO networks play a vital role in disseminating information to a wide range of users. Regional participatory networks, involving national and international governmental organizations as well as NGOs, are also gaining strength. One rather advanced example is the BALLERINA network of the Baltic Sea countries, making use of modern telecommunications technologies.

Summing Up

Compared with many other parts of the world, Europe is in a favourable position in the environmental field with:

- relatively up-to-date, comprehensive environmental data and information;

Box 3.15

Some Guiding Principles Emerging from the European GEO Consultation

- A manageable and reliable method for tracking environmental change and policy impacts is required. A well-chosen set of indicators would be an ideal tool.

- There is always a trade-off between environmental needs and expectations and the economic reality of what can be afforded. It is therefore essential to set priorities, using agreed criteria. When it comes to alternative actions, it makes sense to pick ones that will address several problems at the same time.

- Once environmental problems are recognized, it takes time to get them on to political and policy agendas, especially where environment ministries are the weak cousins in Governments. However, experience has shown that early action benefits not only the environment but also the economy; policies put in place today save money tomorrow.

- Environmental problems are closely interlinked and are an integral part of economic and social systems. Water and coastal zone management are clear examples of socio-economic situations that must be considered together with technical management aspects. Every effort should be made to tackle environmental problems in an integrated way, even though this is conceptually complex and most attempts to date have been crude.

- International cooperation is essential for tackling transboundary environmental issues because these cannot be solved by individual countries. Legal and institutional frameworks must first be in place and multilateral agreements have an important role to play. Progress in the European region is variable:

    - Legal frameworks are generally in place for air quality and hazardous waste disposal, but inadequate for the protection of coastal areas.
    - Institutional frameworks need to be better developed for some river basins.
    - Mechanisms to regulate land use on an international level exist for the European Union; countries with economies in transition still need to establish the necessary institutional and legal frameworks.

    - The protection of biodiversity is governed by an unusually large number of international agreements; specific bilateral and multilateral policies are still required to tackle issues like biosafety, green corridors, and protected areas across international borders.
    - An international framework on sound forestry practices is needed; existing international agreements such as the Framework Convention on Climate Change could be used as an additional protective mechanism.
    - A full assessment of the impacts of the Chernobyl accident is still needed and would assist the many countries in the region still dealing with the aftermath of the event.

- Another set of issues, including many urban and land degradation problems, require national or subnational policy development and action; international collaboration is not necessary in these situations.

- Most successful policies in the region have been driven by sectoral issues. However, with emphasis on end-of-pipe remedial measures, policies have not always been effectively focused. More emphasis is needed on the "input" side of equations and achieving a comprehensive "cradle-to-grave" approach.

- Many problems can now be anticipated far in advance. Whereas many environmental problems of western Europe are linked to life-styles, eastern European countries still have the opportunity to choose their own consumption and production patterns, to evolve a different route towards sustainable development and avoid the mistakes made by the West.

- Current pan-European processes are still weak on linking issues to policy. Driving forces must be the action links between the two.

References

UNEP. 1996. Report of the Regional Consultations held for the first Global Environment Outlook. UNEP. Nairobi.

many well-developed institutional and governmental structures as a basis for environmental policy setting and implementation;

an enviable climate of pan-regional co-operation; and

an impressive range of environmental policy options implemented and tested.

Despite all the efforts of recent decades and many individual national and international achievements, the environment of the region continues to deteriorate, especially in countries in transition (UNEP, 1996). The existing array of policies and actions is still unequal to the task, but there are already many lessons available that should be considered in further policy development within the region (See Box 3.15).

References

EEA. 1995. *Europe's Environment: The Dobříš Assessment.* D. Stanners and P. Bourdeau (eds.). European Environment Agency (EEA). Office for Official Publications of the European Communities. Luxembourg.

EC. 1994. *Compendium of Operational Programmes, 1993.* European Commission.

OECD. 1995. *The St. Petersburg Guidelines on Environmental Funds in the Transition to a Market Economy.* Document OCDE/GD(95)108. Organisation for Economic Co-operation and Development. Paris.

REC. 1994. *National Environmental Protection Funds in Central and Eastern Europe: Case studies of Bulgaria, The Czech Republic, Hungary, Poland and The Slovak Republic.* Regional Environment Centre (REC). Budapest.

REC. 1995a. *Status of Public Participation Practices in Environmental Decision-making in Central and Eastern Europe: Case Studies of Albania, Bulgaria, Croatia, Czech Republic, Estonia, Hungary, Latvia, Lithuania, FYR Macedonia, Poland, Romania, Slovak Republic and Slovenia.* REC. Budapest.

REC. 1995b. *Status of National Environmental Action Programs in Central and Eastern Europe: Case Studies of Albania, Bulgaria, The Czech Republic, Croatia, Hungary, Latvia, Lithuania, FYR Macedonia, Poland, Romania, The Slovak Republic and Slovenia.* REC. Budapest.

Stichting Natuur en Milieu & Foundation for International Environmental Law and Development (FIELD). 1994. *Freedom of Access to Information on the Environment in the United Kingdom: A User's Guide to the Environmental Information Regulations and EU Directive 90/313.*

UN-ECE. 1995. *Conference Proceedings: Environment for Europe.* Third Ministerial Conference. United Nations Economic Commission for Europe (UN-ECE). 23–25 October. Sofia.

UNEP. 1996. Report of the Regional Consultations held for the first Global Environment Outlook. UNEP. Nairobi.

UNEP/DEIA. 1996. *State of the Environment Reporting: Source Book of Methods and Approaches.* UNEP/DEIA/TR.96.1. Nairobi.

LATIN AMERICA AND THE CARIBBEAN

Since the United Nations Conference on Environment and Development (UNCED) in 1992, significant improvements in the definition of environmental policies, the implementation of related programmes, and the passage of legislation have taken place in Latin America and the Caribbean (LAC). Newly established environmental institutions, ministries, and commissions set up to oversee environmental policy and action have greatly assisted policy implementation. These improvements result partly from national commitments to environmental issues and an interest in the principles of sustainable development on the part of both governmental agencies and non-governmental organizations (NGOs), and partly from the impetus provided by international financing agencies such as the Inter-American Development Bank and the World Bank (UNEP, 1996).

Economic and social changes over the past two decades have also brought policy changes that had implications for the environment. In particular, structural adjustment programmes led Governments in the region to cut social and environmental spending. This has meant the suspension of many Government-supported activities, including the abandonment of environmental planning in some countries. The pressure to raise foreign exchange has also meant that sectoral legislation (on forests, fisheries, and industry, for example) often did not incorporate environmental criteria, but was instead oriented towards the expansion of short-term productivity. Problems associated with the growth of industrial megacities, such as the lack of adequate waste treatment or disposal, have also been exacerbated by the reduction in public spending (UNEP, 1996).

In some countries, economic liberalization has also resulted in the increased concentration of land tenure in the hands of few landowners. Those with only small landholdings, unable to compete on the new open markets, have been forced to sell their land as a result. This has generated population migrations towards marginal lands and the subsequent expansion of agricultural frontiers (UNEP, 1996).

National Initiatives

Most national initiatives for the environment in LAC revolve around command-and-control mechanisms, particularly legislation. The major instruments in the legislative framework are new and improved environmental institutions, such as ministries to co-ordinate environmental management and enforce laws; the inclusion of environmental matters in the constitution; the setting of environmental standards and norms through legislation; the use of economic instruments; and increased public participation and education.

Environmental Institutions

The creation of specific ministries of the environment in many countries and the adaptation and empowerment of existing bodies have been important steps towards the conservation of environmental quality in the region. The establishment of appropriately empowered Government agencies helps ensure that environmental issues become part of a Government's agenda and decision-making process. Moreover, the establishment of these institutions will help pave the way for a more holistic and coherent approach to environment and development issues and minimize the problems that arise from fragmented and unco-ordinated institutional regimes (UNEP, 1995b).

The new generation of state agencies responsible for the environment in the region include: the Ministry of Sustainable Development and Environment in Bolivia; the Secretariat of Environment, Natural Resources, and Fisheries (SEMARNAP) in Mexico; the Natural Resources Conservation Department of Jamaica; the National Environmental Commissions (CONAMAs) in Chile and Guatemala; the Secretariat of Natural Resources and Human Environment (SERNAH) in Argentina; and the Secretariats of the Environment in El Salvador and Honduras (UNEP, 1995b; WRI, 1995). Similar initiatives have taken place in many other countries of the region.

Most of these institutions have multiple roles, ranging from the drafting of legislation to the enforcing of pollution standards. For example, in Honduras, the General Law on the Environment in 1993 established a State Secretariat in the Department of the Environment. The duties of the Secretariat are monitoring compliance with and enforcing environmental legislation, formulating and co-ordinating national policies on the environment, supervising their fulfilment, and co-ordinating public and private institutions dealing with the environment (UNEP, 1995b). Through bodies of this type, numerous legislative measures have been taken to set air and water quality standards, emission standards, and impact assessment guidelines.

Aside from the multi-purpose environmental ministries, some countries have created separate bodies to deal with specific environmental sectors. Examples include the protection of natural patrimony through specific organizations, such as the National Commission for Knowledge and Use of Biodiversity (CONABIO) in Mexico and the National Biodiversity Institute (INBIO) in Costa Rica—two organizations devoted to the survey of the biological richness of their respective national ecosystems. The work of these groups is pointing out gaps in the national networks of protected areas and allowing the incorporation of knowledge derived from research in the areas into specific policies (WRI/UNEP/IUCN, 1995).

There has also been concrete progress in the establishment of national systems of protected areas.

In some countries, alliances have been made with local populations, research groups, NGOs, and international organizations in order to improve the management of protected areas and to implement the protection of reserves legally decreed but not yet managed in practice.

Environmental laws in the region have invested relevant agencies with wide regulatory powers to establish environmental standards and norms. In Mexico, power is given "to establish requirements, conditions, procedures, parameters, and permissible limits that must be observed in development of activities or use and benefit of products which cause, or might cause, ecological imbalance or damage to the environment." Similarly, the Brazilian Law on the National Environment Policy of 1981 entrusts the National Environment Council with the task of setting standards and norms (UNEP, 1995b).

The law enforcement powers granted to these institutions reflect the seriousness with which particular states view problems within their borders. In LAC, broad powers have been granted to pollution control authorities in some countries in an attempt to control polluting activities.

In Mexico, SEMARNAP has authority to confiscate polluting materials or substances and impose the temporary closure of a polluting source where there is an imminent risk to the environment or public health. The sanctions that may be imposed by State or local authorities include fines, temporary or permanent closure of the offending source, administrative arrest for up to 24 hours, and the cancellation of any permits, licences, or concessions (UNEP, 1995b).

In Honduras, it is not the environmental agency but the courts that have the authority to impose fines or jail terms or to close down or suspend activities or facilities that are damaging the environment. The courts may require indemnity to the State or to third parties for damages caused to the environment or natural resources (UNEP, 1995b).

Environmental Amendments to Constitutions

Since the 1972 Conference on the Human Environment in Stockholm, principles of environmental management have increasingly been incorporated into the constitutions of LAC countries. This elevation of environmental concerns to constitutional status is a statement of intent, and may enhance the priority conferred by Governments to sound national environmental management and sustainable development.

All constitutions enacted in LAC in the two decades since Stockholm contain important environmental protection principles, and older constitutions have been amended to incorporate them. For example, the Constitution of Panama states that it is the fundamental duty of the State to safeguard the conservation of ecological conditions by preventing environmental pollution and imbalances in the ecosystems, in harmony with economic and social development (UNEP, 1995b). Since UNCED, six LAC countries (Paraguay, Cuba, Ecuador, Argentina, Costa Rica, and Nicaragua) have incorporated the right to a healthy environment as a constitutional right. Bolivia and Chile incorporated this right into their general environmental laws. Colombia has put the concept of sustainable development into its new Constitutional Charter. In Mexico, the National Commission on Human Rights has urged Government authorities to take action to solve critical environmental problems that are considered to be violating the basic right to a healthy environment.

Environmental Legislation

Legislation dealing with a broad range of environmental issues—pollution, management of hazardous wastes, protection of water resources, and conservation of biodiversity—have increased over the past decade in the region. Effective implementation of the legislation and law enforcement, however, are still weak in most countries, mostly as a result of the lack of financial resources.

Environmental laws existed in the region before the Stockholm Conference. Most were in the form of legislation dealing with the management and sustainable use of specific natural resources such as fisheries. In 1967, for example, Argentina established a legal system for control of fisheries, while laws

passed in the same year in Brazil established penalties for marine pollution and regulated fisheries. In Colombia, several regulations were passed as part of the National Code on Renewable Resources and Environmental Protection, including decrees on hydrobiological resources (1978) and the use of marine resources (1979). In Peru, a Forestry and Wildlife Law and a General Fisheries Law were enacted in 1975.

Following the Stockholm Conference, appreciation of the interrelationships within the ecosystem and the linkages in environmental stresses increased greatly. Since then, there has been a growing realization that a combination of sectoral "resource-oriented" legislation and anti-pollution laws are not sufficient to safeguard the quality of the environment or to guarantee sustainable development. As a result, more "system-oriented" legislation has emerged, aimed at the integrated planning and management of the environment. This legislation began to emerge in Latin America with the promulgation of the Colombian Code of Renewable Natural Resources and Environment Protection in 1974, and with the Venezuelan Organic Law on Environment in 1976.

The new basic environmental laws of LAC countries are now the primary instruments for reordering the fragmented and unco-ordinated sectoral approaches to environmental management used thus far. These laws conceptualize the environment as an integrated system that should be managed on the basis of all-embracing environmental principles, policies, and plans. Such laws have been passed in most countries in the region.

Examples include the 1986 Law for the Prevention and Control of Environmental Pollution Decree in Ecuador; the Mexican General Law on Ecological Balance and Environment Protection of 1988, which was added to the 1971 Law to Prevent and Control Environmental Pollution; and the 1986 Guatemalan Law for Environmental Protection and Improvement (UNEP, 1995b).

The move towards more comprehensive environmental laws is apparent in the increase in National Environmental Action Plans. The countries that now have these include El Salvador, Honduras, and Nicaragua in Central America, and Colombia and Ecuador in South America. Numerous countries also have National Conservation Strategies, including Costa Rica, El Salvador, and Nicaragua in Central America, and Colombia, Ecuador, and Peru in South America. Many countries have augmented these national plans with sectoral action plans, such as those for forests. (See Table 3.2.)

Many innovations have taken place as a result of legislative changes, particularly after UNCED, including increased setting of emission standards and greater use of environmental impact assessments. As a result, atmospheric degradation in some of the region's large cities is now not increasing quite so fast. But there have also been numerous counteracting forces. On the one hand, introduction of emission standards and programmes, such as Brazil's efforts to produce energy from biomass, have contributed significantly to the reduction of gasoline emissions and achieved some degree of sustainability in the use of energy. On the other hand, the widespread promotion of the automobile industry in the region as a stimulus for industrial development has generated growing environmental problems in the large cities.

Environmental auditing of industries and comprehensive environmental impact statements are now mandatory in many countries. Environmental impact statements have become prerequisites for large-scale development projects in some nations. Environmental impact assessments (EIAs) are a predominant tool for incorporating environmental considerations into national socio-economic planning. Many countries, such as Chile, apply EIA legislation to both private and public-sector undertakings. In Mexico, the Secretariat of Environment, Natural Resources, and Fisheries is responsible for reviewing environmental impact statements, which must be prepared for specified projects and undertakings. The Secretariat may grant authorization to undertake the work, deny permission, or require modifications in order to avoid or lessen the severity of the environmental impacts associated with ordinary operations (UNEP, 1995b). The EIA process in Jamaica lets the Natural Resources Conservation Authority request an EIA of any permit applicant

or anyone planning to undertake works in prescribed areas (UNEP, 1995b).

Economic and Financial Instruments

The use of economic disincentives to control and prevent pollution has long been part of national legislation in the region. The use of pollution licences and fines for the improper treatment of waste are common examples of such instruments. More innovative economic instruments are also being used in the region to address environmental concerns. These include tax incentives, environment funds, and other tools to promote the "polluter pays" principle.

The Chilean Law on General Basis for the Environment, in 1994, provided for an Environment Protection Fund. This is financed by allocations from the national budget, among other sources, to provide financing for projects and activities to protect or restore the environment, to preserve nature, or to conserve the environmental heritage (UNEP, 1995b).

Numerous countries work with schemes to promote the polluter pays principle. For example, the Jamaican Government requires permits and licences to undertake certain activities that will have a negative impact on the environment. Similarly, Chilean environmental legislation encourages the adoption of economic instruments, including tradeable emissions permits, tradeable water rights, emissions taxes or user charges, and other instruments that encourage environmental improvement and restoration activities (UNEP, 1995b). In Santiago, access rights to certain key city roads for buses and taxis have been auctioned. Costa Rica introduced biodiversity prospecting rights and tradeable reforestation tax credits, and is currently experimenting with internationally tradeable development rights and carbon offsets.

Financial incentive programmes for the protection of the environment also abound in the region. In Honduras, agricultural credits are given to programmes and schemes that protect and conserve valuable soil resources. Investment in filters or other technical equipment used for the prevention of

Table 3.2

National Action Plans and Environmental Information in LAC

Country	National Report for UNCED	National State of the Environment Report	National Environmental Profile	National Biodiversity Profile	National Conservation Strategy	Environ-mental Action Plan	Forestry Action Plan
Central America							
Belize	yes (1992)	no	yes (1984)	yes (1988)	being prepared	no	yes (1989)
Costa Rica	yes (1992)	yes (1988)	yes (1982)	yes (1992)	yes (1990)	no	yes (1990)
El Salvador	yes (1992)	no	yes (1985)	yes (1988)	yes (1994)	yes (1994)	no
Guatemala	n/d	no	yes (1984)	yes (1988)	being prepared	no	yes (1991)
Honduras	yes (1992)	no	yes (1982,1989)	yes (1988,1995)	no	yes (1993)	yes (1988)
Mexico	yes (1992)	yes (1986-90)	no	no	no	no	yes (1994)
Nicaragua	yes (1992)	no	yes (1981)	no	yes (1991)	yes (1994)	yes (1991)
Panama	yes (1992)	yes (1985)	yes (1980)	no	no	no	yes (1990)
Caribbean							
Anguilla	n/d	no	yes (1993)	no	no	no	no
Antigua & Barbuda	yes (1992)	no	yes (1991)	no	no	no	yes (1993)
Bahamas	yes (1992)	no	no	no	no	no	no
Barbados	yes (1992)	no	no	no	no	no	yes (1993)
Cuba	yes (1992)	no	no	no	no	no	yes (1989)
Dominica	n/d	no	yes (1991)	no	no	no	yes (1993)
Rep. Dominican	yes (1992)	no	no	no	no	no	yes (1990)
Granada	n/d	no	yes (1991)	yes (1988)	no	no	yes (1993)
Haiti	yes (1992)	yes	yes (1985)	no	no	being prepared	no
Jamaica	yes (1992)	being prepared	yes (1987)	no	no	no	yes (1990)
Monserrate	n/d	no	yes (1993)	no	no	no	yes (1993)
Saint Kitts & Nevis	yes (1992)	no	yes (1991)	no	no	no	yes (1992)
Saint Lucia	n/d	no	yes (1991)	no	no	no	yes (1993)
St. Vincent & Grenadines	n/d	no	yes (1991)	yes (1986)	no	no	yes (1993)
Trinidad & Tobago	yes (1992)	no	no	no	being prepared	no	yes (1993)
South America							
Argentina	yes (1992)	being prepared	yes (1994)	no	no	no	yes (1989)
Bolivia	yes (1992)	no	yes (1986)	yes (1988)	no	being prepared	yes (1989,1991)
Brazil	yes (1992)	no	yes (1992)	yes (1988)	no	no	no
Chile	yes (1992)	yes (1990,1994)	yes (1990,1995)	yes (1993)	no	no	yes (1993)
Colombia	yes (1992)	no	yes (1990)	yes (1988)	yes (1995)	yes (1991)	yes (1989,1992)
Ecuador	yes (1992)	being prepared	yes (1987)	yes (1988,1995)	yes (1995)	yes (1993)	yes (1990)
Guyana	yes (1992)	no	yes (1982)	no	no	no	yes (1989)
Paraguay	yes (1992)	no	yes (1985)	no	no	no	no
Peru	yes (1992)	no	yes (1986)	yes (1988)	yes (1995)	no	yes (1987,1991)
Suriname	n/d	no	no	no	no	no	no
Uruguay	yes (1992)	yes (1992)	no	no	no	no	no
Venezuela	yes (1992)	yes (1990, 92, 94–95)	no	no	no	no	no

Sources: WRI/UNEP/UNDP (1994); WRI/IIED/IUCN (1992, 1995); CIAT/UNEP, 1995.

pollution in the industrial, agricultural, forest, or other commercial sectors may be deducted from income tax, and such equipment is also exempt from import duties and sales tax (UNEP, 1995b).

Some countries, including Mexico, Costa Rica, Colombia, and Chile, have incorporated estimates of the degradation and loss of their natural resources into their national accounting systems. For methodological reasons, these estimates usually are not incorporated into the financial estimates of economic development. The fact that indicators such as soil erosion or deforestation are presented together with financial estimates of economic growth highlights the growing interest in the region in evaluating the costs of natural resource degradation. (See Box 3.16.)

Public Participation and Education

Non-governmental organizations increasingly participate in the formulation of policies, and some Governments are turning over the management of protected natural areas to NGOs and grassroots groups. Mexico, Colombia, and Chile have passed new laws requiring Governments to establish environmental planning committees with broad social representation at the provincial or local levels (WRI, 1995).

The work of NGOs has been crucial in the creation and management of protected areas in Costa Rica, of biosphere reserves in Mexico, and of the Atlantic Forest Biosphere Reserve in Brazil. In some countries, NGOs have also been important driving forces in the implementation of recycling programmes and in the promotion of alternative sources of energy.

One such example is the Isiboro Secure National Park in El Beni, Bolivia. Most of the park's territory is located in territory traditionally occupied by Indian communities who, after negotiations with the Government, began administering the park in 1992. In other countries, such as Mexico, Guatemala, Honduras, Belize, and Costa Rica, Governments have turned to NGOs to help manage national parks and other protected areas. The Calakmul Bioreserve in Mexico's south-eastern

state of Campeche is one example of such NGO participation (WRI, 1995).

Environmental education programmes are growing at all levels in the region, and the incorporation of an environmental perspective into traditional educational curricula is widespread in the primary, secondary, and tertiary levels of education. Many LAC universities now offer graduate courses in environmental sciences, ecology, and natural resource management.

Environmental Information

A great deal of data and information exists in the LAC region on the state of the environment and natural resources. Most countries have completed either national State of the Environment reports or environmental profiles in some form. (See Table 3.2.) These reports generally include an inventory of natural resources, a summary of the state of the environment, and, in some cases, policies and strategies for natural resource use and conservation. Most countries in the region provided national reports for UNCED in 1992. However, few regularly or periodically publish State of the Environment reports, with the exception of Chile, Mexico, and Venezuela. As a result, there is a lack of continuity and cohesion in environmental monitoring and reporting. Much of the information produced is consequently underused and does not adequately contribute to environmental decision-making and policy setting in the region (CIAT/UNEP, 1995).

Regional Initiatives

The last years have witnessed the growth and strengthening of subregional agreements, initiatives, and alliances in LAC. While these have mainly aimed at developing and promoting regional economic and social issues, they also incorporate environmental and sustainability issues. Such agreements include the Andean Pact (*Pacto Andino*), MERCOSUR, the Andean Corporation for Promotion of Development (*Corporación Andina de Fomento*), the System of Central American Integration (*Sistema de la Integración Centroamericana*), the Initiative for the

Box 3.16
Green Accounting

A number of countries in LAC, including Chile, Colombia, Costa Rica, and Mexico, are using some form of green accounting or natural resource accounting. Green accounting addresses the shortcoming of traditional national accounting, known as the System of National Accounts (SNA). Green accounting is based on the concept that a proper assessment of a country's income and wealth needs to account for the contributions of activities made by all sectors of the economy and their impact on resource depletion and degradation. Traditional SNA ignores the value of resources (on and in the ground) as well as the value of environmental degradation. Therefore, it gives a false impression of income and wealth and often leads policy-makers to ignore or destroy the environment to further economic development. Incorporating the real value of natural resources as well as their depletion and degradation allows for better allocation of priorities, thereby helping to address the causes of current major environmental problems including the over-exploitation of natural resources such as forests.

To date there have been two main approaches to green accounting. The first approach is to create separate or "satellite" accounts alongside the traditional national accounts, which capture changes in natural resources but do not integrate them within the framework of the traditional SNA. Satellite accounts are the most common form of environmental accounting now in use. These accounts allow for the valuation of resource use and depletion as well as estimations of expenditures for environmental protection to be made. This valuation allows countries to maintain accounts of annual resource use and depletion. While satellite accounts are linked to the existing system of national accounts, they are not an integral part of them.

The other approach is to integrate environmental accounts with the traditional SNA. For this approach, countries must modify their existing system of national accounts to incorporate environmental assets, such as subsoil reserves. The integration of natural resources, however, is limited to easily valued resources (such as oil, coal, and timber) and as yet does not account for all environmental aspects, particularly environmental pollution.

The United Nations Statistical Division (UNSD) is co-ordinating the development of a more all-encompassing and integrated green accounting system. In the early 1990s, UNSD proposed a new accounting framework called the Integrated System of Environmental and Economic Accounts (IEEA). The system integrates environmental issues into conventional national accounts. Some countries, such as Colombia and Mexico, have experimented using this system, although in parallel to the traditional SNA rather than as the traditional system. In the long run, the IEEA system could replace the traditional SNA and thereby make the environment an integral part of national accounting systems.

From green accounting systems such as the IEEA, green indicators can be developed to augment traditional economic indicators such as GDP. Green indicators take into account the environment, while traditional indicators such as GDP, drawn from the traditional national accounts system, have little or no consideration for the environment. The eco-domestic product (EDP) is one such green indicator—an environmentally adjusted measure of net domestic product. EDP helps to highlight the value of resource depletion missed by GDP. For example, a country that exports minerals but has limited remaining reserves would show an EDP that is significantly lower than its GDP. Such green indicators would serve as an aid to policy setting and enable more informed decision-making regarding resource allocation and economic development. Of course, better accounting does not necessarily result in better environmental policies.

Americas (*Iniciativa para las Américas*, which includes the United States and Canada), and the North American Free Trade Agreement (NAFTA, which includes Mexico).

In recent years, some specific environmental treaties, conventions, and agreements have also been signed, including the Treaty of Amazon Co-operation (*Tratado de Cooperación Amazónica*), the Caribbean Convention for Environmental Protection, the Caribbean Action Plan for the Sustainable Development of Island States, the Program of Action for Tropical Forestry (*Programa de Acción Forestal Tropical*), and the Permanent Commission of the South Pacific (*Comisión Permanente del Pacífico Sur*).

In Central America, the treaties and alliances include the Central American Alliance for Sustainable Development (*Alianza Centroamericana de Desarrollo Sostenible*), the Central American Commission of Environment and Development (*Comisión Centroamericana de Ambiente y Desarrollo*, CCAD) (see Box 3.17), and the Central American Council of Forests and Protected Areas (*Consejo Centroamericano de Bosques y Areas Protegidas*). With the signature of NAFTA, a North American Commission on Environmental Cooperation has also been created to guarantee that the free trade agreement does not harm the environment.

These alliances, agreements, and commissions indicate growing recognition of the need to confront environmental problems at a regional level and to jointly plan the sustainable use of regional natural resources. Large ecosystems, such as Amazonia, the Andes, the Central American tropical forests, the Southern Pacific, and the Caribbean small island states are similarly considered. The treaties also serve as vital catalysts in sparking international co-operation among NGOs, Governments, and international institutions in designing and implementing environmental policies. Regional and subregional alliances have also played a fundamental role in the preparation of technical documents establishing guiding principles, appropriate management procedures, and strategic policies on regional environmental issues (CCAD, 1992; CDEA, 1992; CDMAALC, 1991; UN, 1994).

An example of the co-operation initiated by these agreements is the Treaty of Amazon Co-operation (*Tratado de Cooperación Amazónica*). With its signature, a Special Commission for the Amazonian Environment was created in 1989, which operates eight environmental programmes in different countries. Important efforts such as the Amazonian Network of Protected Areas (SURAPA) operate as a result of these programmes, allowing for co-ordination of subregional efforts. Through their joint environmental programmes, the Caribbean Countries played an extremely important role in the preparation of the *Programme of Action for Small Island States*

presented at UNCED, and in the organization of the Global Conference on the Sustainable Development of Small Island States held in Barbados in 1994. These two events have played a major role in raising awareness and promoting discussion on the critical problems of sustainability for small island states.

Another positive programme that has emerged from the plethora of agreements in Central America is the Alliance for Sustainable Development (*Alianza Centroamericana de Desarrollo Sostenible*). Initiated in October 1994 by the seven Central American Presidents, this has been instrumental in promoting co-ordinated bilateral or multilateral actions for the management of protected areas, particularly those located along national borders, through the establishment of neighbouring reserves and biological corridors spanning borders. The Alliance has emerged as a forum in which various interested parties discuss and identify priority actions. In 1995, for example, to implement the forestry, biodiversity, and environmental law commitments made by Alliance signatories, CCAD and The World Conservation Union (IUCN) convened a planning workshop in Panama to identify priorities and collaborating organizations across the region. Some 100 representatives from Governments, NGOs, the business sector, research institutions, and grassroots organizations from the seven Central American countries attended (WRI, 1995).

There is also an annual Meeting of the Ministers of the Environment for LAC organized in co-operation with UNEP's regional office for LAC. Its main objectives, as reiterated at the Ninth Meeting in Cuba in 1995, are fourfold: to guide the implementation of the environmental agenda of LAC; to identify opportunities for regional co-operation in environmental matters conducive to the implementation of Agenda 21; to propose measures to achieve greater effectiveness and coherence in the regional planning and implementation of the environmental agendas of international agencies; and to reach agreement on common positions concerning topics of importance to the international environmental agenda with implications for the LAC region (UNEP, 1995a).

BOX 3.17
Central American Commission for Environment and Development (CCAD)

The Central American Commission for Environment and Development (CCAD) is an excellent example of regional-level policy setting in Central America. It was created in 1989 by the Presidents of Central America and is composed of the heads of the ministries and agencies most directly responsible for environmental policy in each of the seven Central American countries.

The organization seeks to influence regional decision-makers by facilitating the exchange of information and by providing a forum in which different interest groups can address specific regional issues. CCAD's principal mission is to promote policy co-ordination, develop new funding, build institutional capacities, make information available, and foster citizen participation in addressing the region's pressing environmental and development problems.

CCAD has expanded from mainly a forum for discussions of issues of common concern among Ministers responsible for the environment to an organization involved in planning related to regional environmental and development issues. The Commission is now building its capacities to gather, organize, and distribute information on environment and development in Central America.

CCAD brings together representatives of Governments, NGOs, grassroots groups, and international institutions to discuss and analyse problems and develop policy recommendations and action plans. It has designed a consultation methodology for elaborating action plans and international conventions across the region. Hundreds of individuals representing diverse interests discuss and rank policy proposals for consideration by Presidents and Parliaments.

Examples of policies discussed include the Central American Tropical Forest Action Plan (PAFTCA) sponsored by CCAD in 1991. This initiative has drawn technical and financial support for better forest management. The Forest Action Plan included the Regional Convention for the Management and Conservation of Natural Forest Ecosystems and the Development of Forest Plantations. Signed in 1993, the convention provides a framework for policy and institutional reform in the forestry sector.

To pave the way for legal reform across the region, CCAD helped create other regional bodies to bridge gaps between Governments and civil organizations. The Central American Inter-Parliamentary Commission on the Environment (CICAD), for instance, brings together representatives of the legislatures from the seven countries to press for ratification of international conventions and policy reforms in national congresses.

Acting on reports of toxic waste dumping, CCAD and CICAD joined forces to help set up regional networks of NGOs and Government bodies to monitor the dumping of wastes. Late in 1992, the seven countries signed an agreement to ban the importation or international transport of a wide range of hazardous materials. Coupled with the networks' information and public education campaigns, the ban is making illegal waste dumping difficult in the region.

Other legal and institutional co-operation mechanisms within CCAD's area of competence are the Central American Convention on Climate Change (signed in May 1995), the Central American Convention on Biodiversity (signed in June 1992), and efforts to promote the adoption of the Central American Development Strategy or Central American Alliance for Sustainable Development in 1994. More recently, CCAD has participated in the creation of the Central American Fund for Environment and Development.

Throughout Central America, CCAD is also helping strengthen national environmental agencies to foster public participation in decision-making. In 1994, it initiated a project to train the staff of Government environment agencies in Central America in participatory methods for policy formulation.

CCAD has access to the highest levels of policy-making. This accounts for its success in getting NGOs, Ministers, and Presidents to endorse its initiatives and proposals. The prestige that Presidential support affords CCAD, the organization's commitment to democratic processes, and its policy to remain small and agile are instrumental to its success.

Reference

WRI. 1995. Policy Hits the Ground: Participation and Equity in Environmental Policy. World Resources Institute. Washington.

International Initiatives

The Governments of the region have strongly supported international environmental agreements to help protect the environment and the natural resources of LAC. Among these topics, the regional ramifications and implications of the following are of particular relevance: the effective implementation of Agenda 21 and its commitments, the Biodiversity Convention and the property rights of genetic resources, the Convention on Climate Change and the conservation of the regional forests, and the Antarctic Treaty. Regional priority issues such as the sustainable management of native forests, the restoration of degraded areas, or the establishment of biogeographic corridors at a subcontinental level present opportunities for further international cooperation.

Several countries have participated in the development of international conventions and treaties, though many of these have not been ratified. At the Ninth Meeting of the Region's Environment Ministers in 1995, countries confirmed their commitment to the majority of global environmental conventions. The Ministers fully supported the implementation of the regional application of the Desertification Convention for LAC and the provisions of the Convention on Biodiversity. There was also support for the objectives and actions of the Declaration of Non-Legally Binding Principles on Forests established by UNCED and the Intergovernmental Panel on Forests, as well as for the preparation of the Protocol on Land-Based Sources of Pollution in the wider Caribbean region, within the UNEP Regional Seas Programme. To help combat the increase in marine pollution and the resulting drop in fishing harvests, Governments are also promoting an action programme on land-based sources of pollution (UNEP, 1995a).

Other pre-UNCED conventions—such as Ramsar, the Convention on International Trade in Endangered Species of Wild Flora and Fauna, the Convention on the Law of the Sea, the Montreal Protocol on Substances that Deplete the Ozone Layer, and the Basel Convention on the Control of Transboundary Movement of Hazardous Waste—have received the full participation of the majority of the LAC countries.

A number of innovative initiatives have also taken place in support of environmental protection in the region. One such initiative is debt-for-nature swaps in countries with both debt and environmental problems. These have had a mixed reception. In countries like Costa Rica the outcome has been positive, with substantial funds swapped for external debt being channelled into environment programmes. Other international initiatives that have had some success include Trust Funds that have been launched in countries such as Mexico and Bolivia for the financing and management of protected areas, which are supported by international organizations.

References

CCAD. 1992. *Agenda Centro-Americana de Ambiente y Desarrollo*. Comisión Centroamericana de Ambiente y Desarrollo(CCAD). United Nations Development Programme, World Resources Institute, World Conservation Union, and Conservation International.

CDEA. 1992. *Amazonia Without Myths*. Comisión de Desarrollo y Medio Ambiente para la Amazonía (CDEA). Inter-American Development Bank. United Nations Development Programme. Amazon Cooperation Treaty.

CDMAALC. 1991. *Nuestra Propia Agenda*. Comisión de Desarrollo y Medio Ambiente de América Latina y el Caribe (CDMAALC). Inter-American Development Bank and UNDP.

CIAT/UNEP. 1995. *Capacidad Institucional para la producción y analysis de datos ambientales en los paises de América Latina y el Caribe*. Prepared by Manuel Winograd. Cali, Colombia.

UN. 1994. *Earth Summit. Programme of Action for Small Island States*. Global Conference on the Sustainable Development of Small Island Developing States. 26 April-6 May. Bridgetown, Barbados.

UNEP. 1995a. *Final Report of the Ninth Meeting of Ministers of the Environment of LAC*. 21–26 September. Havana, Cuba.

UNEP. 1995b. *UNEP's New Way Forward: Environmental Law and Sustainable Development*. Chapter 12. Emerging Trends in National Environmental Legislation in Developing Countries. UNEP Environmental Law Unit. Nairobi.

UNEP. 1996. Report of the Regional Consultations held for UNEP's first Global Environment Outlook. UNEP. Nairobi.

WRI. 1995. *Policy Hits the Ground; Participation and Equity in Environmental Policy-Making.* World Resources Institute. Washington.

WRI/IIED/IUCN. 1992. *Country Environmental Studies.* INTERASIE Project. Washington.

WRI/IIED/IUCN. 1995. *Country Environmental Studies.* INTERASIE Project. Washington.

WRI/UNEP/IUCN. 1995. National biodiversity planning: guidelines based on early experiences around the world.

WRI/UNEP/UNDP. 1994. *World Resources 1994–95.* Oxford University Press. New York and London.

NORTH AMERICA

In the early 1970s, both Canada and the United States moved swiftly to respond to public outcries about the environmental issues in North America. In 1970, the United States Environmental Protection Agency (EPA) was created, and in 1971, the Government of Canada established a Federal Department of Environment, now known as Environment Canada. In the years since these major milestones, both countries have established strong records in terms of the application of command-and-control policies as well as the use of economic instruments to achieve environmental results.

Both Canada and the United States are Federal systems and, as such, depend heavily on an effective partnership with other levels of Government (Federal, State, provincial, and municipal). This collaboration includes legislation, research and monitoring, and enforcement measures to combat environmental deterioration and protect the health and safety of their citizens and their environment. Success on many fronts is thus largely due to efforts undertaken at all levels of government. The United States and Canada are widely regarded for the environmental legislation they have designed and enacted and for the establishment of scientifically based environmental and pollutant standards.

In recent years, concern has grown about the capacity for legislative measures alone to deal with the delicate balancing act of environment and economy. Conflicts over natural resources have sometimes exceeded the capacity of established institutions, legislation, and regulations to resolve them. Historically, many environmental regulations were developed and applied to specific sectors for specific substances. This fragmented approach resulted in pollution shifting rather than pollution prevention in certain circumstances. Rather than eliminating the substance, the pollutant would, for instance, move from land to air to water. Further, frustration

also grew because the complex network of environmental regulatory processes was delivering too little environmental protection at too high a cost (EPA, 1994a).

As the more obvious problems such as eutrophication of Lake Erie were being resolved, scientists in both countries discovered that command-and-control regulations did not necessarily address other stresses threatening ecological resources and general well-being (for example, the Great Lakes ecosystem). In a recent report, EPA expressed concern that command-and-control approaches to mitigating pollution have sometimes proved to be blunt instruments—overregulating in some areas, undercontrolling in others (EPA, 1996). Evidence has been seen in the failure of regulations to halt the decline of salmon populations in the Pacific Northwest and oyster stocks in the Chesapeake Bay; to control toxic contamination of the beluga whale population in the St. Lawrence River estuary; and to protect migratory bird populations generally. Such problems underscore the substantial limits of present knowledge of the earth's natural systems and the ways in which human activities affect these systems.

Market incentives and participatory processes are being tried as ways of addressing the shortcomings of command-and-control strategies. Increased efforts have been made to use them in environmental protection and natural resources management programmes throughout the region. However, both the U.S. and Canadian Governments recognize that such efforts have their own limitations and are not universally effective in dealing with all environmental threats. For example, measures to deal with human exposure to highly toxic chemicals do not appear to be amenable to this form of policy action. Many environmental problems still require compliance to specific rules and regulations to achieve acceptable standards and ensure protection of public health and the environment (PCSD, 1996).

Against this background, policy in North America seems to be coalescing around three themes: first, strengthen and streamline sectoral environmental policies; second, test the potential for more comprehensive management and creative partnerships with local decision-makers (businesses and communities); third, focus national research and technology where the long-term potential for great scientific discovery compensates for a lack of immediate commercial interest.

New Approaches to Sectoral Environmental Policies

In both Canada and the United States, sectoral environmental policies that address land, forest, water, biodiversity, and waste are being developed and applied. For the most part, these initiatives build on previously enacted legislation, pollution standards, and monitoring programmes. An exception is the Canada Oceans Act, now before Parliament, billed as the world's first example of a national law and policy aimed at all aspects of oceans governance. The act will be largely founded on collaborative planning and management, avoiding the confrontational approach of earlier legislation, and solidly based on the principle of integrated resource management and sustainable development, tempered by the precautionary approach.

Land Conservation

The Canadian Federal Department of Agriculture, known as Agriculture and Agri-Food Canada (AAFC), is expected to release its sustainable development strategy by December 1996. With its primary focus on land-management issues, the strategy promises to show the improved ability of AAFC to measure the impacts of agriculture on the environment. This ability results from environmental assessments carried out on three of its major programmes: the Gross Revenue Insurance Program, the Net Income Stabilization Account, and Crop Insurance. The new sustainable development strategy addresses

a shortcoming found in the previous programmes— their ineffectiveness in mitigating negative impacts on environmental resources.

A number of Canadian agricultural policies, such as the Wheat Board quota system, government-subsidized wetland drainage, and land pricing and taxation systems, have been criticized for placing special production pressures on all farms regardless of site-specific environmental factors. Subsequently, in the early 1990s, under the auspices of Canada's Green Plan, resources to encourage site-specific resource assessments were put into place. How effective these will be in reversing the negative impact of main agricultural policies is yet to be assessed.

In the United States, to promote sustainable agricultural practices, the Government is encouraging actions consistent with integrated farming systems at the Federal and State levels. Some of the key elements include strengthened conservation requirements, protection of prime farmland from conversion to non-agricultural use, environmentally friendly pest management techniques, minimization of water pollution from animal wastes, and reduced consumption of non-renewable energy sources (PCSD, 1996). The U.S. Conservation Reserve Program has been credited with reducing soil erosion on croplands by more than a billion tons a year from 1982 to 1992 (USDA, 1996).

Forest Management

Important steps have been taken in North America to chart an effective course towards sustainable forestry management. Under Canada's 1991 Model Forest Programme, suggested approaches and actions are being tested in 10 sites across the nation. The following year, Canada released a National Forest Strategy that identified 96 actions for sustainable forestry management. Initiatives have been taken to develop criteria and indicators of sustainable forest development that will let Canada assess the health of its forests (Government of Canada, 1995). The Strategy was endorsed by all stakeholders, with Aboriginal organizations playing a leading role (Canadian Dept. of Foreign Affairs and International Trade, 1996).

The commitment of the United States to achieve sustainable management of all U.S. forests by the year 2000 is important but complex since it extends to forestlands beyond the Federal Government's direct control. A positive aspect is that surveys are finding non-industrial private forest landowners care about the environment and indicate they want to do the "right thing." This category of owners cares for 59 per cent of U.S. timberland and was responsible for 41 per cent of the trees planted in the United States in 1993 (Comanor, 1994).

Biodiversity

Public awareness and participation are playing a key role in the protection of biodiversity. Semi-natural areas situated between densely populated urban land and protected wildlands are especially important to preserve. Voluntary partnerships with private owners of such lands are being tried as a complement to the existing system of laws to safeguard the environment on both public and private lands. Conservation areas and preserves are an important basis for biodiversity protection across the region (PCSD, 1996).

The U.S. National Biological Service was created in 1993 to provide scientific knowledge to balance the compatible goals of ecosystem protection and economic progress. Research needed to meet short-term, technical, and long-term strategic needs is conducted at 16 Science Centers and 81 Field Stations, as well as at 44 Cooperative Research Units in 40 states (NBS, 1996).

A recent Canadian development is the establishment of a comprehensive national network of protected marine areas. These will incorporate existing national marine parks and wildlife reserves, and may eventually also embrace existing marine conservation programmes operated by the provinces (Can. Dept. of Foreign Affairs and International Trade, 1996). Further, Canada—all levels of Government and stakeholders—has finalized a Canadian National Biodiversity Strategy. The Federal and provincial environment and wildlife ministers agreed on a national framework for protection of endangered species. Soon Federal endangered species legislation will be introduced in the Canadian

Parliament. Both the national framework and the legislation are the product of widespread consultation with Aboriginal groups, non-governmental organizations, industry leaders, and private citizens. It is hoped that through this new framework there will be increased scope for more successful recovery programs, like the return to Southern Canada of the peregrine falcon, which had disappeared from this area but is now increasing in numbers due to a Federal-provincial recovery project.

Toxic Contaminants, Pollution Control, and Waste

Innovative measures to tackle the problem of toxic contaminants and waste in the environment and their effects on human health are being implemented. (See Box 3.18.) Risk assessment and risk management along with the provision of complete and accurate information to the public are considered key to dealing with harmful effects of toxic substances on human health and the environment. Both Governments have taken significant steps to reduce human exposure to certain pollutants, particularly lead, mercury, and pesticides.

In Canada, efforts are currently under way to update and improve the Canadian Environmental Protection Act (CEPA). The assessment of health risks posed by substances or chemicals with toxic potential and the subsequent control of these substances are the essential concerns of CEPA. Through the renewal of CEPA, the Government plans to shift legislative emphasis from reacting to the toxics and pollution at the end of the pipe to preventing the pollution in the first place. The renewed CEPA will also emphasize a partnership between governments and citizens by allowing citizens to start action in Canadian courts to clean up the environment.

The Government hopes that this legislation will focus on preventing pollution at its source. Also with regard to toxics, Canada has developed a National Pollutants Release Inventory. This is now available on the "Green Lane" Internet site. Information is provided on releases and transfers of pollutants by more than 1,000 industries. Annual reports identify the most significant substances released to the land,

Box 3.18

United States EPA Initiatives in Partnership Programmes Related to Pollution Prevention and Greening Industrial Activities

The Common Sense Initiative

The Common Sense Initiative (CSI) involves EPA, industry, environmental and community groups, labour, and other Federal, State, and local Government agencies in a study of environmental policies facing six industrial sectors in order to recommend changes that will encourage cleaner, cheaper, smarter approaches to environmental management. CSI is focused initially on automobile assembly, computers and electronics, iron and steel, metal finishing, petroleum refining, and printing. These industries account for more than 11 per cent of U.S. gross national product and a slightly higher share of toxic releases (EPA, 1994).

The Star Program

Most U.S. manufacturers of computers, monitors, and printers have joined EPA's Star Program, which promotes equipment that uses 50 per cent less energy, with a potential electricity cost saving of US$70 a year per computer and printer. Nearly 90 per cent of printers and 40 per cent of computers sold in the United States now conform with Energy Star.

The Green Lights Program

The Green Lights Program has attracted 1,612 organizations to focus on more energy-efficient lighting. The participants achieved an average rate of return of 25 per cent on investments and reduced electricity bills by 40 per cent or more.

Project XL

Project XL is an example of how EPA may now grant regulatory flexibility in exchange for an enforceable commitment by a regulated entity to achieve better environmental results. As an example, 3M Corporation's Project XL proposes to obtain "beyond compliance" permits that allow for performance-based permits, establish emission caps below existing regulatory limits, develop a single, simplified multimedia permit, and implement a simplified reporting system and an Environmental Management System (EMS) verification process. Three facilities of 3M would be covered; preliminary stakeholder meetings have been held to gain support on this initiative and obtain input on the format and content of emissions reporting information.

air, and water for Canada as a whole and for each province (Canadian Dept. of Foreign Affairs and International Trade, 1996). The Accelerated Reduction/Elimination of Toxics (ARET) initiative is an example of an effort to address quickly the adverse effects of toxic substances, especially persistent organic pollutants, on human health and the environment.

A good example of non-regulatory policies in action is the use of market incentives in the field of air pollution control. Title IV of the U.S. Clean Air Act Amendments of 1990 calls for a 9-million-metric-ton reduction in annual emissions through the

Acid Rain Program. The centrepiece of this programme is market-based allowance trading, which lets utilities adopt the most cost–effective strategy to reduce sulphur dioxide (SO_2) emissions. Affected utilities are required to install systems that continuously monitor emissions of SO_2, nitrogen oxides (NO_x), and other related pollutants in order to track progress, ensure compliance, and provide credibility to the trading component of the programme.

In Canada, under the Acid Rain Control Programme, the trading of SO_2 emissions occurs between power plants of a particular utility in Ontario, New Brunswick, and Nova Scotia. The programme was formalized in 1985 through Federal-provincial agreements with the seven provinces east of Saskatchewan. Participants agreed to reduce their combined SO_2 emissions to 1.8 million metric tons per year by 1994, but actual reductions went beyond the target to about 1.5 million metric tons. Consequently, total SO_2 emissions in eastern Canada have been reduced by 56 per cent since 1980 (Canadian Dept. of Foreign Affairs and International Trade, personal communication, 1996). Trading of consumption allowances is also being used to manage the phaseout of some ozone-depleting substances (Draper, 1996).

Both countries have set waste-reduction targets and introduced aggressive recycling programmes. A growing realization in the region is that considerable money can be made by finding ways to "mine" wastes. For example, in Canada, gas produced from landfill sites is captured and sold to installations that turn it into electricity. The volume of greenhouse gases diverted from the atmosphere as a result of this is equivalent to removing 500,000 cars from the road every year (Marchi, 1996). There are also some 50 non-profit and for-profit companies in Canada taking advantage of emerging demands to stop dumping used building materials in landfills. They sell and recycle building materials such as doors, windows, plumbing fixtures, wood and asphalt, concrete, and gypsum (Government of Canada, 1996).

Comprehensive Management and Creative Partnerships

There is today a realization throughout the region that an appropriate mix of instruments will achieve the best overall environmental results. Voluntary compliance measures are increasingly seen by nearly all stakeholders as important complements to regulatory and economic instruments for environmental protection. The social and economic benefits of improved environmental performance and the desire to anticipate regulations are driving corporations to "get ahead of legislation." Such voluntary actions by the private sector also demonstrate to Governments and the public that self-regulation is a viable option (EC, 1996a).

Comprehensive Management

Overall, a noticeable shift in North America is taking place away from managing single resources towards managing ecosystems composed of a variety of resources. In Canada, the State of the Environment Report has long championed this concept. Environment Canada is advancing an operational strategy with ecozones as spatial reporting units, emphasizing that people are indeed part of the ecosystem (Government of Canada, 1996).

In the United States, Federal agencies including the Forest Service, Bureau of Land Management, Fish and Wildlife Service, National Park Service, and the EPA have established integrated ecosystem management policies. These guide decisions for achieving various goals, including those set by law. Nearly 150 U.S. examples were identified by the Keystone Center's national policy dialogue on ecosystem management. Such programmes seem to offer the most promise where public and private lands have multiple uses, such as forestry, fisheries, grazing, and recreation (PCSD, 1996).

EPA promotes watershed protection by a holistic framework that addresses complex water quality problems. The strategy is place-based, integrating water quality management activities within hydrologically defined drainage basins (watersheds), rather than in areas defined by political boundaries. There are several key guiding principles for the watershed protection approach, including a place-based focus, stakeholder involvement and partnerships, environmental objectives, problem identification and prioritization, and integrated actions (EPA, 1994b).

In both countries, these initiatives provide some of the best examples of how to achieve sustainable development through a comprehensive ecosystem approach. Key elements essential to its success are partnerships, environmental citizenship, science, and leadership.

The region is also making progress in adopting market mechanisms to improve comprehensive environmental management. In Canada, a baseline study of possible barriers and disincentives was initiated in the 1994 budget that provided for a Task

Force on Economic Instruments and Disincentives to Sound Environmental Practices. The Government has since continued to work to substantially reduce or eliminate many subsidies, grants, and contributions that may inadvertently disadvantage environmental objectives with regard to other goals. For example, business subsidies have been reduced between 1994–95 and 1997–98 by about 60 per cent (Government of Canada, 1996).

The U.S. Pollution Prevention Act of 1990 takes a comprehensive approach towards industry—encouraging manufacturers to modify equipment and processes, redesign products, substitute raw materials, and make improvements in management techniques, training, and inventory control (Gore, 1995). Incentives for continuous environmental improvement are a major feature of the Industry Strategy Division (ISD) created in 1995 by EPA. ISD works towards its goal in a number of ways, including demonstration projects with companies and other stakeholders in Louisiana, New Jersey, and Indiana that focus on four industrial subsectors—metal finishing, chemical manufacturing, photo imaging, and thermoset plastics.

Creative Partnerships

The importance of partnerships, empowered communities, and stewardship in environmental management is now widely recognized. Significant popular mobilization has created an important network of environmental organizations in civil society that have information, advocacy, and watchdog roles. As EPA Administrator Carol Browner noted, "In the final analysis, what is critical in our efforts to advance pollution prevention is a willingness to take chances, to question established practices and to experiment with new ideas and, above all, to cooperate with each other as we try to harmonize environmental protection with economic growth" (EPA, 1994a). Of particular note in both the United States and Canada has been the taking up by industry of voluntary initiatives concerning environmental conservation and protection.

In the United States, for example, EPA has many co-operative programmes targeting specific con-

stituencies. The Common Sense Initiative, the Green Lights Program, and the Star Program are perhaps its most visible efforts to create pollution-prevention partnerships for environmental protection. (See Box 3.18.) There are also initiatives to spur municipal solid waste reduction by large businesses.

Environment Canada is also working to give Canadians the tools to build a greener society. The Department focuses on providing educational and information services, forming partnerships and convenants between government and industry, and ensuring that economic development is environmentally sensitive. National environmental indicators, a system of key indicator bulletins, and the award-winning Green Lane on the Internet are examples of Environment Canada's commitment to engage Canadians in becoming environmental citizens.

One of the most significant institutional changes in Canada in the past year took place under the banner of the "Federal House in Order" initiative. In 1996, the Federal Government established the Office of the Commissioner for the Environment and Sustainable Development. As a result, each Federal department is required to develop sustainable development strategies, including plans for the greening of their operations and policies, progress on which is reported to the Parliament.

In Canada, experience is demonstrating that non-regulatory approaches can achieve measurable environmental results. One particular example is the Accelerated Reduction/Elimination of Toxics Initiative, which is the cornerstone of Environment Canada's pollution prevention efforts. The purpose of ARET is to reduce the potential adverse effects of toxic substances on human health and the environment by accelerating the reduction or elimination of emissions of selected toxic substances. Since the ARET Challenge was launched in March 1994, 300 facilities from 170 major corporations have taken up the cause. These organizations have filed action plans with toxic release reduction commitments of more than 24,000 tons a year by 2000. This reduction represents a 72-per-cent release reduction overall from the base year, 1994.

Another very notable measure is the Toxic Release Inventory (TRI) Program pioneered in the

United States. TRI takes information that manufacturers are required to submit annually to EPA and places it in the public domain. The overall goal of the programme is to enhance the public's ability to monitor industry's releases of contaminants and to serve as a pollution prevention scorecard by tracking toxic chemicals. At the same time, TRI raises the internal awareness of industry and creates strong public-image pressures for companies to reduce wastes. Of the 23,321 facilities that reported to TRI in 1993, 35 per cent implemented source reduction activities (EPA, 1994b).

EPA is also working with stakeholders to design the next generation of the voluntary 33/50 Program. More than 1,300 companies committed themselves in this programme to reducing releases and transfers of 17 high-priority toxic chemicals by 33 per cent in 1992 and 50 per cent in 1995, based on the 1988 TRI benchmark. The programme is expected to include information on the extent to which source reduction and other pollution prevention practices are responsible for documented release reductions.

Regional Initiatives

Because Canada and the United States share one of the most extensive common borders in the world, complex transboundary conservation and pollution issues are among the key concerns for the region. Bilateral ministerial-level meetings and frequent consultations at the working level are regularly held to discuss issues of common concern. Institutional arrangements for the Great Lakes ecosystem and joint action on acid rain have demonstrated the effectiveness for concerted international co-operative action. The North American Free Trade Agreement (NAFTA) and its accompanying side-agreement on Environmental Co-operation (NAAEC) provide an opportunity to strengthen the relationships between trade and environmental policy development and to extend co-operative efforts for mutual economic as well as environmental benefit. Mexico, which is also a signatory to NAFTA and the NAAEC, helps to define the environmental agenda for the region. Regionalization, in turn,

promotes awareness of national possibilities as well as respective responsibilities for global concerns, such as climate change.

The long history of co-operation on environmental issues is exemplified by the multiplicity of programmes under the Great Lakes Water Quality Agreements (GLWQA). The Great Lakes—Superior, Michigan, Huron, Erie, and Ontario—are an important part of the physical and cultural heritage of North America and one of the most modified and studied ecosystems in the world. Spanning more than 1,200 kilometres, they are the largest system of fresh surface water on earth, containing roughly 18 per cent of the world's water supply; the basin is home to more than one tenth of the population of the United States and one quarter of the population of Canada.

In the 1950s, concerns arose in both countries about increasing eutrophication, the impact of overfishing and of the parasitic exotic sea lamprey on fish stocks and aquatic ecosystems, and the bioaccumulation of persistent toxic chemicals in fish-eating species. Governmental responses were formalized in a number of agreements and conventions between Canada and the United States as early as the 1955 Convention on the Great Lakes Fisheries and the subsequent GLWQA of 1972 and 1978.

The GLWQA is monitored by the International Joint Commission, an independent international organization established in 1909 to help prevent and resolve disputes between the two countries with respect to waters that cross or lie on the boundary. Revisions to the Water Quality Agreements have been carried out, taking into consideration the successes as well as current concerns, such as control of nutrients and eutrophication, return of certain species, plateauing of pollutant decline despite continued reduction efforts, non-point sources of pollution, and atmospheric inputs. Similar initiatives dealing with the Gulf of Maine on the East Coast and Puget Sound/Georgia Basin on the West Coast illustrate regional integrated coastal zone management in action.

In 1991, a joint Air Quality Agreement was signed to confront the region's acid rain problem. This umbrella agreement currently contains commitments for reductions in SO_2 and NO_x emissions (CEPA, 1996). Its significance and the necessity of a transboundary approach are underlined by the fact that half the acid rain in Canada originates in the United States (Marchi, 1996).

On the international level, both countries are addressing the climate change issue through action plans to reduce their greenhouse gas emissions. Emissions for the United States have levelled off in recent years. Furthermore, at the Second Conference of the Parties to the United Nations Framework Convention on Climate Change (Geneva, July 1996), the United States announced its support for a binding international agreement requiring the world's industrial nations to reduce greenhouse gas emissions and setting a "realistic, verifiable and binding medium-term target" (Wirth, 1996). Canada also called for accelerated negotiations for a legal instrument by the end of 1997 "that would encompass significant overall reductions" (EC, 1996c).

Co-operation on many fronts highlights the commitment of the people and Governments of Canada and the United States to prevent further environmental degradation within each country, in the region as a whole, and internationally. Environmental protection and conservation have long been a tradition—stemming back to the turn of the century with bilateral agreements on the Great Lakes and other shared ecosystems. Recently, this collaboration has been strengthened through both Governments' commitment to meet environmental responsibilities under NAFTA. Widespread support from the public, non-governmental organizations, and many forward-looking industries has been crucial in these endeavours. The use of regional approaches by both Governments is recognition that environmental problems are not unique to either country. And neither are the solutions.

Focusing Research, Technology, and Education

The ability to achieve sustainable development depends on scientific knowledge of the earth's natural systems and the ways in which human activities affect these systems. Accurate information built on basic scientific research establishes the foundation of knowledge needed for sound decision-making by individuals, businesses, governments, and society as a whole (PCSD, 1996).

North America attaches great importance to research, technology, information, and education. Technology, the so-called engine of economic growth, is considered responsible for as much as two thirds of the increase in U.S. productivity since the Great Depression of the 1930s. Technological advances depend on continuing research and development (R&D) (NSTC, 1996). The U.S. gross domestic expenditure on R&D in 1995 was approximately US\$167 billion, amounting to 2.81 per cent of gross domestic product (GDP). Canadian expenditure on R&D for the same year was about US\$8 billion, 1.51 per cent of GDP (OECD, 1995).

Private funds have become increasingly important in this area as Federal programmes in both Canada and the United States feel the effects of budget constraints. Overall, industry funds nearly 60 per cent of U.S. and 41 per cent of Canadian outlays for R&D. (The average for members of the Organisation for Economic Co-operation and Development in 1995 was slightly more than 50 per cent.) Nonetheless, Government commitments to basic science and energy research remain firm where long-term potential for great scientific discovery compensates for a lack of immediate commercial interest (EC, 1996c; NSTC, 1996).

In recent years, the environmental sector has become a growth industry: world-wide sales in 1992 amounted to US\$300 billion and are expected to reach US\$425 billion by 1997. The United States has the largest segment of the industry, with total estimated domestic and international sales of US\$134 billion (SBA, 1996). The market for prevention technologies rose by almost 15 per cent in 1992 and 1993. Other high-growth areas include technologies for resource recovery and energy conservation. More generally, this sector is dominated by service providers, which account for 74 per cent of total revenues. Most of these services focus on the cleanup of past environmental problems (NSTC, 1996).

The environmental sector in Canada is also one of its fastest-growing industries. With nearly 4,500 mostly small- and medium-sized firms employing more than 150,000 workers and annual sales of about US $8 billion a year, this sector has become a significant contributor to the Canadian economy (Marchi, 1996; CEI, 1996). These companies offer the technologies, products, and services that permit innovative solutions for the treatment and prevention of pollution and state-of-the-art environmental management services. The Technology Partnerships Canada Program of Industry Canada, announced in the 1996 budget, is expected to encourage the development of Canada's increasingly important environmental technology industry. Beyond the US$443 million over three years allocated from the Canadian budget, this programme is designed to leverage more than US$738 million in private-sector investment for new and innovative technologies (Marchi, 1996).

Science and technology (S&T) related activities account for most of Environment Canada's expenditures. About one fifth of S&T is devoted to research and development. Overall, S&T is delivered through three programme activities (Atmospheric Environment, Environmental Protection, and Environmental Conservation) that are conducted through mutually reinforcing strategic business lines: reducing risks to human health and the environment; providing weather forecasts and warnings and emergency preparedness services; and giving Canadians the tools to build a greener society (EC, 1996b; Canadian Dept. of Foreign Affairs and International Trade, personal communication, 1996).

One Canadian S&T initiative is the development of a series of long-term, multidisciplinary research and monitoring sites—the Ecological Monitoring and Assessment Network (EMAN). The aim of EMAN is to understand what changes are occurring in the ecosystem and the specific or multiple causes of those changes. The Network is building on existing sites that have been in operation for years as well as establishing new ones as issues emerge (Can. Dept. of Foreign Affairs and International Trade, 1996b). Across the Federal Government in Canada, there is also progress in working together and collaborating on sustainable development S&T. In 1995, the four natural-re-

source-based departments (Environment Canada, Natural Resources Canada, Fisheries and Oceans, and Agriculture and Agri-Food Canada) signed a Memorandum of Understanding on S&T for Sustainable Development. Through this spirit of interdepartmental co-operation, great efficiencies have been found, and progress is being made on such issues as climate change.

Both countries have initiated educational programmes for schoolchildren about environmental issues. The Government of Canada continues to support Learning for a Sustainable Future, a non-governmental, not-for-profit organization whose long-term goal is to integrate the principles of sustainable development in all aspects of curriculum in the formal education sector. In addition, through its Action 21 Programme, Environment Canada provides financial support to communities to implement local action programmes. Both these initiatives have grown out of the work Environment Canada did in the early 1990s under the banner of its "environmental citizenship" initiative. The U.S. Government has launched the Global Learning and Observations to Benefit the Environment (GLOBE) programme, a concept that has expanded to more than 60 countries. This international environmental, science, and education initiative creates a partnership between students, teachers, and the scientific research community that actively involves the students in data collection and observation.

References

Canadian Dept. of Foreign Affairs and International Trade. 1996. Global Agenda—Canada's Foreign Policy and the Environment. Vol. 4, No. 1. June. Ottawa.

CEI. 1996. A strategy for the Canadian Environmental Industry. Update, March 1996. Industry Canada & Environment Canada.

CEPA. 1996. Canadian Environmental Protection Act. Part III, Chapter 8: International Air Pollution. Ottawa. Address on World Wide Web: <http://www.ec.gc.ca/cepa/govtresp/echap08.html>.

Comanor, J.M. 1994. Ecosystem Management and Its Influence on Private Forest Landowners. Paper presented at the SAF National Convention. September 18–22.

Draper, W. 1996. The Future of Emissions Trading. Speech presented at a *GLOBE 1996* workshop.

EC. 1996a. Achievements of the Past, Commitments to the Future. Environment Canada (EC). Address on World Wide Web: <http://www.doe.ca/ec25/pastfuture_e.html>.

EC. 1996b. Environmental Initiatives, Invest in Science and Technology Advances. EC. Address on World Wide Web: <http://www.doe.ca/EnvironIni/index.html>.

EC. 1996c. Environmental Initiatives: Invest in Science and Technology Advances. EC. Address on World Wide Web: <http://www.doe.ca/EnvironIni/index.html>.

EPA. 1994a. EPA Pollution Prevention Accomplishments. U.S. Environmental Protection Agency (EPA). Address on World Wide Web: <http://es.inel.gov/program/epaorgs/oa/epa-acmp.html>.

EPA. 1994b. 1994 Annual Urban Air Quality Trends Report. Washington. EPA. Address on World Wide Web: <http://politicsusa.com/CVC/cafe/air_quality.html>.

EPA. 1996. The Inside Story: Indoor Air—Basic Facts. EPA. Address on World Wide Web: <http://www.medaccess.com/pollution/con_polltoc.html>.

Gore, A. 1995. Statement by the Vice-President of the United States of America. Made on Earth Day. 22 April.

Government of Canada. 1995. Sustaining Canada's Forests. Environment Canada. National Environmental Indicators Bulletin No. 95-4.

Government of Canada. 1996. The State of Canada's Environment Report. Ottawa.

Marchi, S. 1996. Speech presented at the Municipal Clean Air Summit. June 4. Toronto.

NBS. 1996. A Biological Survey for the Nation. National Research Council. National Biological Survey. Address on World Wide Web: <http://www.its.nbs.gov/>.

NSTC. 1996. National Environmental Technology Strategy. NSTC. Address on World Wide Web: <http://vm1.hqadmin.doe.gov/nepp/ch6bx2.html>.

OECD. 1995. OECD in Figures—Statistics on the member countries. Supplement to The OECD Observer. No. 194 June/July. Organisation for Economic Co-operation and Development. Paris.

PCSD. 1996. The President's Council on Sustainable Development: Sustainable America. A New Consensus for Prosperity, Opportunity, and a Healthy Environment for the Future. President's Council on Sustainable Development. U.S. Government Printing Office. Washington.

SBA. 1996. Bridging the Valley of Death: Financing Technology for a Sustainable Future. United States Small Business Administration. Address on World Wide Web: <http://web.miep.org/sba/index.html>.

USDA. 1996. 1996 Farm Bill Conservation Provisions: Summary. United States Department of Agriculture (USDA) Natural Resources Conservation Service.

Wirth, T.E. 1996. Statement on behalf of the United States of America—Second Conference of the Parties Framework Convention on Climate Change. July 17. Geneva.

WEST ASIA

National Initiatives

Great strides have been taken in the West Asia region over the past two decades in the development and strengthening of environmental institutions and legislation.

Initiatives to protect the environment at the national level have depended mainly on command and control mechanisms, particularly legislation. The main avenues for the implementation of environmental policy in the region have been national institutions co-ordinating environmental management and enforcing laws (e.g., Ministries, General Directorates and the Environment Protection Councils or Secretariats) and the setting of standards and norms through legislation.

Recent socio-economic changes have also brought policy changes that had environmental implications. Unprecedented urban and industrial growth in the region, particularly in the Gulf States, has resulted in increased demand for natural resources and rates of waste generation (both domestic and industrial). In addition, structural adjustment programmes have led the governments of some countries in the region to suspend many government-supported activities, including environmental planning.

In addition, the hostilities in the region over the last two decades have caused large population migrations towards marginal land and water resources. This, along with the lack of adequate waste disposal and/or treatment, has also posed a serious threat to the environment and human health in the region.

Environmental Institutions

All countries of the region now have environmental institutions or ministries in place, with many countries having restructured these institutions in the recent past. (See Table 3.3.) In some countries the newly established or restructured institutions were given higher political standing. At present four countries have ministers for environment in their cabinets, namely Oman (Ministry of Regional Municipalities and Environment), Jordan (Ministry of Municipal and Rural Affairs and Environment), Bahrain (Ministry of Housing, Municipalities and Environment), and Syria (Minister of State for the Environment heading the General Commission for Environmental Affairs).

Of these countries, Oman was the first to establish a Ministry for Environment and Water in 1984. This Ministry, along with the Council for Conservation of the Environment and Prevention of Pollution were then merged into a new Ministry of Regional Municipalities and Environment in 1991. The Syrian Government created a Ministry of State for Environmental Affairs to act as the advisory body for co-ordinating environmental issues between the Ministries, setting environmental standards, carrying out environmental studies, monitoring pollution, and developing environmental guidelines.

Most other countries of the region have also established environmental institutions, although not necessarily at Cabinet levels. General Directorates for environment or similar governmental bodies were established in Iraq, the United Arab Emirates, and Yemen. Environmental Protection Councils have been replaced by Environmental Authorities at the General Directorate level in Bahrain and Kuwait.

The United Arab Emirates issued a federal law in 1993 creating the Federal Environment Agency, which is the first country-wide institution with legal powers to protect and conserve the environment (UNEP, 1995). Recently, the Palestine Authority also established a central institution for

Table 3.3

Governmental Environment Institutions and Agencies in West Asia

Country	Policy Institutions	Executive Agency
Bahrain	Environmental Protection Commission	Ministry of Housing, Municipalities, and Environment
Iraq	National Council for the Protection and Improvement of Environment	Ministry of Health
Jordan	Council of Ministers; Ministry of Municipalities, Rural Affairs, and Environment	General Corporation for Environmental Protection
Kuwait	Environmental Protection Council	Various Ministries
Lebanon	Ministry of Environment	Various Ministries
Oman	Council of Ministers	Ministry of Provisional Municipalities and Environment
Qatar	Council of Ministers (Permanent Commission for Environmental Protection)	Ministry of Municipalities and Agriculture
Saudi Arabia	Ministerial Committee on Environment	Meteorology and Environmental Protection Administration
Syrian Arab Republic	Ministry of State for Environmental Affairs	General Authority for Environmental Affairs
United Arab Emirates	Council of the Federation	Federal Environmental Agency
West Bank & Gaza Strip	Council of Ministers	Ministry of Agriculture
Yemen	Council of Ministers	Environmental Protection Council

Source: Compiled and provided by the ESCWA Secretariat. 1996. Based on national sources.

environmental management and introduced legislation for resource protection.

In Lebanon, the Ministry of Environment was established in 1993. Saudi Arabia established the Meteorology and Environmental Protection Administration (MEPA) by Royal Decree in 1981. MEPA is now the central agency responsible for environment at the national level. Saudi Arabia has also established environmental sections in other relevant ministries, namely, in the Ministry of Agriculture and Water, the Ministry of Petroleum and Mineral Resources, the Ministry of Municipalities and Rural Affairs, the Ministry of Industry and Electricity, and the Ministry of Health. Some countries in the region have also created separate bodies to deal with specific environmental sectors (for example, the national committees and commissions for wildlife conservation and development in Saudi Arabia, Bahrain, Oman, Jordan, Kuwait, and Syria).

Despite the plethora of new institutions, however, programmes, laws, and institutions have often been created haphazardly and are generally sectoral. In most countries, different institutions are responsible for agriculture, water, fisheries, mineral resources, development, human settlements, industry, transport, and tourism.

Recent recognition of the inter-sectoral nature of many environmental concerns has led to an increasing number of Governments developing cross-cutting policy institutions. These commonly take the form of inter-ministerial or interdepartmental committees, and national environmental strategies developed with sectoral departments.

Only a few Governments, however, have created high-level, cross-cutting bodies under the direct control of the Head of Government (in Oman, for instance) or a senior minister (ESCWA, 1996). Due to this weakness in organizational structure, as well as shortcomings of the consultative machinery, there has been a lack of national integrated environmental policy in some countries. Furthermore, environmental departments almost everywhere have limited staff and budgets in relation to the demands made on them. There is therefore a lack of resources for implementing agreed policy or enforcement of law (ESCWA, 1996).

Environmental Legislation

The countries in West Asia have passed numerous laws dealing with the environment. In Kuwait, as early as 1964, the first law was passed to protect navigable water from oil pollution. Articles 15, 16, and 21 of the constitution of Kuwait were subsequently amended in 1976 and in 1980 to incorporate environmental protection principles and to establish mechanisms to enforce the implementation of environmental laws.

Despite the often fragmented nature of organizational responsibilities for the environment, legislation in the region has been fairly cross-sectoral and all-encompassing since the 1980s. These laws, sometimes known as framework laws, have helped countries reorder fragmented approaches to environmental management.

Framework laws in the region include:

- the Decree for Establishment of the Environmental Protection Committee in Bahrain (1980);

- Iraq's Environment Protection and Improvement Act (1986);

- the Law Protecting the Environment in Kuwait (1980);

- the Decree Creating the Council for Protection of Environment and Pollution Control (1979) and the Act for Environment Protection and Pollution Control in Oman (1979, amended 1985);

- Saudi Arabia's Environmental Protection Standards (1982); and

- the Decree Concerning Establishment of the Supreme Committee for Environment and Its Mandate in the United Arab Emirates (1981).

More recent attempts at harmonization of environmental legislation and institutions have also taken place. For example, the Jordanian Parliament ratified an environmental law in 1995 establishing an independent General Corporation for Environment Protection. Yemen has elaborated and ratified environmental laws and established national or independent authorities for environmental protection. Recently, the Palestinian Authority established a central institution for environmental management and introduced legislation for resource protection. Lebanon has also reviewed all existing environmental legislation. A legal environment code and a law for the protection of natural sites and

monuments were developed. Moreover, an environmental impact assessment decree and procedural guidelines have been prepared. All these laws have been discussed in national consultations.

The enforcement of existing laws is critical for the protection of the region's environment. Many states have imposed new types of liability or increased penalties for environmental offences in order to secure better environmental quality. In Bahrain, for example, any person found guilty of causing oil pollution in the marine environment or of dumping in territorial waters wastes from ships or land-based sources is liable to large fines. Violators are also responsible for the cleanup of the contaminated area within a specific time (UNEP, 1995).

Although most countries of the region have adequate legislation, there remains a need for revision, amendment, and the introduction of new legislation. Norms, standards, and monitoring are generally inadequate, and most countries and the region require assistance to remedy the situation and put into place effective enforcement mechanisms (UNEP, 1995).

Environmental Action Plans

West Asian countries have made substantial efforts at the national level to integrate environmental dimensions into their development schemes and strategies. While prior to the 1990s these plans simply concentrated on development strategies, some countries now incorporate environmental policies and resource management principles. However, while most countries have developed strategies and action plans, they continue to lack adequate resources for their implementation.

In Jordan's five-year development plan for 1986–90, the environment appeared for the first time as an independent sector. In addition, in 1996 a National Environment Action Plan was formulated for the Kingdom. Oman also has a comprehensive environmental planning and management system that ensures that development takes into account environmental concerns.

With desertification being a major concern in the region, countries have responded by launching national action plans to combat desertification. Their main elements include assessment of desertification and improved land management, public corrective measures against droughts and their impacts, institutional arrangements for building the capacity of personnel, and international co-operation. The National Action Plan for Combating Desertification in Bahrain, for instance, emphasizes appropriate land management practices, water management measures, strengthening of science and technology, and international action and co-operation.

Similarly, because water issues are a major concern, several national action plans have been initiated and implemented. For example, in Oman, the Government has started several regional activities to conserve and protect water resources from pollution and to increase public awareness of such pressing environmental issues as the scarcity of water resources and the importance of protecting biodiversity. In Kuwait, a water quality monitoring programme was established in 1986 in parallel with an air quality monitoring programme. Sea water quality monitoring sites have been established in the coastal areas, especially around desalination plants. A monthly monitoring programme of drinking-water quality is implemented in accordance with World Health Organization (WHO) drinking-water monitoring guidelines. The countries of the East Mediterranean region, such as Lebanon and Syria, have begun to elaborate integrated coastal management programmes and regional environmental assessment initiatives, in line with environmental assessment initiatives and priorities in their respective countries.

Syria has initiated the preparation of background papers on the environmental situation at all seven national river basins to be used to compile a sustainable development strategy and to develop relevant action plans required to respond to the identified needs and priorities. The papers are being prepared through an interactive participatory approach involving various governmental, academic, and research institutions, as well as local authorities and groups. The environmental effects of industrial, agricultural, and domestic activities, as well as socio-economic issues, are assessed in these papers.

To help combat the pressures on the region's biodiversity, particularly due to habitat destruction, some countries of the region have begun to establish protected areas. Protected areas now total over 24 million hectares, some 6 per cent of the total area of the West Asia region (ESCWA/FAO, 1995). (See Table 3.4.)

Economic and Financial Instruments

Various economic instruments are also in use in the region to help promote sustainable development. In Bahrain, Oman, UAE, and Kuwait, for example, soft loans are available for introducing water-saving irrigation techniques (e.g., drip irrigation) to relieve some of the pressure on groundwater resources. Some countries have also implemented programmes to promote intensive protected agriculture (e.g., greenhouses) in order to help improve water productivity.

Instruments using the polluter pays principle also exist in the region. In Syria, for example, a municipal service operation levy has been introduced for domestic and private institutions with regard to the collection of solid wastes. These rates differ according to quantities of waste generated and collected. In Lebanon, preparations are underway to introduce economic tools, such as taxation and incentives, for air pollution management. These tools will be integrated within the action plan and legislation for air pollution.

Public Participation and Capacity Building

A growing number of non-governmental organizations (NGOs) are found in most countries of the region. However, their role in planning and implementation needs to be strengthened. In addition, there is a need for capacity building to increase the involvement of NGOs as well as other institutions and the private sector in the environmental policy-making and action cycle. Although in most countries initiatives for capacity building are in place, these need to be turned into reality (UNEP, 1996). The United Nations Development Programme (UNDP) has initiated various programmes in the

Table 3.4
National Parks and Protected Areas in the West Asia Region

Country	Area (square kilometres)	Total Protected Area (hectares)	Percentage of Area under Protection
Bahrain	691	1,325	1.92
Iraq	434,924	541	-
Jordan	83,750	119,829	1.43
Kuwait	24,280	30,000	1.24
Lebanon	10,452	4,512	0.43
Oman	212,379	2,836,900	13.36
Qatar	10,360	100	0.01
Saudi Arabia	2,144,969	21,210,740	9.89
Syrian Arab Republic	185,680	103,240	0.56
United Arab Emirates	86,449	14,650	0.17
West Bank & Gaza Strip	10,161	-	-
Yemen	485,273	-	-
TOTAL	3,689,368	24,321,837	6.59

Source: ESCWA/FAO. 1995.

region for environmental management that are more specifically addressing capacity building issues in the context of UNDP's Capacity 21 efforts. The UNDP Regional Bureau for Arab States has assisted in the initiation of projects funded by the Global Environment Facility, with strong capacity building components in the areas of biodiversity, climate change, and international waters.

Environmental technology transfer is still at a limited level in the region. Some initiatives, however, are in existence. One initiative is to circulate successful examples of environmental technologies by the Council of Arab Ministers Responsible for Environment (CAMRE). Adequate technology transfer should be considered in parallel with the development of improved capacities and human resources.

A recent survey of tertiary-level environmental training institutions in the West Asia region revealed that more than 35 university research and training institutions are engaged in environmental training programmes. Collectively, these institutions teach more than 290 regular undergraduate and graduate environment courses as well as providing training courses and seminars. Graduate studies of environmental issues are available at 12 universities in the region. Courses on environment have also been incorporated into the teaching programmes of schools in most countries of the region (UNEP/ROWA, 1994).

Environmental Information

There is a general lack of data and information on the environment in West Asia. Where information is available in the region, there is a lack of continuity and cohesion in the environmental monitoring and reporting. Much of the information produced is also under-utilized (UNEP, 1996).

At the national level, some countries have prepared state of the environment reports (SOE) or environmental profiles of some form. Kuwait, for example, has completed four SOE-type reports (1984, 1986, 1988, and 1992) (Environment Protection Council, 1992). Most of the countries of the region have not regularly published such reports.

Specific environmental reports dealing with certain environmental issues are also available in some countries. For example, reports on desertification and plans of action to combat desertification have been prepared in Oman, Bahrain, UAE, Jordan, Syria and Yemen. These reports also include some information on the state of environment in the respective countries.

Another common problem in the region is that environmental data are scattered among numerous public and private-sector institutions, with little or no collaboration or co-ordination. As a result, there are gaps and duplication in data and the countries of the region need to compile and standardize their information (Olivier and Tell, 1995).

There is also little networking and integration of data for environmental assessment, except occasionally at the sectoral level, such as for water. Initiatives for the development of information for problem solving and networking have been undertaken in Syria and Lebanon, largely due to UNDP's Sustainable Development Network and Capacity 21 Projects. Nevertheless, effective environment information networks for the dissemination of data nationally and regionally still need to be put in place in much of the region (Olivier and Tell, 1995).

Regional Initiatives

Numerous regional institutions and initiatives deal directly and indirectly with the environment in the West Asia region. These are generally either associated with one of the four seas in the region (the Mediterranean, Arabian, and Red seas and the Persian Gulf) or with subregional groupings—the Mediterranean subregion (Lebanon, Syria, Jordan, and Palestine) and the Arabian Peninsula region (Bahrain, Iraq, Kuwait, Oman, Qatar, the Kingdom of Saudi Arabia, the United Arab Emirates, and Yemen).

Regional Institutions

West Asian countries have made substantial joint efforts at the regional level to help protect natural resources and the environment. At the highest political level is the Council of Arab Ministers Responsible for Environment and the Gulf Cooperation Council (GCC) Secretariat.

CAMRE adopted the Arab Declaration on Environment and Development and Future Prospects in 1991 and agreed on principles and directives for the protection and improvement of the environment in the region. It established the Joint Committee on Environment and Development in the Arab Region (JCEDAR) to enhance co-operation and co-ordination among Arab regional and national organizations.

Heads of States of the GCC member countries (Bahrain, Kuwait, Oman, Qatar, Saudi Arabia, and the United Arab Emirates) approved environmental principles in 1985. The GCC Secretariat now encompasses a regional Directorate of Man and Environment that organizes regional surveys, assessments, education, and training and information exchange at the GCC subregional level, as well as with other regional and national institutions.

Regionally binding agreements have also led to the establishment of regional organizations to co-ordinate implementation efforts, such as the Regional Organisation for the Protection of the Marine Environment (ROPME). (See Box 3.19.) Despite these achievements, efforts towards co-operation among regional organizations need to be strengthened and co-ordinated. Although there has been a growth in declarations on environmental protection, such as the Regional Organization for the Conservation of the Environment of the Red Sea and Gulf of Aden (PERSGA), with many involving the formulation of umbrella agreements stating the general goals of the Parties, not all have imposed a mechanism that obliges them to achieve the goals.

There are also many technical organizations dealing with the regional environment, including the Arab Centre for Studies of Arid Zone and Dry Lands (ACSAD), the Centre for Environment and Development for the Arab Region and Europe (CEDARE), the Programme for the Environment of the Red Sea and the Gulf of Aden, the Gulf Area Oil Companies Mutual Aid Organisation, the Marine Emergency Mutual Aid Centre, and other Arab specialized organizations. Almost all provide technical assistance and respond to capacity building needs. Universities and other research institutions and NGOs play a supportive role in the region.

Among United Nations bodies and programmes in the region are the United Nations Environment Programme Regional Office for West Asia (UNEP/ROWA), the Economic and Social Commission for West Asia (ESCWA), WHO's Regional Centre for Environmental Health Activities, UNDP's Capacity 21, and the UNEP-initiated Mediterranean Action Plan. There is also the Mediterranean European Technical Assistance Programme, a regional partnership of the European Commission, the European Investment Bank, the World Bank, UNDP, and countries of the region

Box 3.19

Policy in Action: the Regional Organisation for the Protection of the Marine Environment

The Regional Organisation for the Protection of the Marine Environment (ROPME) provides a good example of a regional body working on multiple levels to help policy setting and planning for the region's marine environment. ROPME was established in 1982 as the secretariat providing technical coordination to the Kuwait Action Plan by eight member states surrounding the Persian Gulf and Gulf of Oman (Bahrain, Iran, Iraq, Kuwait, Oman, Qatar, Saudi Arabia, and the United Arab Emirates). Its programmes cover environmental monitoring, management, legislation, preparation of protocols, awareness building (especially in schools), and training.

Among its monitoring and training work, ROPME has supported regional laboratories to purchase equipment and has provided training for organizations to carry out monitoring of coastal waters. In terms of management, it has supported member states' assessments of land-based sources of pollution. In terms of regional legal environmental instruments and arrangements, ROPME has prepared and adopted numerous protocols, including the Mutual Assistance in Marine Environmental Pollution Resulting from the Exploration and Exploitation of the Continental Shelf (1989) and the Protocol for the Protection of the Marine Environment from Pollution Resulting from Land Based Sources (1990). The latter was a recognition by the member states of the urgent need to protect the region's marine environment against pollution from land-based sources. In 1995, the ROPME Council followed up by approving a Regional Programme of Action for the Protection of the Marine Environment from Land-Based

Activities. The programme of action is to be implemented in parallel with the Global Plan of Action on Land-Based Activities.

The programme of action seeks first to update surveys of source categories, impacts, and capabilities, and second to develop guidelines, standards, and criteria for the management of land-based sources of pollution. The surveys are to define the problematic contaminants and sources of pollution and to identify vulnerable resources and areas of concern in the region. The guidelines are designed to prevent, reduce, and control pollution of the marine environment through regulations on pollution abatement through source control. The Programme is also developing a river basin management programme for the major rivers of the region, which contribute significant amounts of contaminants and sediments into the ROPME sea area. This involves Syria and Turkey in addition to ROPME member states. Finally, the programme is completing a pilot study on persistent organic pollutants—their manufacture, use, and effect on the ROPME region.

ROPME's mandate at a high political level, the cross-cutting nature of its work, and its ability to tailor global agreements and action plans into programmes relevant to the region have made it a success in the field of environmental policy setting and action planning for the marine environment in the region.

Reference

ROPME Secretariat, personal communication, 1996.

---

that mobilize grant funds for technical assistance, to strengthen environmental management and establish environmentally sound policies.

Regional Information Sharing

The lack of general data and information at a national level is echoed at the regional level. Although some regional organizations have initiated actions for information management and networking, the dissemination and accessibility to data banks remains insufficient and there needs to be improved co-ordination among relevant organizations.

Among the limited existing initiatives are the Arab Environmental Information Network, initiated by CAMRE and JCEDAR, with technical support

Table 3.5

Status of West Asian Countries Regarding Selected International Treaties on the Environment

Country	Trade in Endangered Species 1973	Montreal Protocol on Substances that Deplete the Ozone layer 1987	Basel Convention on the Transboundary Movement of Hazardous Wastes & Disposal 1992	Biological Diversity 1992
Bahrain		❖	❖	
Iraq				
Jordan	❖	❖	❖	❖
Kuwait		❖	❖	
Lebanon		❖	❖	❖
Oman			❖	❖
Qatar			❖	
Saudi Arabia	❖	❖	❖	
Syrian Arab Republic		❖	❖	
United Arab Emirates	❖	❖	❖	
Yemen				

from CEDARE and UNEP/ROWA. Other initiatives include the ACSAD's arid zones and drylands information network, ROPME's database development, and UNDP's Sustainable Development Networking Programmes. The Mediterranean Action Plan also has a mechanism for information dissemination that plays an important role in the promotion of the implementation of the Plan by its contracting parties (including Lebanon and Syria).

Regional technical organizations also have some limited information management and networking. For example, ACSAD has published, jointly with UNESCO, the hydrogeological map of the Arab region and the adjacent areas. It is also preparing a water resources database, including an integrated data base management system that stores and retrieves data related to the assessment of water resources in the region.

At present, various plans exist for the creation of a World-wide Web site under the auspices of one of the regional organizations to help increase information dissemination in the region. Each country would then provide information for the site, which could be a basis for sharing information and experience. The centre for monitoring and administering the Web site could also be the information centre for standardized data collection and analysis of all environmental data for the West Asia region. Reports could be produced and distributed in hard copy as well as through the Web site (UNEP, 1996).

International Initiatives

The level of participation by the countries in West Asia in international agreements and conventions related to the environmental issues is rather sporadic. (See Table 3.5.) Three countries have ratified the Convention on Biological Diversity and the Convention on International Trade in Endangered Species of Wild Flora and Fauna. Agreements related to the prevention and control of pollution include the Framework Convention on Climate Change, which has been ratified by five countries of the region; the International Convention to Combat Desertification, which has been ratified by Lebanon and Syria; the Basel Convention on the Control of Transboundary Movements of Hazardous Wastes and their Disposal, ratified by nine countries; and the Montreal Protocol on Substances that Deplete the Ozone Layer, ratified by seven.

The relatively low level of representation in many international conventions and the priority given to their implementation is partly due to the shortcomings of domestic legislation. It is also due to the large amount of professional and administrative expertise and resources needed to implement the complicated legal and administrative requirements of conventions.

Nevertheless, regional mechanisms to follow up implementation of these conventions have been initiated, such as the Regional Committees for the

Table 3.5 continued

Status of West Asian Countries Regarding Selected International Treaties on the Environment

Country	Climate Change 1992	Desertification 1994	Action Plan for the Protection of the Mediterranean Sea Against Pollution (MAP) 1975	Kuwait Action Plan 1978	Red Sea and Gulf of Aden Action Plan 1982
Bahrain	❖			❖	
Iraq				❖	
Jordan					❖
Kuwait	❖			❖	
Lebanon	❖	❖	❖		
Oman	❖			❖	❖
Qatar				❖	
Saudi Arabia	❖		❖	❖	❖
Syrian Arab Republic		❖			
United Arab Emirates				❖	
Yemen					❖

Source: Compiled and provided by the ESCWA Secretariat, 1996.

Montreal Protocol and the Basel Convention. A subcommittee for the Climate Change Convention has also been established in CAMRE, and at the subregional level, for the GCC countries. ACSAD has been nominated as the regional co-ordinator for the Convention to Combat Desertification and the Convention on Biodiversity.

References

Environment Protection Council. 1992. The National Report. Government of Kuwait.

ESCWA. 1996. Personal correspondence with the UNEP/GEO Team. United Nations Commission on Economic and Social Commission for Western Asia (ESCWA).

ESCWA/FAO. 1995. Wildlife Conservation for Sustainable Development in Arab Countries. Report No. E/ESCWA/AGR/1994/11. ESCWA and the United Nations Food and Agriculture Organization (FAO).

Olivier R., and S. Tell. 1995. The development and integration of environmental information management, assessment and decision support capacities in West Asia. Internal UNEP report from fact finding mission.

UNEP. 1995. *UNEP's New Way Forward: Environmental Law and Sustainable Development.* Chapter 12: Emerging Trends in National Environmental Legislation in Developing Countries. UNEP/Environmental Law Unit. Nairobi.

UNEP. 1996. Report of the Regional Consultations held for the first Global Environment Outlook. UNEP. Nairobi.

UNEP/ROWA. 1994. Regional Directory for Tertiary Level Environmental Training Institutions in West Asia. UNEP Regional Office for West Asia. Bahrain.

POLAR REGIONS

THE ARCTIC

International Co-operation

The environmental concerns of the Arctic tend to be common and shared by all Arctic countries. While individual nations have their own programmes for their particular parts of the Arctic, the region is characterized, like the Antarctic, by international co-operative policy and action.

The most extensive international Arctic co-operative programme is the Arctic Environmental Protection Strategy (AEPS) adopted by the eight Arctic countries—Russia, the United States (Alaska), Canada, Greenland/Denmark, Iceland, Norway, Sweden, and Finland—in Rovaniemi in 1991 (also referred to as the Rovaniemi Process). A number of other countries and international organizations have observer status in the AEPS. The objectives of the AEPS are to protect the Arctic ecosystems; to provide for the protection, enhancement, and restoration of natural resources; to recognize the traditional and cultural needs, values, and practices of the indigenous peoples; to review regularly the state of the Arctic environment; and to identify, reduce, and, as a final goal, eliminate pollution.

The AEPS has established five working groups:

- Arctic Monitoring and Assessment Programme (AMAP), focusing on contaminants and their effects in the Arctic environment;

- Protection of the Arctic Marine Environment (PAME), to assess the need for further actions or legal instruments to prevent pollution of the Arctic marine environment;

- Emergency, Prevention, Preparedness and Response (EPPR), addressing accidental pollution and emergencies;

- Conservation of Arctic Flora and Fauna (CAFF), to facilitate initiatives to conserve

the diversity and habitats of Arctic flora and fauna; and

- Sustainable Development and Utilization (SDU), with particular reference to the use of natural resources (EEA 1996).

At the Third AEPS Ministerial meeting, in March 1996, held in Inuvik, Canada, the eight countries agreed to a set of work priorities for the Arctic and to the establishment of an Arctic Council with the involvement of Arctic indigenous communities and other Arctic inhabitants. The Council is designed to promote co-operation and co-ordination on particular issues of sustainable development and environmental protection; to co-ordinate programmes established under the AEPS; and to encourage research. Canada currently has the lead on the Arctic Council, which was established in September 1996 (Canadian Dept. of Foreign Affairs and International Trade, personal communication, 1996; WWF, 1996).

Subregional co-operation on Arctic issues is also ongoing, mainly in Europe. The Euro-Arctic Barents Region has launched an initiative to develop industry, trade, and local co-operation in the northern regions of Norway, Sweden, Finland, and western Russia. The initiative includes efforts to deal with industry and nuclear waste in north-western Russia, and an environmental action plan was adopted in 1994 as part of the larger programme.

The Arctic environmental policies currently in place (and the activities to implement these policies) focus on environmental protection. International agreements are a driving force for both. A set of progressive and coherent measures exist to protect the marine environment. Important global conventions for Arctic marine pollution include the Convention on the Prevention of Marine Pollution by

Dumping of Waste and other Matter (London, 1972) and the MARPOL 73/78 International Convention for the Prevention of Pollution from Ships (London, 1973, plus the 1978 Protocol).

Two further agreements relate specifically to the Atlantic and Arctic oceans north of latitude 36°N—the Oslo (1972) Convention for the Prevention of Marine Pollution by Dumping from Ship and Aircraft, and the Paris (1974) Convention for the Prevention of Marine Pollution from Land-Based Sources. These have now been negotiated into a single legal instrument, known as the 1992 OSPAR Convention for the Protection of the Marine Environment of the North-East Atlantic, which will replace the other two as soon as it comes into force (Norwegian Ministry of Environment, 1993). The harvesting of fish and marine mammals is addressed by a further set of conventions, some global and others specific to northern oceans.

The United Nations Economic Commission for Europe's Convention on Long-Range Transboundary Air Pollution (Geneva, 1979) is considered to be an appropriate mechanism for addressing the transfer of airborne contaminants to the Arctic. Steps are under way to establish further protocols under this convention to address heavy metals and discharges of persistent organic pollutants (AMAP, 1996), both of which are a major concern in the Arctic. A number of existing international agreements and programmes concerning nuclear safety (EEA, 1996) should help to minimize radioactive pollution in the Arctic.

A new, relevant international initiative, the Global Programme of Action for the Protection of the Marine Environment from Land-based Activities, was adopted by Governments in November 1995 in Washington, D.C. (UNEP, 1995). One hundred and nine countries were represented at the meeting, including the eight Arctic countries.

During the negotiations of the Global Programme of Action, the need to address persistent organic pollutants, which are contaminating all oceans including those in the Arctic, was specifically recognized. The Secretariat of the Programme is to promote and facilitate its implementation at the national, subregional, regional, and global levels through, in particular, a revitalization of the Regional Seas Programmes.

Arctic wildlife and habitats will benefit from the global conventions that focus on biodiversity, migratory species, endangered species, and wetlands. In addition, the Arctic is covered by some regional agreements, such as the Berne 1979 Convention on the Conservation of European Wildlife and Natural Habitats. Polar bear hunting is limited to sustainable levels by the Oslo 1973 Agreement on Conservation of Polar Bears, though the Convention has been less useful in protecting their habitats (EEA, 1996).

As mentioned in Chapter 2, all countries in the region have established protected areas. In 1995, a total of 285 such areas covered a little over 14 per cent of the Arctic. About half of this total area is located in the Northeast Greenland National Park (972,000 square kilometers).

The current set of protected areas is considered inadequate to maintain the biodiversity of the region. CAFF has recently prepared a strategy and action plan for developing an adequate and well-managed Circumpolar Protected Area Network incorporating the current areas. The network, which would involve local and indigenous peoples and their needs, concerns, and knowledge, would aim to provide relatively strict protection to at least 12 per cent of each Arctic ecozone (CAFF, 1996).

Regional Data Collection and Information Sharing

Since 1991, AMAP has been implementing a programme to monitor the levels and effects of a number of priority anthropogenic contaminants in all components of the Arctic environment. Members of this collaborative programme include the Arctic rim countries, indigenous people's organizations, observing countries, observing and co-operating international organizations, and other AEPS working groups (AMAP, 1996).

Much of the monitoring is carried out by national monitoring programmes (known as AMAP National Implementation Plans [NIPs]) of the eight Arctic rim countries. For example, the Canadian NIP is largely based on the Northern Contaminants

Programme (NCP), which addresses contaminants in traditionally harvested foods in the Canadian Arctic. Carried out over the past six years in conjunction with five northern Aboriginal organizations, the NCP has found elevated levels of toxic substances in a number of the Arctic's fish and wildlife, which are important foods in the diets of many northerners, particularly aboriginal peoples. Those research findings have, on a number of occasions, led to health advisories in both Canadian territories and restrictions on the consumption of certain foods.

Because Arctic contamination has global dimensions, Canada uses the research of the NCP to pursue action at the international level and to provide scientific substitution for global controls, phase-outs, and bans in countries that still use these chemicals (Canadian Dept. of Foreign Affairs and International Trade, personal communication, 1996).

A number of international processes are under way to prepare status reports on the Arctic. Two AMAP reports are due for completion in 1996–97. The AMAP Assessment Report will be a comprehensive scientific and technical assessment of all validated data on the status of the Arctic environment related to the AMAP mandate. The State of the Arctic Environment Report, addressed to Ministers, will present the main assessment findings, conclusions, and recommendations for action (AMAP, 1996). AMAP is preparing a CD-ROM–World Wide Web version of the State of the Arctic Environment Report, through UNEP GRID-Arendal.

Other projects under way to improve the availability of Arctic information include the Nordic Council of Minister's report on the Nordic Arctic Environment, a report on the State of the Barents Sea Environment by the Russian-Norwegian Marine Environment Group (EEA, 1996), and a Wilderness Quality mapping project for the Euro-Arctic Barents Region. This latter report was undertaken as a joint project by UNEP GRID-Arendal, the Norwegian Directorate for Nature Management, and the National Remote Sensing Centre (Husby, 1995).

THE ANTARCTIC

International Agreements

With no internationally recognized state sovereignty in the Antarctic, the international agreements of the Antarctic Treaty System play the key role in controlling human activities in the region. The Antarctic Treaty is central among these agreements. It was adopted in Washington in 1959, by 12 States that had all actively participated in the 1957–58 Antarctica Programme of the International Geophysical Year (Argentina, Australia, Belgium, Chile, France, Japan, New Zealand, Norway, South Africa, the Russian Federation, the United Kingdom, and the United States). Together with an additional 14 States that have ratified the Treaty and are also conducting substantive research activities in the Antarctic (Brazil, China, Ecuador, Finland, Germany, India, Italy, Republic of Korea, Netherlands, Peru, Poland, Spain, Sweden, and Uruguay), these States are known as the Consultative Parties. An Antarctic Treaty Consultative Meeting (ATCM) is convened annually to adopt recommendations relating to the management of the polar region south of latitude 60°S.

The objectives of the Antarctic Treaty are to ensure that Antarctica is used for peaceful purposes and for international co-operation in scientific research and that it does not become the scene and object of international discord. The Treaty prohibits military manoeuvres and weapons testing in Antarctica, ensures freedom of scientific research and information sharing, and freezes territorial claims by Parties. The Treaty also bans the disposal of radioactive waste within the Treaty area. Under the Antarctic Treaty, a recommendation was made in 1964 on Agreed Measures for the Conservation of Antarctic Fauna and Flora. These are intended to protect indigenous mammals, birds, and plants on the continent and to prohibit the introduction of exotic species into the region. Provision is also made for the establishment of protected terrestrial and marine sites.

Although some seals were afforded protection under the Agreed Measures, the Convention for the

Conservation of Antarctic Seals, which entered into force in 1978, extended that protection to all seals inhabiting seas south of 60°S. Concern over an unregulated fishery for Antarctic krill, along with past exploitations of whales and fur seals, resulted in the adoption of the Convention on the Conservation of Antarctic Marine Living Resources (CCAMLR). CCAMLR entered into force in 1982, and stringent conservation measures to halt the further decline of fish stocks were implemented by 1989 (Kock, 1994). By protecting the lower species in the food chain and extending coverage beyond the areas addressed by the existing agreements, CCAMLR aims to encompass the whole Antarctic ecosystem.

Protection of the Antarctic environment is further strengthened by the Protocol to the Antarctic Treaty on Environmental Protection (the Madrid Protocol), adopted in 1991 by States Parties to the Antarctic Treaty. The protocol builds on and rationalizes existing measures with the aim to ensure comprehensive protection of the Antarctic environment and dependent and associated ecosystems, including its value as an area for the conduct of scientific research. The Madrid Protocol has been ratified by 23 of the States that were party to its negotiation. As of November 1996, three further states must ratify the agreement for it to enter into full international legal effect.

Key aspects of the Madrid Protocol include provisions for environmental impact assessment, conservation of Antarctic fauna and flora, waste disposal and waste management, prevention of marine pollution, and the protection and management of special areas. The Madrid Protocol prohibits mineral resource enterprises other than for scientific research. In the interim, while waiting for the Madrid Protocol to enter into force, States Parties to the Antarctic Treaty have agreed to implement voluntarily, and as far as practicable, the provisions of the agreement as adopted in 1991.

A number of global instruments that are not part of the Antarctic Treaty System also have relevance to the Antarctic. Of particular note is the 1946 International Convention on the Regulation of Whaling.

Regional Data Collection and Information Sharing

The Antarctic Treaty provides for the unrestricted exchange and access of data and information on the Antarctic. This need was endorsed by the consensus text of Chapter 17 of Agenda 21, on the protection of oceans, seas, and their living resources.

Several collaborative, long-term data collection and exchange programmes are under way in the Antarctic. States Parties to the Antarctic Treaty convened the First Meeting of Experts on Environmental Monitoring in Antarctica in Buenos Aires, Argentina, in June 1992. The group made recommendations, among other matters, on the representation of monitoring sites, data management, the need to develop data standards, and international co-ordination. A further workshop has since been held in two sessions (17–20 October 1995 in Oslo, Norway, and 25–29 March 1996 in College Station, Texas, United States), the report of which will be submitted to the 1997 session of the ATCM.

Another item on the ATCM agenda is the preparation of a comprehensive state of the environment report for the Antarctic. States Parties to the Antarctic Treaty requested the Scientific Committee on Antarctic Research (SCAR) of the International Council of Scientific Unions (ICSU) to consider and provide advice on this matter at the Twentieth ATCM in May 1996. At the August 1996 SCAR Meeting, the production of a state of the Antarctic environment report was discussed. It was considered both appropriate and essential that SCAR undertake the challenge in concert with other interested parties to produce an authoritative assessment of this key region. SCAR expects to appoint a small steering committee in the very near future to initiate discussions with other organizations on the scope and content of such a report. SCAR will report back on these discussions to the 1997 ATCM.

Such a report would for the first time draw together into an accessible and easily interpreted form a wide variety of data dispersed throughout the Antarctic literature and environmental databases world-wide. Such a report would also provide a means of communicating with all members of the global community and informing them about Antarctica.

A second long-term data collection programme involves the Intergovernmental Oceanographic Commission (IOC) of UNESCO, which has a Regional Committee for the Southern Ocean that addresses a variety of issues including pollution and human impact. The IOC is strengthening international research programmes in co-operation with other organizations (ICSU/Scientific Committee on Oceanic Research/SCAR, CCAMLR, the International Whaling Commission [IWC], World Meteorological Organization [WMO], and UNEP) to improve ocean observations and data exchange in the Southern Ocean. The IOC aims to meet requirements of Agenda 21 (Chapter 17), the Framework Convention on Climate Change, the Convention on Biological Diversity, and the Madrid Protocol.

CCAMLR has a Working Group on Ecosystem Monitoring and Management. This group has constructed a framework that will allow information collected from established monitoring programmes to be integrated into management advice (CCAMLR, 1996).

In 1996, the IWC broadened the scope of its monitoring programme with the introduction of the Southern Ocean Whale and Ecosystem Research Programme, which will include research into the effects of environmental change on cetaceans. Other research programmes in the Southern Ocean target blue, humpback, and southern right whales. The IWC also aims to improve collaboration with organizations working on related issues in the Southern Ocean, such as CCAMLR, SCAR, the IOC, and the Intergovernmental Panel on Climate Change.

With 37 land-based stations operated by 15 countries, the Antarctic is an important component of WMO observing systems. The stations contribute to the World Weather Watch programme and some of them also monitor trace gas constituents such as carbon dioxide and ozone as part of the Global Atmosphere Watch. WMO has noted that financial constraints may threaten the continuity of some stations with valuable long-term climatic records.

References

AMAP. 1996. *Report to Ministers. AMAP Interim Report to the Third Ministerial Conference, Arctic Environmental Protection Strategy. Inuvik, Canada.* AMAP Report 96:1. Arctic Monitoring and Assessment Programme(AMAP). Oslo, Norway.

CAFF. 1996. *Circumpolar Protected Areas Network (CPAN)—Strategy and Action Plan.* Habitat Conservation Report No. 6. Conservation of Arctic Flora and Fauna. Directorate for Nature Management, Trondheim, Norway.

CCAMLR. 1996. *CCAMLR Newsletter 1996.* Convention for the Conservation of Arctic Marine Living Resources. Hobart, Australia.

EEA. 1996. *The State of the European Arctic Environment.* J.R. Hansen, R. Hansson, and S. Norris (eds). EEA Environmental Monograph No. 3. European Environment Agency (EEA). Also published as Norsk Polarinstitutt, Meddelelser No. 141. Copenhagen, Denmark.

Husby, E. 1995. *Wilderness Quality Mapping in the Euro-Arctic Barents Region.* DN-rapport 1995-4. Direktoratet for Naturforvaltning, Trondheim, Norway.

Kock, K-H. 1994. Fishing and conservation in southern waters. *Polar Record.* 30(172):3.

Norwegian Ministry of Environment. 1993. *International Environmental Cooperation in the Northern Seas.* Oslo, Norway.

UNEP. 1995. Global Programme of Action for the Protection of the Marine Environment from Land-Based Activities. UNEP (OCA)/LBA/IG. UNEP. Nairobi.

WWF. 1996. The Arctic Council to be inaugurated on September 19 in Ottawa. *Arctic Bulletin* 3.96:4–5. World Wide Fund for Nature. Gland, Switzerland.

chapter 4

LOOKING TO THE FUTURE

T he results of the model-based analysis on the current and possible future state of the global environment described in this chapter highlight the integrated nature of the environment and the need to study linkages among environment, economic, social, institutional, and cultural sectors and among different environmental issues, such as biodiversity, climate, land, and water.

The chapter illustrates that, assuming conventional development, despite declining global birth rates since 1965 and recent policy initiatives towards more efficient and cleaner resource use in some regions, large global increases in population and expanding economies in industrializing countries will continue to increase global resource and energy consumption, generate burgeoning wastes, spawn environmental contamination and degradation, and put increased pressures on remaining biodiversity and natural ecosystems. If no fundamental changes occur in the amount and type of energy used, global carbon dioxide emissions will increase and declining trends in acidifying sulphur and nitrogen concentrations may be reversed. If, however, currently best available technology is applied all over the world, a global energy system by 2050 with carbon dioxide emissions well below current levels is feasible. Given the projected impacts of climate change in the not-too-distant future, contingency plans will be required, including the development of drought-resistant crops, increases in water use efficiency, interlinking remaining natural areas, and an improvement of the capabilities in all regions to adapt to climate change impacts.

If only moderate application of improved agricultural management and technology in developing regions continues in the future, the need to feed growing populations and the increasing burden of poverty may well lead to substantial expansion of agricultural activities into often marginal lands at the expense of remaining wilderness and associated biodiversity. Although the projections in this chapter show adequate global availability for water and food, regional deficiencies might well emerge or be aggravated in the near future. The combination of increased pressure on land by expanding urbanization and the loss of productive land through degradation and unsustainable management practices may well lead to shortages in arable land and water, impeding development in several regions. Although global food trade can supplement these regional shortfalls, it will create dependencies and require that importing countries engage in other development activities to finance the necessary food imports.

INTEGRATED MODELLING TECHNIQUES AND SCENARIOS CAN BE EXCELLENT TOOLS FOR ENVIRONMENT AND DEVELOPMENT POLICY SETTING AND PLANNING.

Although global sufficiency in water and food is expected to have a positive impact on the health of the global population, sharp regional differences may remain, and poverty may be aggravated in several regions. If global economic gains are not accompanied more explicitly by reinvestment in education, in social development, and in environmental protection, a move towards a more equitable, healthy, sustainable future for all sectors of society will be difficult to realize, and existing urban and pollution-related health problems may worsen while new ones are also appearing.

Integrated modelling techniques and scenarios can be excellent tools for environment and develop-

ment policy setting and planning, for instance, by simulating risks of continuing current global development patterns. The methodology, however, will need to be further developed and adapted to the realities and expectations of diverse regions, incorporating alternative policy strategies and development scenarios. The GEO Working Groups dealing with models and scenarios will also need to expand the scope of the analysis to address social and institutional issues. Furthermore, environmental quality issues (such as water pollution or forest degradation) need more attention as compared with environmental quantity only (such as water availability or forest area). Data, scale, and sensitivity of

Table 4.1
Selected Base Year Data and Assumptions for GEO Analysis: Absolute Figures

Population (millions)	Total				Average Annual Change (per cent)		
	1950	1990	2015	2050	1950–90	1990–2015	2015–2050
Africa	218	639	1,256	2,198	2.7	2.7	1.6
Asia & Pacific	1,321	2,926	4,070	5,161	2.0	1.3	0.7
Europe	572	790	862	894	0.8	0.4	0.1
Latin America	164	446	639	820	2.5	1.5	0.7
North America	166	277	320	330	1.3	0.6	0.1
West Asia	69	202	411	726	2.7	2.9	1.6
World	2,510	5,280	7,560	10,129	1.9	1.4	0.8

Gross domestic product (billion 1990 US$)	1950	1990	2015	2050	1950–90	1990–2015	2015–2050
Africa	102	413	1,009	4,300	3.6	3.6	4.2
Asia & Pacific	395	4,661	11,990	30,753	6.4	3.9	2.7
Europe	1,719	8,143	15,063	27,274	4.0	2.5	1.7
Latin America	184	1,145	2,431	6,905	4.7	3.1	3.0
North America	1,722	6,031	13,075	21,625	3.2	3.1	1.4
West Asia	73	570	1,572	6,905	5.3	4.1	4.3
World	4,195	20,964	45,140	95,954	4.1	3.1	2.2

Primary energy consumption (petajoules)	1950	1990	2015	2050	1950–90	1990–2015	2015–2050
Africa	1,231	7,396	16,528	58,859	4.6	3.3	3.7
Asia & Pacific	4,814	68,663	185,143	336,144	6.9	4.0	1.7
Europe	30,691	129,933	185,490	205,483	3.7	1.4	0.3
Latin America	1,938	14,323	25,067	55,405	5.1	2.3	2.3
North America	37,398	88,824	132,650	121,604	2.2	1.6	-0.2
West Asia	389	11,424	26,431	59,097	8.8	3.4	2.3
World	76,459	320,563	571,309	836,592	3.6	2.3	1.1

Energy Intensity (megajoules per 1990 US$)	1950	1990	2015	2050	1950–90	1990–2015	2015–2050
Africa	12	18	16	14	1.0	-0.4	-0.5
Asia & Pacific	12	15	15	11	0.5	0.2	-1.0
Europe	18	16	12	8	-0.3	-1.0	-1.4
Latin America	11	13	10	8	0.4	-0.8	-0.7
North America	22	15	10	6	-1.0	-1.5	-1.7
West Asia	5	20	17	9	3.4	-0.7	-1.9
World	18	15	13	9	-0.4	-0.8	-1.1

the analysis will need to be improved. In all this work, active involvement by the regions will be of paramount importance.

THE GENERAL SETTING

The present chapter contains quantitative analyses of the status of and trends in selected environment and development issues—current and future, regional and global. For selected issues, it describes events likely to occur in the relatively short time-frame considered in this report if no policy reforms are implemented.

Computer modelling techniques were used for the analyses in an attempt to capture the many complex interactions between the environment and the socio-economic fabric of life, especially for analysing potential future developments. The preparation of the chapter required the integration of

diverse sets of information from different sources and disciplines. The basic data used for this chapter were also used to prepare the projections in the Department for Policy Coordination and Sustainable Development Trends Report.

A few important considerations should be kept in mind when reading a modelling effort like the one presented here: the analysis is not intended to predict the future—even though it may seem so because only one scenario has been analysed so far. Besides, the current generation of modelling tools, although much improved since the early 1970s, is still limited. For instance, social factors, institutional practices, and the rate and type of technological development remain critical uncertainties. Furthermore, the ability of models to reflect reality in all its facets will always be limited by the possibilities of measurement as well as by gaps in knowledge about the interactions of biochemical cycles and human

Table 4.1 continued

Selected Base Year Data and Assumptions for GEO Analysis: Absolute Figures

Agricultural production of maize (thousand metric tons)	Total				Average Annual Change (per cent)		
	1970	1990	2015	2050	1970–90	1990–2015	2015–2050
Africa	21,356	36,651	82,669	186,751	2.7	3.3	2.4
Asia & Pacific	49,219	116,612	220,479	296,467	4.4	2.6	0.8
Europe	46,094	70,506	91,799	120,956	2.1	1.1	0.8
Latin America	36,778	55,931	91,592	153,744	2.1	2.0	1.5
North America	125,322	202,070	224,076	251,521	2.4	0.4	0.3
West Asia	1,827	3,086	4,288	3,784	2.7	1.3	-0.4
World	280,596	484,856	714,903	1,013,223	2.8	1.6	1.0

Caloric intake (billion kilocalories per day)	1970	1990	2015	2050	1970–90	1990–2015	2015–2050
Africa	789	1,511	3,210	6,236	1.6	3.1	1.9
Asia & Pacific	4,129	7,252	10,821	14,071	1.4	1.6	0.8
Europe	2,290	2,717	2,952	3,060	0.4	0.3	0.1
Latin America	703	1,192	1,778	2,391	1.3	1.6	0.9
North America	732	1,009	1,170	1,191	0.8	0.6	0.1
West Asia	278	585	1,217	2,167	1.9	3.0	1.7
World	8,921	14,265	21,148	29,116	1.2	1.6	0.9

Total water withdrawal (cubic kilometres per year)	1950	1990	2015	2050	1950–90	1990–2015	2015–2050
Africa	n.a.	145	199	280	n.a.	1.3	1.0
Asia & Pacific	n.a.	1,298	1,654	2,048	n.a.	1.0	0.6
Europe	n.a.	715	871	912	n.a.	0.8	0.1
Latin America	n.a.	179	241	302	n.a.	1.2	0.7
North America	n.a.	511	582	574	n.a.	0.5	0.0
West Asia	n.a.	130	168	211	n.a.	1.1	0.7
World	n.a.	2,978	3,715	4,327	n.a.	0.9	0.4

Sources: Historical data from Klein Goldewijk and Battjes (1995); assumptions about the future from Raskin *et al.* (1996).

Note: n.a. = not available.

and environmental systems. And finally, results are always open to different interpretation by different groups of people.

In this chapter, present and future socio-economic driving forces are analysed, the resulting future conditions of the atmosphere and land are analysed, and the potential impacts on natural habitats and human health are projected.

Most assumptions in this chapter about future developments have been formulated by a team led by the Stockholm Environment Institute (SEI). It is a conventional development scenario, i.e., it does not consider any major future policy reforms. Tables 4.1 and 4.2 list the data used (Klein Goldewijk and Battjes, 1995; Raskin *et al.,* 1996). Of course, there are many other "possible" futures. Some work on this is briefly illustrated in Figure 4.1.

Data used for the integrated modelling efforts in this chapter were previously collected by countries and compiled into international databases by

the United Nations and other international organizations such as the United Nations Department of Economic and Social Information and Policy Analysis, the Food and Agriculture Organization, the United Nations Development Programme, the World Bank, the World Meteorological Organization, and the World Resources Institute.

Complex processing of such base data then usually takes place during modelling exercises to derive value-added data sets such as population density, air emissions, or land cover. Details on data used for this chapter are given in van Woerden *et al.* (1995), while UNEP/UNDPCSD (1996) elaborates further on the core data issue.

For information on the models and the assumptions used to derive the analysis, the reader is referred to a separate Technical Report prepared by the National Institute of Public Health and the Environment (RIVM) in the Netherlands. Some of the models used (IMAGE, RAINS, AIM, TAR-

Table 4.2

Selected Base Year Data and Assumptions for GEO Analysis: Per Capita Figures

Gross domestic product per capita (1990 US$)	Per Capita				Average Annual Change Per Capita (per cent)		
	1950	1990	2015	2050	1950–90	1990–2015	2015–2050
Africa	468	646	803	1,956	0.8	0.9	2.6
Asia & Pacific	299	1,593	2,946	5,958	4.3	2.5	2.0
Europe	3,004	10,309	17,465	30,518	3.1	2.1	1.6
Latin America	1,124	2,569	3,804	8,425	2.1	1.6	2.3
North America	10,376	21,809	40,830	65,530	1.9	2.5	1.4
West Asia	1,059	2,823	3,821	9,508	2.5	1.2	2.6
World	1,671	3,971	5,971	9,473	2.2	1.6	1.3

Primary energy consumption per capita (gigajoules)	1950	1990	2015	2050	1950–90	1990–2015	2015–2050
Africa	6	12	13	27	1.8	0.5	1.4
Asia & Pacific	4	23	45	65	4.8	2.7	1.7
Europe	54	164	215	230	2.8	1.1	0.6
Latin America	12	32	39	68	2.5	0.8	1.2
North America	225	321	414	368	0.9	1.0	0.2
West Asia	6	57	64	81	5.9	0.5	0.6
World	30	61	76	83	1.7	0.9	0.5

Energy intensity per capita (joules per thousand 1990 US$)	1950	1990	2015	2050	1950–90	1990–2015	2015–2050
Africa	55	28	13	6	-1.7	-3.0	-2.5
Asia & Pacific	9	5	4	2	-1.5	-1.1	-1.4
Europe	31	20	14	8	-1.1	-1.4	-1.4
Latin America	64	28	16	10	-2.0	-2.2	-1.7
North America	131	53	32	17	-2.2	-2.1	-1.9
West Asia	77	99	41	12	0.6	-3.5	-3.5
World	7	3	2	1	-2.3	-2.2	-2.0

GETS) have been extensively peer-reviewed and are therefore not documented in this chapter. Others (models for water satisfaction at drainage basin level, biodiversity pressures) are still being developed, so brief explanations are included in the text.

GEO-1 concentrates on the world while at the same time taking into account regional differences. The six regions used in the model-based analysis roughly match the UNEP regional divisions used elsewhere in this report. (See Figure 4.2.) Considering the many differences within some of the regions, subdivisions should be considered for future GEO Reports.

FORCES DRIVING CHANGE

The primary driving forces of future developments considered in the models and analysis throughout this chapter are mainly related to population growth and the economy. These two forces in turn generate demand for food, water, energy, and so on.

Population Growth

The dynamics of human populations are sufficiently well understood to estimate fairly precisely the expected development over the next two to three decades. (See Figure 4.3.)

More than 86 million people are now added to the world each year, and world population is likely to increase at this rate until 2015. The projected growth in world population of 4.7 billion by the middle of the next century, with 95 per cent of the increase in developing countries, produces a total global population of just over 10 billion (Raskin *et al.*, 1996). In other words, despite a decline in birth rates in many countries, large increases in popula-

Table 4.2 continued
Selected Base Year Data and Assumptions for GEO Analysis: Per Capita Figures

Agricultural production of maize per capita (kilograms)	Per Capita				Average Annual Change Per Capita (per cent)		
	1970	1990	2015	2050	1970–90	1990–2015	2015–2050
Africa	98.0	57.3	65.8	85.0	-2.6	0.6	0.7
Asia & Pacific	37.3	39.9	54.2	57.4	0.3	1.2	0.2
Europe	80.6	89.3	106.4	135.3	0.5	0.7	0.7
Latin America	224.3	125.4	143.3	187.6	-2.9	0.5	0.8
North America	755.0	730.7	699.7	762.2	-0.2	-0.2	0.2
West Asia	26.5	15.3	10.4	5.2	-2.7	-1.5	-2.0
World	111.8	91.8	94.6	100.0	-1.0	0.1	0.2

Caloric intake per capita (kilocalories per person per day)	1970	1990	2015	2050	1970-90	1990-2015	2015-2050
Africa	2,193	2,363	2,555	2,837	0.4	0.3	0.3
Asia & Pacific	2,066	2,479	2,658	2,726	0.9	0.3	0.1
Europe	3,260	3,439	3,423	3,424	0.3	0.0	0.0
Latin America	2,478	2,674	2,781	2,917	0.4	0.2	0.1
North America	3,234	3,647	3,653	3,609	0.6	0.0	0.0
West Asia	2,415	2,893	2,960	2,964	0.9	0.1	0.0
World	2,416	2,704	2,799	2,871	0.6	0.1	0.1

Total water withdrawal per capita (cubic meters per year)	1950	1990	2015	2050	1950-90	1990-2015	2015-2050
Africa	n.a.	227	159	127	n.a.	-1.4	-0.6
Asia & Pacific	n.a.	444	406	397	n.a.	-0.4	-0.1
Europe	n.a.	905	1,010	1,020	n.a.	0.4	0.0
Latin America	n.a.	401	376	369	n.a.	-0.3	-0.1
North America	n.a.	1,847	1,817	1,740	n.a.	-0.1	-0.1
West Asia	n.a.	641	409	291	n.a.	-1.8	-1.0

Sources: Historical data from Klein Goldewijk and Battjes (1995); assumptions about the future from Raskin *et al.* (1996).
Note: n.a. = not available

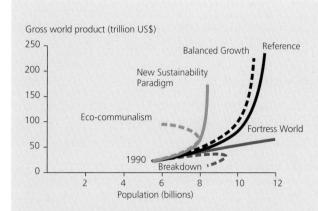

Gross world product (trillion US$)

Figure 4.1. Population and economic growth from 1990–2100 under different development scenarios.

Source: Gallopin *et al.* (forthcoming).

A Global Scenario Group (GSG), which also serves UNEP's GEO Scenario Working Group and is co-ordinated by the Stockholm Environment Institute (SEI), has so far focused on qualitative contours of three classes of scenarios: a central "Conventional Worlds" class; a pessimistic "Barbarization" class; and an optimistic "Great Transitions" class.

Conventional Worlds

Reference or Conventional Development scenario: already developed; analysed in this chapter.

Balanced Growth: stronger policy interventions; strong political will to implement policy reforms, strengthen management systems, and ensure widespread use of better technology; all to provide greater social equity and environment protection; many of the same patterns of production and consumption, notions of global governance, and political and cultural values as the Reference scenario.

Barbarization Scenarios

Breakdown: an extreme case of destructive anarchy; governmental and social failures, unchecked population growth, and environmental and social deterioration lead to scarcity, violence, and possible massive migration; eventually leading to economic collapse, a drastic fall in global population levels, loss of institutions, productive capacity, and technological wisdom.

Fortress World: an authoritarian "solution"; a minority of the elite in privileged enclaves protect their way of life by forcibly imposing limits and social controls on the impoverished majority, by seizing control of critical natural resources for their exclusive use, and by restricting access to information and technology; instability of a "Fortress" system may push the world into a "Breakdown" situation.

Great Transitions

Eco-communalism: a deep green utopian vision that emphasizes bio-regionalism, localism, face-to-face democracy, small technology, and economic autarky; population and economic scales diminish, environmental conditions improve dramatically.

New Sustainability Paradigm: seeks to alter the character of urban industrial civilization rather than to replace it; to build a more humane and equitable global civilization rather than to retreat into localism; a dramatic decrease of per capita material flows through behavioural changes and technology improvements, a resilient and high-quality environment, and high, well-distributed welfare with economic activity oriented towards services.

Although such futures may be viewed as utopian or unrealistic, the contrary hypothesis may be entertained as well, namely that attempting sustainability without such changes is quixotic.

The discussion of alternative futures raises a host of profound questions. Which of these pathways are self-consistent and plausible? Can the policy reforms of "Balanced Growth" achieve sustainability, or at least solve the urgent problems in many regions as identified in this GEO? What critical points could kick the system into global or regional "Barbarization" and what policies and actions are needed to reduce this risk? Can new values and policies transform industrial society as assumed in the "New Sustainability Paradigm"? And last but not least, the practical question for next GEO Reports: what actions are implied?

tion appear to be inevitable in the near future.

The geographical distribution of populations has also changed: notably, various economic, technological, and social factors have resulted in increasing urbanization (see Figure 4.4) and an associated concentration of populations. This trend will probably continue.

The quality of human life is as important for the future as the absolute numbers of people, and health is one important quality aspect. Two indicators widely used are life expectancy at birth and disability-adjusted life years. These are determined by a complex pattern of social and economic changes, ranging from income distribution and literacy to access to safe water, sanitation, and medical services. In the past, correlations have been observed between such patterns and a general indicator of economic welfare such as gross domestic product (GDP) per capita.

The Economy

The economic system is the second major driving force for analyses of the human-environment system. It has industrial, agricultural, manufacturing, and servicing components, and is supported by an infrastructure of roads, schools, hospitals, and other facilities. Together, these constitute the stocks of economic capital.

Adequate functioning of "economic capital" has to be accompanied by other, less tangible forms of "human capital," including aspects such as education, and of "social capital," such as community and governance structures (see also World Bank, 1995a). The economic system can only be sustained by a continuous influx of energy and material derived from "environmental capital." History has repeatedly shown that a proper balance among these four forms of capital and their use is an important

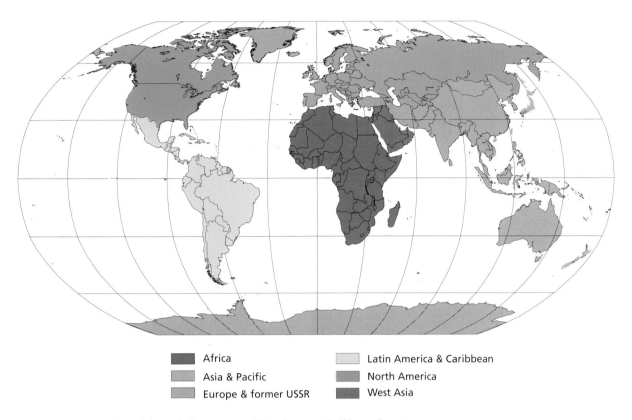

Africa	Latin America & Caribbean
Asia & Pacific	North America
Europe & former USSR	West Asia

Figure 4.2. Regional breakdown used in the modelling chapter.

Source: United Nations Environment Programme.
Note: The six regions shown here are more or less the same as the regions described in Chapters 2 and 3, except that the Polar Regions have been handled separately in these two chapters.

condition for a healthy, fulfilling, prosperous life. Experience has also shown that as countries become wealthier, there is generally a transition from a largely agricultural to an industrial economy and then towards a service and information-oriented economy—the economic transition described earlier. (See also Maddison, 1991.)

For members of the Organisation for Economic Co-operation and Development (OECD), it is assumed in this analysis that the service sector will continue to grow at the expense of agricultural and industrial contributions to GDP. Non-OECD regions are assumed to follow patterns similar to those in OECD countries. Per capita incomes in Latin America and East Asia are projected to exceed current levels in OECD Europe in the second half of the next century. Per capita incomes in Asia and the Pacific are assumed to rise faster than in industrial countries during the 1990–2050 period. In

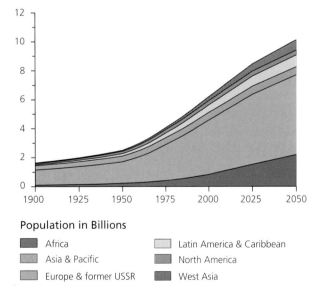

Population in Billions

Africa	Latin America & Caribbean
Asia & Pacific	North America
Europe & former USSR	West Asia

Figure 4.3. Recent and projected trends in population growth.

Sources: Alcamo *et al.* (1994); Berry (1990); UN (1992); WRI/UNEP/UNDP (1986, 1992, 1994); Klein Goldewijk and Battjes (1995).
Note: One billion represents 10^9 or one thousand million.

Percentage of Total Population

----- Urban
──── Rural

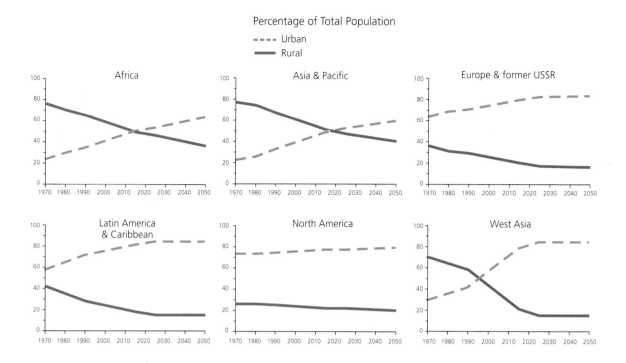

Figure 4.4. Recent and projected trends in urbanization.

Source: Raskin *et al.* (1996).

Africa, Latin America and the Caribbean, and West Asia, they are projected to rise more slowly from 1990 to 2015 (due to the slower decline of population growth, among other factors). In spite of these projected growth rates, the income gap between developing and industrial countries is likely to increase in the near future.

Convergence between per capita income levels in industrial and developing countries by 2050 (assuming a 1 to 1.5 per cent annual growth in GDP in industrial countries) would necessitate an average annual growth of 6 per cent in developing countries throughout the period. For Africa to catch up with North America, a 9 per cent regional growth rate would be needed. If GDP grows at 2 per cent per year in industrial countries, these figures would have to be 7 per cent overall in developing countries and 10 per cent for Africa (recent growth rates of 8 per cent have been observed in some African countries, but this is exceptional so far).

Given the commonly accepted near-term developments of population and economic growth, it is possible to project future demands for food, water, and energy. A number of additional features have

to be taken into consideration when doing this. These are detailed in the following sections, which deal with selected issues.

CLIMATE CHANGE AND ACIDIFICATION

This section focuses on climate change, acidification of the environment, and the interaction of these two problems. The results illustrate the importance of studying linkages between environmental problems.

Past and Present Trends

Since its establishment in 1988 by UNEP and the World Meteorological Organization, the Intergovernmental Panel on Climate Change (IPCC) has published a series of assessment reports, the latest of which concluded that "the balance of evidence suggests a discernible human influence on global climate." The detection of the resulting impacts on ecosystems remains difficult, however (IPCC, 1996).

Acidification of the environment occurs when two key conditions exist. First, a region has a high level of economic activity with extensive use of fossil fuels leading to large atmospheric emissions of acidifying pollutants that are transported both locally and for long distances. Second, soil, forest, and aquatic ecosystems in a region are susceptible to these acidifying pollutants. Up to now, most developing countries have not experienced acidification because only the second condition exists, whereas acidification has been well established in North America and Europe for at least the last two decades (see also Tolba *et al.,* 1992). Now, however, certain regions in Asia that have rapidly expanding economies (see, for example, Khemani *et al.,* 1989; Shindo *et al.,* 1994; Zhao and Seip, 1991) also fulfil the first condition for being at risk of acidification.

Rodhe *et al.* (1988) identified schematically areas in which acidification might represent a serious threat in the future on the basis of expected emissions, population density, and soil sensitivity. Areas at potential risk at that time included the northern and south-western parts of South America, the south-eastern part of Brazil and the La Plata region, and the southern part of West Africa (Kuylenstierna *et al.,* 1995).

Recent assessments have identified the northern and central part of Europe (Hettelingh *et al.,* 1995a), the eastern part of China, and southern parts of Asia (Hettelingh *et al.,* 1995b and 1995c) as being the regions at the greatest risk of damage.

Climate change and acidification are recognized as current or potential problems in both industrial and developing countries. Recently, a better understanding of how these two problems overlap and interact has emerged (see, for example, Houghton *et al.,* 1995).

First, greater combustion of fossil fuels increases the emissions of many acidifying pollutants as well as greenhouse gases. Second, changes in weather patterns stimulated by climate change will alter the intensity and distribution of acid deposition. Third—and perhaps most important, because it complicates projections of climate change—emissions of acidifying pollutants, especially sulphur dioxide, lead to the accumulation in the upper atmosphere of aerosols that partly mask the effects of greenhouse gases (IPCC, 1996).

The two important global issues addressed here—climate change and acidification—have the same underlying cause: a high level of economic activity that results in the emission of huge amounts of polluting substances into the atmosphere. Industrial activities—particularly energy production from the burning of fossil fuels and raw material use—release into the atmosphere acidifying gases, sulphur dioxide, and nitrogen oxides, and greenhouse gases, nitrous oxide, carbon dioxide, halocarbons, and other unwelcome by-products. They are, therefore, important sources of both acidifying gases and the greenhouse gases that are closely associated with climate change. In 1990, the burning of fossil fuels accounted for more than 80 per cent of the global emissions of carbon dioxide, the main greenhouse gas (IPCC, 1992), and about 94 per cent of the emissions of sulphur dioxide in Europe, the main cause of the acidification of the environment in that region (EEA, 1995).

Energy consumption in industrial regions has increased almost exponentially with the growth of population and economies. As Figure 4.5 illustrates, the cause of this environmental pressure has not been distributed equally world-wide.

Only in the last 10–20 years have there been signs of a decoupling between economic activity and the use of energy and materials in industrial countries. This is associated with their transition into service-based, less resource-intensive economies, as well as efficiency improvements. Concerns about human health and more recently about the natural environment have induced governments of industrial countries to develop and enforce environmental regulations to curb the level of atmospheric emissions. Initially, this involved lowering concentration levels by dilution and dispersion (through high chimneys, for example); later, it entailed so-called end-of-pipe technologies, preventing pollutants from entering the environment, and an increased use of cleaner and more efficient production technologies; recently, improved efficiency has been obvious in some parts of the world.

Figure 4.6 shows that as a consequence of these measures, global emissions of sulphur compounds have lately decreased, the emissions of nitrogen

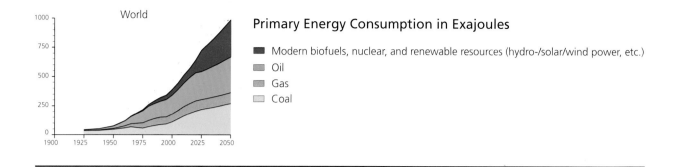

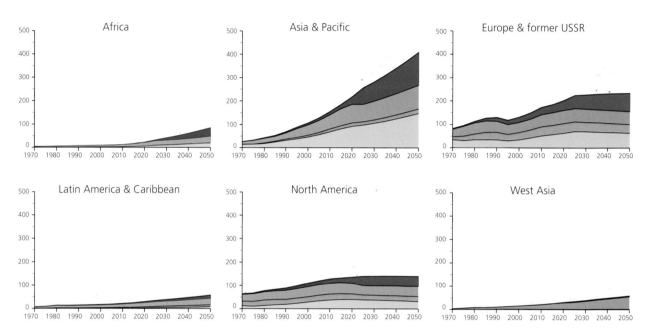

Figure 4.5. Recent and projected trends in primary energy consumption.

Sources: Alcamo *et al.* (1996b); Darmstadter (1971).

Note: Primary energy consumption is used here only for purposes of comparison and includes coal; oil; gas; and modern biofuels, nuclear, and renewable resources such as hydropower, solar power, and wind power.

oxides have more or less stabilized, but carbon dioxide emissions continue to grow. These global trends, however, mask important regional differences: emissions are decreasing in Europe, but significantly increasing in Asia.

The growth in the number of motor vehicles world-wide is among the factors responsible for continuing high levels of nitrogen oxides emissions despite technological advances in the design of car engines. Agricultural activity is another important source of emissions. Expansion of this sector often leads to forest clearance and the burning of trees and the shrub layer; together, these release large amounts of carbon dioxide and other greenhouse gases into the atmosphere. Other agricultural sources of

greenhouse gases are methane emitted by livestock and released from wet rice fields, and nitrogen oxides from crop fertilizers. As a result of the growth of energy use, deposits of acidifying substances have more than quadrupled compared to pre-industrial levels.

Projected Trends

Energy demands are projected to grow significantly both globally and across all regions (Raskin and Margolis, 1995). In particular, economic development in industrializing countries will require a spectacular increase in energy consumption. For Africa, West Asia/Middle East, and Asia, this increase is assumed to be by a factor of five or more by the year 2050, despite the assumption that energy intensity will decline in all regions. The increased energy demand is expected to continue to be met primarily by fossil fuels. Figure 4.5 shows key aspects of the energy scenario, which assumes that development is not constrained by limited availability of energy resources. Various estimates of future sulphur dioxide emissions for selected countries or regions are reported in the literature. (See Table 4.3a.) For the purpose of this analysis, the global emission estimates given in Posch *et al.* (1996) were applied. (See also Table 4.3b.)

Two different levels of sulphur dioxide emissions have been assumed: uncontrolled growth and partial controls (agreed-upon emission reductions in OECD countries and for most other countries a linear reduction of emission factors to about 50 per cent in 2050). No additional emission controls have been assumed beyond those already agreed on internationally.

The analysis does not necessarily include all the latest and planned national-level policies. At the global level, the growth in developing countries' economies outweighs the decrease or stabilization of carbon dioxide emissions in industrial countries. Not only do global carbon dioxide emissions continue to move upwards, but the declining trend in emissions of sulphur and nitrogen compounds will also be reversed.

Climate Change Trends

Most impact assessments of climate change to date have centred on industrial countries at medium and high latitudes. This is partly because most computer models project that the largest temperature changes are likely to occur at these latitudes, and partly because ecosystems at these latitudes are often particularly vulnerable to climatic changes. Nevertheless, the models also indicate that developing countries in low latitudes may experience important changes in climate as well, including crucial revisions in rainfall patterns (IPCC, 1990, 1996). Moreover, developing countries may be more vulnerable in other respects (e.g., agriculture or housing) because their less developed economies and infrastructures impede adapta-

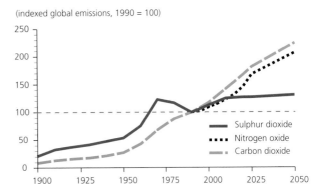

(indexed global emissions, 1990 = 100)

Figure 4.6. Index of global emissions of sulphur dioxide, nitrogen oxide, and carbon dioxide.

Sources: Alcamo and Kreileman (1996); Gschwandtner *et al.* (1985); Hameed and Dignon (1988); Keeling (1973, 1994); Klein Goldewijk and Battjes (1995); Marland and Rotty (1984); Marland *et al.* (1994); Mylona (1993); Overrein *et al.* (1981); Placet and Streets (1987); WRI/UNEP/UNDP (1994).
Notes: Data for carbon dioxide emissions before 1990 are derived from Keeling (1994); data after 1990 are assumed and are from Posch *et al.* (1996). No reliable historical data are available for nitrogen oxide emissions.

tion to new climate patterns. Recently completed studies indicate the special vulnerability of developing countries to impacts such as more frequent droughts and coastal flooding (IPCC, 1996).

Although overall global food production may not be harmed by projected climatic changes, according to IPCC (1996) there will be large regional differences. (See also "Use of Land" below.) Figure 4.7 provides an example of one possible impact of climate change on food production between 1990 and 2050. It indicates the major current areas of maize cultivation that are projected to experience higher or lower yields as a result of changes in temperature and precipitation.

In some areas, production may rise, but in other vulnerable areas, negative impacts may occur. These risks are particularly important for developing countries in semi-arid zones because they are less able to adapt to change than industrial countries are. Food imports from less affected regions may be an important mechanism for dealing with the impacts of climate change on crop yields. The analyses here highlight the fact that it is important to focus on regional "redistribution" of climate (with the associated changes in agricultural productivity and trade patterns) as well as on globally averaged climatic changes.

Table 4.3a

Sulphur Dioxide Emission Estimates from Different Sources

Region	Emissions (megatons) 1990	2000	2010	2050	Data Source
Europe	38	22	14	n.a.	(1)(2)
	44	30	27	22	(3)
	44	46	63	71	(4)
	46	39	38	48	(6)
Asia	34	53	78	n.a.	(1)
	35	n.a.	n.a.	n.a.	(5)
	35	53	77	84	(3)
	35	53	77	162	(4)
	31	36	42	75	(6)
USA	21	15	14	n.a.	(1)
	22	17	15	13	(3)
	22	30	37	32	(4)
	21	21	20	18	(6)
China	22	34	48	n.a.	(1)
	19.5	n.a.	n.a.	n.a.	(5)
	23	34	49	46	(3)
	23	34	49	92	(4)
	21	23	26	41	(6)
India	4.5	6.6	10.9	n.a.	(1)
	3.8	n.a.	n.a.	n.a.	(5)
	3.9	6.4	11.3	21.7	(3)
	3.9	6.4	11.3	43.5	(4)
	3.2	3.9	5.1	13.4	(6)
Other	7.5	12.4	19.1	n.a.	(1)

Sources:

1. Foell, W., M. Amann, G. Carmichael, M. Chadwick, J.-P. Hettelingh, L. Hordijk, and D. Zhao. 1995a. *RAINS-Asia: An Assessment Model for Air Pollution in Asia.* World Bank. Washington.
2. ECE/EB.AIR/40. 1994. *Protocol to the 1979 Convention on Long-Range Transboundary Air Pollution on Further Reduction of Sulphur Emissions.* United Nations Economic Commission for Europe. Geneva.
3. IMAGE 2.1 Baseline-A, with sulphur dioxide protocol.
4. IMAGE 2.1 Baseline-A without sulphur dioxide protocol.
5. Barrett, M. 1992. Environmental impacts of fossil fuels. In: Ramani, K.V., P. Hills, G. George (eds.). *Burning Questions: Environmental Limits to Energy Growth in Asian-Pacific Countries During the 1990s,* APDC/WWF, Asian and Pacific Development Centre. Kuala Lumpur, Malaysia.
6. Matsuoka, Y. 1992. Future projections of global anthropogenic sulfur emissions and their environmental effects. *Environmental Systems Research,* 22:359–368. (The Asian Pacific Integrated Model - AIM.)

Note: n.a. = not available.

Acidification Trends

Integrated assessment models have been used for the areas most affected to date—Europe (Amann *et al.,* 1995) and Asia (Foell *et al.,* 1995a and 1995b; Morita *et al.,* 1995). For this chapter, atmospheric models have been used to estimate how winds will transport and redistribute acidifying pollutants throughout Asia (Arndt and Carmichael, 1995) and Europe (Barrett and Seland, 1995). This information has been combined with estimates of the deposition levels that are considered acceptable (critical loads) for local ecosystems (Downing *et al.,* 1993; Hettelingh *et al.,* 1991 and 1995a; Posch *et al.,* 1995). Based on sulphur dioxide emissions shown in Table 4.3b, the results of this simulation indicate that, even under partial controls, substantive risks of acidification exist in Asia.

A comparison with other modelling studies, such as the Asian-Pacific Integrated Model of

Table 4.3b

Emissions of Sulphur Compounds Assumed Under Conventional Development (teragrams)

Region	1990	Hypothetical Benchmark No Controls Assumed 2015	2050	2100	Partial Controls Assumed 2015	2050	2100
Africa	2	5	17	41	5	8	21
Asia & Pacific	17	46	80	131	43	40	65
Europe & former USSR	25	37	41	34	19	15	12
Latin America & Caribbean	4	6	14	14	6	7	7
North America	12	21	18	12	9	7	5
West Asia	2	5	11	20	5	5	10

Source: Posch *et al.* (1996).

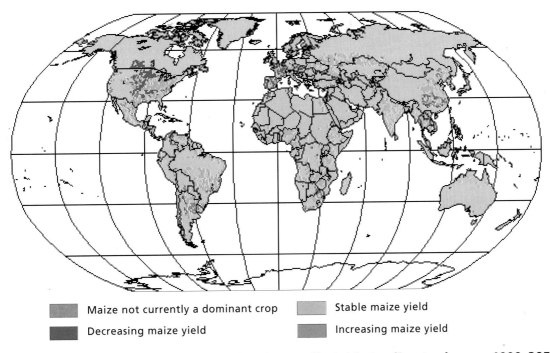

Maize not currently a dominant crop

Decreasing maize yield

Stable maize yield

Increasing maize yield

Figure 4.7. Projected changes in yields of maize attributable to climate change, 1990–2050.
Source: Alcamo and Kreileman (1996).
Note: Only major areas where maize is currently grown are shown.

Morita *et al.* (1995), finds comparable results for the Asia region. Woodlands in some developing areas could deteriorate rapidly, endangering supplies of fuelwood and other products. In some areas acid deposition will lead to the release of toxic metals to ground and surface water, further contaminating drinking water supplies. Agricultural crops become increasingly subject to risk because of the excess of critical loads in soils and high sulphur dioxide concentrations in the air (exceeding critical levels), resulting in lower cereal yields.

Unlike the situation with climate change, re-ductions in emissions of acidifying gases lead rela-tively quickly to lower deposition levels, followed after some time by rehabilitation of the ecosystems affected (typically this would take one to five dec-ades, provided that biogeochemical balances were not distorted too much when the depositions took place). Taking into account the impact of the imple-mentation of international treaties on acidification as well as future trends in energy use and the economy in Europe, it has been estimated that the ecosystem area affected by sulphur-based acid depo-sition in Europe may decrease from 19 per cent in

1990 to 10 per cent in 2010 (Hettelingh et al., 1995a).

Interactions Between Climate Change and Acidification

To consider the interaction of climate change and acidification, the IMAGE 2, RAINS Europe, and RAINS Asia models were used, focusing on Europe and Asia (Posch *et al.,* 1996).

Emissions of acidifying pollutants, especially sulphur dioxide, lead to the accumulation of parti-cles in the upper atmosphere, which partly masks the climate change caused by greenhouse gases. If global emissions of sulphur dioxide increase in par-allel with the use of fossil fuels in developing coun-tries, then the mass of those particles in the atmos-phere will also increase, moderating this warming trend. (See Figure 4.8.)

Nevertheless, global average temperature is still projected to increase significantly even if sulphur dioxide emissions grow uncontrollably (which would have separate, adverse effects on the environ-ment), and important shifts in global weather sys-

(degrees Celsius)

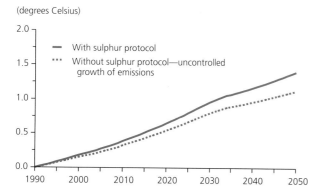

Figure 4.8. **Projected changes in average global surface temperatures for varying levels of control of sulphur dioxide emissions, 1990–2050.**

Source: Alcamo *et al.,* (1994).

(million metric tons per year)

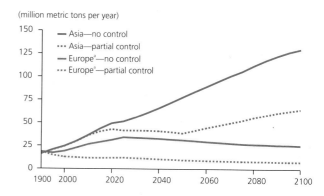

Figure 4.9. **Projected trends in sulphur dioxide emissions in selected regions with partial control of emissions and with no control.**

Sources: Alcamo *et al.* (1996a); Posch *et al.* (1996).
Note: a. Includes those countries in the European part of the former USSR.

tems could occur. If emissions of acidifying gases were reduced while those of greenhouse gases were not, decreasing sulphur dioxide particle concentrations would "unmask" the warming caused by greenhouse gases, leading to even greater increases in global temperature affecting both industrial and developing nations. This underscores the importance of studying the interactions among environmental problems rather than just looking at, for example, acidification and climate change in isolation.

Trends in emissions of sulphur dioxide in two regions for two different sets of assumptions (no controls and partial controls) are depicted in Figure 4.9.

Land areas that could be affected by both acidification and climate change in Europe and Asia in 2015 and 2050 according to the model simulations are shown in Figure 4.10. It is predicted that 12.5 per cent of Europe and 7.3 per cent of Asia are liable to be affected by both problems in the year 2050 (Alcamo *et al.,* 1995; Posch *et al.,* 1996).

Trend Implications

The time-frame required to adjust the climate system to a different level of emissions ranges from decades to centuries. Even if emissions were immediately and sharply reduced, some climate change would still occur because of inherent inertia in the system. This underlines the importance of system

inertia when evaluating impacts and response options.

The Framework Convention on Climate Change stipulates the goal of stabilizing greenhouse gas concentrations. For the short term, as a first step, Annex I countries (industrialized countries, including those in transition to a market economy) are required to bring their greenhouse gas emissions in 2000 back to the 1990 level. An even more stringent protocol is set to be adopted in 1997. In contrast with the emissions of some other pollutants (such as sulphur dioxide and particulate matter), emissions of greenhouse gases have not been demonstrated to decrease as national income levels rise. Even if best efforts are made to reduce greenhouse gas emissions, some degree of climate change will inevitably occur. This is due to lags in the climate system and to the difficulty in reducing global greenhouse gas emissions because of inertia in socio-economic systems.

Experiments with the model illustrate that the longer responses to climate change are delayed, the more drastic will emission reductions need to be to achieve the same results that could have been realized if measures had been adopted early (Alcamo and Kreileman, 1996). There are significant interim impacts caused by emissions during any period of delay in initiating action. Early action has additional advantages of keeping options open, increasing flexibility, and avoiding a shift of the responsibility

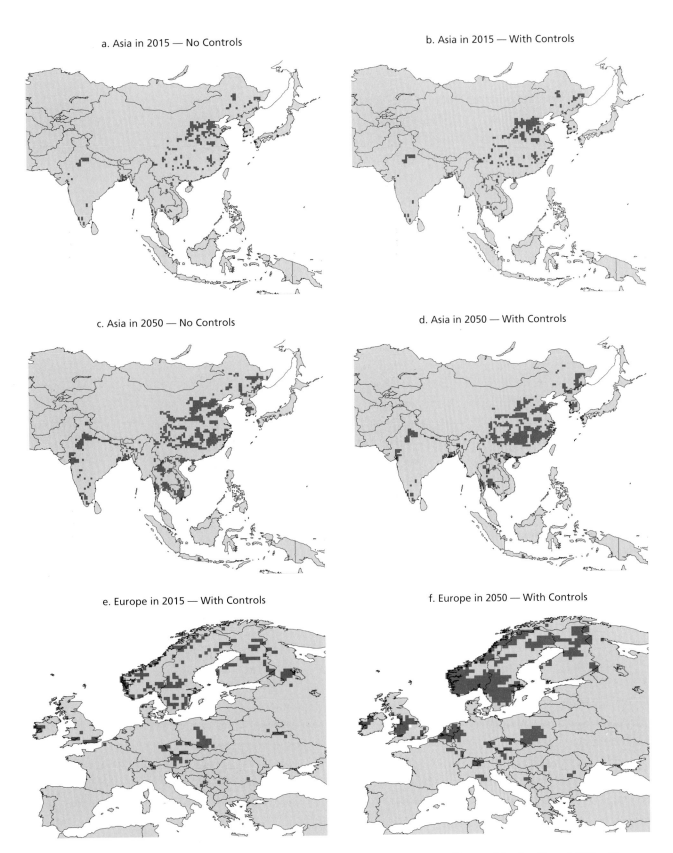

a. Asia in 2015 — No Controls

b. Asia in 2015 — With Controls

c. Asia in 2050 — No Controls

d. Asia in 2050 — With Controls

e. Europe in 2015 — With Controls

f. Europe in 2050 — With Controls

Figure 4.10. Areas in Asia and Europe projected to be seriously affected by both acidification and climate change by 2015 and 2050.

Source: Posch et al. (1996).

to future generations to act on a problem caused by past and present generations. Delaying responses may make the costs of reclaiming lost resources, including agricultural areas, prohibitive for future generations. On the other hand, delaying further emission reductions can have advantages, according to some economic analyses: technological developments and the discounting, in economic terms, of response measures both make any responses in the future cheaper, and avoid premature retirement of current capital goods (see, for example, Wigley *et al.,* 1996).

Contingency plans are required to adapt to impacts of climate change such as coastal and river flooding, alterations in water availability, changes in the occurrence of extreme meteorological events, shifts in natural vegetation zones and crop zones, and other developments that will have a major effect on people and the natural environment. Important examples of such useful adaptations are the development of drought-resistant crop varieties, increases in the efficiency of water use, and avoidance of the fragmentation of ecosystems.

The issues discussed in this section all stem from a high level of economic activity that produces enormous amounts of emissions of polluting substances to the atmosphere. The most important source of these is the burning of fossil fuels. Hence, modifying the amount or type of fossil fuels burned is an effective strategy for mitigating all these problems at the same time. This could be considered as the next great transition in the world's energy system.

The so-called LESS scenario (Low CO_2-Emitting Energy Supply System) developed by IPCC (1996) indicates that a global energy system with emissions of carbon dioxide below current levels by 2050, which is compatible with stabilization of carbon dioxide concentrations well below twice pre-industrial levels, is feasible with current technology. The importance of paying serious attention to energy issues at the global scale is echoed in an International Institute for Applied Systems Analysis/World Energy Council study, which states that "the single most important conclusion is that, given the expected divergence of development paths post-

2020, and the foreclosure of potentially desirable options unless relevant policies are initiated and decisions taken long before then, action needs to start now" (Nakicenovic and Jefferson, 1995).

USE OF LAND

The main pressure on land use is caused by an expanding economy and the demand for food by a growing population and changing diets. A model is used here to address the impact of these factors on the production of food, on remaining natural land, and on the balance between food self-sufficiency and imports.

Global food production can be increased either through intensification (using multicropping, raising cropping intensity by shortening fallow periods, or applying other inputs such as fertilizers to raise yields) and improved technology or through land expansions (cultivating additional land, primarily by converting forest or rangeland into farmland). This modelling study considered several factors, such as the availability of suitable land, the quality of the land, socio-economic conditions, and the availability of needed inputs. Regional food production can be supplemented by imports, which have an effect on food production in exporting regions.

Past and Present Trends

Global human food consumption figures show that the daily average world per capita intake of 2,700 kilocalories is substantially above the critical daily level needed for a healthy life (1,900 kilocalories). This suggests that there is enough food to feed the current global population. Yet there is a major difference in caloric intake between developing and industrial regions—2,470 kilocalories a day per capita compared with 3,400 kilocalories (FAO, 1992).

Food production has not always kept pace with population growth. In most of Africa, Latin America, and about half of Asia, less food was produced per capita at the end of the 1980s than at the beginning of the decade (IFPRI, 1995). From 1985 to 1994, the amount of grain produced per person globally has fallen (FAO, 1995b). In addition, increases in rice and wheat yields are beginning to level off in some major producing regions. The expansion in world grain production has slowed from 3 per cent a year in the 1970s to 1.3 per cent a year in the 1983–1993 period (IFPRI, 1995).

In the past, food production rose mainly due to a more intensive use of the land and to expansion of agricultural land (Leach, 1995), but area expansion is becoming less and less an option to boost output (Gardner and Peterson, 1996). In almost three decades, agricultural land area in the industrial and developing worlds has increased by 2.9 and 15.4 per cent respectively, yielding a global figure of 9.2 per cent. But these numbers mask considerable regional variations: increases in Africa of 20 per cent; in Latin America, 27 per cent; and in South and South-East Asia, 13 per cent. Nor do they include pasture land, the main contributor to the total land extension in many regions. In Latin America, for example, five to six times as much land is used for pasture as for arable purposes. The mainstay of agricultural production growth in the more recent past has been increased yields through intensification, from the application of new varieties and of technologies derived from scientific discovery and improvements in management (FAO, 1995b). But these increases are levelling off also.

The International Food Policy Research Institute (IFPRI) reported that in 1990 about 800 million people were "food insecure"—that is, lacking economic and physical access to the food required to lead healthy and productive lives—and that some 185 million children under the age of six were seriously underweight for their age (IFPRI, 1995). Food insecurity and child malnutrition are mainly concentrated in South Asia and are increasing in sub-Saharan Africa (FAO, 1995b; IFPRI, 1995).

According to the U.N. Food and Agriculture Organization (FAO), however, food security and nutrition have improved significantly in most developing regions, mainly due to increased domestic production and food imports. Yet sub-Saharan Africa, parts of South Asia, and Latin America and the Caribbean are still in a difficult position (FAO, 1995b).

At present (except in cases of civil strife), malnutrition is caused less by a global shortage of food than it is by poverty—the lack of income to buy food or the lack of means (land or capital) to grow enough. More than 1.1 billion people in the developing world live in absolute poverty, with incomes of US$1 a day or less per person. The gap between rich and poor has become larger since 1960. The share of global income obtained by the poorest 20 per cent of the world's population decreased dramatically—from 2.5 per cent in the 1960s to 1.3 per cent in 1990 (IFPRI, 1995).

Projected Trends

Caloric Intake

It is projected that, globally, nutrition will continue to improve. Figure 4.11 shows the projections for six regions with respect to caloric intake, indicating a convergence towards the diets in western industrial countries—an average of 2,840 kilocalories per day per capita in 2015 and 3,000 kilocalories in 2050. Due to low (albeit increasing) assumed income levels and high population growth, improvement is projected to be slowest in Africa.

After 2050, food intake per capita is projected to slowly level off as the amount reaches the saturation point. There is an observed trend, particularly in areas with growing economies, of a shift in diet composition towards luxury and processed food products, especially animal products (which have a lower ecological efficiency). In developing regions, the share of animal products in the diet is assumed to rise by 30 per cent to reach about 13 per cent of the total caloric intake by 2015 and about 17 per cent by 2050 (Leach, 1995). In industrial regions, it is expected to remain stable at around 30 per cent. The required additional production for higher caloric intake and diverse diets would have to come from a combination of intensification (primarily increasing inputs), expansion (land conversion), and imports.

Demand–Supply Ratio (Import–Export)

Contrary to past experience, global food supply is likely to increase faster than global demand. In some major regions, however, particularly in Africa and West Asia, the need to import food in order to meet the demands for basic staples will continue and probably increase in the future (Leach, 1995). To offset this, more developed regions, particularly North America, Europe, and the former USSR, are projected to produce more food.

In large parts of Asia and the Pacific, West Asia, and Africa, current results indicate a gap between demand and supply by 2015. The continuing degradation of soils and the possibly insufficient access of farmers to technology might even increase the rate of land conversions and dependence on food imports. On the other hand, additional increases in productivity, notably in livestock management and production on marginal lands, could have the opposite effect. These projections are in line with the *FAO 2010* study, which indicates that the already large, current differences in self-sufficiency ratios between industrial and developing regions will widen still further (FAO, 1995b).

In the 2010 report, FAO indicates that the expectation that the world would now be on a firm path towards eliminating hunger and malnutrition has proved to be over-optimistic, despite the availability of adequate food at the global level. Studies by IFPRI for 2020 also project that the current uneven path in food security and nutrition is likely to continue (IFPRI, 1995). Table 4.4 provides the actual and projected amounts of food products required in developing and industrial regions and the world as a whole (Leach, 1995).

As discussed in the preceding section, climate change may also become a factor that has both negative and positive impacts on food production, as may regional disasters. These effects will differ by region.

Intensification of Agriculture

An agricultural transition to intensive but not necessarily sustainable land use is assumed. It is projected that in developing regions, cropping intensity will increase by 15–20 per cent by 2050, both for irrigated and rainfed agriculture. A slower increase, mainly to produce more food for export to food-

deficient regions, is projected for industrial regions. This is again in line with the *FAO 2010* report, which states that intensification in land use will continue, especially in regions where arable land is scarce, such as South Asia, West Asia, and North Africa (FAO, 1995b).

Improved yields have a greater impact on productivity growth than increases in cropping intensity do. Sustained increases in yield are expected up to 2050. With the exception of China, the yields in developing regions will not exceed those in the leading industrial countries today. It is assumed that the generally poor yield performance in Africa in the past will be improved.

Food Production

Global growth in agricultural production is expected to fall to around 1.5 per cent per annum. Table 4.5 shows the projected crop yields for wheat plus coarse grains in 2025 and 2050. It indicates a relatively higher increase for developing regions, although in absolute terms the yields are lower there. The strongest relative increase in yield is assumed to take place in the first 35 years.

Figure 4.12 indicates the amount of total cereals produced for 1970–90 (historical) and 1990–2050 (projections), based on information on demand (population, economy, and intake); self-sufficiency; quality of the resources (climate, land, water, and so on); and management characteristics.

Land Use/Land Cover

Figure 4.13 shows land use/land cover changes. Globally, agricultural land (for this study, defined as arable, pasture, and marginal land) currently occupies approximately 37 per cent of total land area; about one third of this 37 per cent is arable land (that is, used for cultivation). Agriculture's share of the land is projected to increase to 46 per cent by 2015 and to around 50 per cent by 2050, whereas the ratio between pasture and arable lands is expected to remain relatively stable over time.

These global changes mask quite distinct regional differences in land use changes. In industrial

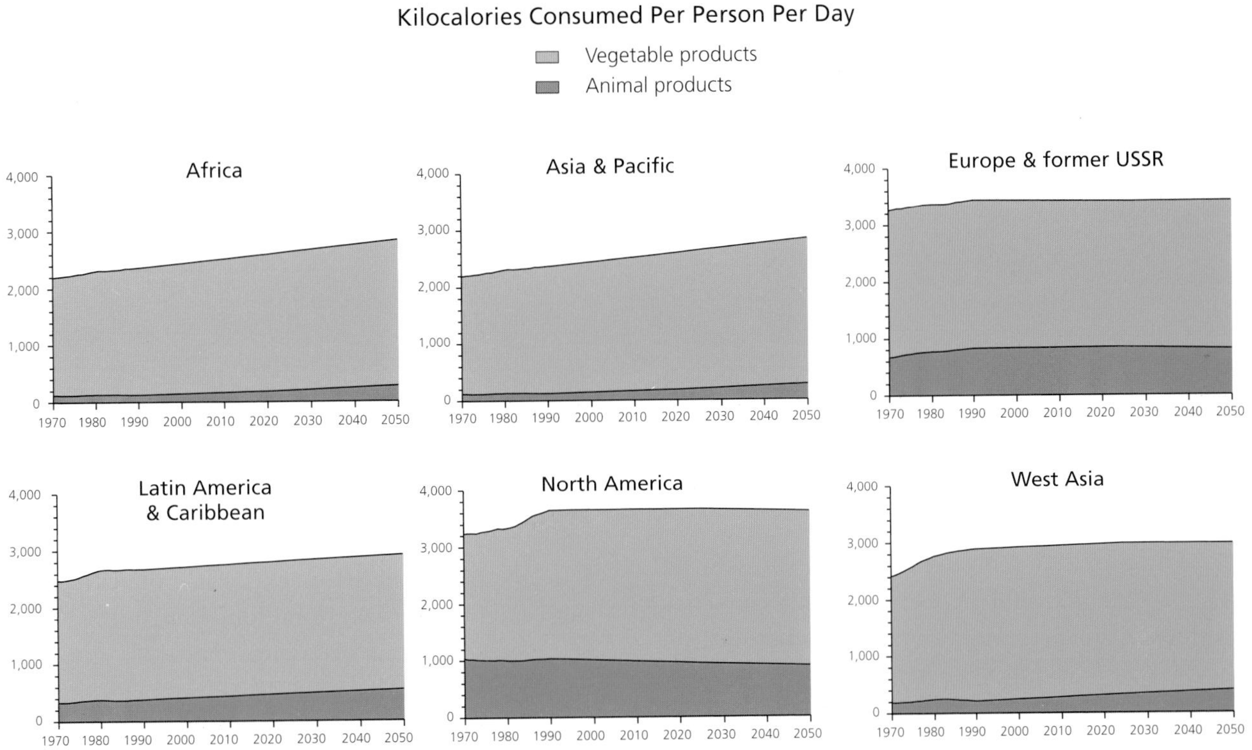

Kilocalories Consumed Per Person Per Day

▢ Vegetable products
▢ Animal products

Figure 4.11. Recent and projected trends in caloric intake from vegetable and animal products.

Sources: Alcamo *et al.* (1996b); Leach (1995).
Notes: Caloric intake data for 1970–90 are based on FAO statistics (FAO, 1992) and projected for 1990–2050. Vegetable products include temperate cereals, rice, maize, tropical cereals, roots and tubers, pulses, oil crops, and others; animal products include meat from cattle, pigs, sheep, and goats, meat and eggs from poultry, and milk from cattle.

regions, agricultural land is projected to increase from its 1990 level by about 3 per cent by 2015 and 10 per cent by 2050. In North America, the percentage increase is 4 per cent by 2015 but only 2 per cent by 2050, while in Europe and the former USSR the figures are 4 per cent by 2015 and 18 per cent by 2050.

Developing regions, in contrast, show a projected increase in agricultural land area of about 33 per cent by 2015 and 45 per cent by 2050 compared with 1990. The lowest increases are expected in Latin America and the Caribbean—about 10 per cent by 2015 and 20 per cent by 2050—whereas the figures in Asia and the Pacific are about 28 per cent by 2015 but only 24 per cent by 2050. In the latter case, the reduced increase is related to the limited options for further expansion of agricultural land. In Africa and West Asia, increases in agricultural area are projected to be much higher—about 55 and 57

per cent by 2015, respectively, and 90 and 95 per cent by 2050. These figures include extensive use of grassland.

The large increases in the area of cultivated land in Africa and West Asia result from a very sharp rise in demand, but they presume only moderate developments in agricultural management and technology. In particular, it is assumed that traditional animal husbandry systems, which require considerable grazing land, will be continued. More elaborate traditional farming systems, requiring more inputs and better management but with higher output/input ratios, are highly likely to lead to far less dramatic land use changes by 2050.

In summary, to meet future food demands, a considerable extension of the area currently used for agriculture is needed, in addition to improvements in yields, unless more drastic changes take place in societies. It is projected that this extension will

Table 4.4

Animal Products and Crops Demanded by an Increasing World Population
(million metric tons)

	Cereals			Other crops			Animal products		
	1989	2025	2050	1989	2025	2050	1989	2025	2050
Developing	940	1,882	2,419	1,870	3,950	5,502	307	903	1,405
Developed	754	952	961	1,110	1,298	1,262	565	666	660
World	1,694	2,834	3,380	2,980	5,248	6,764	872	1,569	2,065

Source: Leach (1995).

Note: Values are reported at 2025 rather than at 2015.

principally affect developing regions and some parts of North America, Europe, and the former USSR. In all areas, any extension of agricultural area is projected to occur at the expense of remaining natural areas.

The projected land use changes and associated intensification would have other significant environmental impacts. For example, if intensification (as the main driving force behind increases in productivity) is not managed properly, it has negative consequences for environmental quality. These can include land degradation, overexploitation of freshwater resources (for irrigation), pollution of ground water (with nutrients and/or pesticides), and increased demand for fossil energy and other resources

(to make fertilizers, for example, or as energy for tractors).

Regional Summary

Due to the projected increases in population and per capita food intake, total food demand in Africa is projected to grow 120 per cent by 2015 and more than 300 per cent by 2050. The combination of this strong increase in agricultural demands, an assumed additional supply from food imports, and a moderate development in agricultural technology translates into an increase of 55 per cent in the total agricultural area by 2015 and almost a doubling by 2050. Again, this assumes no major changes in the way Governments and people handle their land. From 2020 onwards, the area of suitable land is projected to become scarce, and the food supply will come under more and more pressure, mainly because of the expected low average yields. To overcome these threats, a strong agricultural development is needed in Africa that would lead to a faster increase in regional productivity and greater security regarding food supply. In addition, if there is to be money available to pay for food imports, much more revenue needs to be generated from non-agricultural activities.

The projected increase of the population of North America and the static or even slightly decreasing average daily food intake there means only 15 per cent more food production is needed by 2050. The slight increase in total production in North America that is foreseen is mainly caused by demand for exports to developing regions. Because of the assumed continuity in technological development in agriculture, it is expected that the in-

Table 4.5

Projected Yields of Wheat and Coarse Grains for Selected Regions
(metric tons per hectare)

Region[a]	Wheat and Coarse Grain Yields[b]		
	1989	2025[c]	2050
Africa	1.2	2.2	2.7
Latin America	2.0	3.0	3.3
Middle East	1.2	2.5	3.0
China and centrally planned Asia[d]	3.2	5.1	5.7
S & SE Asia	1.5	2.8	3.2
North America	3.9	6.0	6.3
Western Europe	3.9	6.0	6.3
Eastern Europe	3.7	5.5	6.0
OECD Pacific	1.7	2.6	2.8
Former USSR	1.9	3.3	3.5

Sources: Leach (1995) and Raskin *et al.* (1996).

Notes:

a. Regions as applied in SEI scenario work.

b. Coarse grains following the FAO classification: maize, rye, oats, barley, millet, and sorghum.

c. Values are reported at 2025 rather than at 2015.

d. Includes Kampuchea, the Democratic People's Republic of Korea, Laos, Mongolia, and Vietnam.

crease in regional demand, including for export, will not lead to a substantial call for new agricultural land.

In Latin America and the Caribbean, with both population and per capita food intake expected to increase, the total food demand will grow by 50 per cent by 2015 and will more than double by 2050. The combination of an increase in agricultural demands and a successful implementation of agricultural technology is expected to lead to a 10-per-cent increase in the total agricultural area by 2015 and about a 20-per-cent increase by 2050.

The same picture emerges for Asia and the Pacific: an expected increase in food demand of about 50 per cent by 2015 and about 100 per cent by 2050. Combined with an assumed additional supply from food/feed imports and a continuation in implementation of agricultural technology, total agricultural area is due to increase almost 28 per cent by 2015, and then drop to 24 per cent by 2050. Large parts of Asia have areas with dense populations that are projected to run out of suitable agricultural land from 2000 onwards. To overcome growing shortages in land area, likely solutions for Asia are further implementation and development of agricultural technologies and an increase in imports (to be paid for from non-agricultural revenues).

Given the small projected increase of the population of Europe and the former USSR and an unchanged daily food intake per capita, only 13 per cent more food production would be needed in this region by 2050. The projected increase in total production is mainly caused by demand for exports to developing regions. Notwithstanding an assumed continuity in technological development in agriculture, it is expected that the increase in regional demand, including for exports, will lead to some extra demand for agricultural land—4 per cent more by 2015 and about 18 per cent by 2050.

Due to the projected increase of population in many countries of West Asia (including Turkey, Iran, and Afghanistan) and a small increase in per capita food intake, total food demand in the region is to increase 110 per cent by 2015 and almost 300 per cent by 2050. This strong increase in demand, combined with presumably high additional supplies

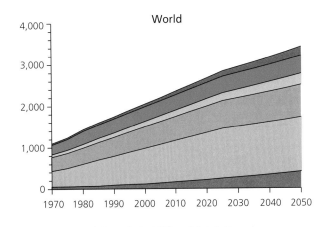

Figure 4.12. Recent and projected trends in the production of total cereals.

Sources: Alcamo *et al.* (1994 and 1996b) based on FAO (1995c); Leach (1995).

from imports and a moderately fast implementation of agricultural technology, leads to a 57-per-cent increase of the total agricultural area by 2015 and almost a doubling by 2050. The results show that from 2020 on, the area of available suitable land is completely used and the food supply comes under increasing pressure.

Global Summary

Total global food demand is expected to increase by 50 per cent by 2015 and by more than 110 per cent by 2050. The combination of the increase in agricultural demands, changes in consumption patterns (less staple foods and more luxury products, which require more inputs), and ongoing technological development in agriculture will lead to a 27-per-cent increase of the total agricultural area by 2015 and about a 42-per-cent increase by 2050.

Several compounding factors have not yet been addressed in this summary, however. First, soil degradation is currently estimated to affect some 1.2 billion hectares of land world-wide (that is, 10 per cent of the current agricultural land area). Water and wind erosion account for just over 1 billion hectares of the total area degraded (FAO, 1995b; IS-RIC/UNEP, 1991). The main causes of degradation

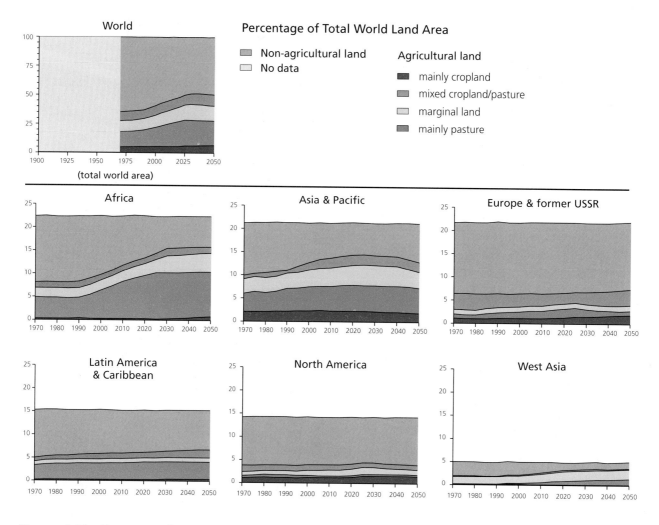

Figure 4.13. Recent and projected changes in land use and land cover.

Source: Alcamo *et al.* (1996b).

Notes: Regional graphs show the percentage of total world land area; while the world graph shows the total world area. Results are simulated for 1970–90 and projected for 1990–2050.

   Non-agricultural land here includes forest, tundra, ice, desert, savannah, steppe, scrubland, and urban areas. *Agricultural land* is comprised of cropland, mixed cropland/pasture, marginal land, and pasture.

   In contrast to agricultural land, *domesticated areas* are comprised of cropland, pasture, and urban areas. (See Figure 4.16.) All other areas are considered *non-domesticated*. Thus, there is overlap between land classified as agricultural and land classified as domesticated, but there are also differences.

are deforestation, overgrazing, and the mismanagement of arable land. Such activities lead to nutrient depletion (Smaling, 1993), salinization, and desertification (UNEP, 1991), and ultimately affect food production and socio-economic structures. Estimates indicate that each year 5–6 million hectares are lost through severe soil degradation. If this continues, several million hectares of additional land would be needed every year to offset the loss of land to degradation.

   Another factor that affects agricultural production is urbanization, since land areas suitable for

agriculture are often converted for urban land use. This puts pressure on non-domesticated areas.

   Many reputable research institutes and organizations have addressed the issues discussed in this section. Generally speaking, there are two perspectives. The somewhat optimistic reports and publications (such as FAO, 1995b) assume that if technology and enhanced management are implemented successfully, demand can be met without reaching the biophysical limits of global food production. The pessimistic voices (such as Brown, 1996) express the view that technological developments do not look so promising and will lead to non-sustainable agricultural practices, that technologies are unevenly spread across the world, that developing regions will depend increasingly on imports, and that a growing number of people are likely to lack food security and be malnourished in the future.

The difference in perspective can be largely attributed to varying assumptions about the future availability of suitable soil and water resources, about the way these resources will be used or misused (Gardner and Peterson, 1996), about the impact of environmental pollution on agriculture (due to climate change, acidification, and water pollution), and about agriculture's own contribution to the general pollution of water, air, and soil.

The results depicted here are optimistic in that they assume significantly higher productivity and efficiency in agriculture, but pessimistic because they assume a reduction in self-sufficiency in some developing regions. They assume that the needed extensions of agricultural land will have negative effects on remaining natural habitats and hence on biodiversity, highlighting again the need to address interlinkages among different sectoral assessments.

Because food security is one of the most basic human needs, the clear differences in assumptions and vision among leading experts about achievable developments require much more international attention, research co-operation, and integrated systems analysis.

PRESSURES ON NATURAL HABITATS

Habitats the world over are under threat, with dire consequences for plant and animal species. The distribution and sizes of populations of many species are declining significantly, leading to local or regional extinctions and ultimately to global extinction. At the same time, a small number of mostly opportunistic species are increasing substantially. According to the *Global Biodiversity Assessment*, species have been becoming extinct since 1600 at 50–100 times the average estimated natural rate, while the extinction rate is expected to rise to between 1,000 and 10,000 times the natural rate (UNEP, 1995a).

The *Global Biodiversity Assessment* identifies the five major causes of biodiversity loss as the fragmentation, degradation, or outright loss of habitats (through the conversion of land for agriculture, infrastructure, or urbanization, for example); overexploitation; the introduction of non-native species; pollution; and climate change (UNEP, 1995). (See Figure 4.14.) Some positive initiatives have also been identified, however, such as the establishment of protected areas, habitat regeneration, and measures that mitigate pressures from human activities.

This section provides the results of a specific study on the projected changes in pressures that will affect biodiversity at the regional and global levels as a result of possible socio-economic developments. This is predominantly achieved by quantifying the projected conversion of non-domesticated into domesticated land and by assessing some of the pressures on the remaining natural habitat that affect its quality.

The domestication of land is one of the major causes of biodiversity loss on a global scale. For the purpose of this study, non-domesticated land is defined as those areas not dominated by human activity, irrespective of whether they are pristine or degraded. Examples of this include virgin land; nature reserves; all forests, also production forest, except wood plantations planted with exotic species; areas with shifting cultivation; all fresh-water areas and land covered with ice (excluding Antarctica); and extensive grasslands (marginal land used for grazing by nomadic livestock).

Past and Present Trends

The results in this section are based on the same calculations as used in the previous section ("Use of Land"), but they focus on non-domesticated areas, a somewhat different classification compared with agriculture and non-agriculture, as was included there.

Between 1700 and 1980, the amount of non-domesticated area decreased globally by more than one third—from about 95 per cent to about 65 per cent. (See Figure 4.15.) This was mainly due to the conversion of natural forests and grassland into cropland and pasture. Hannah *et al.* (1994) found estimates of a similar order of magnitude today for the globe, and Mackinnon and Mackinnon

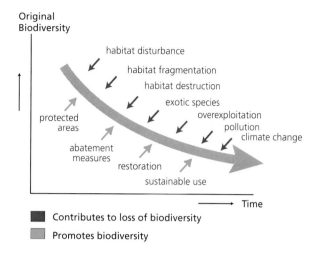

Figure 4.14. Main causes of biodiversity losses and gains.

Source: RIVM/UNEP (1997).

(1986a,b) found similar estimates for Indo-Malayan and Afrotropical realms. Any differences can be explained by different definitions of habitat loss and regional divisions.

In densely populated subregions, such as the western part of Europe (that is, excluding the Nordic countries and Greenland), the losses in non-domesticated area have been considerably larger. Here, the remaining area is less than 30 per cent (Kaales, 1996). And in the Netherlands, only about 20 per cent of the land is not domesticated, of which 9 per cent consists of terrestrial ecosystems and 11 per cent of fresh-water ecosystems (van der Ven, 1996).

The total loss of global forest area (that is, forest and woodland) in the period 1700–1980 is estimated at one fifth, from 47 per cent of the global area in 1700 to 38 per cent in 1980 (Richards, 1990). In temperate zones considerable decline in forest area had already taken place before 1700, especially in the Mediterranean Basin and the Indus Valley (areas occupied by ancient Egyptian, Indian, Greek, and Roman civilizations) and in northern and north-western China (FAO, 1995a). Considerable declines also occurred in north-western Europe during the Middle Ages (Idema *et al.*, 1993).

In contrast to the Mediterranean region, in North America development did not lead to the almost complete loss of forest. Over some 150 years, an initial rapid conversion of forested land was followed by a slowing down in clearance rates, and eventually by a stabilization. In recent decades, there has even been an expansion in the area of forested land, with a considerable amount of the original forest remaining. This reversal reflects a major transition in attitudes and a changing perception of the forest resource, ultimately placing an increasing value on the recreation and wilderness qualities of forests in North America (Mather, 1990). This can be seen as a positive trend, although newly planted forest and wood plantations cannot replace the ecological values of virgin forests.

Currently, primary or old-growth forest (more than 200 years old) is only a small part of the total forest area. Primary forest cover has been greatly reduced in most industrial countries and is rapidly decreasing in developing ones. Old-growth forest is about 1 per cent of the total forest area in Western Europe, about 2 per cent in Scandinavia, about 1 per cent in China, about 15 per cent in the United States, about 25 per cent in New Zealand, and about 52 per cent in Canada (Dudley, 1992).

In developing regions, the average annual decline in forest area between 1980 and 1990 was 0.43 per cent, but the loss of natural forest was 0.8 per cent per annum (FAO, 1995a). The histories of the Mediterranean region (a negative example) and North America (a positive example) illustrate the different patterns of forest use that countries could expect, depending on the approach they follow.

Increasing pressure as a result of production, consumption, and population growth will generally lead to a loss of ecosystem quality. For example, forests are losing vitality due to acid rain in parts of Europe, Asia, and North America (NAPAP, 1991). The combined loss of area (quantity) and of ecosystem quality leads to considerable declines in the distribution or population numbers of many plant and animal species.

Projected Pressures on Natural Habitats

Projections were made for the changes in total quantity and geographic distribution of non-domesticated areas. These areas have been broken down into six groups—one group for areas covered by ice plus five vegetation categories: all forest, including tropical woodland and regrowth forest; grassland/savannah, which includes steppe and shrubland but excludes extensively used grassland; extensively used grassland, including all (marginal) land used for grazing; tundra and wooded tundra; and hot desert. [Note that marginal land used for grazing has been defined and included here as "non-domesticated" but has also been included as agricultural land in the previous section ("Use of Land").]

The percentages of non-domesticated land for each region for 1990, 2015, and 2050 are summa-

rized in Table 4.6. Figure 4.16 then shows the extent for each of the six non-domesticated land categories from 1970 to 2050, as well as for domesticated land; both for the world and for each region. (For 1970–80, these figures differ from those in Figure 4.15, because two different data sources have been used.) Figure 4.17 shows the geographical distribution of domesticated and non-domesticated areas in 1990, 2015, and 2050.

Quantification of combined pressures on the remaining non-domesticated areas allows projections of the future risks for global and regional biodiversity. The four pressures used in this analysis are population density, consumption and produc-

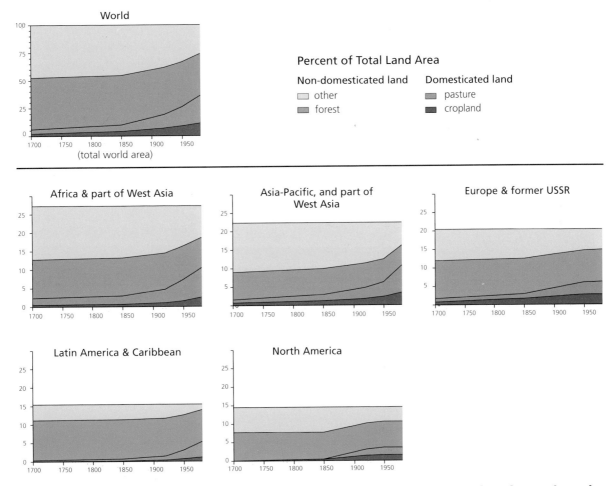

Figure 4.15. Habitat loss due to conversion of land from non-domesticated to domesticated areas, 1700–1980.

Source: Derived from Richards (1990) and FAO (1992), as described in detail in Klein Goldewijk and Battjes (1995).
Notes: Regional graphs show the percent of total world land area; while the world graph shows the total world area. Also note that the time scale for these graphs differs from previous regional and world diagrams. For this graph only, data for West Asia were included in Africa and in Asia and the Pacific.

Table 4.6

Non-Domesticated Land as a Percentage of Total Regional Land Area, 1990–2050

Region	1990	2015	2050
Africa	70	55	45
Asia & Pacific	60	50	55
Europe & former USSR	75	75	70
Latin America & Caribbean	70	65	60
North America	80	80	80
West Asia	90	75	70
World	70	65	60

Source: RIVM/UNEP (1997).
Note: Totals are rounded to 5 per cent intervals.

tion rates (gross national product per square kilometer per year), forest clearance for timber, and climate change.

The individual pressures were determined and given a preliminary grading from 0 to 10 for each non-domesticated area grid cell. A class of 0 meant no pressure, whereas class 10 meant extremely high pressure and subsequent high chances of extremely poor biodiversity compared with the original state. The total pressure was calculated by aggregating the four pressures per grid cell, which could theoretically result in a cumulative pressure class of 40 (though this value was never reached). The smaller the remaining non-domesticated area and the higher the total pressures on it, the greater the risk of poor biodiversity quality. A similar pressure-based

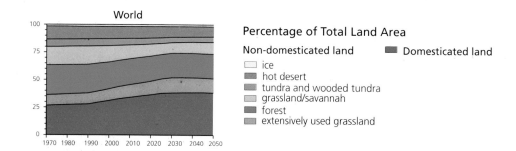

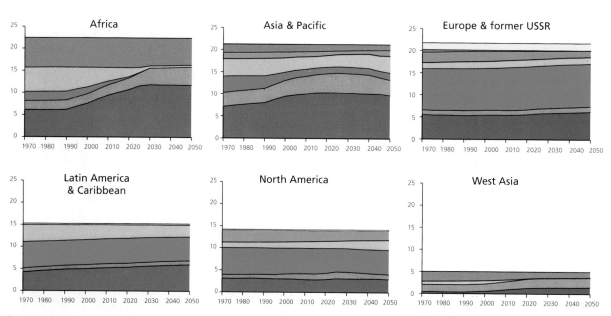

Figure 4.16. Recent and projected extent of domesticated and non-domesticated land, 1970–2050.

Source: RIVM/UNEP (1997).

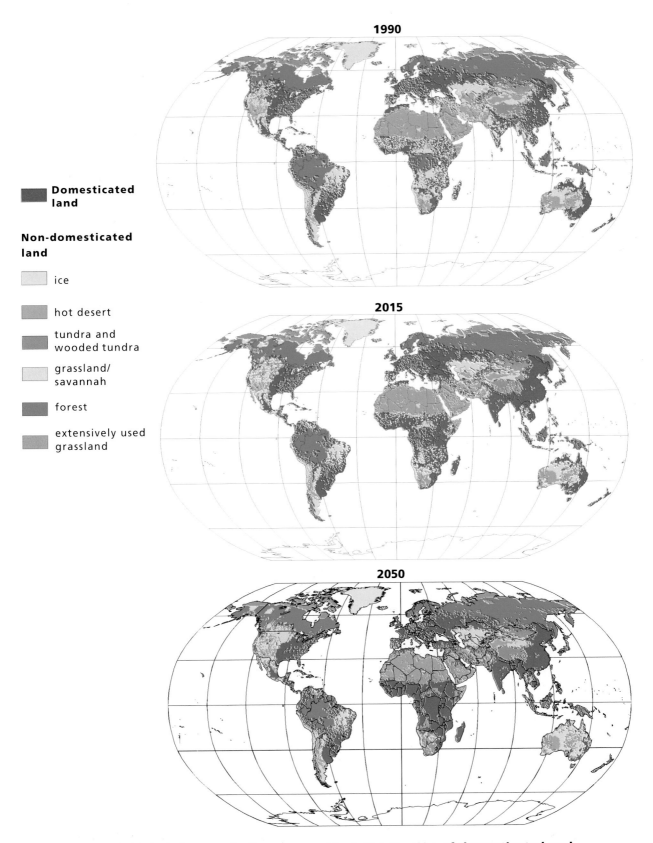

**Domesticated
land**

**Non-domesticated
land**

ice

hot desert

tundra and
wooded tundra

grassland/
savannah

forest

extensively used
grassland

1990

2015

2050

**Figure 4.17. Projected changes in the geographical distribution of domesticated and
non-domesticated land, 1990–2050.**

Source: RIVM/UNEP (1997).

approach has also been applied by Hannah *et al.* (1994) and Bryant *et al.* (1995) for, respectively, the current situation of natural habitats and coastal ecosystems.

Figure 4.18 shows the share of non-domesticated land globally that is under pressure in 1990, 2015, and 2050, based on the aggregated pressures of population density, consumption and production rate, forest clearance, and climate change.

Regional Summary

Africa's current natural habitat is projected to be at risk in terms of both quantity and quality. A large portion of the non-domesticated area, especially forests and grassland/savannah, are projected to be converted to agricultural land, implying a decrease in non-domesticated area from the current 70 per cent to about 55 per cent in 2015 and 45 per cent in 2050. Grassland/savannah (mainly non-domesticated open rangeland) would largely be converted to permanent pasture (which is domesticated area). Forests would to a great extent disappear. The remaining non-domesticated area would be largely arid and semi-arid land.

Pressure on Africa's remaining non-domesticated area will on average nearly double in intensity. Climate change is the dominant one of the four considered pressures. The area used for extensive grazing will also double, putting extra pressure on the remaining non-domesticated area.

The current natural habitat in West Asia is projected to be at risk, both in terms of quantity and quality. The non-domesticated area is expected to decrease from the current 90 per cent to about 75 per cent in 2015 and then to 70 per cent in 2050. Grassland/savannah (so far, mainly non-domesticated open rangeland) will be converted largely to permanent pasture (domesticated area). The remaining non-domesticated area will be to a great extent arid and semi-arid land.

Pressure on the remaining non-domesticated area in West Asia will on average double in intensity. Population density and, to a lesser extent, climate change are the dominant pressures. Moreover, the area used for extensive grazing will increase by one third (from about 30 per cent to 38 per cent in 2015 and 40 per cent in 2050), adding to the pressure on the non-domesticated area.

Natural habitat in Asia and the Pacific region is projected to be at risk, since the non-domesticated area is expected to decrease from the current 60 per cent to around 50 per cent in 2015, although it would then increase slightly to 55 per cent in 2050, mainly due to expansion and subsequent regression of arable land. By 2015, the forest area would be reduced from the current 12 per cent to about 7 per cent of the total area, which is one fifth of the 35 per cent forested land in 1700 (Richards, 1990). (The figure for 1700 is differently defined and not entirely comparable with those used for present and future forested area.) The remaining non-domesticated area will be less suitable for human settlement and agriculture because it is largely in mountainous areas or arid or semi-arid zones.

In many Asian countries, the area of agricultural land is currently fairly stable. Continuing economic and population growth would lead to higher demands for food that would be met primarily by intensification of agriculture, as well as by increasing imports and further land conversions. Better results in terms of intensification or increased imports would lead to lower conversions of land.

Pressure on the remaining non-domesticated area in Asia and the Pacific will increase by 50 per cent on average. Climate change and, to a lesser extent, population density are the dominant pressures. The extensive grassland area, used for grazing, will increase 25 per cent, pressuring the remaining non-domesticated area further.

In Europe and the former USSR, natural habitat is projected to be at risk, especially due to climate change. The non-domesticated area is expected to be fairly stable until 2015, and then to decrease slightly from the current 75 per cent to around 70 per cent in 2050, mainly due to an increase in food exports from Europe. The non-domesticated area is to a large extent situated in the boreal and subpolar areas in the former USSR and the Nordic countries. Pressure on the non-domesticated area will on average almost double in intensity. Climate change is the dominant pressure.

Figure 4.18. Percentage of non-domesticated land area projected to be under different degrees of pressure from human population and associated activities.

Source: RIVM/UNEP (1997).

Notes: Non-domesticated land under pressure is expressed as a percentage of total regional area. Pressure is calculated for areas that are non-domesticated during the whole period 1990–2050.

Pressure categories—The following linear functions were used:

i)   Population density: 0 to 100 persons per square kilometre.

The maximum pressure values for population density are derived from Hannah *et al.* (1994). Harrison (1992) and Terborch (1989) mentioned similar levels.

ii) Consumption and production rate: US$0 to US$6,000,000 gross national product (GNP) per square kilometre per year.

The GNP per square kilometre value is an approximation of the production and consumption rate and the related use of, and pressure on, non-domesticated areas such as emissions, extraction, physical disturbances, and fragmentation. The maximum GNP per square kilometre is similar to values found in highly populated and highly industrialized countries such as Germany and the Netherlands.

iii) Forest clearance for timber: not logged since 100 to 0 years ago.

The maximum pressure value for forest clearance for timber is set at 0 years ago, assuming total ecosystem destruction; the minimum value at 100 years, assuming no pressure and total regeneration of the forest ecosystem. Generally a longer period for forest regeneration is assumed. For example, "old growth forest" is generally defined as more than 200 years (Dudley, 1992).

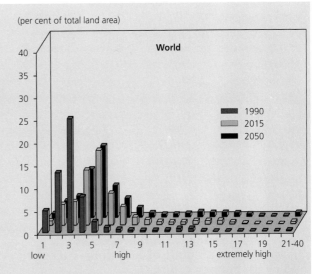

(per cent of total land area)

iv) Climate change: a change in mean temperature of 0 degrees to 2.0 degrees Celsius within a 20-year period. For example, an increase in mean temperature of 0.2 degrees Celsius in 20 years results in a pressure rating of 1, while an increase of 2.0 degrees Celsius in 20 years results in a pressure rating of 10).

This rate is based on the still rudimentary understanding of the vulnerability of ecosystems to historical temperature changes. The maximum value of 2.0 degrees Celsius over two decades is high in comparison with the maximum temperature increase of 2.0 degrees Celsius, which is suggested as the "absolute limit beyond which the risks of grave damage to ecosystems, and of non-linear responses, are expected to increase rapidly" (Jäger, 1987 and 1990).

Current natural habitat in Latin America and the Caribbean is at relatively moderate risk in comparison with Asia and Africa because of the comparatively low population pressure and the projected increase in agricultural production through intensification. The non-domesticated area is projected to decrease from 70 per cent to some 65 per cent in 2015 and to 60 per cent in 2050. This decrease is mainly at the expense of forest and grassland/savannah.

Pressure on the remaining non-domesticated area in this region is expected to double in intensity, although the current pressure is relatively low. Climate change and, to a lesser extent, population density are the dominant pressures. Climate change will particularly affect the temperate zones.

North America's natural habitat is at risk, according to this study, due to climate change and the associated spatial shift in land use. The non-domesticated area fluctuates only a few percentage points around 80 per cent from 1990 to 2050. Nevertheless, it is expected to shift considerably

from the east to the midlands due to climate change. The forested areas in the east are expected to be converted into arable land, while the arable land in the north-west will be reconverted into extensively used grassland. In 2050, the greater part of the non-domesticated area could be situated in the mountainous West, the dry midlands, and the boreal and subpolar North. Following a pattern comparable to Europe and the former USSR, pressure on the remaining non-domesticated area will on average double in intensity, largely due to climate change.

Global Summary

Overall, the world's natural habitat is projected to be at serious risk. Non-domesticated area is projected to drop from its current 70 per cent to about 65 per cent in 2015 and then to 60 per cent in 2050, mainly due to the increased need for land to grow food. Although this change may seem small, many individual species-rich ecosystems in the tropical and

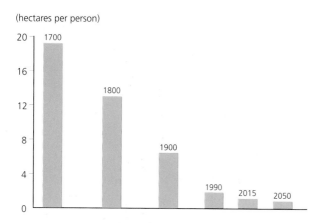

(hectares per person)

Figure 4.19. Historical and projected changes in the amount of non-domesticated land available per capita.

Source: RIVM/UNEP (1997).

subtropical zones are at serious risk, particularly from conversion to agricultural land. In the 20 countries with highest species diversity (WCMC, 1994), about 25 per cent of the current non-domesticated area will be converted until 2050. A great deal of the remaining non-domesticated area would be situated in mountainous, boreal/subpolar, arid, and semi-arid zones, which are generally less suitable for human settlement. The amount of non-domesticated area per person is expected to decline from the current 1.8 hectares to 1.1 hectares in 2015 and to 0.8 hectares in 2050. (See Figure 4.19.)

Pressure on the remaining non-domesticated area world-wide will on average roughly double in intensity. Of the four pressures considered here, this is largely due to climate change, particularly in the northern temperate and boreal zones, and to a lesser extent due to population growth, particularly in the tropics and subtropics. Moreover, the area used for extensive grazing will increase by almost one third (from about 10 per cent to 12 per cent in 2015 and 13 per cent in 2050), intensifying the pressure on the remaining grassland and savannah area.

The world's centres of origin of the main crop plants are not limited to one specific region. They are important from an agricultural point of view: through the process of domestication, wild plants have become sources of new crop species, and they are an invaluable source of genes needed to improve

the world's crops. Therefore, preliminary calculations have been made about future pressures on these centres of origin, based on the map published in *Global Biodiversity* (WCMC, 1992). It is expected that, compared with about 45 per cent of the total area of these centres being domesticated in 1990, some 60 per cent will be domesticated in 2015 and 65 per cent in 2050. Further, the pressure due to climate change would increase by two thirds.

Protecting Natural Habitats

The analysis in this section underlines the important impact on biodiversity of economic and population growth, with the associated need for the conversion of non-domesticated land to agricultural land in order to satisfy food demands, and of projected climate change. Remaining natural habitats can only be protected effectively if appropriate measures are taken to allow increased agricultural production by means other than the conversion of natural lands.

Although area protection, for instance, in nature reserves, appears to be a prerequisite for conserving nature and its diversity, climate change will be a serious threat if these areas are isolated and fragmented. It is estimated that climate change would alter the vegetation in 44 per cent of the world's current conservation areas (Alcamo *et al.*, 1995). The natural vegetation in these areas might be unable to adapt to these changed climate conditions (Alcamo *et al.*, 1995). Migration is a common response of many species to climate change, and hence connections (such as vegetation corridors and bridges) between natural areas are needed to reduce biodiversity losses. The design of Regional Ecological Corridors of interconnected natural areas (that is, linking remaining natural areas) might be an efficient response to this problem (as is being done in the Middle America Biological Corridor GEF project, currently in its preparatory phase).

An integrated, cross-sectoral approach to dealing with the impact of increasing food demands and climate change on biodiversity appears to be essential. Linking the assessment work conducted by the different secretariats responsible for international conventions is a first step in this direction.

HUMAN HEALTH

This section presents the results of a specific study on the relative importance of environment-related determinants of health and looks at how the state of global health might develop. The results presented here are based on a preliminary version of the health submodel of TARGETS (Niessen *et al.*, 1996). This model is being developed to analyse issues related to sustainable development at a global level (Rotmans and de Vries, forthcoming).

The analysis looks at relative changes in disability-adjusted life expectancies (DALEs) due to environmental pressures and other health-related factors. DALEs are a measure of years lived adjusted for for each year lived in incomplete health (assessing complete health as 100 per cent).

The information considered in this study has a direct or indirect bearing on human health and welfare (such as literacy rate, educational status, gross national product, and poverty issues including malnourishment and access to safe water). Since the model used for this study cannot differentiate data for the six regions addressed in the rest of this chapter, three countries were selected to illustrate the characteristics of regions at different stages of the health transition: India (see Hutter *et al.*, 1996), Mexico, and the Netherlands.

Past and Present Trends

Over the last four decades, there has been an enormous and continuing improvement in human health world-wide, although regional situations still vary. The main determinants of human health can be grouped as follows:

- medical care (van der Velden *et al.*, 1995; World Bank, 1993b);

- water sanitation, storage, supply, and sewage systems (Cairncross and Feachem, 1983; Pollitzer, 1959; World Bank, 1993a);

- education, insight, and rational behavior (McKeown, 1976; World Bank, 1993b);

- economic situation and income status; and

- environmental factors (such as water quality and chemical pollution).

In industrial regions, health improvements occurred at a constant pace over the last 200 years, and often determinants came in sequential order, facilitating the study of their relative influence. Medicine, for instance, did not contribute to the enormous health improvements in north-western Europe in the nineteenth century, when life expectancy increased about 20 years, but it did play a role in the gain of another 20 years during the twentieth century (through vaccination programmes and the use of antibiotics, for instance).

In currently developing regions, a multitude of health determinants have an influence at the same time. There are important negative impacts of environmental factors, as well as more positive impacts, of which economic situation and family income, education and insight, and behavioural changes appear to be dominant influences. One example is the large improvement in the health of children under age five in these regions (which cannot only be ascribed to medicine and health engineering).

Thus, major improvements in health have been achieved over recent decades in terms of both decreases in overall morbidity and mortality and more specific parameters such as the incidence of infectious diseases or perinatal and infant mortality (WHO, 1993; World Bank, 1993b). Life expectancy has increased nearly everywhere, and this has led to increases in population, despite declining birth rates in many countries (UN, 1994). In some countries, however, this fertility transition is slow or stagnating.

At the moment, children under age five account for more than 25 per cent of global mortalities. (See Figure 4.20.) These occur almost exclusively in developing countries, where 85 per cent of mortality (10.6 million deaths) in children under age 5 is caused by communicable diseases—nearly half of them diarrhoeal diseases. (See Figure 4.21.) Nevertheless, mortality in children under age 5 attributable to communicable diseases in developing countries is declining; if this trend continues, it will lead to significant decreases in global mortality.

Projected Trends

It is projected that the demographic and health transitions already observed for industrial countries can also occur elsewhere if conditions are favourable.

As noted in the section on use of land and food production, it is projected that food supply is likely to be adequate at a global level. An adequate food supply will have a positive effect on the health of the global population. Local famines and malnutrition caused by climate disturbances, poor socio-economic conditions, and inequity within and among nations remain a threat, however.

Despite the projected global availability of adequate water, water scarcity is projected to occur in several regions (Gleick, 1996; Hoekstra and Vis, forthcoming; UN/SEI, forthcoming). Even without considering the problems associated with obtaining adequate water of suitable quality, such local water scarcity problems constitute an even more serious risk for health than food shortages do, partly because it is more difficult and expensive to trade water among regions than it is to trade agricultural products.

Given the crucial importance of water for health and the projected increase in domestic water demand, a special study addressed the "water satisfaction rate." This is the ratio of the per catchment water supply (the result of calculating the monthly surface runoff and ground-water recharge from monthly precipitation and potential evaporation data) to the total demand in the catchment area (domestic, industrial, and agricultural demand).

The rate was calculated for all major (1,165) river basins except those with very low population densities (Klepper et al., 1995; Klepper, forthcoming). Thus, the analysis applies to 53 per cent of the global land area, where 95 per cent of the total population lives. Flows of upstream subbasins to downstream basins and the distribution of supply and demand within a subbasin were taken into consideration. Calculations for each drainage basin were based on monthly averages for the years reported, with the calculations for 2015 and 2050 assuming years with average climate characteristics.

The study results for 1990 show that about 27 per cent of the world population, living in about 12 per cent of the total land area, had (directly or indirectly) severe to moderately severe problems with getting sufficient fresh water; 44 per cent of the world population, living in about 18 per cent of the total land area, had moderate to little water quantity problems. Twenty-four per cent of the world population, living in 22 per cent of the total area, had no water quantity problems. The remaining 5 per cent of the world population, living in the 47 per cent land area with very low population density, has not been included in the study. (See Figure 4.22.) The areas most affected were West Asia and parts of India, Africa, and the United States.

The projected changes in global water demand assuming conventional development (Table 4.1) are as follows: water withdrawal in 2050 compared with 1990 is 2.12 times greater for domestic use; for industrial use, it is 2.37 times greater; and for agricultural use, it is 1.06 times greater. For 2015, preliminary results show that the areas with severe to moderately severe water quantity problems increase slightly (14 per cent). However, areas without water quantity problems decrease significantly (from 22 per cent to 18 per cent), and areas classified as having moderate to few water quantity problems increase (from 18 per cent to 21 per cent). (See Figure 4.22.)

For the period 2015 to 2050, this trend continues. Areas with severe to moderate water quantity problems show a slight increase (from 14 per cent to 16 per cent), areas without water quantity problems continue to decrease (from 18 per cent to 15 per cent), and areas classified as having moderate water quantity problems more or less stabilize (from 21 per cent to 22 per cent). (See Figure 4.22.)

Translating these percentages into absolute numbers of people produces the following: the number of people who will face severe water quantity problems by 2050 will almost double from 1.5 billion in 1990 to 2.1 billion in 2015 to 2.8 billion in 2050; the number of people who will face moderate to almost no water quantity problems will also double (an increase from 2.4 billion in 1990 to 3.4 billion people in 2015 to 4.7 billion in 2050); and the number of people with no water quantity problems will increase less (from 1.3 billion in 1990 to 1.7 billion in 2015 to 2.2 billion in 2050). (See Figure 4.23.)

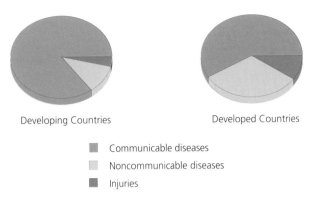

Developing Countries   Developed Countries

■ Communicable diseases
■ Noncommunicable diseases
■ Injuries

Figure 4.21. Causes of death among children under age 5 in developing countries and developed countries, 1990.

Source: World Bank (1993b).
Note: Developed countries include the former socialist economies of Europe and the established market economies.

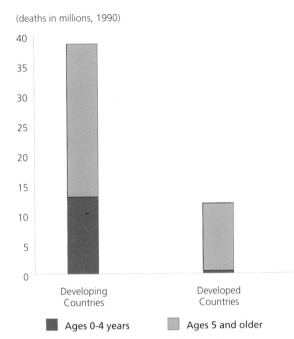

(deaths in millions, 1990)

Developing Countries   Developed Countries

■ Ages 0-4 years   ■ Ages 5 and older

Figure 4.20. Numbers of deaths by age group in developing and developed countries, 1990.

Source: World Bank (1993b).
Note: Developed countries include the former socialist economies of Europe and the established market economies.

Under the assumptions analysed here, the availability of sufficient fresh water will have to be a continuous topic of concern and will affect a growing number of people. The improvements in efficiency that are assumed in the projections do not diminish the overall pressures on fresh-water resources.

For additional studies on the current fresh-water resources situation and the concerns for the future, the reader is referred to the draft *Global Freshwater Assessment* prepared by United Nations agencies and the Stockholm Environment Institute for the fifth session of the Commission on Sustainable Development.

Health and Population Projections

Taking into consideration various assumptions about health determinants, a world population of about 10 billion people by 2050 is projected in this study. However, if investments in health and social development are lower than assumed, this will have a negative impact on health and other factors that influence demographic trends, and more rapid population growth would therefore occur.

Up to 2015, the increase in health and life expectancy may be hampered at local levels by shortages of food and water. But for the world as a whole, the factors enhancing improvements in health will probably outweigh the negative influences. (See Figure 4.24.)

Fertility rates are projected to decline further world-wide. Life expectancy is projected to reach a global average of just over 70 years by 2050, compared with 75 years or more today in industrial countries. The lower global average is due mainly to the persistence of poverty and the remaining large differences in income levels.

Figure 4.25 shows that a global transition to a healthier society will be possible. But many developing countries will lag behind the global average. The results also indicate a likely global decrease in importance over the next decades of health effects related to food and water supplies and to vector-borne diseases, although again with some regional variations. In addition, new diseases associated with environmental change might emerge. Also note that, for instance, chemical pollution effects have not been considered in this study.

The results of the study presented here suggest that improvements in health may well lead to lower population growth than derived from many other long-term (2050 and beyond) projections. Such a

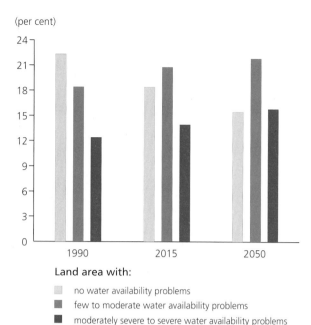

(per cent)

Land area with:

- no water availability problems
- few to moderate water availability problems
- moderately severe to severe water availability problems

Figure 4.22. Availability of fresh water, assuming conventional development: land area by availability of fresh water as a percentage of the total world land area.

Source: RIVM/UNEP (1997); Klepper *et al.* (forthcoming).
Note: The remaining 47 per cent of the world land area concerns catchment areas with extremely low population density where the analysis is not applicable.

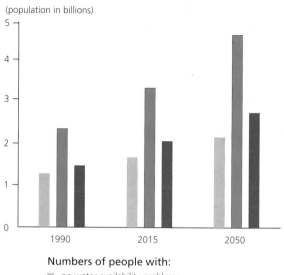

(population in billions)

Numbers of people with:

- no water availability problems
- few to moderate water availability problems
- moderately severe to severe water availability problems

Figure 4.23. Availability of fresh water, assuming conventional development: number of people by availability of fresh water.

Sources: RIVM/UNEP (1997); Klepper *et al.* (forthcoming).
Notes: In 1990, 0.3 billion people lived in extremely low population-density areas that are not included in this study. In 2015, this figure is projected to increase to 0.5 billion; in 2050, to 0.7 billion.

slower projected population growth depends heavily on a mixture of optimistic assumptions about investing part of the increasing wealth in health, the environment (including the agricultural and water sectors), and social services (including education).

Slow Progress Towards Health for All

Despite this optimistic projection, increasing pollution, urbanization, population growth, poverty, and lack of education will continue to hamper progress towards achieving the United Nations goal of "health for all."

Indeed, the results are conditional in that the assumed economic growth will have to be achieved and accompanied by investments in social and environmental development similar to those that have taken place in industrial countries. Without such investments, a move towards a more equitable, healthy, and sustainable future for all sectors of society will be difficult to realize. If the projected growth in population and income is not matched by investments in

social development and environmental protection, environmental degradation may pose a serious threat to human health—either directly (through floods, for example) or indirectly—by reducing the availability of enough healthy food and clean water.

The projected global increase in life expectancy will contribute to a shift towards a population structure with a higher proportion of adults and older people. This raises a new issue. Larger, healthier, and thus, on average, older populations will place additional demands on economies. Hence it is worth considering, especially over the long term, the possible influence of human health on the environment—the reverse of the concern in many developing countries today.

The impact of a number of environmental changes on health were not (and could not be) taken into account at this stage. These include land degradation, the destruction of the centres of origin of the world's staple foods, climate change (which might, for instance, enlarge the areas where vectors of diseases such as malaria and dengue can thrive), acidification, and the hazards of persistent organic pollutants.

ALTERNATIVE POLICIES

The modelling results presented so far in this chapter cover only one set of assumptions about possible future developments, namely that current policies and trends will more or less continue to dominate or shape the future world. What if very different policies were applied, or if consumer attitudes were to change drastically? This would probably result in very different development paths in the future. Models are excellent tools to explore the answers to such questions. As an illustration, the possible impacts of energy and food policy measures aimed at a more efficient use of resources were explored through a semi-quantitative modelling exercise for the globe as a whole. A baseline and two sets of policy strategies were considered:

- current trends, policies, strategies, and attitudes will continue: a business-as-usual baseline situation (Baseline) that resembles the one applied in the earlier sections of this chapter (Alcamo *et al.*, 1996b);

- the best available technology (BAT) is used all over the world both in energy and agriculture: this represents drastic technological changes, especially in developing regions (Variant 1); and

- in addition to the use of BAT, the use of renewable energy sources (especially biofuels) is increased, and a fundamental change is made in human diet (such as lower meat consumption): this represents drastic changes in consumer attitudes (Variant 2).

The results of policy Variants 1 and 2 were compared with the Baseline situation, in particular by exploring the possible effects on resource use (such as energy consumption and agricultural land use) and on environmental degradation (such as carbon dioxide emissions, temperature changes, and change in forest area).

For all three exercises, the same medium population growth and medium economic growth are assumed, and the implementation of the policy

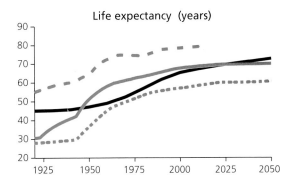

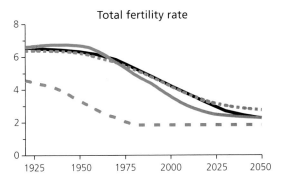

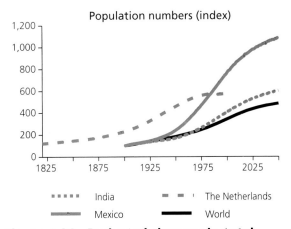

Figure 4.24. Projected changes in total fertility, life expectancy, and resulting changes in population for India, Mexico, the Netherlands, and the world.

Source: Niessen *et al.* (1996).
Note: The following were used to calculate the population index: Netherlands, 1800 = 100; India, Mexico, and the world, 1900 = 100. Total fertility is defined as the average number of children a woman would have if she experienced current fertility during her lifetime.

strategies is assumed to be extremely fast. Any barriers to their implementation have not been taken into account; in reality, therefore, such extremely fast changes would not be really feasible.

For the technological change strategy (Variant 1), it was assumed that within a short transition period of 20 years, developing regions will reach the

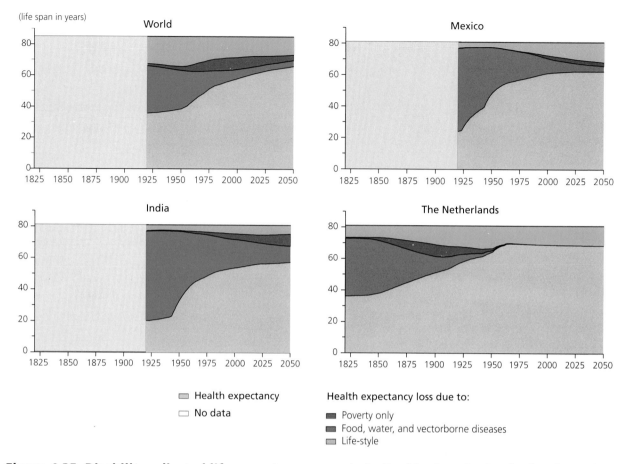

(life span in years)

Figure 4.25. Disability-adjusted life expectancy years in India, Mexico, the Netherlands, and the world.

Source: Niessen *et al.* (1996) (preliminary results).
Note: Disability-adjusted life expectancy (DALE) years are a measure of years lived minus an estimated percentage for each year lived in incomplete health. The number of years lost have been arranged according to the main pressures of food, water, and vectorborne diseases; poverty only; and life-style. Please note that DALE years are different from DALYs (disability-adjusted life years) as used by the World Bank (Murray and Lopez, 1996).

level of efficiency of industrial regions, both for energy and for agriculture. Within the energy sector, for instance, it is assumed that all new industries and power stations all over the world will be as efficient as the best available technology. And, for the agricultural sector, it is assumed that animal husbandry and management practices in developing regions converge to the higher productivity level of the industrial world.

For the fundamental change strategy, Variant 2, it was assumed that in addition to the technological changes assumed in Variant 1, the market share in 2050 of renewables and biofuels within the energy sector will be higher than in the Baseline situation and the best available technology strategy (55 per cent for Variant 2 and 20 per cent for the Baseline

and Variant 1) and that the consumption of meat is much lower compared to the Baseline situation (50 per cent less meat consumed, again realized within a very short 20-year period).

The results of this modelling exercise are shown in Figure 4.26. The strong increase in energy consumption observed in the Baseline situation and also reported on in the preceding sections of this chapter will be drastically reduced.

Carbon dioxide emissions from energy and industry show an even stronger reduction: in 2050 the carbon dioxide emissions of the best available technology variant are about 35 per cent of the Baseline situation; for the fundamental change variant, they are about 20 per cent of the Baseline situation. These results are in line with the potential

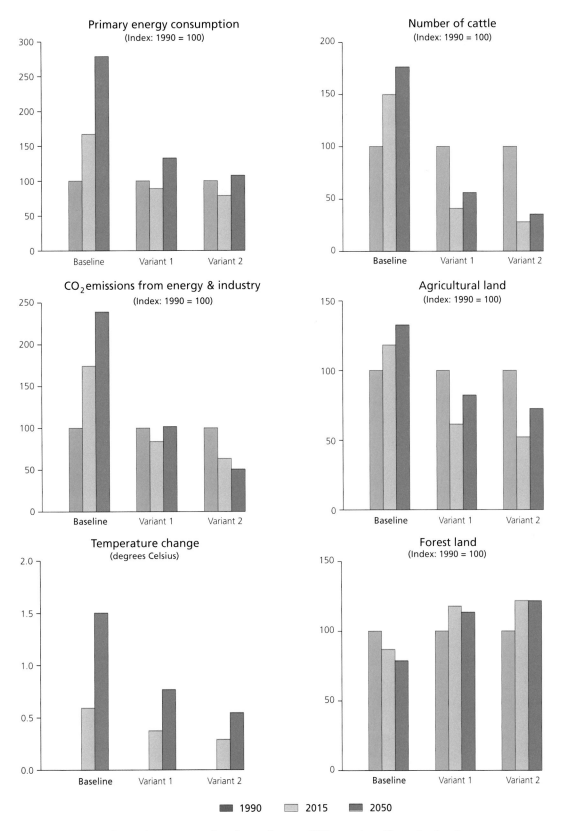

Figure 4.26. Potential environmental gains of two different policy strategies.

Source: RIVM/UNEP (1997).
Note: The figure shows a fast global convergence of energy efficiency and agricultural productivity, and fundamental changes towards renewable energy supply and low meat diets relative to the Baseline situation.

for emission reductions in scenarios of, for instance, the World Energy Council and Shell, as summarized in a recent UNEP/STAP/GEF report on Renewable Energy Technologies (UNEP/STAP/GEF, 1996).

The effect of the different policies on temperature change is based on the combined effects of changes in energy use and projected changes in land use. Taking these assumptions into account, the temperature increase in 2050 would be about one third as large for Variant 2 as for the Baseline situation, and about half as large for the BAT exercise (Variant 1).

The number of cattle is projected to decrease strongly because of the introduction of agro-technological improvements raising animal productivity: by 2050 the number of cattle would be about half of the number in 1990, and some 25–30 per cent of the number projected in the Baseline exercise in 2050. For the fundamental change exercise, the 2050 number becomes about one third of the current 1990 number and about 20 per cent of the Baseline numbers.

By 2050, the Baseline exercise projects a 25-percent increase in land used for agriculture compared with 1990 figures; with the BAT exercise, the increase turns into a decrease of about 20 per cent compared with 1990, while for the third exercise, the decrease would become 25 per cent.

Figure 4.26 shows that the policy measures ensuring best available technology would result in an increase in forest area of about 20 per cent instead of the 25-per-cent decrease projected under the Baseline situation; under the fundamental change exercise, the increase in forest area would be 25 per cent.

The results of the analysis indicate that technology transfer and fundamental changes in attitude can lead to significant changes in future energy consumption, land use, and carbon dioxide emissions, and subsequently in positive changes in land cover and temperature change in the future. The influence of the fundamental change policies on these projected changes is clearest for carbon dioxide emissions. Although this analysis is only a first attempt to explore the possible impacts of certain policy strategies, it clearly demonstrates that reduction of human pressures on the global environment is indeed technically possible if the willingness to change is there.

REFERENCES

Alcamo, J., and G.J.J. Kreileman. 1996. The global climate system: near term action for long term protection. National Institute of Public Health and the Environment (RIVM). Bilthoven, the Netherlands. Background Report (No. 481508001) prepared for the Workshop on Quantified Emission Limitation Reduction Objectives at the Third Meeting of the Ad Hoc Group on the Berlin Mandate Framework Convention on Climate Change. Geneva. 28 February.

Alcamo, J., G.J.J. Kreileman, M.S. Krol, and G. Zuidema. 1994. Modeling the global society–biosphere–climate system: Part I Model description and testing. In: J. Alcamo (ed.). *Image 2.0: Integrated modeling of global climate change.* 14–35. Kluwer Academic Publishers. Dordrecht, the Netherlands.

Alcamo, J., M. Krol, and R. Leemans. 1995. Stabilising greenhouse gases: global and regional consequences. In: S. Zwerver, R. van Rompaey, Kok, and M. Berk (eds.). *Climate Change Research: Evaluation and Policy Implications, Studies in Environmental Science 65A.* Elsevier. Amsterdam.

Alcamo, J., M. Krol, and M. Posch. 1996a. An integrated analysis of sulphur emissions, acid deposition, and climate change. In: *Water, Air, and Soil Pollution* 85: 1539–1550.

Alcamo, J., G.J.J. Kreileman, J.C. Bollen, G.J. van den Born, R. Gerlagh, M. Krol, A.M.C. Toot, and H.J.M. de Vries. 1996b. Baseline Scenarios of Global Environmental Change. In: *Global Environmental Change.*

Amann, M., M. Baldi, C. Heyes, Z. Klimont, and W. Schoepp. 1995. Integrated Assessment of emission control scenarios, including the impact of tropospheric ozone. In: *Water, Air, and Soil Pollution* 85:2595.

Arndt, R.L., and G.R. Carmichael. 1995. Long-range transport and deposition of sulphur in Asia. In: *Water, Air, and Soil Pollution* 85:2283.

Barrett, K., and Ø. Seland. 1995. European Transboundary Acidifying Air Pollution, EMEP Co-operative programme for monitoring and evaluation of the long-range transmission of air pollutants in Europe. Report 1/95. Meteorological Synthesising Centre-West, Norwegian Meteorological Institute. Oslo, Norway.

Barrett, M. 1992. Environmental impacts of fossil fuels. In: K.V. Ramani, P. Hills, and G. George (eds.). Burning questions: environmental limits to energy growth in Asia–Pacific countries during the 1990s. APDC/WWF. Asian and Pacific Development Centre. Kuala Lumpur, Malaysia.

Berry, B.J.L. 1990. Urbanization. In: B.L. Turner II, W.C. Clark, R.W. Kates, J.F. Richards, J.T. Mathews, and W.B. Meyer (eds.). The earth as transformed by human action. 103–120. Cambridge University Press. New York.

Brown, L. 1996. *The State of the World 1996, A Worldwatch Institute Report on Progress Toward a Sustainable Society*. W.W. Norton & Company. New York.

Bryant, D., E. Rodenburg, T. Cox, and D. Nielsen. 1995. Coastlines at Risk: An Index of Potential Development-Related Threats to Coastal Ecosystems. World Resources Institute. Washington.

Cairncross, S., and R.G. Feachem. 1983. Environmental health engineering in the Tropics. J. Wiley & Sons. Chichester, U.K.

Darmstadter, J. 1971. Energy in the world economy. Johns Hopkins University Press. Baltimore.

Downing, R.J., J.-P. Hettelingh, and P.A.M. de Smet. 1993. Calculation and mapping of critical loads in Europe: Status Report 1993. Report to the UN/ECE Convention on Long-Range Transboundary Air Pollution. RIVM. Bilthoven, the Netherlands.

Dudley, N. 1992. Forests in trouble: A review of the status of temperate forests worldwide. World Wildlife Fund. Gland, Switzerland.

ECE/EB.AIR/40. 1994. Protocol to the 1979 Convention on Long-range Transboundary Air Pollution on Further Reduction of Sulphur Emissions. United Nations Economic Commission for Europe. Geneva.

EEA. 1995. *Environment in the European Union*. Report for the Review of the Fifth Environmental Action Programme. European Environment Agency (EEA). Copenhagen.

FAO. 1992. *AGROSTAT-PC*. Food and Agricultural Organisation of the United Nations (FAO). Rome.

FAO. 1995a. *Forest Resources Assessment 1990, Global Synthesis*. FAO Forestry Paper 124. FAO. Rome.

FAO. 1995b. World Agriculture: Towards 2010, an FAO study. N. Alexandratos (ed.). Food and Agricultural Organization of the United Nations and J. Wiley & Sons. Chichester, U.K.

FAO. 1995c. *FAOSTAT-PC*. FAO. Rome.

Foell, W., M. Amann, G. Carmichael, M. Chadwick, J.-P. Hettelingh, L. Hordijk, and D. Zhao. 1995a.

RAINS-Asia, An Assessment of Air Pollution in Asia. The World Bank. Washington.

Foell, W., C. Green, M. Amann, S. Bhattacharya, G. Carmichael, M. Chadwick, J.-P. Hettelingh, L. Hordijk, J. Shah, R. Shresta, D. Streets, and D. Zhao. 1995b. Energy use, emissions, and air pollution reduction strategies in Asia. In: *Water, Air, and Soil Pollution* 85:2277.

Gallopin, G., A. Hammond, P. Raskin, and R. Swart. Forthcoming. Branch Points: Global Scenarios and Human Choice. Draft Perspectives Paper of the Global Scenario Group.

Gardner, G., and J.A. Peterson. 1996. *Shrinking Fields: Cropland Loss in a World of Eight Billion*. Worldwatch Paper 131. Worldwatch Institute. July. Washington.

Gleick, P.H. 1996. Human Population and Water: Meeting Basic Needs in the 21st Century. Prepared for the Conference on Population, Natural Resources, and the Environment. March 13–14. Washington.

Gschwandtner, G., K. Gschwandtner, and K. Eldridge. 1985. *Historic Emissions of Sulfur and Nitrogen Oxides in the United States from 1900 to 1980*. Vol. I. *Results*. Report No. EPA-600/7-85-009a. Air and Energy Engineering Research Laboratory, U.S. Environmental Protection Agency. Washington.

Hameed, S., and J. Dignon. 1988. Changes in the geographical distributions of global emissions of NO_x and SO_x from fossil-fuel combustion between 1966 and 1980. *Atmospheric Environment* 22(3): 441–449.

Hannah, L., J.L. Carr, and A. Lankerani. 1994. Human disturbance and natural habitat: a biome level analysis of a global data set. *Human Disturbance of Biomes*. Conservation International. Washington.

Harrison, P. 1992. *The Third Revolution. Environment, Population and a Sustainable World*. In association with the World Wildlife Fund. I.B. Taurus & Co. Ltd. London.

Hettelingh, J.-P., R.J. Downing, and P.A.M. de Smet. 1991. *Mapping Critical Loads for Europe*. Report to the UN/ECE Convention on Long-Range Transboundary Air Pollution. RIVM. Bilthoven, the Netherlands.

Hettelingh, J.-P., M. Posch, P.A.M. de Smet, and R.J. Downing. 1995a. The use of critical loads in emission reduction agreements in Europe. In: *Water, Air, and Soil Pollution* 85:2381.

Hettelingh, J.-P., H. Sverdrup, and D. Zhao. 1995b. Deriving critical loads for Asia. In: *Water, Air, and Soil Pollution* 85:2565.

Hettelingh, J.-P., M.J. Chadwick, H. Sverdrup, and D. Zhao. 1995c. Assessment of environmental effects of acidic deposition in Asia. In: Foell *et al.* 1995b. Energy use, emissions, and air pollution reduction strategies in Asia. In: *Water, Air, and Soil Pollution* 85:VI/1-VI/64.

Hoekstra, A., and J.W.D. Vis. Forthcoming. *The Aqua Zambezi Model.*

Houghton, J.T., L.G. Meira Filho, T. Bruce *et al.* 1995. Climate Change. 1994. Radiative forcing of climate change and an evaluation of the IPCC 1992 emission scenarios. Cambridge University Press. Cambridge.

Hutter, I., F.J. Willekens, H.B.M. Hilderink, and L.W. Niessen. 1996. *Fertility Change in India.* Global Dynamics and Sustainable Development Programme. GLOBO Report Series No. 13. Population Research Centre, University of Groningen, Groningen; and RIVM. Bilthoven, the Netherlands.

Idema, R.J., J.N.M. Dekker, and A. Stijkel. 1993. Een verkenning van de biovoorraden: vis en hout als voorbeelden. University of Utrecht. Report No. 93010 (in Dutch). Utrecht.

IFPRI. 1995. A 2020 Vision for Food, Agriculture, and the Environment: the Vision, Challenge, and Recommended Action. International Food Policy Research Institute (IFPRI). Washington.

IPCC. 1990. *Climate Change: The IPCC Scientific Assessment.* Cambridge University Press. Cambridge.

IPCC. 1992. *Climate Change 1992: The Supplementary Report to the IPCC Scientific Assessment.* Cambridge University Press. Cambridge.

IPCC. 1996. *Climate Change 1995. Impacts, Adaptations and Mitigation of Climate Change: Scientific-Technical Analysis: Contribution of Working Group II to the Second Assessment Report of the Intergovernmental Panel on Climate Change.* R.T. Watson, M.C. Zinyowera, and R.H. Moss (eds.). Cambridge University Press. Cambridge.

ISRIC/UNEP. 1991. World Map of the Status of Human-Induced Soil Degradation. Global Assessment of Soil Degradation. UNEP. Nairobi.

Jäger, J. 1987. Developing Policies for Responding to Climate Change. WMO/UNEP.

Jäger, J. 1990. Responding to Climate Change: Tools for Policy Development. Stockholm Environment Institute. Stockholm.

Kaales, M.W. 1996. Pilot study on the feasibility of some biodiversity indicators at the regional and global level, applied to Europe. RIVM. Bilthoven, the Netherlands.

Keeling, C.D. 1973. Industrial production of carbon dioxide from fossil fuels and limestone. *Tellus* 25(2):174–198.

Keeling, C.D. 1994. Global historical CO_2 emissions. In: T.A. Boden, D.P. Kaiser, R.J. Sepanski, and F.W. Stoss (eds.). ORNL/CDIAC-65, ESD Pub. No. 4195. *Trends '93: A Compendium of Data on Global Change.* Carbon Dioxide Information Analysis Center (CDIAC). Oak Ridge National Laboratory. Oak Ridge, Tennessee.

Khemani, L.T., G.A. Momin, P.S. Prakasa Rao, P.D. Safai, G. Singh, and R.K. Kapoor. 1989. Spread of acid rain over India. *Atmospheric Environment* 23/4:757–762.

Klein Goldewijk, C.G.M., and J.J. Battjes. 1995. The IMAGE 2 Hundred Year (1890–1990) Data Base of the Global Environment (HYDE). Report No. 481507008. RIVM. Bilthoven, the Netherlands.

Klepper, O., C.R. Meinardi, and A.H.W. Beusen. 1995. A quantitative assessment of water resources in Africa: Identifying constraints for sustainability development in the coming decades. Discussion paper, a contribution to the UNEP Water Study. CWM memo 001/95.

Klepper, O. Forthcoming. A quantitative assessment of water resources at catchment level: Identifying constraints for sustainable development in the coming decades. RIVM. Bilthoven, the Ntherlands.

Kuylenstierna, J.C.I., H. Cambridge, S. Cinderby, and M.J. Chadwick. 1995. Terrestrial ecosystem sensitivity to acidic deposition in developing countries. *Water, Air, and Soil Pollution* 85:23–81.

Leach, G. 1995. Global Land and Food in the 21st Century. Trends and Issues for Sustainability. Stockholm Environment Institute (SEI). Polestar Series Report No. 5. Stockholm.

Maddison, A. 1991. *Dynamic Forces in Capitalist Development—A Long-run Comparative View.* Oxford University Press. Oxford.

Marland, G., and R.M. Rotty. 1984. Carbon dioxide emissions from fossil fuel: A procedure for estimation and results for 1950–1982. *Tellus* 36B(4):232–261.

Marland, G., R.J. Andres, and T.A. Boden. 1994. Global, regional and national CO_2 emissions. In: T.A. Boden, D.P. Kaiser, R.J. Sepanski, and F.W. Stoss (eds.). ORNL/CDIAC-65, ESD Pub. No. 4195. *Trends '93: A Compendium of Data on Global Change.* Carbon Dioxide Information Analysis Center (CDIAC). pp. 505–584. Oak Ridge National Laboratory. Oak Ridge, Tennessee.

Mather, A.S. 1990. *Global Forest Resources.* Belhaven Press/Pinter Publishers. London.

Matsuoka, Y. 1992. Future projections of global anthropogenic sulfur emissions and their environmental effects. In: *Environmental Systems Research.* 22:359–368. (The Asia Pacific Integrated Model-AIM).

McKeown, T.F. 1976. The role of medicine—dream, mirage or nemesis. Nuffield Provincial Hospitals Trust. London.

Morita, T., M. Kainuma, H. Harasawa, K. Kai, and Y. Matsuoka. 1995. Long-term global scenarios based on the AIM model. AIM Interim Paper IP-95-03. Global Warming Response Team, Global Environment Group, National Institute for Environmental Studies. Tsukuba, Japan.

Murray, C-J. L. and A.D. Lopez. 1996. The global burden of disease. Vols. I & II. Cambridge University Press. Cambridge.

Mylona, S. 1993. Trends of sulphur dioxide emissions, air concentrations and depositions of sulphur in Europe since 1880. EMEP/MSW-W Report 2/93. Meteorological Synthesizing Centre–West. The Norwegian Meteorological Institute. Blindern.

Nakicenovic, N., and J.M. Jefferson. 1995. Global energy perspectives to 2050 and beyond. IIASA Working Paper WP-95-127. Laxenburg, Austria.

NAPAP. 1991. Integrated assessment report. Office of the Director. National Acid Precipitation Assessment Programme (NAPAP). Washington.

Niessen, L., and H.B.M. Hilderink. 1996. Roads to health, modelling the health transition: the TARGETS generic population and health modelling framework, Version 1.0. RIVM. Bilthoven, the Netherlands.

Overrein, L.N., H.M. Seip, and A. Tollan. 1981. Acid precipitation—effects on forest and fish. Research Report 19|80. Final report of the SNSF-project 1972–1980. Norges landbruksvitenkapelige forkningsråd. Oslo.

Placet, M., and D.G. Streets. 1987. The causes and effects of acidic deposition. Vol. II: Emissions and Control. National Acid Precipitation Assessment Program (NAPAP).

Pollitzer, R. 1959. Cholera. World Health Organization (WHO). Geneva.

Posch, M., J.-P. Hettelingh, J. Alcamo, and M. Krol. 1996. Integrated scenarios of acidification and climate change in Europe and Asia. In: *Global Environmental Change.*

Posch, M., P.A.M. de Smet, and J.-P. Hettelingh. 1995. Calculation and mapping of critical thresholds in Europe: Status report 1995. Report to the UN/ECE Convention on Long-Range

Transboundary Air Pollution. RIVM. Bilthoven, the Netherlands.

Raskin, P., M. Chadwick, T. Jackson, and G. Leach. 1996. The Sustainability Transition: Beyond Conventional Development. Polestar Series Report No. 1. Stockholm Environment Institute. Stockholm.

Raskin, P., and R. Margolis. 1995. Global Energy in the 21st Century: Patterns, Projections and Problems. Stockholm Environment Institute (SEI). Stockholm.

Richards, J.F. 1990. Land Transformations. In: *The Earth as Transformed by Human Action, Global and Regional Changes in the Biosphere Over the Past 300 Years.* B.L. Turner II *et al.* (eds.). Cambridge University Press. London.

RIVM/UNEP. 1997. The Future of the Global Environment: A Model-based Analysis Supporting UNEP's First Global Environment Outlook.

Rodhe, H., E. Cowling, I.E. Galbally, J.N. Galloway, and R. Herrera. 1988. Acidification and regional air pollution in the tropics. In: Rodhe, H., and R. Herrera (eds.). *Acidification in tropical countries.* Scope 36. J. Wiley & Sons. New York.

Rotmans, J., and H.J.M. de Vries (eds.). Forthcoming. *Perspectives on Global Futures.* Cambridge University Press. Cambridge.

Shindo, J., A.K. Bregt, and T. Hakamata. 1994. Application and evaluation of critical load methods for acid deposition in Gunma, Japan. Report of the National Institute of Agro-Environmental Sciences. Tsukuba, Japan.

Smaling, E.M.A. 1993. An agro-ecological framework for integrated nutrient management, with special reference to Kenya. Thesis. Wageningen Agricultural University. Wageningen, the Netherlands.

Terborch, J. 1989. *Where Have All the Birds Gone?* Princeton University Press. Princeton, New Jersey.

Tolba, M.K., O. El-Kholy, E. El-Hinnawi, M.W. Holdgate, D.F. McMichael, and R.E. Munn (eds.). 1992. The world environment 1972–1992. UNEP. Chapman & Hall. London.

UN. 1992. *UN World Population Prospects 1950–2025 (The 1992 Revision).* United Nations (UN). Washington.

UN. 1994. Report of the International Conference on Population and Development. Cairo. 1–13 September. (Document 94-40486 (E) 091194).

UN/SEI. Forthcoming. Global Freshwater Assessment. United Nations/Stockholm Environment Institute.

UNEP. 1991. Status of desertification and implementation of the UN plan of action to combat desertification. Governing Council, Report to the Executive Director, 3rd Special Session, 1992. Nairobi.

UNEP. 1995. *Global Biodiversity Assessment.* Cambridge University Press. Cambridge.

UNEP/STAP/GEF. 1996. The Outlook for Renewable Energy Technologies, Public Policy Issues, and Roles for the Global Environment Facility. Executive Summary of Two Reports on Renewable Energy for Developing Countries. UNEP Scientific and Technical Advisory Panel, Global Environment Facility. Nairobi.

UNEP/UNDPCSD. 1996. Report of the First Integrated Environment Assessment/GEO Core Data Working Group Meeting. 22–23 January. New York.

Velden, K. van der, J.K.S. Van Ginneken, J.P. Velema *et al.* 1995. Health matters: Public Health in North-South Perspective. Royal Tropical Institute. Amsterdam.

Ven, T.L. van der. 1996. Pilot studies on the feasibility of some biodiversity indicators at regional and global level, applied to the Netherlands. (in Dutch). RIVM. Bilthoven, the Netherlands.

WCMC. 1992. Global Biodiversity: Status of the Earth's Living Resources. World Conservation Monitoring Centre (WCMC). Chapman & Hall. London.

WCMC. 1994. Biodiversity Data Resource Book. World Conservation Press, Cambridge.

WHO. 1993. Implementation of the Global Strategy for Health for All by the Year 2000. Eighth Report on the World Health Situation. World Health Organization (WHO). Geneva.

Wigley, T.M.L., R. Richels, and J.A. Edmonds. 1996. Economic and environmental choices in the stabilization of atmospheric CO_2 concentrations. *Nature* 379:240–243.

Woerden, J.W. van, J. Diederiks, and K. Klein Goldewijk. 1995. Data Management in Support of Integrated Environment Assessment and Modelling at RIVM. RIVM Report No. 402001006. RIVM. Bilthoven, the Netherlands.

World Bank. 1993a. *World Tables.* Washington.

World Bank. 1993b. *Investing in health: World Development Report.* Oxford University Press and the World Bank. Washington.

World Bank. 1995a. Monitoring Environmental Progress. Washington.

World Bank. 1995b. *World Health Statistics Quarterly.* Vol. 48 (3/4).

WRI. 1986. *World Resources, 1986.* World Resources Institute. Basic Books. New York.

WRI/UNEP/UNDP. 1992. *World Resources, 1992–1993.* World Resources Institute (WRI), United Nations Environment Programme (UNEP), and United Nations Development Programme (UNDP). Oxford University Press. New York.

WRI/UNEP/UNDP. 1994. *World Resources, 1994–1995.* WRI/UNEP/UNDP. Oxford University Press. New York.

Zhao, D., and H.M. Seip. 1991. Assessing effects of acid deposition in south-western China using the MAGIC model. In: *Water, Air, and Soil Pollution* 60:83–97.

APPENDIX 1. ACRONYMS

AAFC	Agriculture and Agri-food Canada
ACSAD	Arab Centre for Studies of Arid Zones and Drylands
ADB	African Development Bank
ADB	Asian Development Bank
AEC	African Economic Community
AEPS	Arctic Environmental Protection Strategy
AGROSTAT-PC	FAO agricultural statistics database for PC
AIM	Asia Pacific Integrated Model
AMAP	Arctic Monitoring and Assessment Programme
AMCEN	African Ministerial Conference on the Environment
ARET	Accelerated Reduction/Elimination of Toxics
ASEAN	Association of South-East Asian Nations
ASOC	Antarctic and Southern Ocean Coalition
ASOEN	ASEAN Senior Officials on the Environment
ATCM	Antarctic Treaty Consultative Meeting
BAT	best available technology
CAFF	Conservation of Arctic Flora and Fauna
CAMRE	Council of Arab Ministers Responsible for the Environment
CCAD	Central American Commission on Environment and Development
CCAMLR	Convention on the Conservation of Antarctic Marine Living Resources
CCIAD	Central American Inter-Parliamentary Commission on the Environment
CDIAC	Carbon Dioxide Information Analysis Center of ORNL
CD-ROM	compact disk—read only memory
CEC	Commission for Environmental Cooperation under NAAEC
CEC	Commission of the European Communities
CEDARE	Centre for Environment and Development in the Arab Region and Europe
CEE	Central and Eastern Europe
CEPA	Canadian Environmental Protection Act
CFC	chlorofluorocarbon
CGIAR	Consultative Group on International Agricultural Research
CIAT	Centro Internacional de Agricultura Tropical
CIESIN	Consortium for International Earth Science Information Network
CILSS	Inter-state Committee for Drought Control
CIS	Commonwealth of Independent States
CO$_2$	carbon dioxide
COMEMIS	Coastal and Marine Environment Management Information System
CONABIO	National Commission for the Knowledge and Use of Biodiversity, Mexico
CSD	Commission on Sustainable Development of the UN
CSI	Common Sense Initiative
DALE	disability-adjusted life expectancy
DEIA	Division of Environment Information and Assessment of UNEP
DESIPA	Department of Economic and Social Information and Policy Analysis of the UN
DPCSD	Department for Policy Coordination and Sustainable Development of the UN
EAS	East-Asian Seas (Action Plan)
EATR	Environment Assessment Technical Report of DEIA
EC	Environment Canada
EC	European Commission
ECA	Economic Commission for Africa of the UN
ECE	Economic Commission for Europe of the UN
EDP	eco-domestic product
eds.	editors
EEA	European Environment Agency
EFTA	European Free Trade Association
EGAT	Electricity Generating Authority, Thailand
EIA	environmental impact assessment
EIS	environmental information systems
ELMS	Environment and Land Management Sector of SADC
EMEP	European Monitoring and Evaluation Programme
ENRIN	Environmental and Natural Resources Information Network of UNEP
EOP	Executive Office of the President, USA
EPA	Environmental Protection Agency, USA
EPPR	Emergency Prevention, Preparedness and Response
EQA	Environmental Quality Act, Malaysia
ESCAP	Economic and Social Commission for Asia and the Pacific of the UN
ESCWA et al.	Economic and Social Commission for West Asia of the UN and others
EU	European Union
FADINAP	Fertilizer Advisory, Development and Information Network for Asia and the Pacific
FALCAP	Framework for Action on Land Conservation in Asia and the Pacific
FAO	Food and Agriculture Organization of the UN
FDI	foreign direct investment
FSU	former Soviet Union
GAP	Ganga River Action Plan
GATT	General Agreement on Tariffs and Trade
GCC	Gulf Cooperation Council
GEF	Global Environment Facility
GEMS	Global Environmental Monitoring System
GEO	Global Environment Outlook
GESAMP	Joint Group of Experts on the Scientific Aspects of Marine Environment Protection
GDP	gross domestic product
GDR	German Democratic Republic
GNP	gross national product
GLASOD	Global Assessment of Soil Degradation
GLWQA	Great Lakes Water Quality Agreements
GRID	Global Resource Information Database
GTZ	German development assistance agency
Habitat	United Nations Centre for Human Settlements (UNCHS)
IAATO	International Association of Antarctic Tour Operators
IAEA	International Atomic Energy Authority
ICIMOD	International Centre for Integrated Mountain Development
ICRISAT	International Crops Research Institute for the Semi-Arid Tropics
ICSU	International Council of Scientific Unions
ICZM	Integrated Coastal Zone Management
IE	Industry and Environment Office of UNEP
IEEA	Integrated System of Environmental and Economic Accounting
IFPRI	International Food Policy Research Institute
IIASA	International Institute of Applied Systems Analysis
IIUE	International Institute for the Urban Environment
IFFWS	Inland Fisheries, Forestry and Wildlife Sectors of SADC
IGAD	Inter-Governmental Authority on Development
ILO	International Labour Organization
IMAGE	Integrated Model to Assess the Greenhouse Effects
IMERCSA	The India Musokotwane Environment Resource Centre for Southern Africa
INBIO	National Biodiversity Institute, Costa Rica

INC	Intergovernmental Negotiating Committee	RIOD	Reseau International des Organisations Non-governmental sur Desertification
INFOTERRA	a global environmental information exchange and referral system	RIVM	National Institute of Public Health and the Environment, the Netherlands
IOC	Intergovernmental Oceanographic Commission of UNESCO	ROPME	Regional Organisation for the Protection of the Marine Environment
IPCC	Inter-Governmental Panel on Climate Change	ROWA	Regional Office for West Asia of UNEP
IRPTC	International Register of Potentially Toxic Chemicals	SACEP	South Asia Cooperative Environment Programme
ISRIC	International Soil Reference and Information Centre	SADC	Southern African Development Community
IUCN	World Conservation Union	SAF	Society of American Foresters
IWC	International Whaling Commission	SARDC	Southern African Research and Documentation Centre
JCEDAR	Joint Committee on Environment and Development in the Arab Region	SCAR	Scientific Committee on Antarctic Research
LAC	Latin America and the Caribbean	SEI	Stockholm Environment Institute
LRTAP	Long-range Transboundary Air Pollution	SNA	system of national accounts
MARPOL	International Convention for the Prevention of Pollution from Ships	SO_2	sulphur dioxide
		SOE	State of the Environment
MERCOSUR	Mercado Comun del Sur	SPREP	South Pacific Regional Environment Programme
MoE	Ministry of Environment	SSO	Sahara and Sahel Observatory
MOSTE	Ministry of Science, Technology and Environment of Malaysia	TARGETS	Tool to Assess Regional and Global Environmental and Health Targets for Sustainability, developed by RIVM
MRC	Mekong River Commission	TERI	Tata Energy Research Institute
NAAEC	North American Agreement on Environmental Cooperation	TRI	Toxic Release Inventory program
		UAE	United Arab Emirates
NAFTA	North American Free Trade Agreements	UN	United Nations
NAPAP	National Acid Precipitation Assessment Programme	UNCED	United Nations Conference on Environment and Development
NBS	National Biological Service, USA		
NCP	Northern Contaminants Programme, Canada	UNCHS	United Nations Centre for Human Settlements (Habitat)
NEAPs	National Environment Action Plans		
NEPA	National Environment Protection Agency, China	UNDP	United Nations Development Programme
NESDA	Network for Environment and Sustainable Development for Africa	UNDP/UNSO	United Nations Sahelian Office of UNDP
		UNEP	United Nations Environment Programme
NGO	non-governmental organisation	UNESCO	United Nations Educational, Scientific and Cultural Organisation
NIP	National Implementation Plan		
NO_x	nitrogen oxides	UNFCCC	UN Framework Convention on Climate Change
NOWPAP	North-West Pacific Action Plan	UNFPA	United Nations Population Fund
NRAP	National River Action Plan	UNICEF	United Nations Children's Fund
NRC	National Register of Chemicals	UNITAR	United Nations Institute for Training and Research
NSF	National Science Foundation	UNSD	United Nations Statistical Division
NSTC	National Science and Technology Council, USA	US	United States
OAU	Organization of African Unity	USA	United States of America
OECD	Organisation for Economic Co-operation and Development	USAID	US Agency for International Development
		USDA	United States Department of Agriculture
OEPP	Office of Environmental Policy and Planning, Thailand	US-EPA	United States Environmental Protection Agency
ORNL	Oak Ridge National Laboratory	USSR	Union of Soviet Socialist Republics
OSPAR	Convention for the Protection of the Marine Environment of the North-East Atlantic	UV	ultraviolet
		UV-B	ultraviolet-B radiation
OTA	Office of Technology Assessment	VOC	volatile organic compounds
PAHO	Pan American Health Organisation	WB	World Bank
PAME	Protection of the Arctic Marine Environment	WCMC	World Conservation Monitoring Centre
PC	personal computer	WHO	World Health Organization
PCSD	President's Council on Sustainable Development, USA	WMO	World Meteorological Organization
PM	particulate matter	WRI	World Resources Institute
PM-10	fine particulate matter	WTO	World Trade Organization
RAINS	Regional Acidification Information and Simulation, a model developed and maintained by IIASA	WWF	World Wide Fund for Nature
RAPA	Regional Office for Asia and the Pacific of FAO		
REC	Regional Environmental Center for Central and Eastern Europe		

APPENDIX 2. COLLABORATING CENTRES

Arabian Gulf University (AGU)

Mohamed Nabil Alaa El-Din
Vice Dean and Director of Biotechnology Programme
Arabian Gulf University
P.O. Box 26671
Manama, Bahrain

Bangladesh Centre for Advanced Studies (BCAS)

Atiq Rahman
Director
Bangladesh Centre for Advanced Studies
620 Road 10A (New) Dhammondi
GPO Box 3971
Dhaka 1205, Bangladesh

Central European University (CEU)

Ruben Mnatsakanian
Professor
Department of Environmental Sciences and Policy
Central European University
Nador u.9
Budapest H-1051, Hungary

Centre for Environment and Development for the Arab Region & Europe (CEDARE)

Kamal A. Sabet
Chief Technical Advisor
Centre for Environment and Development for the Arab Region &
    Europe
21/23 Giza Street
Nile Tower Building, 13th Floor
P.O. Box 52 Orman
Giza, Egypt

Centro Internacional de Agricultura Tropical (CIAT)

Gilberto C. Gallopin
Leader
Land Management Unit
Centro Internacional de Agricultura Tropical
Apartado aereo 6713
Cali, Colombia

El Colegio de México

Boris Graizbord
Director, LEAD Programme
Centre for Demographic and Urban Development Studies
El Colegio de México
Camino al Ajusco No. 20
Colonia Pedregal de Santa Teresa
C.P. 10740 Mexico D.F. Delegación Tlalpan, México

International Institute for Sustainable Development (IISD)

Nola-Kate Seymoar
International Institute for Sustainable Development
161 Portage Avenue, East
6th Floor
Winnipeg, Manitoba, Canada R3B 0Y4

Moscow State University (MSU)

Genady N. Golubev
Professor
Faculty of Geography
Moscow State University
119899 Moscow, Russia

National Environment Protection Agency (NEPA)

Zhang Shigang
Division Director
Division of International Organisations
National Environmental Protection Agency
No 115 Xizhimen Nei Nanxiaojie
Beijing 100035, The People's Republic of China

National Institute for Environmental Studies (NIES)

Shuzo Nishioka
National Institute for Environmental Studies
Environment Agency of Japan
16-2 Onogawa
Tsukuba
Ibaraki 305, Japan

National Institute of Public Health and the Environment (RIVM)

Fred Langeweg
Director
Environmental Research Division
National Institute of Public Health and the Environment
Antonie van Leeuwenhoeklaan 9
P.O. Box 1
3720 BA Bilthoven, the Netherlands

Network for Environment and Sustainable Development (NESDA)

Clement Dorm-Adzobu
Coordinator
Network for Environment and Sustainable Development in Africa
BP 95 Guichet Annexe BAD
Abidjan, Côte d'Ivoire

Royal Scientific Society (RSS)

Ayman A. Al-Hassan
Director
Environmental Research Centre
Royal Scientific Society
P.O. Box 1438, Jubeiha 11941
Amman, Jordan

Southern African Research and Documentation Centre (SARDC)

Munyaradzi Chenje
Director
India Musokotwane Environment Resource Centre for Southern
Africa, (IMERCSA)
Southern African Research and Documentation Centre Unit
15 Downie Avenue
Belgravia
P.O. Box 5690
Harare, Zimbabwe

Stockholm Environment Institute (SEI)
Paul Raskin
Director
Stockholm Environment Institute, Boston Centre
Tellus Institute
11 Arlington Street
Boston, MA 02116-3411, USA

Tata Energy Research Institute (TERI)
Leena Srivastava
Dean, Policy Analysis
Tata Energy Research Institute
Darbari Seth Block
Habitat Place
Lodhi Road
New Delhi 110 003, India

Thailand Environment Institute (TEI)
Dhira Phantumvanit
President
Thailand Environment Institute (TEI)
210 Sukhumvit 64
Bangchak Refinery Building 4, 2nd floor
Prakanong
Bangkok 10260, Thailand

University of Chile
Osvaldo Sunkel
Coordinator
Sustainable Development Programme
Centre for the Analysis of Public Policy
University of Chile
Diagonal Paraguay 265, Torre 15
Santiago, Chile

World Resources Institute (WRI)
Allen Hammond
Director
Resource & Environmental Information Programme
World Resources Institute
1709 New York Avenue, N.W.
Washington, D.C. 20006, USA

Wuppertal Institute for Climate, Environment and Energy
F. Schmidt-Bleek
Vice President
Wuppertal Institute for Climate, Environment and Energy
Döppersberg 19
42103 Wuppertal, Germany

APPENDIX 3. INTERNATIONAL GEO CONSULTATIONS

REGIONAL GEO CONSULTATIONS

AFRICA

Nairobi, Kenya, 12–16 August 1996. Adel Farid Abdel-Kader, Centre for Environment and Development for the Arab Region and Europe, Egypt; Clement Dorm-Adzobu, Network for Environment and Sustainable Development in Africa, Côte d'Ivoire; Moise Akle, Organization of African Unity, Ethiopia; Munyaradzi Chenje, Environment Resource Centre for Southern Africa, Zimbabwe; Peter K. Chisara, Office of Environment Management, Tanzania; Berhe Debalkew, Inter-governmental Authority on Development, Djibouti; Feisal A.M. Esmael, Egyptian Environmental Affairs Agency, Egypt; Annette Hugo, Department of Environmental Affairs, South Africa; Attia Khalil, International Centre of Environmental Technologies, Tunisia; Celia Maria Ferreira Meneses, Ministry of Environment, Mozambique; Robert Mkwanda, Department of Natural Resources, Zimbabwe; Jobo Molapo, Southern African Development Community—Environment and Land Management Sector, Lesotho; Bore Motsamai, National Environment Secretariat, Lesotho; Robert Tiebilé N'daw, Mali; Boubacar Niane, Ministère de l'environnement et de la protection de la nature, Senegal; Perez M. Olindo, Kenya; Raj Hemansing Prayag, Ministry of Environment and Quality of Life, Mauritius; Winnie Mbala Rogers, Permanent Mission to UNEP, Kenya; Eugene H. Shannon, African Development Bank, Côte d'Ivoire; Vincent Isidore Tchabi, Ministère de l'environnement, Benin.

ASIA-PACIFIC

Association of South–East Asian Nations, Bangkok, Thailand, 21–22 August 1996. Harry Harsono Amir, Office of the State Minister of Environment, Indonesia; Patrick Tan Hock Chuan, Department of Environment, Malaysia; Nguyen Dinh Hai, Embassy of Viet Nam, Thailand; Ho Cheng Hoon, Ministry of Environment, Singapore; Ak Shambary Pg. Dato Hj. Mustapha, Ministry of Development, Brunei Darussalam; Carmelita M. Passe, Environment Management Bureau - DENR, Philippines; Suphavit Piamphongsant, Office of Environmental Policy and Planning, Thailand; Chidchanok Putprasert, Office of Environmental Policy and Planning, Thailand; Prapasit Siribhodi, Environmental Research and Training Center, Thailand; Monthip Sriratana Tabucanon, Department of Environmental Quality Promotion, Thailand; Chalermsak Wanichsombat, Department of Environmental Quality Promotion, Thailand.

Greater Mekong Subregion, Bangkok, Thailand, 30 July 1996. Anette Bjorlin, Mekong River Commission, Thailand; Chuon Chanrithy, Ministry of Environment, Cambodia; Liu Chunyu, National Environmental Protection Agency, China; Malee Hutacharoen, Environmental Research and Training Center, Thailand; Keobang-a Keola, Mekong River Commission, Thailand; Mok Mareth, Minister of Environment, Cambodia; Sein Mya, Mekong River Commission, Thailand; Phonechaleun Nonthaxay, Technology and Environment Policy Division, LAO PDR; Suvat Saguanwongse, Environmental Quality Promotion Department, Thailand; U Nyunt Maung Shein, Myanmar Embassy in Thailand, Myanmar; U Nyi Soe, Myanmar Embassy of Thailand, Myanmar; Monthip Sriratana Tabucanon, Environmental Research and Training Center, Thailand; Truong Manh Tien, Ministry of Science Technology and Environment, Vietnam; Chalermsak Vanitsombat, Department of Environmental Quality Promotion, Thailand; Xayavet Vixay, Department of Environment, LAO PDR; Wang Wenyi, Yunnan Provincial Environmental Protection Agency, China; Yang Weimin, Yunnan Institute of Environmental Science, China.

Southern Asia Cooperative Environment Programme, Kathmandu, Nepal, 23–24 July 1996. Poorna Bhadra Adiga, Ministry of Population and Environment, Nepal; R.S. Ahlawat, Ministry of Environment & Forests, India; Mahfuzul Haque, Ministry of Environment & Forests, Bangladesh; Pradyumna Kumar Kotta, SENRIC Project, Sri Lanka; V.K. Nanayakkara, Environment and Women's Affairs, Sri Lanka; Pramod Pradhan, International Centre for Integrated Mountain Development, Nepal; R. Rajamani, Ministry of Environment & Forests, India; Simad Saeed, Ministry of Planning Human Resources & Environment, Maldives; Hussain Shihab, South Asia Co-operative Environment Programme, Sri Lanka; Basanta Shrestha, International Centre for Integrated Mountain Development, Nepal; S.S. Tahir, Ministry of Environment, Pakistan; Nedup Thsering, National Environment Agency, Bhutan; Batu Krishna Uprety, Ministry of Population and Environment, Nepal.

South Pacific Regional Environment Programme, Tonga, 26 July 1996. Ian Abbil, National Planning Office, Vanuatu; Eric M. Anderson, Australia; Tebao. T. Awerika, Ministry of Foreign Affairs, Republic of Kiribati; S.O. Barnor, Division Commonwealth Secretariat, UK; Christine Douglas, Premier's Office, Niue; Ofiu Isamau, Ministry of Health, Tonga; Maika Kinahoi, Ministry of Health, Tuvalu; Lisia Muller, Central Planning Department, Tonga; M. Nelesone, Department of Foreign Affairs, Tonga; Robert Norombe, Environment & Conservation Department, Papua New Guinea; Komeri Onerio, Environment Impact Assessement, Western Samoa; Esther G. Pavihi, Department of Community Affairs, Niue; Teleke Peleti, Environment Unit, Tulavu; M. Puri, Services Division Commonwealth Secretariat, UK; Peter Raka, Ministry of Foreign Affairs, Papua New Guinea; Seluka Seluka, Environment Unit, Tuvalu; Deve G. K. Talagi, Building & Design Division, Niue; Bale Tamata, Institute of Applied Science, Fiji; Bernard Telei, Ministry of Forest, Energy and Conservation, Solomon Islands; Tua Tipi, Department of Health, Western Samoa; Viliami Tiseli, Ministry of Agriculture and Forestry, Tonga; Ioan Viji, Department of Forestry, Vanuatu; Robert Zutu, Honiara Municipal Authority, Solomon Islands.

EUROPE

Geneva, Switzerland, 22–23 July 1996. Dagmara Berbalk, Federal Ministry for the Environment, Nature Conservation and Nuclear Safety, Germany; Winston H. Bowman, Regional Environmental Center for Central & Eastern Europe, Hungary; Gani Deliu, Minister of Health and Environment, Albania; Stella Dolenec, State Directorate for Environment, Republic of Croatia; Gerard Fauveau, Permanent Mission of France to the United Nations; Juan Manuel Salas Fernández, Permanent Mission of Spain to the United Nations; Genady N. Golubev, Moscow State University, Russian Federation; Marek Haliniak, Ministry of Environmental Protection, Poland; Paul Hofseth, Ministry of Environment, Norway; Shamil Iliasov, Ministry of Environmental Protection, Kyrgyzstan; Catherine Khmaladze, Ministry of Environment, Republic of Georgia; Ionnis Kinnas, Permanent Mission of Greece to the United Nations; Sergey N. Kouarev, Ministry for Environmental Protection and Natural Resources,

Russian Federation; Fred Langeweg, National Institute of Public Health and the Environment, the Netherlands; Geoffrey Lean, Independent on Sunday—Newspaper, UK; Erich Lippert, Ministry of the Environment, Czech Republic; Herman Merckx, Permanent Mission of Belgium to the United Nations; Alla Metelitsa, Ministry for Natural Resources and Environment Protection, Belarus; Reuben Mnatsakanian, Central European University, Hungary; Sona Mrázová, Ministry of Environment, Slovakia; Csaba Nemes, Ministry of Environment and Regional Policy, Hungary; Teodor Ognean, Ministry of Forests and Environment Protection, Romania; Simon Papian, Ministry for Nature and Environment Protection, Armenia; Margareta Petrusevschi, Department for Environmental Protection, Republic of Moldova; Jaime Reynolds, Department of Environment, UK; Jurate Ruoliene, Environmental Protection Unit, Lithuania; Friedrich K. Schmidt-Bleek, Wuppertal Institute, Germany; Nailia G. Shadieva, State Committee for Nature Protection, Uzbekistan; Voldemars Spungis, Ministry of Environmental Protection and Regional Development, Latvia; David Stanners, European Environmental Agency, Denmark; Olof Svanberg, Swedish Environmental Protection Agency, Sweden; Sauli Tapani Rouhinen, Ministry of the Environment, Finland; Anita Velkavrh, Ministry of Environment and Physical Planning, Slovenia; Ulrika Winroth, Swedish Mission, Sweden; Olexander Zakrevsky, Ministry of Environmental Protection, Ukraine; Jolevski Zoran, Permanent Mission of the Former Yugoslav Republic of Macedonia to the United Nations.

LATIN AMERICA & THE CARRIBEAN

Mexico City, Mexico, 7, 9, 10 September 1996. Antonio Elizalde Hevia, Universidad Bolivariana, Chile; Exequiel Ezcurra, Universidad Nacional Autónoma de México, México; Gilberto Gallopín, Centro International de Agricultura Tropical, Colombia; Amalia García Thärn, Swedish International Development Cooperation Agency, México; Nícolo Gligo, Comisión Económica para América Latina y el Caribe, Chile; José Juan González Márquez, Academia Mexicana de Derecho Ambiental, México; Boris Graizbord, El Colegio de México, México; Ricardo Koolen, Argentina; Cuauhtémoc León Diez, El Colegio de México, México; Roberto Messias Franco, Instituto de Geo-Ciencias, Brazil; Jorge Morello, Universidad de Buenos Aires, Argentina; José Pedro de Oliveira Costa, Consejo Nacional de la Reserva de la Biósfera de la Floresta Atlántica, Brazil; Bernardo F. T. Rudorff, Instituto Nacional de Pesquisas Espaciais, Brazil; Ricardo Sánchez, Ministerio de Ciencia, Tecnología y Medio Ambiente, Cuba; Osvaldo Sunkel, Universidad de Chile, Chile; José Velarde Flores, Secretaría Nacional de Recursos Naturales y Medio Ambiente, Bolivia; Manuel Winograd, Centro International de Agricultura Tropical, Colombia.

WEST ASIA

Bahrain, 3–5 September 1996. Abdul Jabbar Abdul Abbas, Ministry of Health, Iraq; Jameel Abdulla Abbas, University of Bahrain, Bahrain; Adel Farid Abdel-Kader, Centre for Environment & Development in the Arab Region & Europe, Egypt; Mahmood Y. Abdulraheem, Regional Organization for the Programme of the Marine Environment, Kuwait; Mohamed Ajjour, The Palestinian National Authority, Palestinian Territories; Dhari Al Ajmi, Kuwait Institute for Scientific Research, Kuwait; Ibrahim A. Alam, Jeddah Municipality, Saudi Arabia; Khalid Ghanim Al Ali, Ministry of Municipal Affairs and Agriculture, Qatar; Ismail El-Bagouri, Arabian Gulf University, Bahrain; Nizar Al-Baharna, University of Bahrain, Bahrain; Elias Baydoun, American University of Beirut, Lebanon; Gert Jan van den Born, National Institute of Public Health and the Environment, the Netherlands; Abdulwahab M. J. Dakkak, Natural

Resources Directorate, Saudi Arabia; M. Nabil Alaa El-Din, Arabian Gulf University, Bahrain; Khalid Fakhro, Environmental Authority, Bahrain; Hussein Al Gunied, Environmental Protection Council, Republic of Yemen; Ahmed Hamza, Egyptian Environmental Affairs Agency, Egypt; Ayman Al-Hassan, Environmental Protection Committee, Jordan; Mohamed Ali Hassan, Environmental Authority, Bahrain; Mirza Khalat, Environmental Authority, Bahrain; Shaker Khamdan, Environmental Authority, Bahrain; M.Z. Ali Khan, World Health Organization, Switzerland; Basim Al-Khatib, Ministry of Municipal and Rural Affairs and the Environment, Jordan; H.H. Kouyoumjian, National Council for Scientific Research, Lebanon; Zahwa Al Kuwari, Environmental Authority, Bahrain; Khalid Abu Laif, Saudi Company for Environmental Works, Saudi Arabia; Ismail M. Al-Madany, Arabian Gulf University, Bahrain; A. Al-Mahmood, Environmental Authority, Bahrain; Essam H. Mahmoud, Arabian Gulf University, Bahrain; Fatima Al-Mallah, Council of Arab Ministers Responsible for the Environment, League of Arab States, Egypt; Lamia Mansour, United Nations Development Programme, Lebanon; Saeed A. Mohamed, University of Bahrain, Bahrain; Faysal Abdel-Gadir Mohammed, United Nations Development Programme, Bahrain; Abdel Hameed Munajjed, Minister of State for Environment, Syria; Sadiq Abdul Hussain Al-Muscati, Ministry of Regional Municipalities & Environment, Sultanate of Oman; Randa Nemer, Ministry of Environment, Lebanon; Ghazi Odat, General Corporation for the Environment Protection, Jordan; Nabil Rofail, Arab Centre for the Studies of Arid Zones & Dry Lands, Syria; A.T. Shanmugam, Gulf Area Oil Companies Mutual Aid Organization, Bahrain; Abdulrazak Tabeishat, Ministry of Municipal & Rural Affairs & the Environment, Jordan; Sufyan El-Tell, Jordan; Mohamed Ali Toure, Islamic Foundation for Science, Technology & Development, Saudi Arabia; Abdul-Elah Al-Wadaee, Environmental Authority, Bahrain.

OTHER INTERNATIONAL CONSULTATIONS

First International Expert Meeting on the Global Environment Outlook Process, Cali, Colombia, 27 February – 2 March 1995.
Chris Anastasi, University of York, UK; Jan Bakkes, National Institute of Public Health and the Environment, the Netherlands; Faye Duchin, New York University, USA; Norberto Fernandez, United Nations Environment Programme, México; Gilberto C. Gallopin, Centro Internacional de Agricultura Tropical, Cali; Genady Golubev, Moscow State University, Russia; Ian Lowe, Griffith University, Australia; Adolfo Mascarenhas,

Institute of Resource Assessment, Tanzania; Michael Norton-Griffiths, Centre for Social and Economic Research on the Global Environment, UK; Paul Raskin, Stockholm Environment Institute, USA; Jan Rotmans, National Institute of Public Health and the Environment, the Netherlands; Youba Sokona, Environmental Development Action in the Third World—Energy, Senegal; Rob Swart, National Institute of Public Health and the Environment, the Netherlands; Sufyan El-Tell, Jordan; Veerle Vandeweerd, United Nations Environment Programme, Nairobi; Manuel Winograd, Centro Internacional de Agricultura Tropical, Cali; Zhang Shigang, National Environmental Protection Agency, China.

Workshop on Information for Sustainable Development and Earthwatch, Geneva, Switzerland, 24 September 1996.
Christine Auclair, United Nations Centre for Human Settlements—Habitat, Kenya; Arnold Bonne, International Atomic Energy Agency, Austria; Jean Yves Bouchardy, Office of the United Nations High Commissioner for Refugees, Switzerland; James L. Breslin, World Meteorological Organization, Switzerland; Carlos Corvalan, World Health Organization, Switzerland; Arthur Dahl, UNEP, Switzerland; Lowell Flanders, Department for Policy Coordination and Sustainable Development, USA; Helmut Forstner, United Nations Industry and Development Office, Austria; Peter Hardi, International Institute for Sustainable Development, Canada; William J. Hartnett III, UN System-wide Earthwatch Coordination Office, Switzerland; Ulrich Hoffmann, United Nations Conference on Trade Development, Switzerland; Mohammad Aslam Khan, Economic and Social Commission for Asia and Pacific, Thailand; Monika Luxem, Department for Policy Coordination and Sustainable Development, USA; Walther Manshard, Institut für Kulturgeographie, Germany; Robert Missotten, United Nations Education, Scientific, and Cultural Organization, France; BedrichMoldan, Charles University Environmental Centre, Czech Republic; John D. Northcut, Information Systems Co-ordination Committee, Switzerland; Merle S. Opelz, International Atomic Energy Agency, Geneva Office, Switzerland; Christina von Schweinichen, Economic Commission for Europe, Switzerland; Mary Pat Williams Silveira, Department for Policy Coordination and Sustainable Development, USA; Pavel Skoda, Permanent Mission of the Czech Republic to the United Nations, Switzerland; Hiko Tamashiro, World Health Organization, Switzerland; Elizabeth Umlas, Office of the United Nations High Commissioner for Refugees, Switzerland; Guennady Vinogradov, Economic Commission for Europe, Switzerland; Fareed Yasseen, Convention on Climate Change, Germany.

Appendix 4. CONTRIBUTORS AND REVIEWERS

Jameel Abdulla Abbas, University of Bahrain, Bahrain

Anwar S. Abdu, Arabian Gulf University, Bahrain

Joseph Alcamo, National Institute of Public Health and the Environment, the Netherlands

Chris Anastasi, University of York, UK

Marina A. Arshinova, Moscow State University, Russia

Ismail Al-Bagouri, Arabian Gulf University, Bahrain

Jan Bakkes, National Institute of Public Health and the Environment, the Netherlands

R. D. Ballhorn, Department of Foreign Affairs and International Trade, Canada with additional inputs from Agriculture and Agri-Food Canada, Department of Fisheries and Oceans Environment Canada, Health Canada, Indian and Northern Affairs Canada, Natural Resources Canada.

Edward Bellinger, Central European University, Hungary

Dagmara Berbalk, Federal Ministry for the Environment, Nature Conservation and Nuclear Safety Division G II4, Germany

Marcel Berk, National Institute of Public Health and the Environment, the Netherlands

Leonard Berry, Florida Center for Environmental Studies, Florida Atlantic University, USA

Preety Bhandari, Tata Energy Research Institute, India

Pieter Bol, National Institute of Public Health and the Environment, the Netherlands

Gert-Jan van den Born, National Institute of Public Health and the Environment, the Netherlands

John Bosch, US Environmental Protection Agency, USA

Winston H. Bowman, The Regional Environmental Center for Central and Eastern Europe, Hungary

Bented ten Brink, National Institute of Public Health and the Environment, the Netherlands

Ernesto Brown, University of Chile, Chile

Jorge Cabrera, Central American Commission on Environment and Development, Guatemala

Ben W.K. Caiquo, Network for Environment and Sustainable Development, Côte d'Ivoire

Michael A. Cairns, US Environmental Protection Agency, USA

Deborah Chapman, Ireland

Peter K. Chisara, Office of Environment Management, Tanzania

Chen Qing, Public Health College of Beijing Medical University, China

Cheng Weixue, National Environmental Protection Agency, China

Munyaradzi Chenje, Environment Resource Centre for Southern Africa, Zimbabwe

Maxwell Chivasa, Environment Resource Centre for Southern Africa, Zimbabwe

Aaron Cosbey, International Institute for Sustainable Development, Canada

Berhe Debalkew, Inter-governmental Authority on Development, Djibouti

Tjeerd Deelstra, International Institute for Urban Environment, the Netherlands

M. Nabil Alaa El-Din, Arabian Gulf University, Bahrain

Clement Dorm-Adzobu, Network for Environment and Sustainable Development, Côte d'Ivoire

Feisal A.M. Esmael, Egyptian Environmental Affairs Agency, Egypt

Deborah Farmer, World Resources Institute, USA

Alexander S. Fetisov, Moscow State University, Russia

David Fig, Group for Environmental Monitoring, Zimbabwe

Gilberto Gallopin, Centro Internacional de Agricultura Tropical, Colombia

Abdul Bar Al-Ghain, The Meteorology & Environmental Protection Administration, Saudi Arabia

Genady Golubev, Moscow State University, Russia

Boris Graizbord, El Colegio de México, México

Guo Xiaomin, National Environmental Protection Agency, China

Nadine El-Hakim, Centre for Environment and Development for the Arab Region and Europe, Egypt

Marek Haliniak, Ministry of Environmental Protection, Natural Resources and Forestry, Poland

Allen Hammond, World Resources Institute, USA

William J. Hartnett, Massachusetts Institute of Technology, USA

Ayman Al-Hassan, Royal Scientific Society, Jordan

Mohamed Ali Hassan, Environmental Protection Committee, Bahrain

Jean-Paul Hettelingh, National Institute of Public Health and the Environment, the Netherlands

Paul Hofseth, Ministry of Environment, Norway

Eric S. Howard, Benchmark Environmental Consulting, USA

Hu Jianxin, Peking University, China

Hu Min, Peking University, China

Jad Isaac, Applied Research Institute, West Bank via Israel

Adel Farid Abdel Kader, Centre for Environment and Development for the Arab Region and Europe, Egypt

Eileen Kane, Department of State, USA

M.A. Kassas, Cairo University, Egypt

Yemi Katerere, International Union for the Conservation of Nature and Natural Resources, Zimbabwe

Nola Kate-Seymoar, International Institute for Sustainable Development, Canada

Zahra Al-Kawari, Environmental Protection Committee, Bahrain

Michael Keating, Canada

Attia Khalil, International Centre of Environmental Technologies, Tunisia

Yasseen Khayatt, Royal Scientific Society, Jordan

Alexandra King, Environment Resource Centre for Southern Africa, Zimbabwe

Ionnis Kinnas, Permanent Mission of Greece to the UN, Greece

Doug Kneeland, USDA Forest Service, USA

Roman Kojder, Permanent Mission of the Republic of Poland to UNEP, Kenya

Eric Kreileman, National Institute of Public Health and the Environment, the Netherlands

Vyacheslav N. Kroutko, Moscow Medical Academy, Russia

Elton Laisi, Environment Resource Centre for Southern Africa, Zimbabwe

Fred Langeweg, National Institute of Public Health and the Environment, the Netherlands

Li Jinlong, Peking University, China

Pedro Lira-González, El Colegio de México, México

Liu Junzhou, Public Health College of Beijing Medical University, China

Tom Loveland, US Geological Survey, USA

Gyde Lund, USDA Forest Service, USA

Ismail Al-Madany, Arabian Gulf University, Bahrain

Clever Mafuta, Environment Resource Centre for Southern Africa, Zimbabwe

Essam Mahmoud, Arabian Gulf University, Bahrain

Pedro Maldonado, University of Chile, Chile

Svetlana M. Malkhazova, Moscow State University, Russia

Anatoly F. Mandych, Russian Academy of Science, Russia

Francisco J. Mata, Earth Council, Costa Rica

Shakespeare Maya, Southern Centre for Energy and Environment, Zimbabwe

Alexander V. Medvedev, Moscow State University, Russia

Celia Maria Ferreira Meneses, Ministry of Environment, Mozambique

Alla Metelitsa, Ministry of Natural Resources and Environment, Belarus

Ruben Mnatsakanian, Central European University, Hungary

Saeed A. Mohamed, Bahrain University, Bahrain

Saidam Mohammed, Royal Scientific Society, Jordan

Abdelkrim Ben Mohammed, Universite Abdou Moumouni, Niger

Wayne Mooneyhan, Universities Space Research Association, USA

Yaroslav Movohan, Ministry for Environmental Protection & Nuclear Safety of Ukraine, Ukraine

Tom Mpofu, United Nations Development Programme, Zimbabwe

Dina Al Naggar, Egyptian Environmental Affairs Agency, Egypt

Vishal Narain, Tata Energy Research Institute, India

Robert Tiebilé N'daw, Mali

Csaba Nemes, Ministry of Environment & Regional Policy, Hungary

Boubacar Niane, Ministère de l'environnement et de la protection de la nature, Senegal

Somrudee Nicro, Thailand Environment Institute, Thailand

Louis Niessen, National Institute of Public Health and the Environment, the Netherlands

Shuzo Nishioka, National Institute for Environmental Studies, Japan

Michael Norton-Griffiths, Centre for Social and Economic Research on the Global Environment, UK

John C. O'Connor, OconECO, USA

R.K. Pachauri, Tata Energy Research Institute, India

Simon Papian, Ministry for Nature and Environment Protection, Armenia

Dhira Phantumvanit, Thailand Environment Institute, Thailand

Bruce Potter, Island Resources Foundation, Virgin Islands

Maggie Powell, World Resources Institute, USA

Raj Hemansing Prayag, Ministry of Environment and Quality of Life, Mauritius

A. Raey, Alexandria University, Egypt

Mahmood Y. Abdul Raheem, Environment Protection Council, Kuwait

Atiq Rahman, Bangladesh Centre for Advanced Studies, Bangladesh

Paul Raskin, Stockholm Environment Institute, USA

Ravendran, Environmental Protection Committee, Bahrain

Ahmed Abdel Rehim, Centre for Environment and Development for the Arab Region & Europe, Egypt

Nabil Rofail, Arab Center for Studies for Arid Zones and Dry Lands, Syria

Kristin Rosendal, Norwegian Institute for Nature Research, Norway

Mohamed Gomaa Al-Rumaidh, Bahrain Centre for Studies and Research, Bahrain

Kamal A. Sabet, Centre for Environment and Development for the Arab Region & Europe, Egypt

M. Sahir, Institute for Political and International Studies, Iran

Isa Bin Salman Al-Khalifa, Arabian Gulf University, Bahrain

Odd Terje Sandlund, Norwegian Institute for Nature Research, Norway

Fernando Santibaanez, University of Chile, Chile

F. Schmidt-Bleek, Wuppertal Institute for Climate, Environment and Energy, Germany

Liz Schmucker, USDA Forest Service, USA

Surya Man Shakya, National Planning Commission Secretariat, Nepal

Shao Min, Peking University, China

Henry M. Sichingabula, University of Zambia, Zambia

Bill Sommers, USDA Forest Service, USA

Kanongnij Sribuaiam, Thailand Environment Institute, Thailand

Leena Srivastava, Tata Energy Research Institute, India

Osvaldo Sunkel, University of Chile, Chile

Rob Swart, National Institute of Public Health and the Environment, the Netherlands

Kiyoshi Takahashi, National Institute for Environmental Studies, Japan

Tang Xiaoyan, Chinese Academy of Sciences, China

Vincent Isidore Tchabi, Ministère de l'environnement, Benin

Sufyan El-Tell, Jordan

Bjorn Age Tommeras, Norwegian Institute for Nature Research, Norway

Camilla Toulmin, International Institute for Environment & Development, UK

Edward L. Towle, Island Resources Foundation, Virgin Islands

Anita Velkavrh, Ministry of Environment and Physical Planning, Slovenia

Diana Vorsatz, Central European University, Hungary

Bert de Vries, National Institute of Public Health and the Environment, the Netherlands

Wang Huiuxiang, Peking University, China

Wang Zaiyong, Beijing Medical University, China

Wang Zhenggang, Public Health College of Beijing Medical University, China

Wang Zhijia, National Environmental Protection Agency, China

Manuel Winograd, Centro Internacional de Agricultura Tropical, Colombia

Jaap van Woerden, National Institute of Public Health and the Environment, the Netherlands

Xia Guang, National Environmental Protection Agency, China

Xie Zhenhua, National Environmental Protection Agency, China

Ye Ruqin, National Environmental Protection Agency, China

Zeng Limin, Peking University, China

Zhang Chongxian, National Environmental Protection Agency, China

Zhang Lixing, Beijing Institute for Anti-tuberculosis/Beijing Muncipal Political Consultation Committee, China

Zhang Shigang, National Environmental Protection Agency, China

Zhang Shiqin, Peking University, China

Zhang Yuanhang, Peking University, China

CONTRIBUTORS AND REVIEWERS IN THE UN SYSTEM

In UNEP: Hussein Abaza; Yinka Adebayo; Johannes Akiwumi; Jacqueline Aloisi de Larderel; Hans Alders; Alex Alusa; Adnan Amin; Maria de Amorim; Ali Ayoub; Alicia Barcena; Francoise Belmont; Hassane Bendahmane; Mona Bjorklund; Aiko Bode; Monica Borobia; Susan Bragdon; Beatrice Bulwa; Lilia Casanova; Dan Claasen; Harvey Croze; Uttam Dabholkar; Arthur Dahl; Dominique Del Pietro; Nickolai Denisov; Elizabeth Dowdeswell; Halifa Drammeh; Anthony Edwards; Norberto Fernandez; Joan Fox-Przeworski; Makram Gerges; Hiremagalur Gopalan; Michael Graber; Kjell Grip; Colin Harris; David Henry; Mario Hernandez; Ivonne Higuero; Taka Hiraishi; Christine Hogan; Sybren de Hoo; Douglas Hykle; Jorge Illueca; Antonella Ingrassia; Sipi Jaakkola; Donald Kaniaru; Bob Kakuyo; Leonid Kroumkatchev; Lars Kullerud; Christian Lambrechts; Sindre Langaas; Enrique Leff; Andrea Matte-Baker; Mark McFarland; Terttu Melvasalo; Danielle Mitchell; Michael Mwangi; Masa Nagai; Takehiro Nakamura; Bruce Noronha; Adel Orabi; John Pernetta; Wimala Ponniah; Walter Rast; Michèle Rattray; Phillippe Rekacewicz; Anders Renlund; Arsenio Rodriguez; Rafa Rodriguez-Capetillo; Iwona Rummel-Bulska; Nelson Sabogal; Vladimir Sakharov; Bernard Schanzenbacher; Frits Schlingemann; Gerhart Schneider; Cyriaque Sendashonga; Surendra Shrestha; Otto Simonett; Ashbindu Singh; Cheikh Sow; Bai Mass-Max Taal; Alexander Timoshenko; Svein Tveitdal; Alessandra Vanzella-Khouri; Omar Vidal; James Willis; Michael Wilson; Peigi Wilson; Ron Witt; Marceil Yeater; Suvit Yodmani; Hamdallah Zedan; Ivan Zrajevskij.

Other UN bodies: John Crayston, International Civil Aviation Organization; Roy M. Green, Intergovernmental Oceanographic Commission; Mathias Hundsalz, Habitat; Michel Jarraud, World Meteorological Organization; Aslam Khan, Economic and Social Commission for Asia and the Pacific; Larry R. Kohler, International Labour Organization; Gwenda Matthews, UN Department of Ocean Affairs and Law of the Sea; Donatus Okpala, Habitat; G. Ozolins, World Health Organization; Jan Rotmans, Department for Policy Coordination and Sustainable Development; Juha Uitto, United Nations University; Mohammed Wahab, Economic and Social Commission for West Asia; Rolf Wichmann, Habitat.